A GUIDE TO THE PCA ARBITRATION RULES

A GUIDE TO THE PCA ARBITRATION RULES

Brooks W. Daly
Evgeniya Goriatcheva
Hugh A. Meighen

OXFORD
UNIVERSITY PRESS

OXFORD
UNIVERSITY PRESS

Great Clarendon Street, Oxford, OX2 6DP,
United Kingdom

Oxford University Press is a department of the University of Oxford.
It furthers the University's objective of excellence in research, scholarship,
and education by publishing worldwide. Oxford is a registered trade mark of
Oxford University Press in the UK and in certain other countries

First published 2014
First published in paperback 2016

Published in the United States of America by Oxford University Press
198 Madison Avenue, New York, NY 10016, United States of America

British Library Cataloguing in Publication Data
Data available

Library of Congress Cataloging in Publication Data
Data available

ISBN 978–0–19–968068–9 (Hbk.)
ISBN 978–0–19–880124–5 (Pbk.)

Abyei Arbitration, The Government of Sudan/The Sudan People's Liberation Movement/Army, PCA Case No 2008-7—Great Hall of Justice, Peace Palace (2009)

CONTENTS

TABLE OF CASES

TABLE OF INTERNATIONAL TREATIES AND CONVENTIONS

TABLE OF NATIONAL LEGISLATION

TABLE OF ARBITRATION RULES

LIST OF DEFINED TERMS

1899 Hague Convention	Convention for the Pacific Settlement of International Disputes, 1899
1907 Hague Convention	Convention for the Pacific Settlement of International Disputes, 1907
1961 Vienna Convention	Vienna Convention on Diplomatic Relations, 1961
1976 UNCITRAL Rules	UNCITRAL Arbitration Rules, 1976
1990s PCA Rules	PCA State/State Rules, State/Non-State Rules, State/International Organization Rules, and International Organization/Private Party Rules
2010 UNCITRAL Rules	UNCITRAL Arbitration Rules, 2010
2012 PCA Rules (or Rules)	PCA Arbitration Rules, 2012
BIT	Bilateral investment treaty
CAFTA-DR	Dominican Republic–Central America–United States Free Trade Agreement
Explanatory Note	Explanatory Note of the International Bureau of the PCA Regarding Time Periods Under the PCA Arbitration Rules 2012
Headquarters Agreement	Agreement concerning the Headquarters of the Permanent Court of Arbitration, 1999
Host Country Agreement	Agreement between the PCA and a host country establishing a legal framework under which PCA-administered proceedings can be conducted in the territory of the host country on an ad hoc basis
IBA Rules	Rules on the Taking of Evidence in International Arbitration of the International Bar Association
ICC	International Chamber of Commerce
ICDR	International Center for Dispute Resolution
ICJ	International Court of Justice
ICSID	International Centre for Settlement of Investment Disputes
LCIA	London Court of International Arbitration
NAFTA	North-American Free Trade Agreement
New York Convention	Convention on the Recognition and Enforcement of Foreign Arbitral Awards, 1958
PCA	Permanent Court of Arbitration
PCA Drafting Committee	PCA Drafting Committee that drafted the 2012 PCA Rules
PCA International Organization/ Private Party Rules	PCA Optional Rules for Arbitration between International Organizations and Private Parties, 1996

PCA Natural Resources/ Environmental Rules	PCA Optional Rules for Arbitration of Disputes Relating to Natural Resources and/or the Environment, 2001
PCA Space Rules	PCA Optional Rules for Arbitration of Disputes Relating to Outer Space Activities, 2011
PCA State/International Organization Rules	PCA Optional Rules for Arbitration Involving International Organizations and States, 1996
PCA State/Non-State Rules	PCA Optional Rules for Arbitrating Disputes between Two Parties of Which Only One is a State, 1993
PCA State/State Rules	PCA Optional Rules for Arbitrating Disputes between Two States, 1992
RIAA	Reports of International Arbitral Awards
UNCITRAL	United Nations Commission on International Trade Law
UNCITRAL Model Law	UNCITRAL Model Law on International Commercial Arbitration, as amended in 2006
UNCLOS	United Nations Convention on the Law of the Sea, 1982
UNTS	United Nations Treaty Series

Part I

INTRODUCTION

1

INTRODUCTION

In December 2012, the Permanent Court of Arbitration (PCA) adopted the PCA Arbitration Rules ('2012 PCA Rules' or 'Rules')—modern procedural rules for arbitration of disputes involving states, state-controlled entities, and intergovernmental organizations. This book is a guide to and commentary on these Rules. **1.01**

The 2012 PCA Rules are based on four sets of PCA procedural rules from the 1990s and the Arbitration Rules of the United Nations Commission on International Trade Law (UNCITRAL). **1.02**

A. The Permanent Court of Arbitration

Established in 1899 during the first Hague Peace Conference, the PCA is the world's oldest intergovernmental organization dedicated to facilitating the peaceful resolution of international disputes. The Conference was convened at the initiative of Czar Nicholas II of Russia 'with the object of seeking the most effective means of ensuring to all peoples the benefits of a real and lasting peace, and above all, of limiting the progressive development of existing armaments'.[1] The creation of the PCA—an 'administrative organization with the object of having permanent and **1.03**

[1] Count Mouravieff, 'Russian Circular Note Proposing the First Peace Conference, St. Petersburg, 12 August 1898', in James Brown Scott (ed.), *The Hague Conventions and Declarations of 1899 and 1907* (Johns Hopkins Press, 1909) xiv.

readily available means to serve as the registry for the purposes of international arbitration'[2]—was the Conference's most important achievement. The PCA's constitutive instruments are the Convention for the Pacific Settlement of International Disputes of 1899 ('1899 Hague Convention')[3] and its 1907 revision ('1907 Hague Convention').[4]

1.04 Originally focused on arbitration and other forms of dispute resolution between states, the PCA now offers a broad range of services for the resolution of disputes involving various combinations of states, state-controlled entities, intergovernmental organizations, and private parties.[5] These services include arbitration, conciliation, fact-finding commissions, good offices, and mediation.

1.05 The PCA administers arbitrations under its own procedural rules, as well as under the UNCITRAL Arbitration Rules of 1976 ('1976 UNCITRAL Rules') and their 2010 revision ('2010 UNCITRAL Rules'). The PCA has also devised ad hoc procedural regimes for arbitrations governed by treaties, such as rules of procedure designed for arbitration pursuant to Annex VII of the United Nations Convention on the Law of the Sea (UNCLOS).[6] In addition, under the UNCITRAL Rules, the PCA Secretary-General may be called upon to designate an 'appointing authority' to, among other purposes, appoint the members of an arbitral tribunal and rule on challenges to arbitrators' independence and impartiality. Parties may also designate the PCA Secretary-General as appointing authority under the UNCITRAL Rules or other instruments.

1.06 PCA services are provided through its secretariat—the International Bureau—which is composed of legal and administrative staff of various geographic origins, and is headed by the Secretary-General of the PCA. The International Bureau has its seat in The Hague.[7] The diplomatic representatives of the PCA's Member States

[2] Shabtai Rosenne, *The Hague Peace Conferences of 1899 and 1907 and International Arbitration: Reports and Documents* (TMC Asser Press, 2001) xxi.

[3] 29 July 1899, 32 Stat 1779, TS 392, reproduced in Appendix II.

[4] Convention for the Pacific Settlement of International Disputes, 18 October 1907, 36 Stat 2199, 1 Bevans 557, reproduced in Appendix III.

[5] The PCA administered its first arbitration between a state and a private party in 1934 (*Radio Corporation of America v China*, Award of 13 April 1935, 3 RIAA 1621). At the time, the broad formulation of Art 26 of the 1899 Hague Convention, which permits the PCA to 'place its premises and its staff at the disposal of the Signatory Powers for the operations of any special Board of Arbitration', was interpreted as encompassing disputes between a state and a non-state actor. More recently, through the adoption of the Optional Rules for Arbitration between International Organizations and Private Parties (1996), the Optional Rules for Arbitration of Disputes Relating to Natural Resources and the Environment (2001), and the Optional Rules for Arbitration of Disputes Relating to Outer Space Activities (2011), the PCA Administrative Council expanded the PCA's mandate to administering arbitrations in some disputes to which no state is a party.

[6] 10 December 1982, 1833 UNTS 397.

[7] 1899 Hague Convention, Art 22(1); 1907 Hague Convention, Art 43.

accredited to the Netherlands make up the PCA's Administrative Council, which has ultimate oversight over the organization.[8]

B. The PCA's Arbitration Rules[9]

The 1899 and 1907 Hague Conventions contain now outdated rules for the conduct of various types of inter-state dispute resolution proceedings. A first set of PCA procedural rules specifically tailored for the arbitration (and conciliation) of disputes between states and private parties was adopted in 1962.[10] **1.07**

In the 1990s, an effort to update the PCA's rules of procedure was undertaken. Thus, in 1992, the PCA Administrative Council adopted the Optional Rules for Arbitrating Disputes between Two States ('PCA State/State Rules') and, in 1993, the Optional Rules for Arbitrating Disputes between Two Parties of Which Only One Is a State ('PCA State/Non-State Rules'). The PCA State/Non-State Rules formally superseded the PCA's rules of 1962.[11] **1.08**

In 1996, the Administrative Council also adopted the Optional Rules for Arbitration Involving International Organizations and States ('PCA State/International Organization Rules') and the Optional Rules for Arbitration between International Organizations and Private Parties ('PCA International Organization/Private Party Rules'). **1.09**

The PCA State/State Rules, State/Non-State Rules, State/International Organization Rules, and International Organization/Private Party Rules (together, the '1990s PCA Rules') were based on the 1976 UNCITRAL Rules with changes made tailoring them to the particular needs of public entities. **1.10**

In addition to the party-specific rules of the 1990s, in 2001 and 2011 respectively, the PCA Administrative Council adopted two sets of procedural rules for arbitration aimed at particular areas of economic activity: the Optional Rules for Arbitration of Disputes Relating to Natural Resources and the Environment ('PCA **1.11**

[8] 1899 Hague Convention, Art 28; 1907 Hague Convention, Art 49. As of October 2013, the PCA had a membership of 115 states. An up-to-date list of PCA Member States is available on the PCA website at <http://www.pca-cpa.org>.

[9] For a complete list of PCA rules of procedure (including rules for conciliation and fact-finding commissions) in force as of October 2013, see Appendix VI. The full text of each set of rules is available on the PCA website at <http://www.pca-cpa.org>. The process that led to the adoption of each set of rules is described in greater detail in PCA, *Basic Documents: Conventions, Rules, Model Clauses and Guidelines* (PCA, 2013), Introduction.

[10] 1962 Rules of Arbitration and Conciliation for Settlement of International Disputes between Two Parties of Which Only One Is a State, drafted by Pieter Sanders.

[11] PCA State/Non-State Rules, introduction.

Natural Resources/Environmental Rules') and the Optional Rules for Arbitration of Disputes Relating to Outer Space Activities ('PCA Space Rules').[12]

C. The PCA Arbitration Rules 2012

1.12 The 1990s PCA Rules having been modelled on the 1976 UNCITRAL Rules; the 2010 revision of the UNCITRAL Rules provided an impetus for the PCA to prepare a set of rules that would reflect both the outcome of the discussion at UNCITRAL and the lessons learned in cases administered by the PCA itself under both the UNCITRAL Rules and its own sets of procedural rules. It was also felt that the PCA's procedural offerings could be simplified by consolidating the party-specific PCA rules of the 1990s into a single set of rules that could apply to all the combinations of parties involved in PCA-administered proceedings. The PCA Administrative Council approved the appointment of a Drafting Committee ('PCA Drafting Committee') for this purpose in May 2011.

1.13 The members of the PCA Drafting Committee were selected on the basis of their professional qualifications, with broad geographic representation, reflecting the PCA's global character. The PCA International Bureau was also represented on the Committee. The Committee was chaired by Professor Jan Paulsson. Its other members were: Ms Lise Bosman, Mr Brooks W Daly, Mr Alvaro Galindo, Professor Alejandro Garro, HE Judge Sir Christopher Greenwood, Mr Michael Hwang, Professor Gabrielle Kaufmann-Kohler, Mr Salim Moollan, Professor Dr Michael Pryles AM, Judge Seyed Jamal Seifi, and Mr Jernej Sekolec.

1.14 The PCA Drafting Committee concluded in favour of consolidating the 1990s PCA Rules into a single document, which would incorporate their distinctive provisions. By May 2012, the Committee had produced a first draft of the Rules, which it submitted to the PCA Member States for review. Comments from the Member States were received throughout the summer. They were reflected in the Committee's second draft, which was presented to the Member States in the autumn and was adopted by the PCA Administrative Council on 17 December 2012. Shortly thereafter, in consideration of observations made by some Member States during the adoption process, the PCA International Bureau issued an explanatory note regarding time periods under the Rules ('Explanatory Note').[13]

[12] For a discussion of these rules, see Dane P Ratliff, 'The PCA Optional Rules for Arbitration of Disputes Relating to Natural Resources and/or the Environment' (2001) 14 *Leiden Journal of International Law* 887; Judge Fausto Pocar, 'An Introduction to the PCA's Optional Rules for Arbitration of Disputes Relating to Outer Space Activities' (2012) 38 *Journal of Space Law* 171.

[13] Explanatory Note of the International Bureau of the Permanent Court of Arbitration Regarding Time Periods Under the PCA Arbitration Rules 2012, reproduced in Appendix I.

The principal features of the 2012 PCA Rules are described in the Rules' introduction, which forms part of their text as adopted by the PCA Administrative Council. This introduction is discussed at the beginning of Part II. **1.15**

D. The Commentary

This book is a guide to and commentary on the 2012 PCA Rules. As such, it approaches the Rules article by article, seeking to provide insight into the rationale and application of each provision. For each article, any differences between the 2012 PCA Rules and the 2010 UNCITRAL Rules are highlighted and explained. The sources of inspiration for these changes (often, the 1990s PCA Rules) and other considerations of the PCA Drafting Committee are brought to the fore.[14] No attempt is made to comment on every aspect of those provisions that are integrally reproduced from the 2010 UNCITRAL Rules. For such coverage, the reader is directed to the wealth of commentary dedicated to the UNCITRAL Rules.[15] **1.16**

As the 2012 PCA Rules are entirely new, it is not currently possible to comment on any cases conducted in accordance with their terms. It is expected, however, that, for shared provisions, existing practice under the UNCITRAL Rules will constitute the starting-point of any interpretation of the 2012 PCA Rules. It is also expected that, under similar provisions, practice under the 2012 PCA Rules will be in line with practice under the 1990s PCA Rules. Accordingly, this book also discusses, in as much detail as the often confidential nature of PCA-administered cases permits, the experience of the PCA under the 1990s PCA Rules and the 1976 and 2010 UNCITRAL Rules. As a result, this book is also a significant source of information on the conduct of proceedings under those sets of rules. **1.17**

The practice of the PCA Secretary-General when requested to act as appointing authority under the UNCITRAL Rules is also the subject of commentary, particularly in the parts of this book addressing provisions that deal with the role of the PCA Secretary-General as appointing authority under the 2012 PCA Rules. **1.18**

In this book, PCA-administered arbitrations that are not confidential are, for ease of reference, identified by their PCA case numbers. Publicly available documents relating to these arbitrations can be found on the PCA's website.[16] When **1.19**

[14] One author of this book was a member of the PCA Drafting Committee; the others assisted the Committee on behalf of the International Bureau.

[15] See eg Peter Binder, Analytical Commentary to the UNCITRAL Arbitration Rules, 4th edn (Sweet & Maxwell, 2013); David D Caron and Lee M Caplan, *The UNCITRAL Arbitration Rules: A Commentary*, 2nd edn (Oxford University Press, 2013); Clyde Croft, Christopher Kee, and Jeff Waincymer, *A Guide to the UNCITRAL Arbitration Rules* (Cambridge University Press, 2013); Thomas H Webster, *Handbook of UNCITRAL Arbitration* (Sweet & Maxwell, 2010).

[16] At <http://www.pca-cpa.org>.

confidential cases are used as examples, information that would allow identification of the case is excluded.

E. The Appendices

1.20 Background and constitutive documents of the PCA are found in the appendices to this book. These include the Explanatory Note to the 2012 PCA Rules, the PCA's founding conventions, a complete list of PCA rules of procedure, a list of the members of the expert groups that drafted the PCA's rules of procedure, the PCA's headquarters agreement with the Netherlands (and the exchange of notes that supplements it),[17] the rules and regulations of the PCA financial assistance fund,[18] the PCA's schedule of fees and costs, and a description of the procedure for requesting the PCA Secretary-General to act as appointing authority.

1.21 Documents relevant to PCA-administered arbitration under the UNCITRAL Rules are also provided: the text of the 1976 and 2010 UNCITRAL Rules, a description of the procedure for requesting the PCA Secretary-General to designate an appointing authority pursuant to the UNCITRAL Rules, and a model clause for PCA-administered arbitration under the UNCITRAL Rules.

1.22 Finally, the appendices contain a model declaration of acceptance and statement of impartiality and independence that can be used in cases under the 2012 PCA Rules and, with minor modifications, under the UNCITRAL Rules, and two sample procedural orders of the sort that arbitral tribunals often issue at the start of proceedings.

[17] See discussion under Art 16.
[18] See discussion under Art 40.

Part II

PCA ARBITRATION RULES 2012

2

THE INTRODUCTION OF THE 2012 PCA RULES

These Rules are for use in arbitrating disputes involving at least one State, State-controlled entity, or intergovernmental organization. They add a new option for arbitration of disputes under the auspices of the Permanent Court of Arbitration (hereinafter the 'PCA') without replacing the previously adopted PCA Rules, which remain valid and available. The Rules are optional and are based on the 2010 UNCITRAL Arbitration Rules with changes made in order to:

(i) Reflect the public international law elements that may arise in disputes involving a State, State-controlled entity, and/or intergovernmental organization;
(ii) Indicate the role of the Secretary-General and the International Bureau of the PCA; and
(iii) Emphasize flexibility and party autonomy. For example:
  (a) The Rules allow for arbitration of multiparty disputes involving a combination of States, State-controlled entities, intergovernmental organizations, and private parties;
  (b) The Rules and the services of the Secretary-General and the International Bureau of the PCA are available for use by all States and their entities and enterprises, and are not restricted to disputes in which the State is a party either to the Hague Convention for the Pacific Settlement of International Disputes of 1899 or that of 1907;
  (c) The Rules allow parties to choose an arbitral tribunal of one, three, or five persons; and
  (d) The choice of arbitrators is not limited to persons who are listed as Members of the PCA.

Model clauses that parties may consider inserting in treaties, contracts, or other agreements to provide for arbitration of existing or future disputes are set forth in the annex to these Rules.

Like previous sets of PCA procedural rules,[1] the 2012 PCA Rules include an introduction providing background information on their purpose and operation. The introduction is not a prescriptive article and does not set out specific procedural duties for the actors in the arbitral proceeding. **2.01**

[1] See the introductions to the 1990s PCA Rules, PCA Natural Resources/Environmental Rules, and PCA Space Rules.

2.02 The chapeau of the introduction specifies that the Rules are intended to be used in arbitrating disputes involving at least one state, state-controlled entity, or intergovernmental organization. Indeed, many of the Rules' provisions have been tailored to the needs of such parties. Nevertheless, some improvements in the Rules should be attractive to private entities as well. As discussed under Article 1(4), the Rules are also available for arbitrations involving exclusively private parties, provided the parties have agreed to arbitration under the Rules. In such cases, the PCA Secretary-General may exercise discretion to determine the PCA's role in the proceedings in light of the PCA's mandate as an intergovernmental organization.

2.03 Further, the chapeau states that the 2012 PCA Rules are optional, emphasizing the consensual nature of arbitral proceedings, whether involving public or private entities. As further discussed under Article 3 of the Rules, parties may express their intention to use the 2012 PCA Rules in a variety of legal documents either before or after a dispute has arisen.

2.04 Finally, the chapeau makes clear that the 2012 PCA Rules do not replace previously adopted sets of PCA procedural rules. The 2012 PCA Rules are an addition to the PCA's procedural offerings, while other PCA rules, such as the 1990s PCA Rules, PCA Natural Resources/Environmental Rules, and PCA Space Rules, remain available. Parties that have chosen to arbitrate their disputes under those sets of rules are entitled to do so.

2.05 The introduction goes on to highlight key characteristics of the 2012 PCA Rules. The Rules' defining feature is that they are based on the 2010 UNCITRAL Rules. However, by incorporating the distinctive provisions of the 1990s PCA Rules or otherwise, the 2012 PCA Rules have also made notable changes to the 2010 UNCITRAL Rules.

2.06 As noted in paragraph (i) of the introduction, changes have been made to 'reflect the public international law elements' that may arise in disputes involving the types of parties for use by which the Rules are intended. For example, the Rules provide that in submitting disputes to arbitration under the Rules, states and intergovernmental parties waive any immunity from jurisdiction they might otherwise enjoy.[2] Where the parties have not agreed on the law applicable to the substance of the dispute, the Rules provide for a different applicable law depending on the nature of the parties: for example, the applicable law for inter-state disputes is based on the Statute of the International Court of Justice (ICJ), while the applicable law for disputes involving both states and private parties is modelled on the 2010 UNCITRAL Rules.[3] The 2012 PCA Rules also provide for the representation of

[2] See discussion under Art 1(2).
[3] See discussion under Art 35.

state parties by agents;[4] a default appointment procedure for five-member tribunals, which are common in inter-state arbitration;[5] and a model arbitration clause for inclusion in treaties.[6]

As mentioned in paragraph (ii) of the introduction, the Rules also provide for the role of the PCA International Bureau and the PCA Secretary-General. Unlike the 2010 UNCITRAL Rules, which do not specify an administrative institution, the 2012 PCA Rules provide for the administration of arbitral proceedings by the PCA. Pursuant to Article 1(3) of the Rules, the PCA International Bureau acts as registry and secretariat, while the PCA Secretary-General is the appointing authority pursuant to Article 6. **2.07**

While many changes to the 2010 UNCITRAL Rules were based on the 1990s PCA Rules, some provisions of the 2012 PCA Rules are completely new. The 2012 PCA Rules tackle the delicate issue of arbitrators' fees by mandating the PCA Secretary-General to review the tribunal's determination of fees and expenses of arbitrators and tribunal-appointed experts in all cases.[7] The Rules also favour procedural flexibility by allowing the PCA International Bureau to extend default time periods provided in the Rules for the constitution of the tribunal and the payment of deposits to cover the costs of arbitration.[8] **2.08**

Paragraph (iii) of the introduction lists four examples intended to highlight the principles of flexibility and party autonomy captured by the 2012 PCA Rules. **2.09**

Paragraph (iii)(a) notes that the Rules have been designed to manage arbitration of multiparty disputes involving a combination of states, state-controlled entities, intergovernmental organizations, and private parties. **2.10**

Paragraph (iii)(c) notes that arbitral tribunals of different sizes may be constituted under the 2012 PCA Rules. While the 1990s PCA Rules also contemplate tribunals of one, three, or five members, the 2012 PCA Rules innovate by providing specific procedures for constituting (and re-constituting) five-member tribunals.[9] **2.11**

Paragraphs (iii)(b) and (iii)(d), which are based on the introductions to previous sets of PCA rules,[10] emphasize that the availability of the 2012 PCA Rules is not limited by the terms of the PCA's constitutive documents—the 1899 and 1907 Hague Conventions. The 2012 PCA Rules, and the services of the PCA International Bureau and Secretary-General provided for therein, are available to states that are not party **2.12**

[4] See Rules, Art 5.
[5] See discussion under Art 9.
[6] See discussion under Art 1.
[7] See discussion under Arts 41 and 43.
[8] See Rules, Arts 4(1), 8(2)(b), 9(3), and 43(4).
[9] See Rules, Art 9.
[10] See introductions to the 1990s PCA Rules, PCA Natural Resources/Environmental Rules, and PCA Space Rules.

to either of the PCA's founding conventions.[11] As with other PCA procedural rules, parties in proceedings under the 2012 PCA Rules are permitted to appoint arbitrators who are not 'Members of the PCA', that is, who are not members of the standing panel of potential arbitrators appointed by PCA Member States pursuant to Article 23 of the 1899 Hague Convention and Article 44 of the 1907 Hague Convention.[12]

[11] A list of states that are party to the 1899 and 1907 Hague Conventions is available on the PCA website at <http://www.pca-cpa.org>.

[12] For a discussion of the role of the standing panel of Members of the Court, see under Art 10(4).

3

SECTION I. INTRODUCTORY RULES

A. Scope of Application—Article 1

1. Where a State, State-controlled entity, or intergovernmental organization has agreed with one or more States, State-controlled entities, intergovernmental organizations, or private parties that disputes between them in respect of a defined legal relationship, whether contractual, treaty-based, or otherwise, shall be referred to arbitration under the Permanent Court of Arbitration Arbitration Rules 2012 (hereinafter the 'Rules'), then such disputes shall be settled in accordance with these Rules subject to such modification as the parties may agree.
2. Agreement by a State, State-controlled entity, or intergovernmental organization to arbitrate under these Rules with a party that is not a State, State-controlled entity, or intergovernmental organization constitutes a waiver of any right of immunity from jurisdiction in respect of the proceedings relating to the dispute in question to which such party might otherwise be entitled. A waiver of immunity relating to the execution of an arbitral award must be explicitly expressed.
3. The International Bureau of the Permanent Court of Arbitration at the Hague (hereinafter the 'International Bureau') shall serve as registry for the proceedings and provide secretariat services.
4. The involvement of at least one State, State-controlled entity, or intergovernmental organization as a party to the dispute is not necessary for jurisdiction where all the parties have agreed to settle a dispute under these Rules. However, where the Secretary-General of the Permanent Court of Arbitration determines that no State, State-controlled entity, or intergovernmental organization is a party to the dispute, the Secretary-General may decide to limit the Permanent Court

of Arbitration's role in the proceedings to the function of the Secretary-General as appointing authority, with the role of the International Bureau under these Rules to be assumed by the arbitral tribunal.

3.01 Article 1 sets out the scope of application of the 2012 PCA Rules. It assures broad access to PCA-administered arbitration for disputes involving at least one state, state-controlled entity, or intergovernmental organization, while limiting the PCA's role in disputes involving exclusively private parties.

3.02 This provision differs from Article 1 of the 2010 UNCITRAL Rules in several respects.

3.03 In Article 1(1), the introductory phrase '[w]here a State, State-controlled entity, or intergovernmental organization has agreed with one or more States, State-controlled entities, intergovernmental organizations, or private parties' encompasses all the combinations of parties for which the 1990s PCA Rules provided individually.[1] This phrase affirms the intention that the 2012 PCA Rules be used primarily for the arbitration of disputes to which at least one party is a state, state-controlled entity, or intergovernmental organization. In keeping with this aim, in many instances the Rules depart from the text of the 2010 UNCITRAL Rules to render them more suitable for dispute resolution involving public entities.[2]

3.04 Disputes involving the combinations of parties targeted by the Rules include:

- inter-state disputes, concerning, inter alia, territorial and maritime boundary delimitation,[3] humanitarian law,[4] environmental protection,[5] and interpretation of treaties;[6]

---

[1] The 1990s PCA Rules concern inter-state disputes, as well as disputes between states and international organizations, states and private parties, and international organizations and private parties.

[2] A number of improvements in the Rules should be attractive to private entities as well. As seen from Art 1(4), there is no prohibition on recourse to the Rules in disputes to which no public entity is a party, provided the parties have agreed to arbitrate under the Rules. As discussed in paras 3.15–3.17, in such cases the PCA Secretary-General may exercise discretion in determining the PCA's role in the proceedings.

[3] See eg *Philippines v China*, PCA Case No 2013-19 (UNCLOS); *Croatia/Slovenia*, PCA Case No 2012-4; *ARA Libertad Arbitration*, Argentina v Ghana, PCA Case No 2013-11 (UNCLOS); *Bangladesh v India*, PCA Case No 2010-16 (UNCLOS); *Guyana v Suriname*, PCA Case No 2004-4 (UNCLOS); *Barbados v Trinidad and Tobago*, PCA Case No 2004-2 (UNCLOS); *Eritrea v Yemen*, PCA Case No 2004-4; *Eritrea-Ethiopia Boundary Commission*, PCA Case No 2001-1 (Rules of Procedure based on PCA State/State Rules).

[4] See eg *Eritrea-Ethiopia Claims Commission*, PCA Case No 2001-1 (Rules of Procedure based on PCA State/State Rules).

[5] See eg *Iron Rhine Arbitration*, Belgium v the Netherlands, PCA Case No 2003-2 (Rules of Procedure based on PCA State/State Rules).

[6] See eg *Ecuador v United States of America*, PCA Case No 2012-5 (1976 UNCITRAL Rules); *Indus Waters Kishenganga Arbitration*, Pakistan v India, PCA Case No 2011-1 (Indus Waters Treaty 1960); *Netherlands v France*, PCA Case No 2000-2.

- investor-state disputes, arising under bilateral[7] and multilateral[8] treaties, national investment statutes,[9] and investment agreements between foreign investors and host states;[10]
- disputes between states or state-controlled entities and private parties, arising under commercial contracts (for example, contracts for the sale of goods, concession agreements, production sharing contracts, financing agreements, construction and other infrastructure project contracts);[11]
- disputes between states and intergovernmental organizations, arising under the founding conventions of intergovernmental organizations, or headquarters agreements[12];
- disputes between intergovernmental organizations and private parties,[13] arising under procurement contracts, or concerning, for example, the rights of parties under employment contracts;

[7] Recent examples include *Philip Morris Asia Limited v the Commonwealth of Australia*, PCA Case No 2012-12 (Hong Kong–Australia BIT) (2010 UNCITRAL Rules); *OAO Gazprom v Republic of Lithuania*, PCA Case No 2012-13 (Russia–Lithuania BIT) (1976 UNCITRAL Rules); *Guaracachi America Inc and Rurelec PLC v Plurinational State of Bolivia*, PCA Case No 2011-17 (China–Mongolia BIT) (2010 UNCITRAL Rules); *1 Chevron Corporation and 2 Texaco Petroleum Company v Ecuador*, PCA Case No 2009-23 (Ecuador–United States BIT) (1976 UNCITRAL Rules).

[8] See eg the North American Free Trade Agreement (NAFTA), 17 December 1992, in force 1 January 1994, (1993) 32 ILM 289, 605; Energy Charter Treaty, 17 December 1994, in force 16 April 1998, 2080 UNTS 95, 34 ILM 360; Central America–Dominican Republic–United States Free Trade Agreement (DR-CAFTA), <http://www.ustr.gov/trade-agreements/free-trade-agreements/cafta-dr-dominican-republic-central-america-fta>. Recent examples of cases include *Detroit International Bridge Company v Canada*, PCA Case No 2012-25 (NAFTA) (2010 UNCITRAL Rules); *Bilcon of Delaware v Canada*, PCA Case No 2009-4 (NAFTA) (1976 UNCITRAL Rules); *1 TCW Group, Inc 2 Dominican Energy Holdings LP v Dominican Republic*, PCA Case No 2008-6 (CAFTA-DR) (1976 UNCITRAL Rules).

[9] See eg *1 Centerra Gold Inc 2 Kumtor Gold Company v Kyrgyz Republic*, PCA Case No 2007-1 (Investment Agreement of 31 December 2003 and Law No 66 'On Investments in the Kyrgyz Republic' of 27 March 2003) (1976 UNCITRAL Rules).

[10] See eg *1 Centerra Gold Inc 2 Kumtor Gold Company v Kyrgyz Republic*, PCA Case No 2007-1 (Investment Agreement of 31 December 2003 and Law No 66 'On Investments in the Kyrgyz Republic' of 27 March 2003) (1976 UNCITRAL Rules).

[11] The overwhelming majority of such cases is confidential. Non-confidential cases include *Eurotunnel Arbitration* 1 The Channel Tunnel Group Limited 2 France-Manche SA v 1 Secretary of State for Transport of the Government of the United Kingdom of Great Britain and Northern Ireland 2 le ministre de l'équipement, des transports, de l'aménagement du territoire, du tourisme et de la mer du Gouvernement de la République française, PCA Case No 2003-5; *Sudan v Turriff Construction Company (Sudan) Limited*, PCA Case No 1966-1, summary in P Hamilton et al., *The Permanent Court of Arbitration: International Arbitration and Dispute Resolution: Summaries of Awards, Settlement Agreements and Reports* (Kluwer Law International, 1999) 164.

[12] See eg Agreement between the Government of the French Republic and the International Criminal Police Organization concerning the Headquarters of INTERPOL and its Privileges and Immunities in French Territory, 1 September 2009, <http://www.interpol.int>, Art 24; Agreement between the Organisation for the Prohibition of Chemical Weapons (OPCW) and the Kingdom of The Netherlands Concerning the Headquarters of the OPCW, 29 April 1997, C-I/DEC.59, Art 26. These agreements provide for the settlement of disputes between the state party and the intergovernmental organization pursuant to the PCA State/International Organization Rules.

[13] See eg *Polis Fondi Immobiliari di Banche Popolare SGRpA v International Fund for Agricultural Development*, PCA Case No 2010-8 (1976 UNCITRAL Rules).

- intra-state disputes, for example between a national government and a political entity from the same state;[14] and
- disputes between intergovernmental organizations.

3.05 Article 1(1) specifies that the arbitration agreement must pertain to a 'defined legal relationship, whether contractual, treaty-based, or otherwise'. This is an adaptation of the new language adopted in the 2010 UNCITRAL Rules and originating in Article II of the Convention on the Recognition and Enforcement of Foreign Arbitral Awards ('New York Convention'),[15] which states that the arbitration agreement must be in respect of a 'defined legal relationship, whether contractual or not'. While the meaning of the two phrases is analogous, the formulation adopted in the 2012 PCA Rules makes explicit that treaties are a potential source of disputes that may be submitted to arbitration under the Rules. As with the 2010 UNCITRAL Rules, the arbitration agreement under the 2012 PCA Rules may be contained in a legal instrument such as a contract or treaty and stipulate the resolution of future disputes through arbitration[16] or may be in the form of an agreement to submit an existing dispute to arbitration (also known as a *compromis*).[17]

3.06 Like the 2010 UNCITRAL Rules, the 2012 PCA Rules provide a model arbitration clause for contracts in an annex.[18] In addition, the annex to the 2012 PCA Rules contains a model arbitration clause for inclusion in treaties and other agreements.[19] The annex suggests that parties should consider stipulating three features of the arbitral proceedings in their arbitration clause: the number of arbitrators, the place (legal seat) of arbitration, and the language of the proceedings.[20] The PCA

---

[14] See eg *Abyei Arbitration*, Government of Sudan/The Sudan People's Liberation Movement/Army, PCA Case No 2008-7 (PCA State/Non-State Rules).

[15] 10 June 1958, 330 UNTS 38.

[16] See Energy Charter Treaty, 17 December 1994, in force 16 April 1998, 2080 UNTS 95, 34 ILM 360.

[17] See Agreement between the Government of the State of Eritrea and the Government of the Federal Democratic Republic of Ethiopia for the resettlement of displaced persons, as well as rehabilitation and peacebuilding in both countries, Algiers, 12 December 2000, 2138 UNTS 94, Arts 4 and 5, establishing the Eritrea-Ethiopia Boundary Commission and the Eritrea-Ethiopia Claims Commission; see also *Croatia/Slovenia*, PCA Case No 2012-4, which was initiated pursuant to a *compromis* between Croatia and Slovenia dated 4 November 2009, press release at <http://www.pca-cpa.org/showpage.asp?pag_id=1443>.

[18] The model arbitration clause for contracts reads as follows: 'Any dispute, controversy or claim arising out of or relating to this contract, or the breach, termination or invalidity thereof, shall be settled by arbitration in accordance with the PCA Arbitration Rules 2012'.

[19] The model arbitration clause for treaties and other agreements reads as follows: 'Any dispute, controversy or claim arising out of or in relation to this [agreement] [treaty], or the existence, interpretation, application, breach, termination, or invalidity thereof, shall be settled by arbitration in accordance with the PCA Arbitration Rules 2012'. A model clause for PCA-administered arbitration under the UNCITRAL Rules is also found in Appendix XVI.

[20] In this respect, the annex to the Rules proposes the following text:

(a) The number of arbitrators shall be . . . [one, three, or five];
(b) The place of arbitration shall be . . . [town or country];
(c) The language to be used in the arbitral proceedings shall be . . . .

Drafting Committee harmonized the model clauses with the Rules' provision for five-member tribunals[21] by including 'five' among the proposed numbers of arbitrators. Unlike the model clause of the 2010 UNCITRAL Rules, the model clauses of the 2012 PCA Rules do not refer to the selection of an appointing authority, as the PCA Secretary-General is the appointing authority under the Rules.[22]

The remainder of Article 1(1) follows the text of Article 1(1) of the 2010 UNCITRAL Rules. Article 1(1) does not contain the requirement, found in the 1976 UNCITRAL Rules, that the arbitration agreement be in writing. Nor does it contain any other formal requirements for the conclusion of an arbitration agreement. The absence of formal requirements in the Rules reflects the choice to leave their specification to the applicable law.[23] Hence, despite the lack of restrictions in the Rules, parties intending to enter an arbitration agreement must consider the formal requirements for valid arbitration agreements.[24] For example, countries that have adopted the UNCITRAL Model Law on International Commercial Arbitration ('UNCITRAL Model Law') require that arbitration agreements be in writing.[25] **3.07**

Furthermore, Article 1(1) recognizes the primacy of party autonomy by allowing agreed modifications to the Rules. In the PCA's experience, parties to inter-state arbitrations in particular expend considerable effort on adapting pre-existing rules to the needs of the case at hand. For example, the PCA State/State Rules have been adopted in modified form in a number of arbitrations.[26] Additional efforts to adapt **3.08**

The importance of these aspects of the arbitral proceedings is touched upon under Arts 9 (number of arbitrators), 18 (place of arbitration), and 19 (language).

[21] See discussion under Art 9.

[22] See discussion under Art 6.

[23] Report of the UNCITRAL Working Group II (Arbitration and Conciliation) on the work of its 45th session, 11–15 September 2006, A/CN.9/614, para 29; Report of the UNCITRAL Working Group II (Arbitration and Conciliation) on the work of its 46th session, 5–9 February 2007, A/CN.9/619, para 29; Report of the UNCITRAL Working Group II (Arbitration and Conciliation) on the work of its 49th session, 15–19 September 2008, A/CN.9/665, para 18.

[24] With respect to the law applicable to the arbitration agreement and the issue of its validity, approaches vary. Depending on the approach, the validity of an arbitration agreement will depend on the law governing the contract, the law of the seat of arbitration, and which of these two laws is most favourable to the recognition of the existence of the arbitration agreement or solely on the common intention of the parties: Alan Redfern, J Martin Hunter, Nigel Blackaby, and Constantine Partasides, *Redfern and Hunter on International Arbitration* (Oxford University Press, 2009) paras 3.09–3.33. On the applicability of national legislation to arbitrations involving only states or intergovernmental organizations, see discussion under Art 1(2).

[25] For a comprehensive list of states that have adopted legislation based on the UNCITRAL Model Law, see <http://www.uncitral.org/uncitral/en/uncitral_texts/arbitration/1985Model_arbitration_status.html>.

[26] See eg *Eritrea-Ethiopia Claims Commission*, PCA Case No 2001-1; *Eritrea-Ethiopia Boundary Commission*, PCA Case No 2001-1. As required by Arts 4(11) and 5(7) of the Agreement between the Government of the State of Eritrea and the Government of the Federal Democratic Republic of Ethiopia for the resettlement of displaced persons, as well as rehabilitation and peacebuilding in both countries, Algiers, 12 December 2000, 2138 UNTS 94, pursuant to which the Eritrea-Ethiopia Claims Commission and the Eritrea-Ethiopia Boundary Commission were established, the Rules of

procedural rules in the inter-state context arise from the magnitude and complexity of the subject-matter at stake, but also from the fact that states often opt for arbitration only once a dispute has arisen. Parties to an existing dispute have the advantage of knowing the nature of the issues between them and can adapt procedural rules to their specific needs in their *compromis*. This stands in contrast with the position of parties that include an arbitration clause in an instrument to cover future disputes the nature of which may be unforeseeable.

3.09 While the PCA favours maximum party autonomy in the adaptation of its rules to individual cases and instruments, the PCA International Bureau should be consulted regarding any contemplated modifications of the PCA's role under the Rules.[27]

3.10 Article 1(2) stipulates that an arbitration agreement constitutes a waiver of immunity from jurisdiction. Equivalent provisions are found in the PCA State/Non-State Rules, International Organization/Private Party Rules, and Natural Resources/ Environmental Rules. Article 1(2) alerts parties that a state's (or an intergovernmental organization's) consent to arbitration constitutes a waiver of immunity to jurisdiction, but not enforcement.[28] Where desired, parties may consider including an additional clause in the arbitration agreement stipulating that the agreement also constitutes a waiver of immunity from execution of the award.

3.11 Article 1(2) refers to 'any' immunity from jurisdiction in order to include both the sovereign immunity of states and functional immunity of intergovernmental organizations. While the 1990s PCA Rules provided for the waiver of immunity 'in respect of the dispute in question', the PCA Drafting Committee replaced this phrase with 'in respect of the proceedings relating to the dispute in question' for greater precision. The new formulation is similar to that found in Article 17 of the United Nations Convention on Jurisdictional Immunities of States and their Property (not yet in force)[29] and section 9 of the UK State Immunity Act 1978.

Procedure of each Commission are based on the PCA State/State Rules, adapted to reflect the respective mandate and workload of each Commission. Another example is the *Iron Rhine Arbitration*, Belgium v The Netherlands, PCA Case No 2003-2 (see Award of 24 May 2005, 27 RIAA 35, para 5; see also the Exchange of Notes constituting an agreement between the Kingdom of the Netherlands and the Kingdom of Belgium on Arbitration concerning the Iron Rhine Railway Line Arbitration Agreement between the Kingdom of Belgium and the Kingdom of The Netherlands, 23 July 2003, LT/sr A.71.92/3110 (Belgium)). See also Treaty Between the Government of the Republic of Namibia and the Government of the Republic of South Africa on the Establishment of the [|Ai-|Ais/ Richtersveld] Transfrontier Park, 17 August 2003, Art 16(2).

[27] For such queries, an email may be sent to bureau@pca-cpa.org.

[28] Redfern, Hunter, and Partasides (n 24), para 11.140.

[29] Adopted by the United Nations General Assembly on 2 December 2004. See General Assembly Resolution 59/38, Annex, Official Records of the General Assembly, 59th Session, Supplement No 49, A/59/49.

Notably, Article 1(2) does not apply to the arbitration of disputes involving only states and intergovernmental organizations. By agreeing to arbitrate these disputes under the Rules, parties may not intend to waive their immunity from national court jurisdiction.[30] In arbitration exclusively between parties that benefit from such immunity, waivers should be express. **3.12**

Article 1(3), calling for the provision of registry and secretariat support services to the proceedings by the International Bureau of the PCA, replicates Article 1(3) of the PCA Space Rules. The 1990s PCA Rules contain similar provisions. This provision includes the variety of services usually provided by the PCA in cases that it administers. As registry, the International Bureau maintains an archive for the proceedings. To facilitate the PCA's work, the Rules provide that all communications between the parties and the tribunal, as well as the notice of arbitration and the response thereto, shall be sent to the International Bureau at the same time as to the other addressees.[31] After the termination of the proceedings, PCA practice is to maintain an archive of any awards rendered indefinitely and to keep one copy of each pleading, procedural order, and item of correspondence for at least five years. Any other documents deposited with the PCA are destroyed in a confidential manner, unless their return is requested by a party or arbitrator. In the Netherlands, the archives of the PCA are inviolable.[32] As secretariat, the International Bureau may serve as the official channel of communication between the parties and the tribunal and provide services such as logistical and technical support for meetings and hearings (including arranging for transcription, video-conferencing, interpretation, catering, and IT equipment), travel arrangements, translation, word-processing, and general secretarial support. Parties in arbitrations administered under the Rules will have free use of hearing and meeting rooms at the Peace Palace in The Hague and at other venues, for example in Costa Rica, Mauritius, and Singapore.[33] Pursuant to Article 43, the International Bureau requests, holds, and disburses the deposits made by parties to cover the costs of arbitration.[34] **3.13**

Article 1(4), first sentence, provides that the involvement in a dispute of a state, state-controlled entity, or international organization is not necessary for tribunal's **3.14**

[30] Similarly, other instruments find no waiver of immunity from national court jurisdiction in the context of arbitration agreements between states. See eg European Convention on State Immunity, 16 May 1972, Art 12(2). See also United Nations Convention on the Jurisdictional Immunities of States and their Property, adopted by the United Nations General Assembly on 2 December 2004, not yet in force, Art 17; General Assembly Resolution 59/38, Annex, Official Records of the General Assembly, 59th Session, Supplement No 49, A/59/49 (on which, see Commentary to Art 17 in (1991) 2(2) *Year Book of the International Law Commission* 55).

[31] See Rules, Arts 3(1), 4(1), 5(3), 17(4), 20(1), 21(1), 37(1), 38(1), 39(1).

[32] Agreement concerning the Headquarters of the Permanent Court of Arbitration, 30 March 1999, in force 8 August 2000 (Netherlands), Art 3(3).

[33] See discussion of Host Country Agreements under Art 16.

[34] See discussion under Art 43.

jurisdiction. This provision takes inspiration from Article 1(1) of the PCA Natural Resources/Environmental Rules[35] and also resembles Article 1(1) of the PCA Space Rules. Its purpose is to prevent jurisdictional objections on the ground that the parties to the dispute fall outside the intended scope of application of the Rules as stated in Article 1(1); specifically, the objection that no state, state-controlled entity, or intergovernmental organization is a party to the dispute. The Rules do not impose any jurisdictional limitation on the type of parties that may use them. Disputes between private parties may be submitted for resolution in accordance with the Rules. The interpretation of the phrase 'State, State-controlled entity, or intergovernmental organization' is therefore irrelevant to the question of jurisdiction.

3.15 However, in view of the PCA's status as an intergovernmental organization,[36] the second sentence of Article 1(4) allows the PCA Secretary-General to limit the administrative role of the PCA in disputes that do not involve at least one entity with partial state control.

3.16 In such cases, the International Bureau may be relieved of its registry and secretariat functions under Article 1(3). The tribunal must then take care of the administrative tasks that would otherwise be undertaken by the International Bureau. However, the Secretary-General remains the appointing authority for all purposes under the Rules in accordance with Article 6(1). The distinction between the attributes of these two roles—that of registry and secretariat, and that of appointing authority—is clearly set out in the Rules. The first role is always denoted by reference to the 'International Bureau'; the second, by reference to the 'appointing authority'.

3.17 The Secretary-General's decision to restrict the PCA's role is a discretionary one, and may take into account the nature of the parties, the factual circumstances of the case, and the policy of the PCA. In particular, there may be cases where the only state, state-controlled entity, or intergovernmental organization party to arbitral proceedings under the Rules ceases to be a party during the course of the arbitration, such as when the arbitral tribunal finds in a preliminary phase that it does not have jurisdiction over that specific entity. In such a case, the Secretary-General may consider allowing the PCA to continue providing administrative services in order to avoid a disruptive transfer of responsibilities, and in particular deposits and financial records, to the arbitral tribunal in mid-proceeding. If the determination of the nature of a party as a state, state-controlled entity, or intergovernmental

---

[35] Article 1(1) of the PCA Natural Resources/Environmental Rules avoids formalistic jurisdictional objections by providing that '[t]he characterization of the dispute as relating to natural resources and/or the environment is not necessary for jurisdiction where all the parties have agreed to settle a specific dispute under these Rules'.

[36] It may be recalled that the PCA was created to deal exclusively with disputes between states and that its areas of competence have since been expanded (see para 1.04, n 5).

organization is relevant to a question before the arbitral tribunal and therefore a matter for the tribunal to decide, the Secretary-General may decline to make any comment on the question.

The 2012 PCA Rules do not feature a presumption for their application such as that found in the 2010 UNCITRAL Rules.[37] The 2012 PCA Rules are not a new version of previous sets of PCA rules and were not drafted to supplant them, but rather to complement the range of dispute resolution instruments made available by the PCA. Thus, the introduction to the Rules states that '[t]hey add a new option for arbitration of disputes under the auspices of the Permanent Court of Arbitration . . . without replacing the previously adopted PCA Rules, which remain valid and available'. The Rules became available on 17 December 2012 when they were adopted by the Administrative Council of the PCA, and will apply whenever they are specifically chosen by the parties to a dispute. The same is true of the previous sets of PCA rules: each set is available on the PCA's website and may be referred to in an appropriate agreement. **3.18**

If an arbitration agreement is unclear in its reference to a particular set of PCA rules, the parties' intentions as to the choice of PCA rules are for the arbitral tribunal to determine. Where the PCA is requested to take action as appointing authority in a case where the parties are in disagreement over the applicable set of procedural rules, the PCA Secretary-General may limit the determination to a prima facie finding that an agreement to the 2012 PCA Rules exists, and leave any further determination to the arbitral tribunal, once constituted. The Secretary-General is also free to decide to take no action with respect to a dispute where there is no prima facie evidence of an agreement to arbitrate vesting some authority to act in the PCA or where any condition precedent to action by the PCA has not been met. **3.19**

The lack of a clear reference in the arbitration agreement to a set of rules or to the PCA Secretary-General was the object of contention in *Marks 3-Zet Ernst Marks GmbH & Co KG v Presstek*. In this case, the arbitration agreement read: 'Any dispute . . . between the Parties arising out of or relating to this Agreement which cannot be settled amicably shall be referred to and determined by arbitration in the Hague under the International Arbitration rules'.[38] The claimant, Marks, requested the Secretary-General of the PCA to designate an appointing authority for the appointment of an arbitrator on behalf of the respondent, Presstek. In its **3.20**

[37] Article 1(2) of the 2010 UNCITRAL Rules provides:

> The parties to an arbitration agreement concluded after 15 August 2010 shall be presumed to have referred to the Rules in effect on the date of commencement of the arbitration, unless the parties have agreed to apply a particular version of the Rules. That presumption does not apply where the arbitration agreement has been concluded by accepting after 15 August 2010 an offer made before that date.

[38] *Marks 3-Zet-Ernst Marks GmbH & Co KG v Presstek*, 455 F.3d 7 (1st Cir 2006) 9.

application, Marks asserted that '[i]t is evident from the choice of The Hague as the forum for the arbitration that the "International Arbitration Rules" referred to in the clause are those formulated by UNCITRAL, since these authorize the Secretary-General of the PCA based in The Hague to appoint members to the tribunal or to nominate a so-called Appointing Authority'.[39] However, Presstek, when asked for comments by the PCA, challenged this assertion, saying that the arbitration provision in the parties' agreement was 'too vague' to support the exercise of the PCA's jurisdiction, and refused to agree to the application of the UNCITRAL Rules in the dispute. The PCA notified the parties that the Secretary-General was 'not satisfied, on the basis of a prima facie screening of the documentation submitted by the parties, that he is competent to act in this matter' and invited the parties 'to seek the interpretation of their arbitration agreement from any court having jurisdiction'.[40] Subsequently, Marks filed a petition in a US district court to compel Presstek to arbitrate the dispute in The Hague under 'the American Arbitration Act's International Rules'.[41]

3.21 Presstek moved to dismiss Marks' petition, arguing that the PCA's letter setting out that the PCA Secretary-General was not competent to act in this matter was an 'award' within the meaning of the New York Convention, and that the US court lacked jurisdiction to vacate, modify, or suspend that award by providing the relief sought. Marks contended that no award was made by the PCA, and that no arbitrators ever considered the dispute. Presstek's motion to dismiss was denied. The court decided that the PCA's letter did not qualify as an 'award' within the meaning of the New York Convention, but nevertheless 'Marks' petition seeking an order compelling arbitration before the PCA [was] moot, based on that prior determination'.[42] The district court dismissed Marks' petition on the ground that 'the relief Marks seeks, an order requiring Presstek to arbitrate their dispute at the PCA under the American Arbitration Act's International Rules, is unavailable'.[43]

3.22 Marks appealed the district court's denial of its motion for reconsideration before the US Court of Appeals, First Circuit.[44] The Court of Appeals affirmed the district court's dismissal of the petition to compel arbitration. With regard to the issue of the district court's inability to grant the relief requested, the judge noted as follows:

> Marks' argument that the district court erred in holding that the relief Marks sought was unavailable is largely based on Marks' reading of the October 21,

[39] *Marks 3-Zet-Ernst Marks GmbH & Co KG v Presstek*, 455 F.3d 7 (1st Cir 2006) 9, 12.

[40] *Marks 3-Zet-Ernst Marks GmbH & Co KG v Presstek*, 455 F.3d 7 (1st Cir 2006) 13–14.

[41] *Marks 3-Zet-Ernst Marks GmbH & Co KG v Presstek*, Order of 20 September 2005, DNH, No Civ 05-CV-121-JD (non-reported), *aff* 455 F.3d 7 (1st Cir 2006).

[42] *Marks 3-Zet-Ernst Marks GmbH & Co, KG v Presstek*, Order of 9 August 2005, DNH 118, No Civ 05-CV-121-JD (non-reported).

[43] *Marks 3-Zet-Ernst Marks GmbH & Co, KG v Presstek*, 455 F.3d 7 (1st Cir 2006) 18.

[44] *Marks 3-Zet-Ernst Marks GmbH & Co KG v Presstek*, 455 F.3d 7 (1st Cir 2006) 18.

> 2003 letter from the PCA, which was rejected by the district court. Marks argues that the district court misconstrued the PCA letter, and that the correct reading is 'that the PCA invited the parties to complete the administration of the case (1) if they stipulate to the UNCITRAL Rules, or, (2) if a court of competent jurisdiction... interpreted the arbitration provision of their Agreement (*no matter what jurisdiction, venue or rules the Court designates under the agreement*).' (emphasis added).
>
> Marks' reading of the PCA letter is strained at best. The letter states in clear terms that the PCA would *be competent* to act in these circumstances '*only* when parties to a contract have agreed that disputes in relation to that contract shall be referred to arbitration *under the UNCITRAL Arbitration Rules*' (emphasis added). Indeed, Marks put into the record the published procedural guidelines of the PCA, which support the court's reading: the guidelines state that '[t]he request for designation of an appointing authority... should be accompanied by... [a] copy of the arbitration clause or agreement *establishing the applicability of the UNCITRAL Arbitration Rules*' (emphasis added).
>
> The district court properly rejected Marks' reading of the letter. It did not clearly err in concluding that the only relief Marks had sought, prior to its motion for reconsideration, was arbitration before the PCA under the American Arbitration Act's International Rules. Nor did the court err in finding that that relief was unavailable, or in dismissing the petition on that ground. There was simply no basis, given the PCA's letter, for the district court to order arbitration before the PCA under any set of rules other than the UNCITRAL Arbitration Rules. Marks has never suggested the PCA was a party or that the court could order the PCA to do that which it already said it had no authority to do.[45]

In apparently treating the PCA's letter of 21 October 2003 as having *res judicata* effect with respect to the determination of the potential applicability of the UNCITRAL Rules, the US courts appear to have overlooked the fact that the PCA had only made a prima facie determination on the documents made available by the parties regarding whether the parties had agreed to empower the PCA Secretary-General to designate an appointing authority, while the US district court could have exercised its competence to arrive at its own interpretation of the arbitration agreement. Although the district court, as the Court of Appeals correctly suggested, could not order the PCA to act, the PCA would have taken its decision into account in deciding whether to act. Indeed, the PCA's letter invited the parties to seek the interpretation of their arbitration agreement before any competent court. **3.23**

It should also be noted that the text of Article 1(3) of the 2010 UNCITRAL Rules, providing that these Rules 'shall govern the arbitration except that where any of these Rules is in conflict with a provision of the law applicable to the arbitration from which the parties cannot derogate, that provision shall prevail', was not included in the 2012 PCA Rules. The purpose of this omission is to avoid the inference that states or intergovernmental organizations intend to waive their immunity **3.24**

[45] *Marks 3-Zet-Ernst Marks GmbH & Co KG v Presstek*, 455 F.3d 7 (1st Cir 2006) 22–3 (emphasis in the original).

from the jurisdiction of national courts, including those of the place of arbitration, in disputes involving only states and intergovernmental organizations when agreeing to the application of the 2012 PCA Rules.[46] However, where non-derogable provisions of law applicable to the arbitration conflict with the Rules, just as under the 2010 UNCITRAL Rules, the applicable law will prevail. Because this is true whether or not the UNCITRAL provision is included (the UNCITRAL provision is more a warning than a substantive rule), the provision was not included in view of the confusion it could cause in the context of arbitration involving only states and intergovernmental organizations.

B. Notice and Calculation of Periods of Time—Article 2

1. A notice, including a notification, communication or proposal, may be transmitted by any means of communication that provides or allows for a record of its transmission.
2. If an address has been designated by a party specifically for this purpose or authorized by the arbitral tribunal, any notice shall be delivered to that party at that address, and if so delivered shall be deemed to have been received. Delivery by electronic means such as facsimile or e-mail may only be made to an address so designated or authorized.
3. In the absence of such designation or authorization, a notice is:
   (a) Received if it is physically delivered to the addressee; or
   (b) Deemed to have been received if it is delivered at the place of business, habitual residence or mailing address of the addressee.
4. If, after reasonable efforts, delivery cannot be effected in accordance with paragraphs 2 or 3, a notice is deemed to have been received if it is sent to the addressee's last-known place of business, habitual residence or mailing address by registered letter or any other means that provides a record of delivery or of attempted delivery.
5. A notice shall be deemed to have been received on the day it is delivered in accordance with paragraphs 2, 3 or 4, or attempted to be delivered in accordance with paragraph 4. A notice transmitted by electronic means is deemed to have been received on the day it is sent, except that a notice of arbitration so transmitted is only deemed to have been received on the day when it reaches the addressee's electronic address.
6. For the purpose of calculating a period of time under these Rules, such period shall begin to run on the day following the day when a notice is received. If the last day of such period is an official holiday or a non-business day at the residence or place of business of the addressee, the period is extended until the first business day which follows. Official holidays or non-business days occurring during the running of the period of time are included in calculating the period.

3.25 Article 2 deals with the permissible means of transmission and deemed date of delivery of notices, and the calculation of time periods.

[46] See n 56.

This provision integrally reproduces Article 2 of the 2010 UNCITRAL Rules. **3.26**

In contrast to previous PCA and UNCITRAL models, the 2012 PCA Rules and 2010 UNCITRAL Rules now expressly recognize, in accordance with modern practice, that notices may be delivered by electronic means, so long as the means chosen provides a record of transmission and the address used is designated by a party or authorized by the tribunal. The extensive discussion of this issue within the UNCITRAL Working Group[47] satisfied the PCA Drafting Committee of the emergence of a best practice in arbitration procedure that is also reflected in other recent procedural rules.[48] **3.27**

C. Notice of Arbitration—Article 3

1. The party or parties initiating recourse to arbitration (hereinafter the 'claimant') shall communicate to the other party or parties (hereinafter the 'respondent') and the International Bureau a notice of arbitration.
2. Arbitral proceedings shall be deemed to commence on the date on which the notice of arbitration is received by the respondent.
3. The notice of arbitration shall include the following:
   (a) A demand that the dispute be referred to arbitration;
   (b) The names and contact details of the parties;
   (c) Identification of the arbitration agreement that is invoked;
   (d) Identification of any rule, decision, agreement, contract, convention, treaty, constituent instrument of an organization or agency, or relationship out of, or in relation to which, the dispute arises;
   (e) A brief description of the claim and an indication of the amount involved, if any;
   (f) The relief or remedy sought;
   (g) A proposal as to the number of arbitrators, language and place of arbitration, if the parties have not previously agreed thereon.
4. The notice of arbitration may also include:
   (a) A proposal for the appointment of a sole arbitrator referred to in article 8, paragraph 1;
   (b) Notification of the appointment of an arbitrator referred to in articles 9 or 10.
5. The constitution of the arbitral tribunal shall not be hindered by any controversy with respect to the sufficiency of the notice of arbitration, which shall be finally resolved by the arbitral tribunal.

[47] See eg Report of the UNCITRAL Working Group II (Arbitration and Conciliation) on the work of its 46th session, 5–9 February 2007, A/CN.9/619, para 50; Report of the UNCITRAL Working Group II (Arbitration and Conciliation) on the work of its 49th session, 15–19 September 2008, A/CN.9/665, paras 23–30.

[48] See eg 2012 ICC Rules of Arbitration, Art 3(2): 'All notifications or communications from the Secretariat and the arbitral tribunal ... may be made by delivery against receipt, registered post, courier, *email, or any other means of telecommunications that provides a record of the sending* thereof' (emphasis added).

3.28 Article 3 of the Rules provides for the commencement of arbitration under the Rules by the communication of a notice of arbitration and specifies the notice's mandatory and optional content.

3.29 This provision includes three amendments to the text of Article 3 of the 2010 UNCITRAL Rules.

3.30 First, Article 3(1) provides that the notice of arbitration must be communicated not only to the respondent, but also to the PCA International Bureau. This amendment recognizes the International Bureau's role, described under Article 1(3), as the keeper of archives for the proceedings. In order to keep an accurate and up-to-date record, the International Bureau must receive copies of communications related to the proceedings contemporaneously with the other addressees. Article 17(4) of the Rules generalizes this rule to all communications between the parties and the tribunal.

3.31 Second, Article 3(3)(d) provides that a notice of arbitration shall include the '[i]dentification of any rule, decision, agreement, contract, convention, treaty, constituent instrument of an organization or agency, or relationship out of, or in relation to which, the dispute arises'. This replicates the text of Article 3(3)(c) of the PCA Natural Resources/Environmental Rules and Article 3(3)(d) of the PCA Space Rules. Article 3(3)(d) of the 1976 UNCITRAL Rules provided that the notice of arbitration had to contain 'a reference to the contract out of or in relation to which the dispute arises', thus implying that contractual agreement is the only valid basis for arbitration under these Rules. The PCA Natural Resources/Environmental Rules, adopted in 2001, expanded this provision to take account of the various non-contractual legal instruments that can and, in cases where states, state-controlled entities, and intergovernmental organizations are parties, often do, contain the parties' agreement to arbitrate. The 2010 UNCITRAL Rules do not retain the exclusive focus on contracts of their previous iteration, stating that the notice of arbitration shall include '[i]dentification of any contract or other legal instrument out of or in relation to which the dispute arises'.[49] Of the two formulations, the PCA Drafting Committee adopted the complete enumeration of potentially relevant instruments of the PCA Natural Resources/Environmental Rules.

3.32 Third, Article 3(4)(a) of the 2010 UNCITRAL Rules, providing that a notice of arbitration may include a 'proposal for the designation of an appointing authority', finds no equivalent in the 2012 PCA Rules. This deletion harmonizes Article 3(4) with Article 6(1) of the 2012 PCA Rules, which stipulates that the Secretary-General of the PCA shall serve as appointing authority. The question of the identity of the appointing authority is therefore decided without any need for the claimant to make a proposal in its notice of arbitration or any further consultation between the parties.

49 See Art 3(3)(d).

The remaining text of Article 3 of the 2012 PCA Rules corresponds to Article 3 of the 2010 UNCITRAL Rules. The wording of this provision was developed by the UNCITRAL Working Group as a compromise among different opinions on the utility of having distinct documents comprising a notice of arbitration and a statement of claim. The UNCITRAL Working Group decided to keep the two documents separate because 'it may be impractical for a party to file a statement of claim together with the notice of arbitration in cases where, for example, there was an urgent need to start arbitral proceedings either due to a limitation period, to the need to seek interim relief, or to precipitate negotiation of a settlement'.[50] Nonetheless, the content requirements of Article 3(3) make it possible for a claimant to elect to treat its notice of arbitration as a statement of claim, as foreseen by Article 20(1).[51] The claimant may therefore expedite the proceedings by filing a notice of arbitration that also complies with the requirements for a statement of claim. **3.33**

Article 3(5) makes clear that any disputes over the sufficiency of the notice of arbitration are for the arbitral tribunal to decide. This does not mean, however, that claimants should necessarily ignore such controversies when they arise, as failure to comply with the Rules may lead the arbitral tribunal, once constituted, to find that it has no jurisdiction and that the claimant has to start again by filing a new notice of arbitration. Nor should this provision be taken to mean that an arbitral tribunal would be constituted where evidence of an arbitration agreement between the parties is lacking. **3.34**

D. Response to the Notice of Arbitration—Article 4

1. Within 30 days of the receipt of the notice of arbitration, or such other period as may be set by the International Bureau, the respondent shall communicate to the claimant and the International Bureau a response to the notice of arbitration, which shall include:
   (a) The name and contact details of each respondent;
   (b) A response to the information set forth in the notice of arbitration, pursuant to article 3, paragraphs 3(c) to (g).
2. The response to the notice of arbitration may also include:
   (a) Any plea that an arbitral tribunal to be constituted under these Rules lacks jurisdiction;
   (b) A proposal for the appointment of a sole arbitrator referred to in article 8, paragraph 1;
   (c) Notification of the appointment of an arbitrator referred to in articles 9 or 10;

[50] Report of the UNCITRAL Working Group II (Arbitration and Conciliation) on the work of its 45th session, 11–15 September 2006, A/CN.9/614, para 49.

[51] Under the 1976 UNCITRAL Rules, a party could include its statement of claim in its notice of arbitration. See eg *Ecuador v United States of America*, PCA Case No 2012-5 (1976 UNCITRAL Rules), Request for Arbitration and Statement of Claim, received 28 June 2011.

(d) A brief description of counterclaims or claims for the purpose of a set-off, if any, including where relevant, an indication of the amounts involved, and the relief or remedy sought;
(e) A notice of arbitration in accordance with article 3 in case the respondent formulates a claim against a party to the arbitration agreement other than the claimant.

3. The constitution of the arbitral tribunal shall not be hindered by any controversy with respect to the respondent's failure to communicate a response to the notice of arbitration, or an incomplete or late response to the notice of arbitration, which shall be finally resolved by the arbitral tribunal.

3.35 Article 4 provides for the filing of a response to the notice of arbitration and its mandatory and optional contents.

3.36 It reproduces the text of Article 4 of the 2010 UNCITRAL Rules with three amendments.

3.37 The requirement of a response to the notice of arbitration was introduced in the 2010 UNCITRAL Rules. It reflects a developing practice in proceedings under the 1990s PCA Rules and PCA-administered proceedings under the 1976 UNCITRAL Rules. For example, in *TCW Group Inc and Dominican Energy Holdings LP v The Dominican Republic*—a PCA-administered case conducted under the 1976 UNCITRAL Rules—the arbitral tribunal considered it useful to request the submission by the respondent of a 'short Reply to the Notice of Arbitration', not to be confused with the statement of claim and statement of defence to be submitted pursuant to Articles 18 and 19 of the 1976 UNCITRAL Rules or the counter-memorial referred to in the free-trade agreement applicable in that case.[52] Notably, as in the 2010 UNCITRAL Rules, Article 4(2)(e) provides for the possibility for the respondent to join a third party (who is also a party to the arbitration agreement) to the arbitral proceedings at an early stage.

3.38 Two of the amendments that distinguish Article 4 of the 2012 PCA Rules from the corresponding provision of the 2010 UNCITRAL Rules mirror the innovations of Article 3. Under Article 4(1), the response, just as the notice of arbitration, must be communicated not only to the claimant, as under the 2010 UNCITRAL Rules, but also to the International Bureau of the PCA, to facilitate the keeping of accurate records in accordance with the International Bureau's role as registry under Article 1(3). The PCA Secretary-General acts as appointing authority pursuant to Article 6(1) of the Rules, so there is no need for a discussion of the identity of the appointing authority in the response to the notice of arbitration.

3.39 Moreover, Article 4(1) provides that the time period for the communication of a response to the notice of arbitration shall be 30 days from receipt of the notice of

[52] PCA Case No 2008-6 (CAFTA-DR) (1976 UNCITRAL Rules), Procedural Order No 1, 23 June 2008, s 2.4.

arbitration or 'such other period as may be set by the International Bureau'. This new text integrates the approaches taken by the 2010 UNCITRAL Rules and the 1990s PCA Rules. Under the 2010 UNCITRAL Rules, a rigid 30-day deadline applies to the filing of the response. Given that, at this stage of the proceedings, the arbitral tribunal is not yet constituted, in an ad hoc arbitration under the UNCITRAL Rules only an agreement between the parties can extend this deadline. Under the 1990s PCA Rules, more generous time periods, usually twice as long as the time periods stipulated in the 1976 UNCITRAL Rules, are set, in recognition of the sometimes slower response time of public entities. In Article 4(1), the 2012 PCA Rules accommodate both approaches.[53] As the purpose of the response is not the provision of a full defence, but rather an initial exchange of information allowing the arbitral tribunal to form a preliminary view of the issues in dispute, the Rules recognize that a period of 30 days is usually sufficient for the filing. Nonetheless, where circumstances justify the extension of this time period, Article 4(1) of the Rules allows the International Bureau to grant extensions upon application by the respondent or on its own initiative. As stated in the Explanatory Note to the Rules, in granting such extensions, the International Bureau will be guided by the time periods provided in the 1990s PCA Rules.[54]

E. Representation and Assistance—Article 5

1. In disputes involving only States and/or intergovernmental organizations, each party shall appoint an agent. Each party may also be assisted by persons of its choice.
2. In other disputes under these Rules, each party may be represented or assisted by persons chosen by it.
3. The names and addresses of agents, party representatives, and other persons assisting the parties must be communicated to all parties, to the International Bureau, and to the arbitral tribunal. Such communication must specify whether the appointment is being made for purposes of representation or assistance. Where a person is to act as an agent or representative of a party, the arbitral tribunal, on its own initiative or at the request of any party, may at any time require proof of authority granted to the agent or representative in such a form as the arbitral tribunal may determine.

Article 5 provides that parties to an arbitration may be represented and assisted by persons of their choice. **3.40**

Article 5(1) stipulates that, in disputes involving only states and international organizations, each party shall appoint an agent. This provision is based on **3.41**

[53] See also Rules, Arts 8(2)(b), 9(3), 43(4).
[54] See Explanatory Note, reproduced in Appendix I.

Article 4 of the PCA State/State Rules and Article 4 of the PCA State/International Organization Rules, and accords with the practice in cases involving such parties.

3.42 Articles 5(2) and (3) are based on Article 5 of the 2010 UNCITRAL Rules, which found broad support from the UNCITRAL Working Group.[55] The last sentence, to the effect that the tribunal may at any time require proof of authority to act as agent or representative, was considered a helpful addition because it captures the varying approaches in different legal systems regarding the proof of authority to act in an arbitral proceeding.[56] The only modification in the 2012 PCA Rules was to add the International Bureau as the recipient of all addresses and names of agents, party representatives, and other persons assisting the parties in order to facilitate the PCA's fulfillment of its role as registry and appointing authority under, respectively, Articles 1(3) and 6(1) of the Rules.

F. Appointing Authority—Article 6

1. The Secretary-General of the Permanent Court of Arbitration shall serve as appointing authority.
2. In exercising its functions under these Rules, the appointing authority may require from any party and the arbitrators the information it deems necessary and it shall give the parties and, where appropriate, the arbitrators, an opportunity to present their views in any manner it considers appropriate.
3. The appointing authority shall have regard to such considerations as are likely to secure the appointment of an independent and impartial arbitrator and shall take into account the advisability of appointing an arbitrator of a nationality other than the nationalities of the parties.

3.43 Article 6 concerns the appointing authority under the Rules.

3.44 In this respect, the 2012 PCA Rules differ from the 2010 UNCITRAL Rules.

3.45 The PCA was the only arbitral institution explicitly mentioned in the 1976 UNCITRAL Rules. It was entrusted with the function of 'designating authority'. The 1976 UNCITRAL Rules provide that in cases where: (i) the parties cannot agree on the choice of a sole arbitrator (Article 6); (ii) the respondent fails to appoint a second arbitrator (Article 7(2)); (iii) the two party-appointed arbitrators cannot agree on the choice of the presiding arbitrator (Article 7(3)); or (iv) when a challenge to an arbitrator needs to be decided (Article 12(1)(c)), and the parties cannot agree on an appointing authority or an agreed appointing authority refuses or fails to act,

[55] Report of the UNCITRAL Working Group II (Arbitration and Conciliation) on the work of its 49th session, 15–19 September 2008, A/CN.9/665, para 43.

[56] Report of the UNCITRAL Working Group II (Arbitration and Conciliation) on the work of its 49th session, 15–19 September 2008, A/CN.9/665, para 43.

then 'either party may request the Secretary-General of the Permanent Court of Arbitration at The Hague to designate an appointing authority'.

At the UNCITRAL Working Group for the revision of the UNCITRAL Rules, **3.46** the option of naming the PCA Secretary-General as a default appointing authority, instead of as a designating authority, was discussed. In this context, the PCA's unique status as an intergovernmental organization with broad membership was emphasized.[57] However, this rule was ultimately not adopted, with the Working Group citing its mandate to only improve what did not work.[58] While there was delay attributable to the 1976 UNCITRAL Rules' procedure, there was no evidence that it did not work.[59] The UNCITRAL Working Group thus only clarified in the 2010 UNCITRAL Rules what often happens in practice, namely that the parties agree on the PCA Secretary-General as the appointing authority.[60]

While not naming the PCA Secretary-General as appointing authority, the **3.47** approach of the 1976 and 2010 UNCITRAL Rules gave the PCA considerable experience in designating and appointing authority matters. The PCA's first UNCITRAL-related task was in 1982, when the Secretary-General was asked to designate an appointing authority for the Iran–United States Claims Tribunal.[61] In the 30 years since this first request, the PCA has been asked to designate an appointing authority or act as appointing authority in over 500 cases.

Pursuant to Article 6(1) of the 2012 PCA Rules, the PCA Secretary-General acts **3.48** as the appointing authority. Under the 2010 UNCITRAL Rules, parties that have not agreed in advance on the identity of an appointing authority may incur delays in the constitution of the tribunal or during subsequent challenges to an arbitrator. For instance, at the outset of the proceedings, the first proposal by one of the parties with respect to the identity of the appointing authority is generally made when it becomes apparent that an appointing authority is necessary, for instance to appoint a second or presiding arbitrator to a three-member tribunal. If the other party does not accept the proposal, the proposing party must await the expiry of a minimum period of 30 days, in accordance with Article 6(2) of the 2010 UNCITRAL Rules,

57 Report of the UNCITRAL Working Group II (Arbitration and Conciliation) on the work of its 46th session, 5–9 February 2007, A/CN.9/619, paras 71, 73.

58 Report of the UNCITRAL Working Group II (Arbitration and Conciliation) on the work of its 46th session, 5–9 February 2007, A/CN.9/619, para 72; see also Report of the UNCITRAL Working Group II (Arbitration and Conciliation) on the work of its 39th session, 19 June to 7 July 2006, A/61/17, para 184.

59 See Jan Paulsson, 'Arbitration Without Privity' (1995) 10 *ICSID Review-Foreign Investment Law Journal* 232, 243–4.

60 See eg Energy Charter Treaty, Lisbon, 17 December 1994, (1995) 34 ILM 381, Art 27(3)(d).

61 The Rules of Procedure of the Iran–United States Claims Tribunal, which confer upon the PCA Secretary-General the authority to designate appointing authorities, were based on the 1976 UNCITRAL Rules. To date, the Secretary-General of the PCA has designated three appointing authorities for the Tribunal. Throughout the years, the PCA International Bureau has served as the secretariat of each appointing authority.

before making a request to the PCA Secretary-General to designate an appointing authority. The PCA will usually solicit the comments of the other party on the request and then search for an appropriate authority for the matter.[62] The new PCA Rules eliminate the need for this procedure. Whenever the need arises for an appointing authority, the parties may directly address the PCA Secretary-General.

3.49 As appointing authority under the Rules, the PCA Secretary-General may, upon request:

- appoint arbitrators (Articles 7–10);
- decide challenges to arbitrators (Article 13(4));
- in exceptional circumstances, directly appoint a substitute arbitrator (Article 14(2)); and
- review and adjust the tribunal's proposal for the determination of its fees and expenses (Article 41(2)).

3.50 Also, in every case under the Rules, the PCA Secretary-General reviews and, if necessary, adjusts the tribunal's determination of its fees and expenses, as well as of the fees and expenses of tribunal-appointed experts (see Article 41(3)).

3.51 Article 6(3) reproduces the formulation of Article 6(7) of the 2010 UNCITRAL Rules and represents the standard practice of the Secretary-General of the PCA with regard to the appointment of arbitrators. A more specific list of appointment criteria was not included to avoid the argument being made at the enforcement stage or in other circumstances that the tribunal was not properly constituted because a particular criterion was not adequately observed by the appointing authority. In general, in addition to the criteria found in the applicable procedural rules, the PCA Secretary-General considers:

- the nationalities of the parties and prospective arbitrators;
- the place of arbitration;
- the language(s) of the arbitration;
- the amounts claimed, the subject-matter, and the complexity of the dispute;
- the qualifications and experience of any prospective arbitrator;
- the place of residence of any prospective arbitrator;
- the language abilities of any prospective arbitrator;
- the fees to be charged by any prospective arbitrator; and,
- the availability of any prospective arbitrator.

It is also possible for the parties to specify relevant criteria for appointment in their arbitration agreement.

---

[62] See *UNCITRAL Arbitration Rules: Report of the Secretary-General of the Permanent Court of Arbitration on its activities under the UNCITRAL Arbitration Rules since 1976*, UNCITRAL Working Group II (Arbitration and Conciliation), 40th session, 25 June to 12 July 2007, A/CN.9/634.

4

SECTION II. COMPOSITION OF THE ARBITRAL TRIBUNAL

A. Number of Arbitrators—Article 7

1. If the parties have not previously agreed on the number of arbitrators, and if within 30 days after the receipt by the respondent of the notice of arbitration the parties have not agreed on the number of arbitrators, three arbitrators shall be appointed.
2. Notwithstanding paragraph 1, if no other parties have responded to a party's proposal to appoint a sole arbitrator within the time limit provided for in paragraph 1 and the party or parties concerned have failed to appoint a second arbitrator in accordance with articles 9 or 10, the appointing authority may, at the request of a party, appoint a sole arbitrator pursuant to the procedure provided for in article 8, paragraph 2 if it determines that, in view of the circumstances of the case, this is more appropriate.

Article 7 supplies the rule regarding the number of arbitrators to be appointed to the tribunal in the absence of agreement by the parties. **4.01**

Article 7(1) is almost identical to Article 7 of the 2010 UNCITRAL Rules. It provides for a three-member tribunal where the parties have not agreed on a different size. A principal issue in deciding the proper default number of arbitrators is to correctly anticipate the size and complexity of potential disputes likely to arise **4.02** under the Rules. A small and simple case may not justify the added expense of a three-member tribunal as compared to a sole arbitrator. However, in the experience of the PCA, it is reasonable to anticipate that many disputes involving states, state-controlled entities, and international organizations will involve complex legal and factual scenarios and significant amounts in dispute. As a result, it was preferred to set the default number of arbitrators to three.[1]

4.03 The only departure from the text of the 2010 UNCITRAL Rules consists of the replacement of the phrase 'the parties have not previously agreed that there shall be only one arbitrator' by 'the parties have not previously agreed on the number of arbitrators'. The purpose of this change is to account for the fact that the Rules, like the PCA State/State Rules, but unlike the 2010 UNCITRAL Rules, contemplate the possibility of five-member tribunals, which are favoured in inter-state arbitration. Article 9(1) of the Rules provides for the manner in which such tribunals are constituted.

4.04 Article 7(2) follows the 2010 UNCITRAL Rules in providing that in cases where the respondent is unresponsive and the circumstances otherwise warrant it, the appointing authority may, upon the request of a party, appoint a sole arbitrator, rather than facilitating the constitution of a three-member tribunal. This provision was included in the 2010 UNCITRAL Rules on the advice given by the PCA after witnessing several small claims forced into three-member tribunals due to the rigid drafting of the 1976 UNCITRAL Rules, which allowed no exceptions to the three-member default rule, even if the amount in dispute was small and the respondent was not participating in the proceedings.[2]

---

[1] This decision aligns with that of the UNCITRAL Working Group, which similarly determined that a default appointment of a sole arbitrator in complex proceedings would be 'unworkable': Report of the UNCITRAL Working Group II (Arbitration and Conciliation) on the work of its 49th session, 15–19 September 2008, A/CN.9/665, para 58.

[2] PCA legal staff attended the meetings of the UNCITRAL Working Group and made recommendations based on the PCA's experience with cases under the 1976 UNCITRAL Rules. With regard to the recommended amendments to Art 7, the PCA was motivated by two cases which occurred in close succession in 2008 while the revision of the UNCITRAL Rules was underway. In one case, the PCA Secretary-General was requested to designate an appointing authority for the appointment of a second arbitrator to a tribunal of three in a case where the amount in dispute was approximately US$330,000 and the respondent was unresponsive. In the second case, the amount in dispute was less than €200,000 and the claimant proposed the appointment of a sole arbitrator. The respondent refused this proposal as part of its general resistance to having any involvement in the constitution of the tribunal on the ground that it had objections to the tribunal's jurisdiction. Constrained by the 1976 UNCITRAL Rules, the Secretary-General ultimately designated an appointing authority for the appointment of a second arbitrator to a three-member tribunal.

B. Appointment of Arbitrators—Articles 8 to 10

1. Article 8

1. If the parties have agreed that a sole arbitrator is to be appointed and if within 30 days after receipt by all other parties of a proposal of an individual who would serve as a sole arbitrator the parties have not reached agreement thereon, a sole arbitrator shall, at the request of a party, be appointed by the appointing authority.
2. The appointing authority shall appoint the sole arbitrator as promptly as possible. In making the appointment, the appointing authority shall use the following list-procedure, unless the parties agree that the list-procedure should not be used or unless the appointing authority determines in its discretion that the use of the list-procedure is not appropriate for the case:
   (a) The appointing authority shall communicate to each of the parties an identical list containing at least three names;
   (b) Within 15 days after the receipt of this list, or such other period as may be set by the International Bureau, each party may return the list to the appointing authority, without copying the other party, after having deleted the name or names to which it objects and numbered the remaining names on the list in the order of its preference;
   (c) After the expiration of the above period of time the appointing authority shall appoint the sole arbitrator from among the names approved on the lists returned to it and in accordance with the order of preference indicated by the parties;
   (d) If for any reason the appointment cannot be made according to this procedure, the appointing authority may exercise its discretion in appointing the sole arbitrator.

Article 8 sets out the mechanism for the appointment of a sole arbitrator by the PCA Secretary-General, who is the appointing authority under the Rules. Pursuant to Article 9(3) of the Rules, the appointment procedure described at Article 8(2) also applies to the appointment by the Secretary-General of a presiding arbitrator to a three-member tribunal and of the three non-party appointed arbitrators to a five-member tribunal.[3] **4.05**

Article 8 of the 2012 PCA Rules improves on Article 8 of the 2010 UNCITRAL Rules in three respects. **4.06**

First, Article 8(1) of the Rules refers to 'a proposal of an individual who would serve as a sole arbitrator', where the equivalent provision of the 2010 UNCITRAL Rules mentions 'a proposal for the appointment of a sole arbitrator'. The PCA Drafting Committee was concerned that the latter phrase could be mistakenly taken to refer to a proposal by a party to submit the dispute to a sole arbitrator rather than to a three-member tribunal, when in fact the phrase is intended to refer to the proposal **4.07**

---

[3] For a discussion of the procedure for the constitution of five-member tribunals, see under Art 9.

of a particular person who could serve as a sole arbitrator.[4] Indeed, the appointment of a sole arbitrator by the PCA Secretary-General pursuant to Article 8(1) is only triggered when:

(i) the parties have previously agreed that the arbitral tribunal will be composed of a sole arbitrator;
(ii) one party has made a proposal of the identity of the sole arbitrator;
(iii) within 30 days of receipt of this proposal by the other party or parties, all parties have not agreed on the identity of the sole arbitrator; and
(iv) one party has made a request to the PCA Secretary-General for the appointment of a sole arbitrator.

4.08 Second, Article 8(2)(b) describes the list-procedure, which is the most commonly used method for the appointment of sole and presiding arbitrators by the appointing authority. It provides that the list of proposed arbitrators communicated by the appointing authority to the parties must be returned '15 days after [each party's] receipt of this list, or such other period as may be set by the International Bureau'.[5] This new text finds a middle ground between Article 8(2)(b) of the 2010 UNCITRAL Rules, which provides for a 15-day deadline for the submission of the list, and the equivalent provisions of the 1990s PCA Rules, which allow a more generous 30-day period.[6]

4.09 In its current drafting, Article 8(2)(b) signals to the parties that 15 days should suffice for the return of the list, but acknowledges that exceptions may be appropriate in certain circumstances. For example, the longer lists of names employed in some cases by the PCA in order to improve the chances for success of a list-procedure may justify allowing the parties more time for the careful evaluation and ranking of each candidate. As stated in the Explanatory Note to the Rules, the time periods set forth in the 1990s PCA Rules will serve as a guideline for the extensions that the International Bureau may decide to grant under Article 8(2)(b) of the Rules.[7]

---

[4] The intended meaning of the phrase is made explicit in the equivalent provision of the 1976 UNCITRAL Rules:

> Article 6
> 1. If a sole arbitrator is to be appointed, either party may propose to the other:
>   (a) *The names of one or more persons, one of whom would serve as the sole arbitrator*;
>
> ...
>
> 2. If within thirty days after receipt by a party of a proposal made in accordance with paragraph 1 the parties have not reached agreement on the choice of a sole arbitrator, the sole arbitrator shall be appointed by the appointing authority...
>
> (emphasis added)

[5] A similar power to change deadlines is available to the PCA International Bureau under Arts 4(1), 9(3), and 43(4) of the Rules.

[6] PCA State/State Rules, Art 6(3)(b); PCA State/Non-State Rules, Art 6(3)(b); PCA State/International Organization Rules, capital Art 6(3)(b); PCA International Organization/Private Party Rules, Art 6(3)(b). See also PCA Natural Resources/Environmental Rules, Art 6(3)(b).

[7] Explanatory Note, reproduced in Appendix I.

An appointment made pursuant to the list-procedure has the potential to reflect the optimal compromise solution, where the appointed arbitrator, while perhaps not being the first choice of either party, is nonetheless acceptable to both parties.[8] A degree of party autonomy is preserved as compared to a direct appointment by the PCA Secretary-General or institutional appointments made under other procedural rules, where the parties would have no knowledge of the identity of the arbitrator prior to the appointment.[9] When directly appointing an arbitrator, the PCA generally takes into account factors such as (in no particular order): **4.10**

- the nationalities of the parties,
- the place of arbitration,
- the language(s) of the arbitration,
- the amount claimed, and
- the subject-matter and complexity of the dispute;

and, with respect to any prospective arbitrator:

- nationality,
- qualifications,
- experience,
- place of residence,
- language abilities, and
- availability.

The PCA also ensures that all prospective arbitrators confirm their independence and impartiality. Nevertheless, the list-procedure allows additional factors to be reflected in the selection, including the degree to which a particular candidate's experience and reputation inspire the confidence of the parties and whether the arbitrator's personal style will result in the right chemistry on the tribunal and with counsel. **4.11**

Third, Article 8(2)(b) of the Rules specifies that each party, having deleted the names of arbitrators it objects to from the list and ranked the remaining names according to its preferences, may return the list to the appointing authority **4.12**

[8] One author describes the list-procedure as the 'ideal system for appointing arbitrators': Pieter Sanders, *The Work of UNCITRAL on Arbitration and Conciliation* (2nd edn, Kluwer Law International, 2004) 6.

[9] In contrast, under the 2012 ICC Rules of Arbitration, the ICC Court appoints sole or presiding arbitrators without divulging their identities prior to appointment (Art 12). Derains and Schwartz note that in ICC proceedings parties most often agree on the identity of presiding arbitrators (if not sole arbitrators), explaining that '[n]o matter how well an arbitral institution such as the ICC may perform its task as an appointing authority, parties increasingly realize that there is no more important choice in connection with an arbitration than the choice of arbitrators, and, to the extent possible, this is therefore not a choice that should be allowed to escape the parties' control': Yves Derains and Eric A Schwartz, *Guide to the ICC Rules of Arbitration* (2nd edn, Kluwer Law International, 2005) 153.

'without copying the other party'. While the 1976 and 2010 UNCITRAL Rules contain no such specification, it is the PCA's experience that parties will, from time to time, copy the other side when returning the list of arbitrators to the appointing authority. Although it would not invalidate the list-procedure, allowing one side to know the other's preferences before submitting its own may influence the outcome of the procedure.

4.13 Consider a case where the PCA circulates to the parties a list of five names, and all names on the list are acceptable to both parties, but the respondent's preferred arbitrator is the one the claimant likes the least. If each party submits the list to the PCA in ignorance of the other's preferences (ie without either party copying the other), the parties' respective lists will reflect their true preferences, for example, as follows:

Claimant	Respondent
Arbitrator A–rank 1	Arbitrator A–rank 2
Arbitrator B–rank 2	Arbitrator B–rank 5
Arbitrator C–rank 3	Arbitrator C–rank 3
Arbitrator D–rank 4	Arbitrator D–rank 4
Arbitrator E–rank 5	Arbitrator E–rank 1

4.14 In this case, the PCA Secretary-General would appoint Arbitrator A as the best compromise between the parties' preferences, given that he is the claimant's first and the respondent's second choice.

4.15 However, if the claimant were to submit its list to the PCA first, and copy the respondent on it, the respondent could manipulate the list-procedure to obtain the appointment of its preferred arbitrator by submitting a list indicating its choices as follows:

Claimant	Respondent
Arbitrator A–rank 1	~~Arbitrator A~~
Arbitrator B–rank 2	~~Arbitrator B~~
Arbitrator C–rank 3	~~Arbitrator C~~
Arbitrator D–rank 4	~~Arbitrator D~~
Arbitrator E–rank 5	Arbitrator E–rank 1

4.16 By striking from the list all the names save that of Arbitrator E, the respondent would ensure that Arbitrator E, its preferred candidate, is appointed. Yet Arbitrator E is the claimant's least favourite candidate. The list-procedure will then have achieved a less desirable result than if Arbitrator A had been appointed.

4.17 Parties also sometimes ask that their comments on the list be kept confidential by the appointing authority for fear of offending an arbitrator whose name has been deleted from the list or who has been ranked below another candidate. The phrase 'without copying the other party' therefore allows parties maximum freedom in the expression of their preferences.

In all other respects, Article 8 of the 2012 PCA Rules mirrors Article 8 of the 2010 UNCITRAL Rules. The application of this provision by the PCA Secretary-General will follow the PCA's existing practices developed under the 1990s PCA Rules and the 1976 and 2010 UNCITRAL Rules. When acting as appointing authority and requested to appoint a sole or presiding arbitrator under the UNCITRAL Rules, the PCA Secretary-General most often provides the parties with a list of five to ten potential arbitrators who have confirmed to the PCA their independence, impartiality, and availability. While both sets of UNCITRAL Rules require only three names to appear on the list, in PCA experience, particularly in cases where parties express strongly divergent views regarding the qualifications that the sole or presiding arbitrator should possess, a longer list increases the chances that one or more candidates will be acceptable to all parties. Where the parties have previously agreed on the profile of the sole or presiding arbitrator (eg they have indicated excluded or preferred nationalities, and required areas of expertise), the PCA Secretary-General endeavours to compile a list composed of arbitrators who fit the parties' agreed profile. If the parties make suggestions but cannot agree on the arbitrator's profile, the PCA Secretary-General takes these suggestions into consideration, without being bound by them. In general, the PCA, in compiling lists of prospective arbitrators, takes into account the same factors (detailed in paragraph 4.10) as in choosing arbitrators for direct appointment. **4.18**

Under the Rules, the PCA Secretary-General may also directly appoint a sole or presiding arbitrator without having recourse to the list-procedure in cases where: **4.19**

- the parties so agree (chapeau of Article 8(2));
- the PCA Secretary-General determines in his or her discretion that the use of the list-procedure is not appropriate for the case (chapeau of Article 8(2)); or
- the appointment cannot be made in accordance with the list-procedure for any reason (Article 8(2)(d)).

When acting as appointing authority under the equivalent provisions of the 1990s PCA Rules and the 1976 and 2010 UNCITRAL Rules, the PCA Secretary-General has generally resorted to a direct appointment only after conduct of the list-procedure had failed due to the absence of overlap between the preferences indicated by the parties (ie where all of the proposed arbitrators on the list had been deleted by at least one of the parties).[10] **4.20**

10 From 2006 to 2012, in the cases where the PCA Secretary-General was requested to appoint a sole or presiding arbitrator, the list-procedure failed twice. In both cases, the request was for the appointment of a sole arbitrator and the Secretary-General had provided the parties with a list of five potential arbitrators. In two more cases, the Secretary-General directly appointed a sole arbitrator because the claimant had made a request for a direct appointment, to which the respondent did not object.

4.21 In order to avoid this outcome, particularly in investment treaty arbitrations, where parties are frequently divided on the appropriate profile for the arbitrator to be appointed, the PCA Secretary-General has on occasion proposed to the parties a modification of the list-procedure described in the 1990s PCA Rules and the 1976 and 2010 UNCITRAL Rules.

4.22 For example, in a recent investment treaty arbitration where the PCA Secretary-General acted as appointing authority by agreement of the parties, the PCA proposed to the parties that the PCA compile a list of ten candidates for appointment as presiding arbitrator, with the name of an eleventh candidate to be withheld by the PCA in case the list-procedure failed and it became necessary to make a direct appointment. The PCA added that, should the parties be willing to agree to delete no more than five names from the list, the PCA would include on the list the names of all 11 candidates. The latter approach would permit the PCA to take into account the parties' respective orders of preference in relation to all candidates who were under consideration for appointment. The prospect of a longer list may make parties more comfortable with limiting the number of names that may be deleted. However, longer lists may be inappropriate in many cases in view of the additional time they may require to constitute or where conflicts of interest or required special expertise limit the pool of qualified potential arbitrators.[11] The modified list-procedure can also be carried out with fewer than 11 names on the list.[12]

2. Article 9

1. If three arbitrators are to be appointed, each party shall appoint one arbitrator. The two arbitrators thus appointed shall choose the third arbitrator who will act as the presiding arbitrator of the arbitral tribunal. If five arbitrators are to be appointed, the two party-appointed arbitrators shall choose the remaining three arbitrators and designate one of those three as the presiding arbitrator of the tribunal.
2. If within 30 days after the receipt of a party's notification of the appointment of an arbitrator the other party has not notified the first party of the arbitrator it has appointed, the first party may request the appointing authority to appoint the second arbitrator.
3. If within 30 days after the appointment of the second arbitrator, or such other period as may be set by the International Bureau, the two arbitrators have not agreed on the choice of the remaining arbitrators and/or the presiding arbitrator, the remaining arbitrators and/or the presiding arbitrator shall be appointed by

[11] Conflicts of interest often limit the ability of the PCA to identify enough qualified candidates to populate longer lists. This is particularly true in cases involving major international corporations or cases where related disputes involving the same parties are the subject of parallel litigation or arbitration proceedings. In such cases, leading practitioners will frequently be acting or have previously acted as counsel, arbitrators or legal experts for one of the parties, or have other contacts with one of the parties that make them inappropriate as candidates for inclusion on the list. The PCA checks each candidate for independence and impartiality before including that person on the list.

[12] In another recent case, the list-procedure was conducted with seven names and each party agreed to strike no more than three.

the appointing authority in the same way as a sole arbitrator would be appointed under article 8, paragraph 2.

Article 9 sets out the procedure for the appointment of an arbitral tribunal composed of three or five members. **4.23**

With regard to the procedure for the appointment of a three-member tribunal, Article 9 modifies the text of Article 9 of the 2010 UNCITRAL Rules in only one respect. Specifically, Article 9(3) of the Rules allows the PCA International Bureau to modify the 30-day period given to the two already appointed arbitrators for the selection of a presiding arbitrator.[13] **4.24**

In this provision, the PCA Drafting Committee chose the 30-day deadline of the UNCITRAL Rules[14] over the 60-day deadline of the PCA State/State Rules, State/International Organization Rules, and International Organization/Private Party Rules.[15] The PCA Drafting Committee considered that, if agreement on the identity of the presiding arbitrator is possible, in most cases 30 days will suffice. However, the Drafting Committee was also of the view that allowing the PCA International Bureau discretion to extend the 30-day deadline would reinforce the fairness and efficiency of the Rules in certain situations, such as where good cause can be shown or where a deadline is missed only by a short period of time. As stated in the Explanatory Note to the Rules, when receiving requests from parties to extend this deadline, the International Bureau will consider the longer deadlines set in corresponding provisions of the 1990s PCA Rules.[16] **4.25**

The 2012 PCA Rules also provide a specific procedure for the appointment of five-member tribunals. In so doing, the 2012 PCA Rules set themselves apart from the 2010 UNCITRAL Rules, as well as from the rules of other arbitral institutions.[17] Under the 2010 UNCITRAL Rules, five-member tribunals are appointed 'according to the method agreed upon by the parties' (Article 10(2)). In the absence of an agreed method, the entire tribunal is constituted by the appointing authority (Article 10(3)). The stipulation of a default procedure for the appointment of five-member tribunals was not necessary in the 2010 UNCITRAL Rules because five-member tribunals are rare in international commercial arbitration. By contrast, they are the norm in inter-state arbitration, where the importance and political sensitivity of the matter in dispute may justify the additional cost and time of a **4.26**

[13] A similar power to extend deadlines is available to the International Bureau under Arts 4(1), 8(2)(b), and 43(4) of the Rules.

[14] 1976 UNCITRAL Rules, Art 7(3), reproduced in Appendix XI; 2010 UNCITRAL Rules, Art 9(3), reproduced in Appendix XII.

[15] PCA State/State Rules, Art 7(3); PCA State/International Organization Rules, Art 7(3); PCA International Organization/Private Party Rules, Art 7(3). See also PCA Natural Resources/ Environmental Rules, Art 7(3) and (5).

[16] Explanatory Note, reproduced in Appendix I.

[17] See eg London Court of International Arbitration (LCIA) Arbitration Rules 1998, Art 5; 2012 ICC Rules of Arbitration, Art 12(1).

five-member tribunal.[18] Given the Rules' objective to provide a dispute resolution mechanism for inter-state disputes, among others, the PCA Drafting Committee chose to include a procedure for the appointment of five-member tribunals. Such tribunals may also be appropriate in complex, high-value, non-inter-state arbitrations.[19] While the Drafting Committee considered phrasing Article 9 in general terms that would cover the case of tribunals of more than five members, it ultimately decided against such a formulation. In practice, parties rarely choose to constitute tribunals of more than five members.[20]

4.27 Accordingly, Article 9(1) provides: 'If five arbitrators are to be appointed, the two party-appointed arbitrators shall choose the remaining three arbitrators and designate one of those three as the presiding arbitrator of the tribunal'. This text first appeared in Article 7(1) of the PCA State/State Rules and was thereafter included in the PCA State/International Organization Rules, Natural Resources/Environmental Rules, and Space Rules.[21] Following this procedure, the arbitrators not appointed by either party outnumber the party-appointed arbitrators. This

[18] Five-member tribunals were constituted in eight of the twelve most recent inter-state arbitrations administered by the PCA: *Philippines v China*, PCA Case No 2013-19 (UNCLOS); *ARA Libertad Arbitration*, Argentina v Ghana, PCA Case No 2013-11 (UNCLOS); *Mauritius v United Kingdom*, PCA Case No 2011-3 (UNCLOS); *Croatia/Slovenia*, PCA Case No 2012-4; *Bangladesh v India*, PCA Case No 2010-16 (UNCLOS); *Case Concerning Land Reclamations by Singapore in and around the Straits of Johor*, Malaysia v Singapore, PCA Case No 2004-5 (UNCLOS); *Guyana v Suriname*, PCA Case No 2004-4 (UNCLOS); *Barbados v Trinidad and Tobago*, PCA Case No 2004-2 (UNCLOS). UNCLOS provides (with some exceptions) for five-member arbitral tribunals (10 December 1982, 1833 UNTS 397, Annex VII, para 3(a)).

[19] The *Eurotunnel* case is one example of a state/private party PCA-administered arbitration with a five-member tribunal: 1 The Channel Tunnel Group Limited 2 France-Manche SA v 1 the Secretary of State for Transport of the Government of the United Kingdom of Great Britain and Northern Ireland 2 le ministre de l'équipement, des transports, de l'aménagement du territoire, du tourisme et de la mer du Gouvernement de la République française, PCA Case No 2003-5, Partial Award of 30 January 2007, PCA Award Series, para 3. This case was particular as it was brought by two private parties against two states under a concession agreement. The dispute resolution clause in the concession agreement referred to a treaty concluded by the states in question. The treaty provided that disputes between the two states would be decided by a three-member arbitral tribunal, whereas in any dispute involving private parties, these parties could appoint two additional arbitrators. The treaty further provided that the two additional arbitrators could not participate 'in that part of the decision relating to the interpretation and application of the Treaty': PCA Case No 2003-5, Partial Award of 30 January 2007, PCA Award Series, para 3, referring to the Treaty between the United Kingdom of Great Britain and Northern Ireland and the Republic of France concerning the Construction and Operation by Private Concessionaires of a Channel Fixed Link, 12 February 1986, 1497 UNTS 335, Art 19(2).

[20] A rare example of a tribunal composed of more than five arbitrators is found in the Indus Waters Treaty 1960, which allocates the use of part of the waters of the Indus river system between India and Pakistan and provides for the resolution of some of the disputes arising under it by a seven-member 'Court of Arbitration' (19 September 1960, 419 UNTS 126, annexure G, para 4). The first Court of Arbitration to be constituted in the 60-year history of the Treaty rendered a Partial Award on 18 February 2013 (*Indus Waters Kishenganga Arbitration*, Pakistan v India, PCA Case No 2011-1).

[21] A similar procedure applies under UNCLOS, with the exception that for the appointment of the three remaining arbitrators UNCLOS provides for an agreement by the parties, rather than by the party-appointed arbitrators (n 103, Annex VII, para 3(d)).

stands in contrast with a procedure wherein each party would appoint two arbitrators and the four party-appointed arbitrators would appoint the presiding arbitrator.[22] Party appointments have been the subject of debate in recent arbitration literature,[23] but PCA experience suggests that, for states in particular, participation in the constitution of the tribunal is one of the most attractive features of international arbitration.

In keeping with Article 9(1), Article 9(3) of the Rules incorporates the necessary wording to apply to the constitution of both three- and five-member tribunals. **4.28**

Apart from the aforementioned departures from the UNCITRAL Rules, and as with Article 8 of the Rules, the PCA Secretary-General will make appointments under Article 9 of the Rules as under the equivalent provisions of the 1990s PCA Rules and the 1976 and 2010 UNCITRAL Rules. Under those rules, the most common requests received by the PCA Secretary-General acting as appointing authority are requests for the appointment of a second arbitrator.[24] Upon receiving a complete request for appointment,[25] the Secretary-General invites the other party to submit its comments within a one-to-two-week period. If all the necessary conditions are met, and on the basis of a prima facie screening of the documents the Secretary-General is satisfied that he or she is competent to act, a second arbitrator is designated upon expiration of the deadline for comments. **4.29**

[22] Examples of five-member tribunals with four party-appointed arbitrators can be found in several PCA-administered arbitrations where the parties modified the PCA State/International Organization Rules or the PCA State/State Rules to this effect. See *Abyei Arbitration*, the Government of Sudan/the Sudan People's Liberation Movement/Army, PCA Case No 2008-7, Arbitration Agreement, Art 5(1); *Eritrea-Ethiopia Claims Commission*, PCA Case No 2001-1; *Eritrea-Ethiopia Boundary Commission*, PCA Case No 2001-1, Agreement between the Government of the State of Eritrea and the Government of the Federal Democratic Republic of Ethiopia for the resettlement of displaced persons, as well as rehabilitation and peacebuilding in both countries, Algiers, 12 December 2000, 2138 UNTS 94, Arts 4(4), 5(2); *Iron Rhine Arbitration*, Belgium v The Netherlands, PCA Case No 2003-2, Rules of Procedure, Art 5(1).

[23] Regarding party appointments, one author notes:

> Disputants tend to be interested in one thing only: winning. They exercise their right of unilateral appointment, like everything else, with that overriding objective in view. The result is speculation about ways and means to shape a favorable tribunal, or at least to avoid a tribunal favorable to the other side—which is logically assumed to be speculating with the same fervor, and toward the same end. Forgotten is the ideal of an arbitrator trusted by both sides.

Jan Paulsson, *The Idea of Arbitration* (Oxford University Press, 2013). It has also been noted that almost all dissenting opinions in international arbitration are made by arbitrators appointed by the losing party (Albert Jan van den Berg, 'Dissenting Opinions by Party-Appointed Arbitrators in Investment Arbitration', in Mahnoush Arsanjani et al. (eds), *Looking to the Future: Essays on International Law in Honor of Michael Reisman* (Martinus Nijhoff, 2010). Such statistics, however, should be approached with some caution, as identifying the winner in an arbitration is not always straightforward, when considering, for instance, a comparison of quantified claims with the quantum of damages actually granted.

[24] See PCA Annual Reports, <http://www.pca-cpa.org/showpage.asp?pag_id=1069>.

[25] For a description of the procedure for requesting the PCA Secretary-General to designate an appointing authority pursuant to the UNCITRAL Rules, see Appendix XIII.

4.30 A recurrent problem under the UNCITRAL Rules is the appointment of an arbitrator by the respondent outside the specified time period, followed by an objection to the late appointment by the claimant. This creates a dilemma: should the late appointment be accepted (which could encourage the non-observance of time periods) or should the appointing authority make an appointment and deny the respondent the opportunity to appoint? In practice, if the respondent has attempted to make its late appointment before the PCA Secretary-General has been able to act, absent concerns regarding (i) further delay, (ii) the independence and impartiality of the arbitrator appointed by the respondent, and (iii) the qualifications of the arbitrator, the PCA Secretary-General generally appoints the same person as was put forward in the late appointment, thus complying with both the requirements of the procedural rules as to time periods and appointing an arbitrator acceptable to the defaulting party.

3. Article 10

1. For the purposes of article 9, paragraph 1, where three or five arbitrators are to be appointed and there are multiple parties as claimant or as respondent, unless the parties have agreed to another method of appointment of arbitrators, the multiple parties jointly, whether as claimant or as respondent, shall appoint an arbitrator.
2. If the parties have agreed that the arbitral tribunal is to be composed of a number of arbitrators other than one, three, or five, the arbitrators shall be appointed according to the method agreed upon by the parties.
3. In the event of any failure to constitute the arbitral tribunal under these Rules, the appointing authority shall, at the request of any party, constitute the arbitral tribunal and, in doing so, may revoke any appointment already made and appoint each of the arbitrators and designate one of them as the presiding arbitrator. The appointing authority may, if it deems it appropriate, reappoint previous appointees.
4. In appointing arbitrators pursuant to these Rules, the parties and the appointing authority are free to choose persons who are not Members of the Permanent Court of Arbitration.

4.31 Article 10 specifies the appointment procedure for cases that are not covered by Articles 8 and 9 of the Rules. The text of the first three paragraphs of Article 10 is mostly drawn from the corresponding provisions of the 2010 UNCITRAL Rules.

4.32 Article 10(1) provides that when appointing arbitrators in multiparty arbitrations, claimants and respondents must jointly appoint their respective arbitrators. The provision applies to cases where there are multiple parties on one or both sides of the dispute.[26]

[26] Report of the UNCITRAL Working Group II (Arbitration and Conciliation) on the work of its 46th session, 5–9 September 2007, A/CN.9/619, para 86.

Article 10(2) states that when parties have agreed to an arbitral tribunal composed of a number of arbitrators other than those anticipated by Articles 8 and 9, the method agreed upon by the parties shall apply to the constitution of the tribunal. This provision acknowledges the fact that, as provided by Article 1(1), the parties may modify the Rules by agreement, and, in particular, agree on a number of arbitrators other than one, three, or five. While parties may agree on an even number of arbitrators, this approach is not recommended, as it may lead to a deadlock within the tribunal and delay or prevent the resolution of the dispute.[27] **4.33**

Article 10(3) provides that the appointing authority may be called upon in the event of any failure to constitute the tribunal in accordance with the Rules. This provision addresses the case where the parties have agreed on a tribunal size other than one, three, or five arbitrators, but have omitted to include a mechanism for the constitution of the tribunal. It also provides the solution to situations where co-respondents or co-claimants are unable to agree upon the identity of an arbitrator under Article 10(1). **4.34**

The well-known ICC case *Dutco v BKMI* illustrates a problem that may arise in the constitution of tribunals in multi-party arbitrations.[28] In this case, one claimant opposed two respondents. The claimant appointed a first arbitrator to the three-member tribunal, but the co-respondents were unable to agree on a second arbitrator. The co-respondents perceived that while they were both on the 'respondent' side of the arbitration, their interests were not aligned. In view of the text of the ICC Rules of Arbitration in force at the time, which did not foresee any particular accommodation for this situation, the ICC insisted that the co-respondents jointly appoint an arbitrator. The co-respondents did so under protest. In an interim award, the arbitral tribunal found that it had been properly constituted and that the arbitral proceedings could validly continue against both respondents. After the final award was rendered, the respondents challenged the award in the French courts, claiming that an irregularity had occurred during the constitution of the tribunal. Ultimately, the French Cour de Cassation (Supreme Court) annulled the award on public policy grounds, ruling that the principle of equality of the parties had been violated when the claimant was able to choose its desired arbitrator while the co-respondents were not.[29] The Cour de Cassation noted that '[t]he principle of equality of the parties in the appointment of the arbitrators is a matter of public policy; one cannot, therefore, waive it until after the dispute has arisen'.[30] **4.35**

[27] See Gary B Born, *International Commercial Arbitration*, vol 1 (Wolters Kluwer, 2009) 1352–4.

[28] See Cass civ (1), *Societés Siemens & BKMI v Societé Dutco*, 7 January 1992, No 89-18708 89-18726 (1992) Revue d'arbitrage 470; for an English translation, see (1993) XVIII YB Com Arb 140.

[29] Cass civ (1), *Societés Siemens & BKMI v Societé Dutco*, 7 January 1992, No 89-18708 89-18726 (1992) Revue d'arbitrage 470; for an English translation, see (1993) XVIII YB Com Arb 140.

[30] The Cour de Cassation noted that 'the principle of the equality of the parties in the appointment of arbitrators is a matter of public policy (*ordre public*) which can be waived only after a dispute has arisen', YB Com Arb 140.

4.36 Where multiple parties on the claimant or the respondent side are unable to agree on a joint appointment, one way to assure the equality of the parties is to allow an appointing authority to make appointments on behalf of both claimants and respondents. If the claimant has already made an appointment when the disagreement arises regarding the co-respondents' joint appointment, the appointing authority is permitted to remove the claimant's appointee from the tribunal. This solution was adopted in recent versions of the ICC Rules of Arbitration,[31] in the 2010 UNCITRAL Rules,[32] and in Article 10(3) of the 2012 PCA Rules. The formulation of the 2010 UNCITRAL Rules was slightly revised in the 2012 PCA Rules for the sake of clarity, but the intention remains to provide a solution to the *Dutco* problem.

4.37 Article 10(4), which provides that arbitrators appointed under the Rules need not be 'Members of the Permanent Court of Arbitration', finds no equivalent in the 1976 and 2010 UNCITRAL Rules, being based on the 1990s PCA Rules.[33] The Members of the Court are a standing panel of arbitrators appointed by the PCA Member States. Pursuant to Article 23 of the 1899 Hague Convention and Article 44 of the 1907 Hague Convention, all the Members must be persons 'of known competency in questions of international law, of the highest moral reputation, and disposed to accept the duties of Arbitrators'. Article 10(4) of the Rules underlines that parties may use the list of Members of the Court to facilitate their search for arbitrators, while specifying that use of this list is not obligatory.[34]

4.38 The relevance of the list for arbitral appointments has been somewhat adversely influenced by the Statute of the ICJ, which gives Members of the Court the role of nominating candidates for election as ICJ judges.[35] A number of PCA Member

[31] 1998 ICC Rules of Arbitration, Art 10(2); 2012 ICC Rules of Arbitration, Art 12(8). In practice, it is reported that these provisions are rarely used, both because of the special circumstances which gave rise to the *Dutco* problem ('the multiple Respondents were unaffiliated companies with different interests, and distinct claims were being made against each of them. In most ICC arbitrations where multiple parties are involved, however, the parties, whether on the Claimant or the Respondent side, are affiliated and their positions and interests are identical') and because parties are generally able to agree on joint appointments, preferring this option to an appointment by the appointing authority (Derains and Schwartz, n 9, 181).

[32] See UNCITRAL Working Group II (Arbitration and Conciliation), *Note by the Secretariat: Settlement of commercial disputes: Revision of the UNCITRAL Arbitration Rules*, 45th session, 11–15 February 2006, A/CN.9/WG.II/WP.143, paras 45–7.

[33] PCA State/State Rules, Art 8(3); PCA State/Non-State Rules, Art 8(3); PCA State/International Organization Rules, Art 8(3); PCA International Organization/Private Party Rules, Art 8(3); see also PCA Natural Resources/Environmental Rules, Art 8(3); PCA Space Rules, Art 10(4).

[34] A current list of Members of the Court is available on the PCA website, <http://www.pca-cpa.org/showpage.asp?pag_id=1041>.

[35] See Statute of the International Court of Justice, 16 June 1945, 59 Stat 1055, Art 4, which provides:

1. The members of the Court shall be elected by the General Assembly and by the Security Council from a list of persons nominated by the national groups in the Permanent Court of Arbitration, in accordance with the following provisions.

States appear only to be considering this use of the list when appointing the Members of the Court, sometimes in apparent contravention of the PCA founding conventions, which require those appointed to be available to act as arbitrators. However, the 1899 and 1907 Hague Conventions do not require parties to choose arbitrators from this list; they may appoint arbitrators of their own choosing.[36] Likewise, the PCA Secretary-General is not confined to this list when requested to appoint arbitrators. Rather, the Secretary-General exercises complete discretion in selecting arbitrators, taking into account the facts of the case and all relevant circumstances.

C. Disclosures by and Challenge of Arbitrators—Articles 11 to 13

1. Article 11

> When a person is approached in connection with his or her possible appointment as an arbitrator, he or she shall disclose any circumstances likely to give rise to justifiable doubts as to his or her impartiality or independence. An arbitrator, from the time of his or her appointment and throughout the arbitral proceedings, shall

---

> 2. In the case of Members of the United Nations not represented in the Permanent Court of Arbitration, candidates shall be nominated by national groups appointed for this purpose by their governments under the same conditions as those prescribed for members of the Permanent Court of Arbitration by Article 44 of the Convention of The Hague of 1907 for the pacific settlement of international disputes.
> 3. The conditions under which a State which is a party to the present Statute but is not a Member of the United Nations may participate in electing the members of the Court shall, in the absence of a special agreement, be laid down by the General Assembly upon recommendation of the Security Council.

[36] 1899 Hague Convention, Art 32, 1907 Hague Convention, Art 55: 'the duties of an Arbitrator may be conferred on one Arbitrator alone or on several Arbitrators selected by the parties as they please, or chosen by them from the Members of the Permanent Court of Arbitration established by the present Convention . . . '. Nevertheless, the list of Members of the Court was used in Art 5(2) of the Abyei Arbitration Agreement as a basis to limit the parties' unilateral appointments to 'current or former members of the PCA or members of tribunals for which the PCA acted as registry who shall be independent, impartial, highly qualified and experienced in similar disputes' (*Abyei Arbitration*, Government of Sudan/ Sudan People's Liberation Movement/Army, PCA Case No 2008-7). The parties were possibly hoping to assure that all appointments would be of individuals who would inspire the mutual confidence of the parties. This unusual provision presented some challenges in implementation. Providing the list of current Members of the Court was straightforward, but the PCA was also required to provide a full list of 'former members of the PCA'. The PCA lists of Members of the Court stretch back over a century; therefore it was clear to the PCA that a 'full list' of former Members (ie including the Members appointed in the early 1900s) would be of little use to the parties. Even with the recent former Members of the Court, the PCA kept no record of their availability to serve as an arbitrator. The requirement to include 'members of tribunals for which the PCA acted as registry' on the list raised similar concerns about availability, but had the further complication that in the majority of PCA-administered cases, the parties had not authorized the PCA to disclose any information about the case, including the identity of the parties or arbitrators. The PCA was nevertheless able to list 55 arbitrators from this last category.

without delay disclose any such circumstances to the parties and the other arbitrators unless they have already been informed by him or her of these circumstances.

4.39 Article 11 of the Rules describes the disclosure obligations of arbitrators.

4.40 This provision replicates Article 11 of the 2010 UNCITRAL Rules, which in turn follows, with minor amendments, the text of Article 12(1) of the UNCITRAL Model Law.[37] This text improves on the 1976 UNCITRAL Rules by referring expressly to the continuous nature of arbitrators' disclosure obligations. To comply with the 2012 PCA Rules, arbitrators must inform the parties of any circumstances likely to give rise to justifiable doubts as to their impartiality or independence both prior to appointment and without delay throughout the duration of the proceedings as any such circumstances arise or become known to them. This amendment was considered necessary by both the UNCITRAL Working Group[38] and the expert group that drafted the PCA Natural Resources/Environmental Rules. The latter contain slightly different language ('An arbitrator, once appointed or chosen, and thereafter promptly, shall disclose . . . ').[39] The PCA Drafting Committee elected the UNCITRAL Model Law formulation as being more precise.

4.41 The 2012 PCA Rules also follow the 2010 UNCITRAL Rules in providing a model statement of impartiality and independence in an annex.[40]

4.42 When acting as appointing authority, the PCA Secretary-General requests potential arbitrators to complete statements of impartiality and independence before including them on a list of proposed arbitrators to be circulated to the parties or considering them for direct appointment. The statement of impartiality and independence is usually circulated by the PCA to prospective arbitrators as a form, in

---

[37] As adopted on 21 June 1985 and amended on 7 July 2006, A/40/17, Annex I, and A/61/17, Annex I, Art 17B.

[38] UNCITRAL Working Group II (Arbitration and Conciliation), *Note by the Secretariat: Settlement of commercial disputes: Revision of the UNCITRAL Arbitration Rules*, 46th session, 5–9 February 2007, A/CN.9/WG.II/WP.145, para 48.

[39] PCA Natural Resources/Environmental Rules, Art 9.

[40] The model statement of impartiality and independence reads as follows:

> No circumstances to disclose: I am impartial and independent of each of the parties and intend to remain so. To the best of my knowledge, there are no circumstances, past or present, likely to give rise to justifiable doubts as to my impartiality or independence. I shall promptly notify the parties and the other arbitrators of any such circumstances that may subsequently come to my attention during this arbitration.
>
> Circumstances to disclose: I am impartial and independent of each of the parties and intend to remain so. Attached is a statement made pursuant to article 11 of the PCA Arbitration Rules 2012 of (a) my past and present professional, business and other relationships with the parties and (b) any other relevant circumstances. [Include statement] I confirm that those circumstances do not affect my independence and impartiality. I shall promptly notify the parties and the other arbitrators of any such circumstances that may subsequently come to my attention during this arbitration.
>
> *Note—Any party may consider requesting from the arbitrator the following addition to the statement of impartiality and independence*:

which they can confirm their willingness to act as arbitrators and the existence or absence of any circumstances requiring disclosure.[41]

2. Article 12

1. Any arbitrator may be challenged if circumstances exist that give rise to justifiable doubts as to the arbitrator's impartiality or independence.
2. A party may challenge the arbitrator appointed by it only for reasons of which it becomes aware after the appointment has been made.
3. In the event that an arbitrator fails to act or in the event of the de jure or de facto impossibility of his or her performing his or her functions, the procedure in respect of the challenge of an arbitrator as provided in article 13 shall apply.
4. If an arbitrator on a tribunal of three, five, or more persons fails to participate in the arbitration, the other arbitrators shall, unless the parties agree otherwise, have the power in their sole discretion to continue the arbitration and to make any decision, ruling or award, notwithstanding the failure of one arbitrator to participate. In determining whether to continue the arbitration or to render any decision, ruling or award without the participation of an arbitrator, the other arbitrators shall take into account the stage of the arbitration, the reason, if any, expressed by the arbitrator for such non-participation, and such other matters as they consider appropriate in the circumstances of the case. In the event that the other arbitrators determine not to continue the arbitration without the non-participating arbitrator, the arbitral tribunal shall declare the office vacant, and, subject to article 14, paragraph 2, a substitute arbitrator shall be appointed pursuant to the provisions of articles 8 to 11, unless the parties agree on a different method of appointment.

Article 12 addresses the grounds for challenging arbitrators as well as options for dealing with non-participating arbitrators. **4.43**

The first three paragraphs of Article 12 of the Rules reproduce Article 12 of the 2010 UNCITRAL Rules. Article 12(1) stipulates the standard for challenges on the ground of conflict of interest: 'if circumstances exist that give rise to justifiable doubts as to the arbitrator's impartiality or independence'. Article 12(2) provides that a party cannot challenge an arbitrator appointed by it, except for reasons that become known after the appointment is made. Article 12(3) makes clear that arbitrators can be challenged not only in cases of conflict of interest, but also in cases where they fail or find it impossible to discharge their functions. **4.44**

In addition to the challenge procedure, Article 12(4), which finds no equivalent in the 2010 UNCITRAL Rules, creates another option for dealing with non-participating arbitrators. Article 12(4) is based on Article 13(5) of the PCA **4.45**

I confirm, on the basis of the information presently available to me, that I can devote the time necessary to conduct this arbitration diligently, efficiently and in accordance with the time limits in the Rules.

[41] For a model form, see Appendix XV.

State/State Rules and equivalent provisions found in other sets of PCA procedural rules.[42]

4.46 Under the 1976 UNCITRAL Rules, a non-participating arbitrator could be removed from the arbitral tribunal only through a challenge procedure initiated by one of the parties.[43] Any vacancy arising on the arbitral tribunal then had to be filled by following the procedure applicable to the initial appointment of the arbitrator being replaced.[44] This rule could be abused by arbitrators and parties to obstruct the arbitral proceedings.[45] For example, an arbitrator could, by not participating in the proceedings,[46] delay the proceedings for the duration of a challenge and, in cases where the challenge was successful, for the duration of the following reappointment procedure as well. Moreover, the party that originally appointed the non-participating arbitrator could then appoint another recalcitrant arbitrator who could continue to obstruct the proceedings. Without robust action by the arbitral tribunal[47] or recourse to national courts, this cycle could continue indefinitely. In any event, the obstructive behaviour of party-appointed arbitrators would cause additional delays when the repetition of oral hearings became necessary following appointment of the substitute arbitrator.

4.47 When a PCA expert group drafted the PCA State/State Rules from 1990 to 1992,[48] it identified these difficulties in the 1976 UNCITRAL Rules and, as a remedy, crafted a provision allowing the remaining members of an arbitral tribunal to decide in their sole discretion to continue the arbitration in the absence of the non-participating member as a so-called 'truncated' tribunal and render any decision, ruling, or award in spite of the non-participation of one of the tribunal members.[49]

4.48 During the revision process of the UNCITRAL Rules in 2006–2010, the UNCITRAL Working Group sought to address the same difficulties by drafting

---

[42] PCA State/Non-State Rules, Art 13(3); PCA State/International Organization Rules, Art 13(3); PCA International Organization/Private Party Rules, Art 13(3); PCA Natural Resources/Environmental Rules, Art 13(3); PCA Space Rules, Art 12(4).

[43] 1976 UNCITRAL Rules, Art 13(2), reproduced in Appendix XI.

[44] 1976 UNCITRAL Rules, Art 12(2), reproduced in Appendix XI.

[45] For a discussion of this issue, see Stephen M Schwebel, *International Arbitration: Three Salient Problems* (Grotius Publications, 1987); Stephen M Schwebel, 'The validity of an arbitral award rendered by a truncated tribunal' (1995) 6(2) *ICC International Court of Arbitration Bulletin* 19.

[46] See eg *Uiterwyk Corp v Islamic Republic of Iran*, Award No 375-381-1 of 6 July 1988, 19 Iran-US Claims Tribunal 107. Or, the party-appointed arbitrator could be prevented against his will from participating in the proceedings. See eg *Himpurna California Energy Ltd Republic of Indonesia*, Final Award of 16 October 1999, (2000) XXV YB Comm Arb 186; *First Investment Corp of the Marshall Islands v Fujian Mawei Shipbuilding Ltd*, 2012 WL 831536 (US CA 5th Circuit).

[47] See eg the tribunal in *Himpurna California Energy Ltd Republic of Indonesia*, Final Award of 16 October 1999, (2000) XXV YB Comm Arb 186, which forged ahead and rendered its final award in the absence of one of the co-arbitrators.

[48] The members of the PCA expert group are identified in Appendix VII.

[49] PCA State/State Rules, Art 13(3).

Article 14(2) of the 2010 UNCITRAL Rules.[50] This provision states that, in exceptional cases, the appointing authority may appoint a substitute arbitrator directly or authorize the remaining arbitrators to proceed with the arbitration as a truncated tribunal. The principal distinction between the two solutions is that the power to decide whether or not the arbitration can proceed with a truncated tribunal is entrusted to different entities: the PCA State/State Rules give it to the arbitral tribunal itself, whereas the 2010 UNCITRAL Rules put the decision in the hands of the appointing authority.

The PCA Drafting Committee drew from both the PCA State/State Rules and 2010 UNCITRAL Rules to craft the solution of the 2012 PCA Rules. On the one hand, the Drafting Committee chose to follow the approach of the PCA State/State Rules in giving the arbitral tribunal rather than the appointing authority the power to decide whether to continue the proceedings in the event of non-participation of a tribunal member. On the other hand, the Drafting Committee retained the possibility, introduced in the 2010 UNCITRAL Rules, for the appointing authority to make a direct appointment to the tribunal. However, unlike under the 2010 UNCITRAL Rules, the appointing authority may only directly appoint a substitute arbitrator after the tribunal has decided not to continue as a truncated tribunal and declared the office of the non-participating arbitrator vacant. **4.49**

As a result, two methods for dealing with non-participating arbitrators are available under the 2012 PCA Rules. First, pursuant to Article 12(3), in the event that an arbitrator fails to act or in the event of the de jure or de facto impossibility of an arbitrator performing his or her functions, any party may request the removal of the arbitrator from the arbitral tribunal in accordance with the procedure for challenges set out in Article 13 of the Rules. If the arbitrator is removed, the mechanism for replacement of arbitrators provided in Article 14 applies—that is, the substitute arbitrator must be appointed or chosen following the procedures that applied to the initial appointment of the arbitrator being replaced. In this case, obstruction to the arbitral proceedings can be avoided by application of the exceptional replacement procedure of Article 14(2), which allows the appointing authority to make direct appointments to the tribunal. Second, pursuant to Article 12(4), the arbitral tribunal may decide to continue the proceedings despite the non-participation of one of its members, or may declare the office vacant. One particularity of this provision is that the arbitral tribunal may act on its own motion, without any request from a party. In some cases the parties may be unaware that one member of the tribunal has ceased responding to communications **4.50**

[50] Report of the UNCITRAL Working Group II (Arbitration and Conciliation) on the work of its 45th session, 25 June to 12 July 2007, A/CN.9/614, paras 67–74; Report of the UNCITRAL Working Group II (Arbitration and Conciliation) on the work of its 46th session, 5–9 September 2007, A/CN.9/619, para 107; 2010 UNCITRAL Rules, Art 14(2), reproduced in Appendix XII.

from the other arbitrators and is unreasonably delaying the tribunal's work. Article 12(4) allows the tribunal to act in such cases. It is also notable that the arbitral tribunal may decide to continue the arbitration despite the non-participation of one of its members at any stage of the proceedings. In contrast, under Article 14(2) of the 2010 UNCITRAL Rules, the appointing authority may authorize the arbitral tribunal to continue as a truncated tribunal only after the closure of hearings. Article 12(4) gives discretion to the arbitral tribunal, providing only that in making its decision it must consider the stage of the proceedings, among other factors. Where national law applies to the arbitration,[51] the tribunal may also wish to consider the attitude toward truncated tribunals of the courts of the place where the arbitration is seated or where the parties are likely to seek enforcement of any award rendered by the tribunal.[52]

4.51 Article 12(4) further specifies that if the office of the non-participating arbitrator is declared vacant, a substitute arbitrator shall be appointed pursuant to the provisions of Articles 8 to 11, subject to Article 14(2). Articles 8 to 11 stipulate the procedure for the initial appointment of arbitrators. Article 14(2) adds a replacement procedure whereby the appointing authority may, in view of the exceptional circumstances of the case, appoint the replacement arbitrator directly.

4.52 It may be noted that the Article 12(4) replacement procedure is essentially the same as that foreseen under Article 14 for all other cases where a replacement is necessary, including cases where an arbitrator is removed by the appointing authority after the arbitrator is challenged by a party under Article 12(3) for failure to act or de jure or de facto impossibility of performing his or her functions.[53]

4.53 Under the 2012 PCA Rules, proceedings can continue with a truncated tribunal only in cases where an arbitrator fails to participate, unlike under the 2010

---

[51] On the applicability of national legislation in the context of arbitrations involving only states or intergovernmental organizations, see discussion under Art 1(2).

[52] While there is little case law on the matter, national courts should normally accept to order the enforcement of awards rendered by truncated tribunals under procedural rules that permit the continuation of proceedings in the absence of an arbitrator, as the truncated tribunal is then part of the bargain struck by the parties in agreeing to arbitration (see Born (n 25) 1587–90). In contrast, where the procedural rules do not provide for this possibility, enforcement can be problematic. See eg *Agence Transcongolaise des Communications—Chemin de fer Congo Ocean v Compagnie Miniere de l'Ogooue*, 1 July 1997, (1999) XXIVa YB Comm Arb 281, where the French Court of Appeals annulled an award rendered by a truncated tribunal after a co-arbitrator had resigned upon receipt of a draft of the award that held against the party which had appointed him. The Court of Appeals reasoned that the truncated arbitral tribunal that rendered the award did not conform to the agreement on which the tribunal's jurisdictional power was based. See also *First Investment Corp of the Marshall Islands v Fujian Mawei Shipbuilding Ltd*, 2012 WL 831536, in which the US Fifth Circuit Court of Appeal was asked to confirm an English arbitral award, enforcement of which had been refused by a Chinese national court on the ground that it was rendered by a truncated tribunal. According to the US Court of Appeal, the arbitrator appointed by the Chinese respondent party had been detained by the Chinese authorities, preventing him from participating in the deliberations preceding issuance of the award.

[53] See discussion under Art 14.

UNCITRAL Rules, which also cover cases where a vacancy arises on the tribunal as a result of a successful challenge, or the resignation or death of an arbitrator.[54] While an award rendered by a truncated tribunal in accordance with the applicable procedural rules is valid and binding, the 2012 PCA Rules seek to ensure that awards are rendered by fully constituted tribunals in as many cases as possible. At the same time, the potential for abuse of the appointment procedure through repeat appointment of recalcitrant arbitrators is avoided, as in all cases the appointing authority may choose to resort to the special procedure of Article 14(2).

3. Article 13

1. A party that intends to challenge an arbitrator shall send notice of its challenge within 30 days after it has been notified of the appointment of the challenged arbitrator, or within 30 days after the circumstances mentioned in articles 11 and 12 became known to that party.
2. The notice of challenge shall be communicated to all other parties, to the arbitrator who is challenged, to the other arbitrators, and to the International Bureau. The notice of challenge shall state the reasons for the challenge.
3. When an arbitrator has been challenged by a party, all parties may agree to the challenge. The arbitrator may also, after the challenge, withdraw from his or her office. In neither case does this imply acceptance of the validity of the grounds for the challenge.
4. If, within 15 days from the date of the notice of challenge, all parties do not agree to the challenge or the challenged arbitrator does not withdraw, the party making the challenge may elect to pursue it. In that case, within 30 days from the date of the notice of challenge, it shall seek a decision on the challenge by the appointing authority.
5. In rendering a decision on the challenge, the appointing authority may indicate the reasons for the decision, unless the parties agree that no reasons shall be given.

Article 13 stipulates the procedure for challenges to arbitrators. **4.54**

This provision follows the text of Article 13 of the 2010 UNCITRAL Rules, with three modifications. **4.55**

First, under Article 13(1), a party may initiate a challenge to an arbitrator within 30 days of receiving notification of the arbitrator's appointment or of learning of the circumstances on which the challenge is based. The 2010 UNCITRAL Rules provide for a shorter 15-day time period. The more generous time period of the Rules accounts for the time that may be required by some states to conduct thorough conflict checks or consider the significance of any disclosure made by the arbitrator. **4.56**

Second, Article 13(2) provides that the challenging party shall send notice of its challenge not only to the other party or parties and all tribunal members, but also **4.57**

[54] See 2010 UNCITRAL Rules, Art 34, reproduced in Appendix XII.

to the PCA International Bureau. This is consistent with the International Bureau's role under Article 1(3) as the keeper of the archives for arbitrations administered under the Rules and allows the PCA to receive advance notice that the challenging party may seek a decision on the challenge from the PCA Secretary-General in his capacity as appointing authority under the Rules.

4.58 Third, Article 13(5), providing that the appointing authority may indicate reasons for its decisions on challenges to arbitrators, is based on Article 13(5) of the PCA Space Rules. This provision reflects the practice of the Secretary-General of the PCA to issue reasoned decisions on challenges. However, it does not make this practice obligatory, as circumstances may favour the rendering of decisions on challenge without reasons in some cases—for example, where there is evidence that a party is using the challenge procedure as a dilatory tactic and where drafting a reasoned decision would unjustifiably delay the proceedings.

4.59 Challenges to arbitrators are particularly frequent in investment arbitrations. One example is found in the challenges saga of the PCA-administered arbitration *Telekom Malaysia Berhad v Ghana*.[55] In this case—an investment dispute conducted under the 1976 UNCITRAL Rules—the parties had, by agreement, designated the Secretary-General of the PCA as appointing authority. During the subsequent hearings before the arbitral tribunal, when Ghana cited the *RFCC v Morocco* award judgment in support of certain of its arguments, Professor Gaillard disclosed that he had been instructed to act as RFCC's counsel in an action seeking the annulment of that award. Ghana challenged Professor Gaillard. The claimant protested against the challenge. The arbitral tribunal decided that the arbitral proceedings should be continued and Professor Gaillard stated that he would not withdraw. Ghana filed its challenge with the Secretary-General of the PCA; this challenge was rejected. Subsequently, Ghana filed the same challenge to Professor Gaillard with the Provisional Measures Judge of the District Court of The Hague pursuant to the Netherlands Arbitration Act 1986.[56] The District Court upheld the motion challenging Professor Gaillard's impartiality, if he did not, within ten days from that judgment, expressly and unreservedly notify the parties to the arbitration that he would resign as attorney in *RFCC v Morocco*.[57] Pursuant to this decision Professor Gaillard notified the parties that he had ceased his activities in *RFCC v Morocco*.

4.60 However, Ghana challenged Professor Gaillard again before the District Court, arguing that the previous decision of the provisional measures judge was based

[55] PCA Case No 2003-3.

[56] The current draft of the new Netherlands Arbitration Act would do away with this second chance to have the challenge decided by a Dutch judge when the parties have agreed that challenges are to be decided by another body.

[57] De Republiek Ghana/Telekom Malaysia Berhad, Rb. 's-Gravenhage, 18 October 2004, (2005) 23:1 ASA Bulletin 186.

on the assumption that Professor Gaillard had not yet taken part in the tribunal's work, which was incorrect. In response to this second challenge, the District Court held that, since there had been no adverse consequences for Ghana arising from such participation by Professor Gaillard and since there were no further grounds to doubt his impartiality, the challenge should be rejected.[58]

D. Replacement of an Arbitrator—Article 14

1. Subject to paragraph 2 of this article, in any event where an arbitrator has to be replaced during the course of the arbitral proceedings, a substitute arbitrator shall be appointed or chosen pursuant to the procedure provided for in articles 8 to 11 that was applicable to the appointment or choice of the arbitrator being replaced. This procedure shall apply even if during the process of appointing the arbitrator to be replaced, a party had failed to exercise its right to appoint or to participate in the appointment.
2. If, at the request of a party, the appointing authority determines that, in view of the exceptional circumstances of the case, it would be justified for a party to be deprived of its right to appoint a substitute arbitrator, the appointing authority may, after giving an opportunity to the parties and the remaining arbitrators to express their views, appoint the substitute arbitrator.

Article 14 sets out the procedure for the replacement of an arbitrator. **4.61**

This provision is based on Article 14 of the 2010 UNCITRAL Rules. The sole **4.62** distinction between the two provisions is that Article 14(2) of the 2012 PCA Rules does not empower the appointing authority to authorize the arbitral tribunal to continue with the arbitration as a truncated tribunal. As explained in the discussion of Article 12, the Rules allow only the arbitral tribunal itself to make this decision.

The procedure stipulated in Article 14 applies to all cases 'where an arbitrator has **4.63** to be replaced during the course of the arbitral proceedings'. The following cases are covered:

- the death of an arbitrator;
- the resignation of an arbitrator, with or without good reason;
- the removal of an arbitrator from the tribunal by the appointing authority upon request by a party because circumstances exist that give rise to justifiable doubts as to his impartiality or independence (Articles 12(1) and 13);
- the removal of an arbitrator from the tribunal by the appointing authority upon request by a party because an arbitrator has failed to act or it is impossible for the arbitrator to perform his or her functions (Articles 12(3) and 13); and

[58] De Republiek Ghana/Telekom Malaysia Berhad, Rb. 's-Gravenhage, 15 November 2004 (unreported).

- the declaration by the arbitral tribunal of the vacancy of the office of a non-participating arbitrator (Article 12(4)).

4.64 Article 14(1) describes the usual procedure for the replacement of an arbitrator, whereby a substitute arbitrator is appointed pursuant to the procedure that was applicable under the Rules to the arbitrator being replaced. As explained under Article 12, this procedure may leave the arbitral proceedings vulnerable to obstruction. Accordingly, the rule is supplemented in Article 14(2), which grants discretionary power to the appointing authority to directly appoint a substitute arbitrator in exceptional cases (in addition to the possibility for an arbitral tribunal to decide to continue with the proceedings in the absence of a non-participating member under Article 12(4) of the Rules).

4.65 The UNCITRAL Working Group originally considered drafting the discretionary power of the appointing authority under Article 14(2) to include only instances where a party had 'abused the challenge procedure repeatedly'.[59] However, the Working Group ultimately avoided this narrow formulation, as did the PCA Drafting Committee in the 2012 PCA Rules. As a result, it is conceivable that the procedure under Article 14(2) of the 2012 PCA Rules and 2010 UNCITRAL Rules could be used for the sole purpose of allowing an arbitral proceeding to proceed faster than it would otherwise.[60]

E. Repetition of Hearings in the Event of the Replacement of an Arbitrator—Article 15

> If an arbitrator is replaced, the proceedings shall resume at the stage where the arbitrator who was replaced ceased to perform his or her functions, unless the arbitral tribunal decides otherwise.

4.66 Article 15 provides a default approach to the resumption of arbitral proceedings following the replacement of an arbitrator pursuant to Article 14.

---

[59] Report of the UNCITRAL Working Group II (Arbitration and Conciliation) on the work of its 46th session, 5–9 September 2007, A/CN.9/619, para 104.

[60] See Report of the UNCITRAL Working Group II (Arbitration and Conciliation) on the work of its 49th session, 15–19 September 2008, A/CN.9/665, para 112:

> 'It was observed that depriving a party of its right to appoint an arbitrator should only occur as a matter of sanction in case a party or an arbitrator misbehaved. In response, it was said that that provision dealt with replacing an arbitrator in the most efficient manner, and was therefore not connected to the notion of sanction. In support of enumerating the cases where a party would be deprived of a right to appoint a substitute arbitrator, it was said that such listing would provide more safeguards to the parties. The prevailing view, however, was that a provision allowing an appointing authority to proceed with the direct appointment of an arbitrator should not extend beyond the cases of improper conduct and should remain generic so as to cover all possible instances.'

This provision follows the text of Article 15 of the 2010 UNCITRAL Rules. Where the 1976 UNCITRAL Rules mandated different consequences for the replacement of a sole or presiding arbitrator and that of 'any other arbitrator',[61] the 2012 PCA Rules and 2010 UNCITRAL Rules treat these situations identically. For the sake of efficiency, both sets of rules provide that no element of the proceedings, including evidentiary hearings, will be repeated, unless the arbitral tribunal decides otherwise. This reverses the starting assumption of the 1976 UNCITRAL Rules, which presumed the repetition of hearings and, in some cases, made it obligatory. **4.67**

Today, leaving the choice whether to repeat proceedings to the tribunal's discretion is in line with the rules of most arbitral institutions.[62] Before the revision of the UNCITRAL Rules, the PCA had already departed from the rigid approach of the 1976 UNCITRAL Rules in its Natural Resources/Environmental Rules, which provide that: 'If one of several arbitrators (including the presiding arbitrator) is replaced, unless the parties agree otherwise or the arbitral tribunal so decides, hearings already held shall not be repeated'. Similarly, in some PCA-administered cases pre-dating the 2010 UNCITRAL Rules, the tribunal and the parties agreed to leave the determination of the consequences of the replacement of an arbitrator to the tribunal's discretion.[63] The 2012 PCA Rules and 2010 UNCITRAL Rules now express the same idea in words inspired by the Swiss Rules of International Arbitration.[64] **4.68**

In deciding whether to repeat any part of the proceedings, and in particular hearings, the arbitral tribunal will consider the cost and time that would be involved, as **4.69**

[61] 1976 UNCITRAL Rules, Art 14: 'If under articles 11 to 13 the sole or presiding arbitrator is replaced, any hearings held previously shall be repeated; if any other arbitrator is replaced, such prior hearings may be repeated at the discretion of the arbitral tribunal'.

[62] Although it used the 1976 UNCITRAL Rules as its model, the Iran–United States Claims Tribunal had already spotted the provision on repetition of hearings as needing improvement when it adopted its Rules of Procedure in 1983. Article 14 of the Tribunal's Rules of Procedure provides that '[i]f a member of the Full Tribunal or of a Chamber is replaced or if a substitute is appointed for him, the arbitral tribunal shall determine whether all, any part or none of the previous hearings shall be repeated'. See also 2009 International Center for Dispute Resolution (ICDR) Rules, Art 11(2): 'If a substitute arbitrator is appointed under either Article 10 or Article 11, the tribunal shall determine at its sole discretion whether all or part of any prior hearings shall be repeated'; 2012 ICC Rules, Art 15(4): 'Once reconstituted, the arbitral tribunal shall determine if and to what extent prior proceedings shall be repeated before the reconstituted arbitral tribunal'.

[63] See eg *Guyana v Suriname*, PCA Case No 2004-4 (UNCLOS), Rules of Procedure, Art 6(2): 'In such an event [replacement of an arbitrator], prior hearings may be repeated in whole or in part, by decision of the Arbitral Tribunal, in consultation with the substitute arbitrator'.

[64] Report of the UNCITRAL Working Group II (Arbitration and Conciliation) on the work of its 45th session, 5 October 2006, A/CN.9/614, para 75. Article 14 of the Swiss Rules of International Arbitration, which were in effect at the time of the drafting of the 2010 UNCITRAL Rules, provided: 'If an arbitrator is replaced, the proceedings shall as a rule resume at the stage where the arbitrator who was replaced ceased to perform his functions, unless the arbitral tribunal decides otherwise'. Almost identical text appears in Art 14 of the 2012 Swiss Rules of International Arbitration.

well as the requirements of procedural fairness. Where the law of the arbitral seat applies to the arbitration,[65] the tribunal should also verify whether it contains any mandatory rules in this regard.[66]

F. Exclusion of Liability—Article 16

> The parties waive, to the fullest extent permitted under the applicable law, any claim against the arbitrators and any person appointed by the arbitral tribunal based on any act or omission in connection with the arbitration.

4.70 Article 16 is a limitation of liability provision for arbitrators and persons appointed by the arbitral tribunal (such as tribunal secretaries and tribunal-appointed experts).

4.71 This provision replicates the text of Article 16 of the PCA Space Rules, which was modelled on Article 16 of the 2010 UNCITRAL Rules,[67] but differs from it in two key respects.

4.72 The first difference pertains to the scope of immunity granted by each set of rules to the relevant persons. The 2010 UNCITRAL Rules exclude cases of 'intentional wrongdoing' from the scope of immunity. This exclusion has been removed from the PCA Space Rules and 2012 PCA Rules, turning Article 16 into an unconditional waiver of liability akin to that contained in the ICC Rules of Arbitration.[68]

4.73 The drafters of the PCA Space Rules considered it superfluous to explicitly exclude 'intentional wrongdoing' from the scope of the waiver. This is because where national law that does not allow waivers of intentional wrongdoing is applicable,[69] the waiver contained in the Rules would have no effect with respect to intentional wrongdoing in any event. Incidentally, the deletion of the reference to intentional wrongdoing will also avert the need for discussion in national courts of the

---

[65] On the applicability of national legislation in the context of arbitrations involving only states or intergovernmental organizations, see discussion under Art 1(2).

[66] While most national laws leave this decision to the arbitral tribunal, some mandatorily require or forbid the repetition of proceedings. Examples can be found in Born (n 25) 1585.

[67] 2010 UNCITRAL Rules, Art 16: 'Save for intentional wrongdoing, the parties waive, to the fullest extent permitted under the applicable law, any claim against the arbitrators, the appointing authority and any person appointed by the arbitral tribunal based on any act or omission in connection with the arbitration'.

[68] 2012 ICC Arbitration Rules, Art 40: 'The arbitrators, any person appointed by the arbitral tribunal, the emergency arbitrator, the Court and its members, the ICC and its employees, and the ICC National Committees and Groups and their employees and representatives shall not be liable to any person for any act or omission in connection with the arbitration, except to the extent such limitation of liability is prohibited by applicable law'.

[69] On the applicability of national legislation in the context of arbitrations involving only states or intergovernmental organizations, see discussion under Art 1(2).

distinction, if any, between 'intentional wrongdoing' within the meaning of the Rules and any equivalent or similar concept in the national law.

The drafters of the PCA Space Rules were also guided by the stated purpose of the UNCITRAL Working Group in adopting Article 16 to 'reinforc[e] the independence of arbitrators'.[70] Article 16 was to 'ensure that arbitrators were protected from the threat of potentially large claims by parties dissatisfied with arbitral tribunals' rulings or awards who might claim that such rulings or awards arose from the negligence or fault of an arbitrator'.[71] By removing the phrase 'save for intentional wrongdoing', the PCA Drafting Committee sought to maximize the protection of arbitrators from suit. **4.74**

The second distinction between the limitation of liability provision of the 2010 UNCITRAL Rules, and that of the PCA Space Rules and 2012 PCA Rules, is that the latter protect from liability arbitrators and persons appointed by them (such as tribunal secretaries or tribunal-appointed experts), but not the appointing authority. This is because the two sets of PCA rules specify that the appointing authority is to be the PCA Secretary-General, and the PCA, as an intergovernmental organization, already enjoys immunity against legal process under international customary law[72] and various agreements. In contrast, under the 2010 UNCITRAL Rules, any individual or private arbitral institution may be designated as appointing authority. While the PCA Secretary-General is assigned a role under the 2010 UNCITRAL Rules (the role of designating appointing authorities),[73] and while early drafts of the 2010 UNCITRAL Rules listed the PCA Secretary-General among the entities protected by the Article 16 waiver,[74] the final text of the 2010 UNCITRAL Rules does not extend the waiver to the PCA Secretary-General, in view of the PCA's existing immunity. **4.75**

In the Netherlands, where its seat is located, the PCA enjoys immunities under the Agreement concerning the Headquarters of the Permanent Court of Arbitration ('Headquarters Agreement').[75] The Headquarters Agreement provides that the PCA and its properties 'shall enjoy immunity from every form of legal process'.[76] The PCA staff are accorded privileges and immunities by reference to the privileges **4.76**

[70] See Report of the UNCITRAL Working Group II (Arbitration and Conciliation) on the work of its 52nd session, 19 February 2012, A/CN.9/688, paras 45–8.

[71] See Report of the UNCITRAL Working Group II (Arbitration and Conciliation) on the work of its 52nd session, 19 February 2012, A/CN.9/688, para 39.

[72] See Abdullah El-Erian, Special Rapporteur, 'Preliminary Report on the Second Part of the Topic of Relations between States and International Organizations', A/CN.4/304 and Corr.1, (1977) II.1 YB Intl L Com 138, paras 57–62.

[73] 2010 UNCITRAL Rules, Art 6.

[74] See UNCITRAL Working Group II (Arbitration and Conciliation), *Note by the Secretariat: Settlement of commercial disputes: Revision of the UNCITRAL Arbitration Rules*, 52nd session, 1–5 February 2010, A/CN.9/WG.II/WP.157, para 41.

[75] 30 March 1999, in force 8 August 2000.

[76] Headquarters Agreement, Art 3(1).

and immunities of members of diplomatic missions under the 1961 Vienna Convention on Diplomatic Relations ('1961 Vienna Convention').[77]

4.77 The Headquarters Agreement also provides immunity to arbitrators in the exercise of their duties, equivalent to the immunity of diplomatic agents under the 1961 Vienna Convention.[78] Other participants in PCA proceedings enjoy 'immunity from criminal, civil and administrative jurisdiction in respect of acts performed in the fulfillment of their duties in PCA Proceedings'.[79] 'Participants' is defined under the Headquarters Agreement to include witnesses, experts, counsel, parties, agents, and other party representatives.[80] The protections afforded by the Headquarters Agreement therefore cover a number of persons who are not covered by Art 16 of the 2012 PCA Rules.

4.78 In 2012, the Headquarters Agreement was supplemented by an exchange of notes that accord witnesses participating in PCA proceedings a broader range of immunities and privileges, including in respect of acts or convictions prior to entry into the Netherlands,[81] upon issuance by the PCA of a document certifying that their

---

[77] Headquarters Agreement, Art 10(1); 1961 Vienna Convention, 500 UNTS 95.

[78] Headquarters Agreement, Art 9(1). The 1961 Vienna Convention reads as follows with respect to the immunities of diplomatic agents:

> Article 29
>
> The person of a diplomatic agent shall be inviolable. He shall not be liable to any form of arrest or detention. The receiving State shall treat him with due respect and shall take all appropriate steps to prevent any attack on his person, freedom or dignity.
>
> Article 30
>
> . . .
>
> 2. His papers, correspondence and, except as provided in paragraph 3 of Article 31, his property, shall likewise enjoy inviolability.
>
> Article 31
>
> 1. A diplomatic agent shall enjoy immunity from the criminal jurisdiction of the receiving State. He shall also enjoy immunity from its civil and administrative jurisdiction, except in the case of:
>   (a) a real action relating to private immovable property situated in the territory of the receiving State, unless he holds it on behalf of the sending State for the purposes of the mission;
>   (b) an action relating to succession in which the diplomatic agent is involved as executor, administrator, heir or legatee as a private person and not on behalf of the sending State;
>   (c) an action relating to any professional or commercial activity exercised by the diplomatic agent in the receiving State outside his official functions.
> 2. A diplomatic agent is not obliged to give evidence as a witness.
> 3. No measures of execution may be taken in respect of a diplomatic agent except in the cases coming under sub-paragraphs (a), (b) and (c) of paragraph 1 of this Article, and provided that the measures concerned can be taken without infringing the inviolability of his person or of his residence....

[79] Headquarters Agreement, Art 9(2).

[80] Headquarters Agreement, Art 1(9).

[81] Exchange of Notes constituting an Agreement supplementing the Agreement concerning the Headquarters of the Permanent Court of Arbitration, 6 June 2012, reproduced in Appendix V. Article 1 reads as follows:

appearance is required by the PCA.[82] This procedure has been successfully used for example at a recent PCA hearing held in The Hague to allow witnesses facing criminal charges in another state to testify in person without the risk of arrest.

The PCA has also adopted a policy of concluding 'Host Country Agreements' with states that are parties to the PCA's founding conventions.[83] The Host Country Agreements serve to ensure that participants in PCA-administered proceedings taking place in the territory of these host countries can perform their functions under similar conditions to those guaranteed under the PCA's Headquarters Agreement. Accordingly, the PCA and participants in PCA-administered proceedings enjoy various privileges and immunities under the Host Country Agreements.[84] **4.79**

Witnesses shall enjoy the following privileges, immunities and facilities to the extent necessary for their appearance in PCA Proceedings for purposes of giving evidence, subject to the production of the document referred to in paragraph 2:

(a) immunity from personal arrest or detention or any other restriction of their liberty in respect of acts or convictions prior to their entry into the territory of the Kingdom of the Netherlands,
(b) immunity from seizure of their personal baggage unless there are serious grounds for believing that the baggage contains articles the import or export of which is prohibited by law or controlled by the quarantine regulations of the Kingdom of the Netherlands;
(c) immunity from legal process of every kind in respect of words spoken or written and all acts performed by them in the course of their testimony, which immunity shall continue to be accorded even after their appearance and testimony in PCA Proceedings;
(d) inviolability of all papers, documents in whatever form and materials relating to their testimony;
(e) for purposes of their communications in relation to PCA Proceedings and with their counsel in connection with their testimony, the right to receive and send papers and documents in whatever form;
(f) exemption from immigration restrictions or alien registration when they travel for purposes of their testimony;
(g) the same repatriation facilities in time of international crisis as are accorded to diplomatic agents under the Vienna Convention.

82 Exchange of Notes constituting an Agreement supplementing the Agreement concerning the Headquarters of the Permanent Court of Arbitration, 6 June 2012, Art 2, reproduced in Appendix V.

83 To date, the PCA has concluded Host Country Agreements with Argentina, Costa Rica, Mauritius, Singapore, South Africa, India, and Chile.

84 PCA Host Country Agreements also secure the provision by the host country of the facilities and services required for PCA-administered proceedings, such as office and meeting space and secretarial services. They may also establish a permanent PCA facility in the territory of the host country. On this, see discussion under Art 18.

5

SECTION III. ARBITRAL PROCEEDINGS

A. General Provisions—Article 17

1. Subject to these Rules, the arbitral tribunal may conduct the arbitration in such manner as it considers appropriate, provided that the parties are treated with equality and that at an appropriate stage of the proceedings each party is given a reasonable opportunity of presenting its case. The arbitral tribunal, in exercising its discretion, shall conduct the proceedings so as to avoid unnecessary delay and expense and to provide a fair and efficient process for resolving the parties' dispute.
2. As soon as practicable after its constitution and after inviting the parties to express their views, the arbitral tribunal shall establish the provisional timetable of the arbitration. The arbitral tribunal may, at any time, after inviting the parties to express their views, extend or abridge any period of time prescribed under these Rules or agreed by the parties.
3. If at an appropriate stage of the proceedings any party so requests, the arbitral tribunal shall hold hearings for the presentation of evidence by witnesses, including expert witnesses, or for oral argument. In the absence of such a request, the arbitral tribunal shall decide whether to hold such hearings or whether the proceedings shall be conducted on the basis of documents and other materials.

4. All communications to the arbitral tribunal by one party shall be communicated by that party to all other parties and the International Bureau. Such communications shall be made at the same time, except as otherwise permitted by the arbitral tribunal if it may do so under applicable law.
5. The arbitral tribunal may, at the request of any party, allow one or more third persons to be joined in the arbitration as a party provided such person is a party to the arbitration agreement, unless the arbitral tribunal finds, after giving all parties, including the person or persons to be joined, the opportunity to be heard, that joinder should not be permitted because of prejudice to any of those parties. The arbitral tribunal may make a single award or several awards in respect of all parties so involved in the arbitration.

5.01 Article 17 concerns the conduct of arbitral proceedings.

5.02 Except for one addition in Article 17(4), this provision follows the text of Article 17 of the 2010 UNCITRAL Rules, incorporating its many improvements from the 1976 UNCITRAL Rules.

5.03 Article 17(1) establishes the arbitral tribunal's control of the procedure within the fundamental safeguards of equality between the parties and each party's right to be heard. The tribunal's discretion is otherwise unlimited. For example, it was suggested within the UNCITRAL Working Group that the tribunal's broad discretion under Article 17(1) would allow it to issue preliminary orders (in the meaning of the UNCITRAL Model Law),[1] despite the absence of a specific provision empowering the tribunal in this respect.[2] The safeguards are phrased in general terms, and are thus also subject to the tribunal's assessment in every situation. Notably, Article 17(1) specifies that each party must be given a reasonable opportunity to present its case, but only 'at an appropriate stage of the proceedings', as determined by the tribunal.

5.04 The arbitral tribunal is also under a duty to maximize the efficiency of the proceedings. The second sentence of Article 17(1) was added in the 2010 UNCITRAL Rules to make this duty explicit. This text resembles that found in the procedural rules of a number of arbitral institutions.[3] While noting that

---

[1] A preliminary order is an order issued by the tribunal during its consideration of an interim measures application directing a party not to frustrate the purpose of the requested interim measure. See UNCITRAL Model Law, as adopted on 21 June 1985 and amended on 7 July 2006, A/40/17, Annex I, and A/61/17, Annex I, Art 17B.

[2] UNCITRAL Working Group II (Arbitration and Conciliation), *Note by the Secretariat: Settlement of commercial disputes: Revision of the UNCITRAL Arbitration Rules*, 49th session, 15–19 September 2008, A/CN.9/WG.II/WP.151/Add.1, para 15; see also Report of the UNCITRAL Working Group II (Arbitration and Conciliation) on the work of its 49th session, 15–19 September 2008, A/CN.9/665, para 127.

[3] See eg LCIA Rules 1998, Art 14.1, referring to the arbitral tribunal's 'general duties at all times . . . to adopt procedures suitable to the circumstances of the arbitration, avoiding unnecessary delay or expense, so as to provide a fair and efficient means for the final resolution of the parties' dispute'.

it was not strictly necessary for the exercise of the arbitral tribunal's discretionary powers, the UNCITRAL Working Group believed that including this language could 'provide leverage for arbitrators to take certain steps both vis-à-vis other arbitrators and the parties'.[4] For the sake of expediency, in many cases, the tribunal proposes that a first procedural order include a provision authorizing the presiding arbitrator to issue procedural decisions alone, either for all procedural matters or only in cases of emergency.[5] Pursuant to Article 33 of the Rules, any decision made by the presiding arbitrator alone is subject to revision by the arbitral tribunal.

5.05 Article 17(2) promptly sets the proceedings in motion by requiring that a procedural calendar be fixed shortly after the tribunal is constituted. The UNCITRAL Working Group considered that this provision 'enhance[s] efficiency and reflect[s] good practice'.[6]

5.06 In many cases, the tribunal and the parties will meet or hold a teleconference to discuss procedural matters on the basis of an agenda or a draft procedural order circulated to the parties by the tribunal. After the meeting or teleconference, the tribunal will issue a procedural order confirming the issues on which the parties have agreed and deciding matters on which agreement could not be reached.[7] In other cases, the tribunal will not hold a procedural conference call or meeting, but will instead solicit the views of the parties in writing on a number of procedural questions. The tribunal will then prepare a draft procedural order. Issues such as the place of arbitration, the language(s) of the proceedings, and the potential need for bifurcation of the proceedings between various phases (for instance between jurisdiction and merits, or between liability and quantum) may be discussed in addition to the timetable for the submission of pleadings, witness statements, and expert reports, document production, and hearings, if any. Some of these issues, such as bifurcation or the setting of dates for a hearing, may be deferred for discussion at a later stage after further submissions by the parties.

[4] UNCITRAL Working Group II (Arbitration and Conciliation), *Note by the Secretariat: Settlement of commercial disputes: Revision of the UNCITRAL Arbitration Rules*, 46th session, 5–9 February 2007, A/CN.9/WG.II/WP.145/Add.1, para 3.

[5] An example of such a provision included in a first procedural order in one PCA-administered arbitration is as follows: 'Procedural decisions shall be issued by the presiding arbitrator after consultation with his co-arbitrators or, in cases of urgency or if a co-arbitrator cannot be reached, by him alone'.

[6] Report of the UNCITRAL Working Group II (Arbitration and Conciliation) on the work of its 52nd session, 1–5 February 2010, A/CN.9/688, para 85; see also Jan Paulsson and Georgios Petrochilos, *Revision of the UNCITRAL Arbitration Rules*, September 2006, paras 120–4, <http://www.uncitral.org/uncitral/uncitral_texts/arbitration/2010Arbitration_rules_travaux.html>.

[7] For examples of such procedural orders, see Appendices XVII and XVIII.

5.07 The second sentence of Article 17(2) gives the arbitral tribunal the power to modify periods of time set by the 2012 PCA Rules or agreed by the parties. In respect of periods of time, the tribunal is therefore in a position to override the parties' agreement. Notably, under Article 17(2), an arbitral tribunal will for example be able to extend an unrealistic deadline set in the arbitration agreement for the issuance of an award. It remains the case that the tribunal's discretion is limited by its duty under Article 17(1) to treat the parties with equality and give each of them a reasonable opportunity to present its case.

5.08 The arbitral tribunal's power to change time periods begins only with its full constitution. Therefore, under the 2010 UNCITRAL Rules, the time periods for actions to be taken prior to constitution of the tribunal (such as for the filing of a response to the notice of arbitration or the appointment of arbitrators) are fixed and cannot be modified except by agreement of the parties.[8] The UNCITRAL Working Group considered allowing the appointing authority to modify these time periods, but ultimately rejected this possibility.[9] The 2012 PCA Rules go further in ensuring the full flexibility of the procedure by giving the PCA International Bureau the power to modify many of the time periods for actions to be taken before constitution of the tribunal, similar to the Article 17(2) power of the tribunal to modify time periods after the tribunal's constitution.[10]

5.09 Article 17(3) concerns the tribunal's choice between holding oral hearings or conducting the proceedings on a purely documentary basis. While the phrasing of the provision suggests that upon the request of a party, the tribunal must hold a hearing, the specification that the request be made 'at an appropriate stage of the proceedings' retains for the arbitral tribunal the right to refuse a request for a hearing when it would compromise the efficiency of the proceedings.[11]

5.10 Article 17(4) deals with communications between the parties and the arbitral tribunal. Article 15(3) of the 1976 UNCITRAL Rules mandated that all documents and information supplied to the tribunal by one party be communicated at the same time to the other party. The UNCITRAL Working Group considered a proposal to omit the words 'at the same time' in the 2010 UNCITRAL Rules, to

[8] See 2010 UNCITRAL Rules, Arts 4(1), 8(1),(2)(b), 9(2), (3).

[9] Report of the UNCITRAL Working Group II (Arbitration and Conciliation) on the work of its 46th session, 5–9 February 2007, A/CN.9/619, para 135.

[10] See eg Rules, Arts 4(1), 8(2)(b), 9(3).

[11] See discussion in Report of the UNCITRAL Working Group II (Arbitration and Conciliation) on the work of its 45th session, 11–15 September 2006, A/CN.9/614, para 77. A tribunal could not refuse to hold hearings under the 1976 UNCITRAL Rules (see Art 15(2): 'If either party so requests at any stage of the proceedings, the arbitral tribunal shall hold hearings for the presentation of evidence by witnesses, including expert witnesses, or for oral argument. In the absence of such a request, the arbitral tribunal shall decide whether to hold such hearings or whether the proceedings shall be conducted on the basis of documents and other materials').

account for cases where a party wishes to apply to the tribunal for a preliminary measure on an ex parte basis. While such a radical amendment was ultimately excluded, it was accepted to provide for simultaneous communications 'except as otherwise permitted by the arbitral tribunal if it may do so under applicable law' as a compromise position that both preserves the original rule and allows the tribunal to modify it when necessary in the circumstances, if authorized under applicable law.[12]

Article 17(4) of the 2012 PCA Rules differs from the equivalent provision of the 2010 UNCITRAL Rules in that communications from a party to the arbitral tribunal must be copied not only to the other party, but also to the International Bureau of the PCA. This allows the institution to stay abreast of developments in the case and also enables it to fulfill its function under Article 1(3) as the keeper of archives. **5.11**

One further trend in arbitrations conducted under PCA auspices has been to interpose the PCA International Bureau as the sole channel of communication between the parties and the tribunal. This is particularly common in inter-state proceedings. A provision to this effect can be included in a first procedural order issued by the tribunal.[13] Among other benefits, such a provision reduces the risk that emails not intended for the parties, containing, for instance, the tribunal's internal discussions, accidentally end up in the parties' inboxes. The International Bureau's role as intermediary also facilitates the making of simultaneous submissions by the parties. When so instructed, the International Bureau, having received submissions from each party at different times prior to the expiration of the deadline, can forward these submissions to the tribunal (and all the parties) at the same time. Another provision regarding communications frequently included in a first procedural order is a restriction on the range of correspondence on which the parties are permitted to copy the tribunal.[14] **5.12**

Article 17(5) reproduces a new provision of the 2010 UNCITRAL Rules. It provides for the joinder to the proceedings of third persons who are also parties to the arbitration agreement. The tribunal may or may not allow the joinder in its discretion, after evaluating the potential prejudice to the parties involved. A key factor influencing the decision will be the stage of the proceedings, and whether any **5.13**

[12] Report of the UNCITRAL Working Group II (Arbitration and Conciliation) on the work of its 49th session, 15–19 September 2008, A/CN.9/665, para 127.

[13] For example, the first procedural order in one PCA-administered case provided as follows: 'The Parties shall send all communications for the attention of the Tribunal by e-mail simultaneously to opposing counsel and the PCA. The PCA shall promptly transmit all communications received from the Parties to each member of the Tribunal'.

[14] An example of such a provision from one PCA-administered case is as follows: 'The Parties shall send copies of correspondence between them to the PCA only if such correspondence relates to a matter where the Tribunal is required to take action or to abstain from acting or if it gives notice of a relevant event that the Tribunal and the PCA should be apprised of'.

parallel proceedings have already been initiated. The tribunal considers the joinder upon request of a party. Notably, the consent of the third person to the joinder is not necessary, and the third party may be joined to the proceedings after full constitution of the tribunal, thus not having had a chance to participate in the choice of the arbitrators. The third person's agreement to an arbitration clause providing for dispute resolution under the 2012 PCA Rules or the 2010 UNCITRAL Rules implies its consent to the application of the joinder provision and to the possibility of the tribunal being constituted without its participation.[15]

5.14 In contrast, like the 2010 UNCITRAL Rules, the 2012 PCA Rules do not contain any provision for the consolidation of proceedings, and so the consolidation of proceedings conducted pursuant to different arbitration agreements would require the consent of all parties.

B. Place of Arbitration—Article 18

> 1. If the parties have not previously agreed on the place of arbitration, the place of arbitration shall be determined by the arbitral tribunal having regard to the circumstances of the case. The award shall be deemed to have been made at the place of arbitration.
> 2. The arbitral tribunal may meet at any location it considers appropriate for deliberations. Unless otherwise agreed by the parties, the arbitral tribunal may also meet at any location it considers appropriate for any other purpose, including hearings.

5.15 Article 18 concerns the legal seat of the arbitration and the physical location of the proceedings.

5.16 This provision reproduces the text of Article 18 of the 2010 UNCITRAL Rules without any modification.

5.17 The new language of the 2012 PCA Rules and 2010 UNCITRAL Rules clarifies that there is a distinction to be made between the legal seat of the arbitration (called in the Rules the 'place of arbitration', following the usage in the UNCITRAL Model Law[16]) and the physical location at which hearings or meetings take place—often called the 'venue'.[17] The award is deemed to be rendered at the legal seat—a rule

---

[15] See Report of the UNCITRAL Working Group II (Arbitration and Conciliation) on the work of its 49th session, 15–19 September 2008, A/CN.9/665, para 130.

[16] 1985, with amendments as adopted in 2006, Art 20.

[17] See UNCITRAL Working Group II (Arbitration and Conciliation), *Note by the Secretariat: Settlement of commercial disputes: Revision of the UNCITRAL Arbitration Rules*, 46th session, 15–19 September 2008, A/CN.9/WG.II/WP.151, para 38 ('The proposed draft seeks to distinguish between the place of arbitration (meaning the legal seat) and the location where meetings could be held, in terms similar to those adopted under article 20 of the UNCITRAL Model Law on International Commercial Arbitration').

which serves to avoid uncertainty in cases where the award is physically signed at a location other than the place of arbitration.[18] The place where the award is made may also be important for the applicability of the New York Convention,[19] as some 73 states, on the basis of reciprocity, apply the Convention only to the recognition and enforcement of awards made in the territory of other contracting states.[20] Except in cases involving only states and intergovernmental organizations, the place of arbitration also determines the *lex arbitri*—the law that applies to the procedure adopted in the arbitration—and the courts with supervisory jurisdiction over the arbitration.[21] The arbitral proceedings themselves (including hearings and tribunal deliberations) can take place at one or multiple locations other than the place of arbitration. Because the place of arbitration and the venue need not be the same, the parties should consider each choice independently of the other. The choice of the place of arbitration requires the consideration of legal factors, while the choice of the venue requires the consideration of practical factors.[22] Parties may find it preferable to stipulate the place of arbitration in their arbitration agreement, but to defer the choice of the venue until all relevant variables, such as the identity of arbitrators, the nature of the dispute, and the location of witnesses and evidence, are known.

The understanding of the place of arbitration is different in proceedings involving only states and intergovernmental organizations. In such cases, the parties generally do not intend to waive their immunity from the jurisdiction of national courts when agreeing to arbitration.[23] Specifically, when agreeing to a place of arbitration, they should not be assumed to have waived their immunity from the jurisdiction of **5.18**

---

[18] See UNCITRAL Working Group II (Arbitration and Conciliation), *Note by the Secretariat: Settlement of commercial disputes: Revision of the UNCITRAL Arbitration Rules*, 46th session, 15–19 September 2008, A/CN.9/WG.II/WP.151, para 10.

[19] 1958, 330 UNTS 38.

[20] New York Convention, 10 June 1958, 330 UNTS 38, Art I(3), see up-to-date list of parties that apply the Convention on the basis of reciprocity at <http://www.uncitral.org/uncitral/en/uncitral_texts/arbitration/NYConvention_status.html>.

[21] For a more detailed discussion of the importance of the choice of the place of arbitration, see Gary B Born, *International Commercial Arbitration*, vol 1 (Wolters Kluwer, 2009) 1679–86; Jan Paulsson et al. (eds), *The Freshfields Guide to Arbitration Clauses in International Contracts* (Kluwer Law International, 2010), 31–9.

[22] The UNCITRAL Notes on Organizing Arbitration Proceedings 1996, para 22 list the following relevant 'factual and legal factors' in deciding on a place of arbitration:

(a) suitability of the law on arbitral procedure of the place of arbitration;
(b) whether there is a multilateral or bilateral treaty on enforcement of arbitral awards between the State where the arbitration takes place and the State or States where the award may have to be enforced;
(c) convenience of the parties and the arbitrators, including the travel distances;
(d) availability and cost of support services needed; and
(e) location of the subject-matter in dispute and proximity of evidence.

The authors of this Guide would suggest that only factors (a) and (b) are relevant to the choice of the place of arbitration, while factors (c)–(e) should be considered in choosing the venue or venues for hearings and meetings.

[23] See discussion under Article 1(2).

the courts of the place of arbitration. In line with this intention, in some inter-state proceedings, the parties and the tribunal elect not to stipulate a place of arbitration at all. And where a place of arbitration is chosen, it is understood as a reference to the expected physical location of the proceedings.[24]

5.19 The place of arbitration may be agreed by the parties in their arbitration agreement, for example by using the model arbitration clauses found in the annex to the 2012 PCA Rules.[25] If the parties have not agreed on a place of arbitration in their arbitration agreement, Article 3(3)(g) of the Rules instructs the claimant to include a proposal for a place of arbitration in its notice of arbitration. Article 4(1)(b) of the Rules then instructs the respondent to reply to the claimant's proposal, either by accepting it or by making a proposal of its own. If the parties agree, the tribunal will record their agreement in a procedural order. If the parties are unable to agree, the tribunal will decide on the place of arbitration pursuant to Article 18(1). Should the positions of the parties on the choice of the place of arbitration not have been explained to the satisfaction of the tribunal in the notice of arbitration and the response thereto, the tribunal may request brief written submissions on the question from the parties, or invite discussion of the matter in a teleconference or at a procedural meeting with the parties. A tribunal decision on the place of arbitration is typically recorded in a procedural order.

5.20 Article 18(2) provides that '[u]nless otherwise agreed by the parties, the arbitral tribunal may also meet at any location it considers appropriate for any other purpose, including hearings'. Pursuant to Article 18(2), it is therefore clear that the parties may jointly decide on the venue for hearings and other aspects of the proceedings. Absent agreement by the parties, the tribunal is free to select 'any location' as the venue. It is advisable for the tribunal to exercise caution in ascertaining whether there is agreement between the parties as to the venue. Despite the conceptual separation of the place of arbitration from the venue intended by the drafters of the 2012 PCA Rules and 2010 UNCITRAL Rules, in fact many parties, when stipulating a place of arbitration in their arbitration agreements, think of this term as importing both legal consequences, such as an applicable *lex arbitri*, and practical consequences, such as a venue for hearings. Parties who have agreed on a place of arbitration may therefore also be understood as having 'agree[d] otherwise' regarding the location of hearings for the purpose of Article 18(2) of the Rules. As a result, tribunals may wish to avoid selecting a venue that differs from the agreed place of

---

[24] See eg *Indus Waters Kishenganga Arbitration*, Pakistan v India, PCA Case No 2011-1, Procedural Order No 1, 21 January 2011, Art 1.1, reproduced in Partial Award, 18 February 2013, para 23, which provides for The Hague as the 'seat of the arbitration'. All meetings and hearings to date have been held at the Peace Palace in The Hague.

[25] Reproduced in Ch 3, nn 18–19.

arbitration, against the objection of one of the parties.[26] In contrast, the parties cannot dictate the location of the tribunal's deliberations.[27]

While the PCA's headquarters are in The Hague,[28] under the 2012 PCA Rules neither the place of arbitration nor the venue of any part of the arbitral proceeding is tied to this location. **5.21**

Under the 1990s PCA Rules and PCA Natural Resources/Environmental Rules, The Hague is the place of arbitration unless the parties agree otherwise.[29] This is not the case under the 2012 PCA Rules, under which there is no default place of arbitration; the parties or the arbitral tribunal must come to a decision on this matter. **5.22**

The 1990s PCA Rules and PCA Natural Resources/Environmental Rules also provide that if the parties choose a place of arbitration other than The Hague, the International Bureau will 'inform the parties and the arbitral tribunal whether it is willing to provide' secretariat and registry services. Under the 2012 PCA Rules, no such limitation applies: the role of the PCA International Bureau remains unchanged regardless of the place of arbitration or venue chosen for the proceedings. **5.23**

The PCA International Bureau regularly organizes hearings and meetings at a variety of locations worldwide.[30] While the parties and the arbitral tribunal are entirely free to choose their preferred location, one relevant consideration in selecting a venue or venues may be that for PCA-administered proceedings, the PCA **5.24**

[26] Nevertheless, some courts have recognized the power of arbitral tribunals to do just that. See *Republic of Indonesia v Himpurna California Energy Ltd, Patuha Power Ltd v Jan Paulsson, Antonino Albert de Fina v Priyatna Abdurrasyid, President, Arrondissementsrechtbank*, Court of First Instance, The Hague, 21 September 1999, in Albert Jan van den Berg (ed), 2000 *Yearbook of Commercial Arbitration* 443*ff*, where a Dutch court rejected the request of the respondent in an international arbitration to prohibit the three members of the arbitral tribunal from holding hearings at the Peace Palace in The Hague, on the ground that the parties' contractually agreed place of arbitration was Jakarta. While the court's reasoning was limited to stating that the tribunal's power to hear witnesses and hold meetings at any place it deems appropriate 'is not limited by the [1976] UNCITRAL Rules', it is worth noting that this decision was rendered in circumstances where the respondent had obtained an injunction from an Indonesian court ordering the claimants to abstain from all activities in furtherance of the arbitral process, on pain of a daily penalty of US$1 million for non-compliance.

[27] UNCITRAL Working Group II (Arbitration and Conciliation), *Note by the Secretariat: Settlement of commercial disputes: Revision of the UNCITRAL Arbitration Rules*, 50th 9–13 February 2009, A/CN.9/WG.II/WP.154, para 43.

[28] 1899 Hague Convention, Art 22(1); 1907 Hague Convention, Art 43.

[29] PCA State/State Rules, Art 16(1); PCA State/Non-State Rules, Art 16(1); PCA State/International Organization Rules, Art 16(1); PCA International Organization/Private Party Rules, Art 16(1), PCA Natural Resources/Environmental Rules, Art 16(1) see also 1899 Hague Convention, Art 25, 1907 Hague Convention, Art 60.

[30] Recent PCA hearing and meeting locations include Berlin, Brussels, Cologne, Dar es Salaam, Delhi, Dubai, Georgetown (Guyana), The Hague, Hong Kong, Houston, Kuala Lumpur, London, Montreal, Mumbai, New York, Ottawa, Paris, San José (Costa Rica), Srinagar (India), Stockholm, Toronto, Vienna, Washington DC, Windhoek (Namibia), Zagreb, and Zurich. Singapore has also been chosen as the venue in several pending PCA cases.

can make hearing and meeting space available at no cost at the Peace Palace in The Hague and at venues in Costa Rica, Mauritius, and Singapore. The PCA has also concluded agreements with other arbitral institutions for use of their facilities in PCA-administered proceedings, including the Hong Kong International Arbitration Centre, the International Centre for Settlement of Investment Disputes (ICSID), and the American Arbitration Association. The availability of PCA Host Country Agreements may also be considered.[31]

C. Language—Article 19

1. Subject to an agreement by the parties, the arbitral tribunal shall, promptly after its appointment, determine the language or languages to be used in the proceedings. This determination shall apply to the statement of claim, the statement of defence, and any further written statements and, if oral hearings take place, to the language or languages to be used in such hearings.
2. The arbitral tribunal may order that any documents annexed to the statement of claim or statement of defence, and any supplementary documents or exhibits submitted in the course of the proceedings, delivered in their original language, shall be accompanied by a translation into the language or languages agreed upon by the parties or determined by the arbitral tribunal.

5.25 Article 19 provides for a determination by the arbitral tribunal of the language or languages of the proceedings and for the translation of documents.

5.26 This provision replicates Article 19 of the 2010 UNCITRAL Rules, which, in turn, tracks the language of the equivalent provision of the 1976 UNCITRAL Rules.

5.27 In revising the UNCITRAL Rules, the UNCITRAL Working Group considered removing the possibility for the arbitral tribunal to elect more than one language as the language of the proceedings, but ultimately decided to retain this option.[32] The same decision was made in the drafting of the 2012 PCA Rules, as the use of more than one language is not uncommon in PCA-administered proceedings.

5.28 Conduct of proceedings in a single language is preferable from the standpoint of speed and cost. Pursuant to Article 19(1), the choice of a language of the proceedings applies to all written statements by the parties (including the statement of claim and statement

[31] See eg *Philip Morris Asia Limited v Australia*, PCA Case No 2012–12 (Hong Kong–Australia BIT) (2010 UNCITRAL Rules), Procedural Order No 3, 26 October 2012, where the arbitral tribunal, in selecting Singapore over London as the place of arbitration, specifically mentioned that 'the PCA, which is administering the present arbitration, has concluded a Host Country Agreement with Singapore, but not with the UK or an institution in London'. PCA Host Country Agreements are described under Art 16.

[32] UNCITRAL Working Group II (Arbitration and Conciliation), *Note by the Secretariat: Settlement of commercial disputes: Revision of the UNCITRAL Arbitration Rules*, 49th session, 15–19 September 2008, A/CN.9/WG.II/WP.151/Add.1, para 39; Report of the UNCITRAL Working Group II (Arbitration and Conciliation) on the work of its 49th session, 15–19 September 15–19, 2008, A/CN.9/665, paras 140–1.

of defence). In practice, any communications between the parties and the tribunal, as well as the tribunal's procedural orders and awards, will be in the language of the proceedings. Generally, the tribunal will exercise its power under Article 19(2) to order the party filing documents in another language to provide translations.[33] If any witnesses are required to appear who do not speak or do not feel confident speaking in the language of the proceedings, their testimony will be interpreted.

It may, however, be necessary to conduct all or part of the proceedings in multiple—usually, two—languages. 5.29

Some proceedings are conducted in two languages that are equally authoritative. For example, where a treaty has been drafted and signed in two authoritative languages, the parties may not wish to give one language precedence over the other in the arbitral proceedings. For example, in the PCA-administered *Eurotunnel* arbitration, which was initiated pursuant to an arbitration agreement found in a bilingual treaty,[34] the procedural rules agreed by the parties provided as follows: 5.30

> Article VII—Language of the Arbitration
>
> 1. The parties and the arbitrators shall use the English or the French language during the arbitration. If necessary there shall be simultaneous translation of oral proceedings.
> 2. Any award shall be made both in the English and French languages.[35]

The tribunal's first procedural order completed this rule by providing for the English or French translation of pleadings.[36] 5.31

In other cases, parties are mostly concerned with access to translations from a practical perspective, and, while requiring bilingual proceedings, accept that one of the languages of the proceedings be selected as the authoritative language, such 5.32

[33] Nevertheless, in some cases, in the context of document production, the tribunal will allow parties to produce documents in their original language, with only those documents that are relied upon by the parties in their submissions requiring translation.

[34] 1 The Channel Tunnel Group Limited 2 France-Manche SA v 1 Secretary of State for Transport of the Government of the United Kingdom of Great Britain and Northern Ireland 2 le ministre de l'équipement, des transports, de l'aménagement du territoire, du tourisme et de la mer du Gouvernement de la République française, PCA Case No 2003-5, Partial Award of 30 January 2007, PCA Award Series, para 12. Treaty between the French Republic and the United Kingdom of Great Britain and Northern Ireland Concerning the Construction and Operation by Private Concessionaires of a Channel Fixed Link, 12 February 1986, 1497 UNTS 335. The Treaty indicates that it was 'done in duplicate... in the English and French languages, both texts being equally authoritative'.

[35] Treaty between the French Republic and the United Kingdom of Great Britain and Northern Ireland Concerning the Construction and Operation by Private Concessionaires of a Channel Fixed Link, February 12, 1986, 1497 UNTS 335, Annex to the Exchange of Letters of 29th July Relating to the Arbitration Rules Concerning the Channel Fixed Link agreed by the Parties, 29 July 1987, Art VII.

[36] *Eurotunnel Arbitration* 1 The Channel Tunnel Group Limited 2 France-Manche SA v 1 Secretary of State for Transport of the Government of the United Kingdom of Great Britain and Northern Ireland 2 le ministre de l'équipement, des transports, de l'aménagement du territoire, du tourisme et de la mer du Gouvernement de la République française, PCA Case No 2003-5, Partial Award of 30 January 2007, PCA Award Series, para 12.

that whenever there is a discrepancy between two language versions of the same document, the version in the authoritative language will prevail. For example, the first procedural order in one PCA-administered arbitration provided that 'English and Spanish will be the official languages of the arbitration and, as between them, English will be the authoritative language'.

5.33 The choice of one authoritative language in bilingual proceedings may make it possible to provide for a delay between the circulation of documents in their original language and in translation. Thus, in one bilingual French/English PCA-administered arbitration, the tribunal's first procedural order provided that 'all notifications and correspondence with the Tribunal and the [PCA] shall be drafted in English and French', and that all written submissions by the parties 'shall be drafted in English or French, accompanied by a translation in the other language... to be submitted within 21 days after the date of filing of the original submission'. In a bilingual English/Spanish PCA-administered arbitration, the first procedural order provided that '[c]ommunications by the Tribunal (including orders, decisions and awards) and all submissions and communications by the parties' would be in English, including 'translations in full of any witness statements prepared in Spanish and translations in relevant part of documentary evidence and legal authorities in a language other than English', and that Spanish translations of the award and the parties' written pleadings on the merits would be submitted no more than six weeks after the original submission, while the translations into Spanish of all other writings would be submitted 'with the writings or as soon as possible thereafter, but in no event later than three weeks after their submission or communication'.

5.34 In another category of cases, the tribunal or the parties may decide that two languages *may*, but are not required to be used in the proceedings, and that each party may unilaterally decide which language to use for any aspect of the proceedings. In such cases, correspondence and submissions made in one of the two permitted languages do not require translation. Such proceedings allow for cost savings, but naturally are possible only where the members of the arbitral tribunal and counsel are all sufficiently proficient in both languages.

5.35 Finally, in some cases, there is only one language of the arbitration, but courtesy translations are provided. For example, in the *Abyei* arbitration, the parties' arbitration agreement provided that English was the language of the proceedings, but also required the International Bureau to ensure that any award would be made available in Arabic translation shortly after being issued.[37]

[37] *Abyei Arbitration*, the Government of Sudan/the Sudan People's Liberation Movement/Army, PCA Case No 2008-7 (PCA State/Non-State Rules), Arbitration Agreement, Arts 7, 9(3). An Arabic translation of the award was produced and is available on the PCA's website. The PCA's press release announcing and summarizing the award was also issued in both English and Arabic (see <http://www.pca-cpa.org/showpage.asp?pag_id=1306>).

5.36 While it appears self-evident that the arbitral tribunal and counsel should have adequate knowledge of the language of the arbitration, this is not always the case and has caused difficulties in various PCA-administered proceedings. In one investor-state arbitration, where the tribunal's first procedural order decided that English would be the language of the arbitration, the tribunal held a preliminary procedural hearing by teleconference with the parties in English. Thereafter, the tribunal circulated to the parties a draft procedural order setting out a timetable, which the tribunal had understood to have been agreed to by the parties during the procedural hearing. The respondent state immediately wrote to the tribunal, denying having agreed to the proposed timetable. Yet the transcript of the teleconference clearly showed the state's representative as having said 'Yes' to the tribunal's proposed procedural calendar. It quickly became apparent that the state's internal counsel, who had represented it on the teleconference, was not fully fluent in English and had not understood the proposal. Ultimately, the tribunal revised the procedural calendar after considering the respondent state's comments provided in its post-hearing letter.

5.37 In another PCA-administered arbitration, an early procedural order provided that the language of the arbitration would be English. From that time, the parties and the tribunal corresponded in English, and the parties made all their written submissions in English as well. When requested to comment on the date for a pre-hearing conference call, counsel for the claimant wrote to the tribunal to 'point out, that this conference call as well as the hearing itself shall be held in three languages: English, German, and Bulgarian'. It appeared from further correspondence between the parties and the tribunal that counsel for the claimant did not feel comfortable making opening and closing statements in English. In a procedural order, the tribunal confirmed that the language of the arbitration was English and ruled that should the claimant require translation of any part of the hearing other than the testimony of its witnesses, the claimant would provide its own Bulgarian/English or German/English interpreters and bear the full costs of any such interpretation.

5.38 Where documents are translated, it is common for the parties to agree or the arbitral tribunal to rule that there will be no requirement that the translations be certified or conform with any other formal constraint, unless a party objects to the accuracy of the translation.

5.39 The PCA International Bureau routinely arranges for translation of tribunal communications (including correspondence, procedural orders, and awards) and interpretation during hearings and meetings. Interpretation can be simultaneous or consecutive at the choice of the parties and the tribunal.[38] If interpretation booths

[38] Interpretation is simultaneous when the interpreter renders the message in the target language at the same time as the speaker speaks in the source language. The interpreter usually sits in a sound-proof booth, with the interpretation being transmitted to the audience via headphones. In consecutive interpretation, the speaker has to pause after each short segment of speech, allowing the interpreter to speak.

are available, simultaneous interpretation is usually preferred, as it greatly reduces the duration of hearings. In multilingual proceedings, transcription of hearings in several language versions may be required.

D. Statement of Claim—Article 20

1. The claimant shall communicate its statement of claim in writing to the respondent, to the International Bureau, and to each of the arbitrators within a period of time to be determined by the arbitral tribunal. The claimant may elect to treat its notice of arbitration referred to in article 3 as a statement of claim, provided that the notice of arbitration also complies with the requirements of paragraphs 2 to 4 of this article.
2. The statement of claim shall include the following particulars:
   (a) The names and contact details of the parties;
   (b) A statement of the facts supporting the claim;
   (c) The points at issue;
   (d) The relief or remedy sought;
   (e) The legal grounds or arguments supporting the claim.
3. A copy of any rule, decision, agreement, contract, convention, treaty, constituent instrument of an organization or agency, or relationship out of, or in relation to which, the dispute arises, and of the arbitration agreement shall be annexed to the statement of claim.
4. The statement of claim should, as far as possible, be accompanied by all documents and other evidence relied upon by the claimant, or contain references to them.

5.40 Article 20 stipulates the requirement that the claimant(s) file a statement of claim, and further specifies the content of the statement of claim and its mandatory and recommended accompanying documents.

5.41 This provision departs from the text of Article 20 of the 2010 UNCITRAL Rules in two respects.

5.42 Article 20(1) includes the PCA International Bureau among the recipients of the statement of claim, allowing the International Bureau to fulfill its function under Article 1(3) of the Rules as the keeper of the archive of the proceeding.

5.43 Article 20(3) lists the types of documents which must accompany the statement of claim. It differs from the equivalent list in the 2010 UNCITRAL Rules so as to align with the list in Article 3(3)(d) of the 2012 PCA Rules. The requirements for the notice of arbitration in Article 3(3)(d) and for the statement of claim in Article 20(3) must correspond so as to project a unified idea of the documents out of, or in relation to which, a dispute may arise under the Rules.[39] This correspondence

[39] Similarly, the UNCITRAL Working Group considered that 'the drafting of the provision on the communication of the contract and arbitration agreement under Articles 3 and 18 [now 20] should be aligned': Report of the UNCITRAL Working Group on Arbitration and Conciliation on the work of its 46th session, 5–9 February 2007, A/CN.9/619, para 147.

between the two provisions is also necessary given that, pursuant to Article 20(1), the claimant has the option of treating its notice of arbitration as a statement of claim, provided that it complies with the requirements of paragraphs 2 and 4 of Article 20. The list at Articles 3(3)(d) and 20(3) of the 2012 PCA Rules expands upon the 2010 UNCITRAL Rules' formulation to take account of the variety of legal instruments that can, and in cases where states, state-controlled entities, and intergovernmental organizations are parties, often do, contain the parties' agreement to arbitrate under the Rules.[40]

Article 20(4) encourages, but does not require, that the statement of claim be accompanied by the evidence on which the claimant intends to rely. It is for the arbitral tribunal, therefore, to decide on the deadline for the filing of evidence by the parties. **5.44**

E. Statement of Defence—Article 21

1. The respondent shall communicate its statement of defence in writing to the claimant, to the International Bureau, and to each of the arbitrators within a period of time to be determined by the arbitral tribunal. The respondent may elect to treat its response to the notice of arbitration referred to in article 4 as a statement of defence, provided that the response to the notice of arbitration also complies with the requirements of paragraph 2 of this article.
2. The statement of defence shall reply to the particulars (b) to (e) of the statement of claim (article 20, paragraph 2). The statement of defence should, as far as possible, be accompanied by all documents and other evidence relied upon by the respondent, or contain references to them.
3. In its statement of defence, or at a later stage in the arbitral proceedings if the arbitral tribunal decides that the delay was justified under the circumstances, the respondent may make a counterclaim or rely on a claim for the purpose of a set-off provided that the arbitral tribunal has jurisdiction over it.
4. The provisions of article 20, paragraphs 2 to 4 shall apply to a counterclaim, a claim under article 4, paragraph 2(e), and a claim relied on for the purpose of a set-off.

Article 21 stipulates the requirement that the respondent file a statement of defence, specifies the content of the statement of defence by reference to Article 20, and provides for counterclaims and set-off. **5.45**

The only feature that distinguishes Article 21 of the 2012 PCA Rules from the equivalent provision of the 2010 UNCITRAL Rules is that it requires the statement of defence to be copied to the PCA International Bureau, thus enabling the International Bureau to keep the archive of the proceeding in accordance with Article 1(3). **5.46**

[40] See discussion under Article 3.

5.47 Article 21 of the 2012 PCA Rules reflects much of the language and reasoning that is captured in Article 20. In particular, mirroring the possibility under Article 20 for the claimant to treat its notice of arbitration as a statement of claim, Article 21 allows the respondent to treat its response to the notice of arbitration as a statement of defence, provided it includes the necessary particulars referred to in Article 21(2).

5.48 To increase the efficiency of the proceedings, Article 21(3) of the 2010 UNCITRAL Rules was drafted to allow the tribunal to determine set-off claims arising in a wider range of situations than those captured by the text of the equivalent provision of the 1976 UNCITRAL Rules, which provided that the respondent could make a set-off claim only if it arose 'out of the same contract'. The UNCITRAL Working Group considered substituting the words 'out of the same contract' with a number of different formulations, including 'arising out of the same legal relationship, whether contractual or not'.[41] This formulation was ultimately rejected in favour of the provision 'the respondent may make a counterclaim or rely on a claim for the purpose of a set-off provided that the arbitral tribunal has jurisdiction over it', which received support because it is 'broad enough to encompass a wide range of circumstances', but does not 'require substantive definitions of the notions of claims for set-off and counterclaims'.[42] In light of the different instruments from which disputes between the intended users of the 2012 PCA Rules may arise, the broader, more flexible language of the 2010 UNCITRAL Rules was adopted in the 2012 PCA Rules.

5.49 A corresponding reference to set-offs was added to Article 23(2) of the 2010 UNCITRAL Rules to enable the arbitral tribunal to fully and properly assess its jurisdiction over set-offs, and this reference is similarly present in Article 23(2) of the 2012 PCA Rules.

F. Amendments to the Claim or Defence—Article 22

During the course of the arbitral proceedings, a party may amend or supplement its claim or defence, including a counterclaim or a claim for the purpose of a set-off, unless the arbitral tribunal considers it inappropriate to allow such amendment or

[41] Working Group Sessions, A/CN.9/WG.II/WP.145/Add.1, para 16; Report of the UNCITRAL Working Group II (Arbitration and Conciliation) on the work of its 45th session, 11–15 September 2006, A/CN.9/614, paras 94–6. See also Report of the UNCITRAL Working Group II (Arbitration and Conciliation) on the work of its 50th session, 9–13 February 2009, A/CN.9/669, paras 27–31.

[42] Working Group Sessions, A/CN.9/WG.II/WP.145/Add.1, para 16; Report of the UNCITRAL Working Group II (Arbitration and Conciliation) on the work of its 45th session, 11–15 September 2006, A/CN.9/614, paras 94–6. See also Report of the UNCITRAL Working Group II (Arbitration and Conciliation) on the work of its 50th session, 9–13 February 2009, A/CN.9/669, paras 31–2.

> supplement having regard to the delay in making it or prejudice to other parties or any other circumstances. However, a claim or defence, including a counterclaim or a claim for the purpose of a set-off, may not be amended or supplemented in such a manner that the amended or supplemented claim or defence falls outside the jurisdiction of the arbitral tribunal.

Article 22 provides for the amendment of the parties' claims and defences. **5.50**

This provision replicates the text of Article 22 of the 2010 UNCITRAL Rules. It is drafted so as to be consistent with Article 21(3) regarding the jurisdiction of the tribunal to hear set-off claims. As compared to the equivalent provision of the 1976 UNCITRAL Rules, it also accounts for multiparty arbitrations (referring to 'prejudice to other parties' rather than 'prejudice to the other party'). **5.51**

While Article 22 provides that a claim or defence may not be supplemented 'in such a manner that the amended or supplemented claim or defence falls outside the jurisdiction of the arbitral tribunal', when faced with a request to amend or supplement a claim or defence before it has considered whether it has jurisdiction over the claims and defences as initially stated, arbitral tribunals may allow the requested amendment or supplement without prejudice to the other party's right to object on jurisdictional grounds. **5.52**

G. Pleas as to the Jurisdiction of the Arbitral Tribunal—Article 23

1. The arbitral tribunal shall have the power to rule on its own jurisdiction, including any objections with respect to the existence or validity of the arbitration agreement. For that purpose, an arbitration clause that forms part of a contract, treaty, or other agreement shall be treated as an agreement independent of the other terms of the contract, treaty, or other agreement. A decision by the arbitral tribunal that the contract, treaty, or other agreement is null, void, or invalid shall not entail automatically the invalidity of the arbitration clause.
2. A plea that the arbitral tribunal does not have jurisdiction shall be raised no later than in the statement of defence or, with respect to a counterclaim or a claim for the purpose of a set-off, in the reply to the counterclaim or to the claim for the purpose of a set-off. A party is not precluded from raising such a plea by the fact that it has appointed, or participated in the appointment of, an arbitrator. A plea that the arbitral tribunal is exceeding the scope of its authority shall be raised as soon as the matter alleged to be beyond the scope of its authority is raised during the arbitral proceedings. The arbitral tribunal may, in either case, admit a later plea if it considers the delay justified.
3. The arbitral tribunal may rule on a plea referred to in paragraph 2 either as a preliminary question or in an award on the merits. The arbitral tribunal may continue the arbitral proceedings and make an award, notwithstanding any pending challenge to its jurisdiction before a competent authority.

Article 23 governs the procedure for objections to the arbitral tribunal's jurisdiction. **5.53**

5.54 This provision follows the text of Article 23 of the 2010 UNCITRAL Rules with three changes aimed at orienting the 2012 PCA Rules toward the arbitration of disputes involving states and intergovernmental organizations. Article 23 of the 2010 UNCITRAL Rules, in turn, mainly follows the language of Article 16 of the UNCITRAL Model Law.

5.55 Article 23(1) establishes the principle of competence-competence—that is, the arbitral tribunal's power to decide whether or not it has jurisdiction to decide the merits of the dispute at hand. It also provides for the separability of the arbitration agreement from the legal instrument (whether contract, treaty, or other) of which it may form part. Both principles serve the efficiency of the arbitral process and, in arbitrations involving private parties,[43] reduce the need for recourse to national courts.[44] One consequence of the separability of the arbitration agreement, as provided in Article 23(1), is that the validity of the arbitration agreement is not necessarily tied to the validity of the legal instrument in which it may be contained. Another consequence is that, particularly in the context of contracts, a different national law (or rules of law) may be applicable to the arbitration agreement than to the underlying legal instrument, which may protect the arbitration agreement from challenges to its validity on the basis of idiosyncratic or discriminatory national laws.[45]

5.56 The 2010 UNCITRAL Rules state the doctrine of separability with reference to contracts ('an arbitration clause that forms part of a *contract* shall be treated as an agreement independent of the other terms of the *contract*'),[46] but make no statement as to the status of arbitration agreements found in other legal instruments, such as treaties. The UNCITRAL Working Group considered adding the words 'or legal instrument' after 'contract' in the second and third sentences of Article 23(1), noting that such addition would 'avoid limiting the types of disputes that parties could submit to arbitration, and could in particular usefully address disputes arising under international investment treaties'.[47] Ultimately, the proposal was rejected, because the UNCITRAL Working Group did not wish to take any 'position as to whether the substantive rights conferred to investors by a treaty,

[43] In cases involving only states and intergovernmental organizations, the parties in any event will likely not have submitted to the jurisdiction of any national courts by virtue of their agreement to arbitrate (see discussion under Art 1(2)).

[44] However, the interaction between the competence of the arbitral tribunal to rule on its own jurisdiction and the competence of national courts to decide on the jurisdiction of arbitral tribunals and to review their jurisdictional decisions depends on the national law applicable to the arbitral proceeding.

[45] Gary B Born, *International Commercial Arbitration*, vol 1 (Wolters Kluwer, 2009) 354–7. While the absence of an agreement on the applicable law may require the arbitral tribunal to choose from a number of options in the context of contracts, the applicable law in treaty disputes would be the same for the arbitration clause and the rest of the treaty, unless otherwise agreed by the parties.

[46] Article 23(1) (emphasis added).

[47] Report of the UNCITRAL Working Group II (Arbitration and Conciliation) on the work of its 50th session, 9–13 February 2009, A/CN.9/669, para 36.

including the right to refer a dispute to arbitration, would be extinguished when the treaty terminated'. The UNCITRAL Working Group noted in this context that the UNCITRAL Rules were not intended to 'attempt regulating such matters of public international law'.[48]

The PCA Drafting Committee took a different approach. The 2012 PCA Rules **5.57** are primarily intended for the arbitration of disputes involving at least one state, state-controlled entity, or intergovernmental organization. While some of these disputes arise under contracts, many are based on dispute resolution clauses incorporated in other legal instruments. To maximize the efficiency of the proceedings in all cases, while avoiding to the extent possible recourse to national courts (which, in cases involving only states and intergovernmental organizations, are usually unavailable in any event),[49] the PCA Drafting Committee extended the scope of Article 23 to cover legal instruments other than contracts. The 2012 PCA Rules accordingly stipulate that an arbitration agreement found 'in a contract, treaty or other agreement' shall be treated as independent from said agreement. Article 23 is thus aligned with Article 1(1) of the 2012 PCA Rules, which emphasizes that arbitration agreements may be found in legal instruments other than contracts.

The broadening of Article 23 to encompass cases where the arbitration agreement **5.58** is found in a treaty required another modification of the language of this article. The 2010 UNCITRAL Rules replaced the reference to the contract being 'null and void' of the UNCITRAL Model Law by a reference to the contract being 'null'. The UNCITRAL Working Group stated that the defects that would be referred to in Article 23(1) should be 'construed as broadly as possible to cover all situations where a contract could be considered null, void, non-existent, invalid or non-effective'.[50] It then expressed the view that 'the term "null" was wide enough to cover all [these] contractual defects'.[51] Similarly, the PCA Drafting Committee considered that the third sentence of Article 23(1) of the 2012 PCA Rules should cover all possible defects of a 'contract, treaty or other agreement'. It viewed the term 'null' as sufficient to address the case of contracts, but preferred to deal with the case of treaties by using the language of the Vienna Convention on the Law of Treaties, which does not refer to treaties being 'null', but only 'invalid' or 'void'.[52] The 2012 PCA Rules therefore refer to the 'contract, treaty or other agreement' being 'null, void or invalid'.

---

[48] Report of the UNCITRAL Working Group II (Arbitration and Conciliation) on the work of its 50th session, 9–13 February 2009, A/CN.9/669, para 37.

[49] See discussion under Art 1.

[50] Report of the UNCITRAL Working Group II (Arbitration and Conciliation) on the work of its 50th session, 9–13 February 2009, A/CN.9/669, paras 40–2.

[51] Report of the UNCITRAL Working Group II (Arbitration and Conciliation) on the work of its 50th session, 9–13 February 2009, A/CN.9/669, para 42.

[52] Vienna Convention on the Law of Treaties, 23 May 1969, 1155 UNTS 331, Art 69(1).

5.59 Article 23(2) prescribes the deadlines for the submission of objections to the tribunal's jurisdiction. While the deadline for raising objections to jurisdiction is the time of filing of the statement of defence (or, with respect 'to a counterclaim or a claim for the purpose of a set-off, ... [the time of filing of] the reply to the counterclaim or to the claim for the purpose of a set-off'),[53] in practice the respondent often raises objections at an earlier date, for example in its response to the notice of arbitration. Under the 2012 PCA Rules and 2010 UNCITRAL Rules, the respondent can also notify its intention to make jurisdictional objections when expressing its views on the provisional timetable to be established under Article 17(2).

5.60 Although no waiver of jurisdictional objections can be implied by a failure to state them before the filing of the statement of defence, some respondents let it be known from the outset that they do not accept the arbitral tribunal's jurisdiction. Early notice is welcome to the tribunal as it informs its view of the complexity of the proceedings, and alerts it to a potential need to bifurcate the proceedings. When requested to designate or act as an appointing authority under UNCITRAL or PCA rules for the appointment of an arbitrator (that is, at a time before the tribunal is constituted), the Secretary-General of the PCA is occasionally informed by the respondent of its jurisdictional objections. The PCA, however, confines itself to a review of the dispute settlement provisions of the documents that are submitted as the basis for arbitral jurisdiction, in order to establish the prima facie existence of an arbitration agreement, which is without prejudice to the tribunal's determination of its jurisdiction, once constituted. In this context, respondents may benefit from being reminded that participation in the constitution of the arbitral tribunal does not entail recognition of its jurisdiction. This principle is expressly stated in the second sentence of Article 23(2) of the 2012 PCA Rules and 2010 UNCITRAL Rules.

5.61 Article 23(2) also provides that the arbitral tribunal may admit an objection to jurisdiction made after the submission of the statement of defence if the delay is justified. In the PCA's experience, applications for leave to make jurisdictional pleas at this late stage of the proceedings are rare.

5.62 Article 23(3) addresses the timing of the arbitral tribunal's determination of its jurisdiction. The tribunal may choose to hear and decide the question of jurisdiction as a preliminary matter or with the merits of the case. Unlike in the 1976 UNCITRAL Rules, which favoured the taking of decisions on bifurcation as a preliminary matter, there is no presumption as to which is the preferred approach in the 2012 PCA Rules and the 2010 UNCITRAL Rules. On the one hand, deciding on jurisdiction at a preliminary stage will eliminate the need for and expense

[53] The exception to the rule is found where the arbitral tribunal grants a time extension for the filing of the statement of defence, but asks for any objections to jurisdiction to be made within the original deadline.

of dealing with a case on the merits if the tribunal finds that it lacks jurisdiction over the dispute. On the other hand, it may be inefficient to separate jurisdiction from merits, particularly when the claims raise common questions of fact and law.

Since their adoption, the 2010 UNCITRAL Rules appear to have influenced proceedings conducted under the 1976 UNCITRAL Rules. Until recently, in most PCA-administered cases, the parties agreed on whether or not to bifurcate the proceedings. In the few cases where the tribunal was asked to rule on bifurcation, the application was most often granted without reasons. When the tribunal decided against bifurcation, it would provide brief reasons. For example, in one case, the arbitral tribunal denied the respondent's request to bifurcate the proceedings between a jurisdiction and a merits phase because it would have to investigate the full set of facts to decide on the issue of jurisdiction, which meant that bifurcation would not 'appear... to be the most efficient and time-saving way to structure the proceedings'. **5.63**

Since 2010, new trends have emerged. Recently, tribunals have more frequently denied bifurcation requests, provided more detailed reasons, and deferred the decision whether to bifurcate until receipt of substantive submissions by the parties. **5.64**

Out of 13 bifurcation requests received in PCA-administered cases under the 1976 UNCITRAL Rules since 2010,[54] seven tribunals have bifurcated the proceedings, in three cases with reasons. **5.65**

In one case, the respondent requested bifurcation of the proceedings in relation to its jurisdictional objections that: (i) the claimants did not have a protected investment under the applicable treaty; and (ii) the tribunal did not have jurisdiction to resolve some of the claimants' claims by virtue of the most-favoured nation clause. The tribunal decided to bifurcate the proceedings with respect to the respondent's second objection, stating that it would 'serve the interests of economy and efficiency'. **5.66**

In another case, the tribunal chose to bifurcate the proceedings after a detailed review of the issues. The tribunal stated that it should have regard not only to 'efficiency; to the practicality of separating jurisdiction from the merits; and to likely savings in costs and time' but also to 'the less quantifiable, but real, "costs" of requiring a party who disputes the tribunal's jurisdiction to litigate a case on the merits before having its jurisdictional objections resolved by any decision-maker'. The tribunal concluded that, while the case for bifurcation was not compelling on grounds of efficiency alone, the proceedings should be bifurcated because: **5.67**

> the extent to which determination of the Claimant's tax liability is a matter which is within the jurisdiction of this Tribunal [was] of central importance to the claim as a whole;...
>
> the early determination of the jurisdictional questions [would] greatly assist both the Parties and the Tribunal itself by clarifying the scope of the present arbitration

[54] As of May 2013.

> and the relationship between it and the ongoing judicial proceedings in [the respondent State];...
>
> and the core questions regarding jurisdictional objection were 'not so inextricably interwoven with the merits as to be incapable of preliminary determination'.

5.68 In the third decision with reasons, the tribunal decided to hear an objection to jurisdiction concerning the interpretation of the dispute resolution clause of the relevant bilateral investment treaty in a preliminary phase while joining all other jurisdictional objections to the merits. The tribunal stated that the first objection was 'a purely jurisdictional one, entirely separate from the merits'. In relation to efficiency, the tribunal noted that determining this early objection could 'dispose of [the] entire dispute'. The other jurisdictional objections were found to be 'intertwined with the merits of the case'.

5.69 The tribunal explained its reasons in a larger proportion of cases—five out of six—where the request for bifurcation was denied.

5.70 In one case, the tribunal decided not to bifurcate in light of the efficient conduct of the proceedings. In particular, the tribunal considered: 'whether any prejudice may be suffered by either Party as a result of bifurcating or not bifurcating the proceedings; the quality and extent of written pleading submitted to date by both Parties on jurisdiction and the merits; and the provisional timetables established in [the tribunal's procedural orders], including the proximity of the hearing dates scheduled in respect of jurisdiction, in the case of a bifurcated proceeding, and the merits, in the case of a non-bifurcated proceeding'. The tribunal concluded that 'the most efficient course in these proceedings' was not to bifurcate the proceedings, and that the respondent would not 'suffer prejudice as a result of the decision'.

5.71 Another tribunal explicitly followed the 'three fold test' adopted by the tribunal in *Glamis Gold v United States.*[55] After confirming that the case met the first and second

[55] *Glamis Gold Ltd v United States of America* (NAFTA) (1976 UNCITRAL Rules), Procedural Order No 2, 31 May 2005. In this case, the tribunal stated that Art 21(4) of the 1976 UNCITRAL Rules contained a 'three fold test': (1) 'in considering a request for the preliminary consideration of an objection to jurisdiction, the tribunal should take the claim as it is alleged by Claimant'; (2) 'the "plea" must be one that goes to the "jurisdiction" of the tribunal over the claim'; (3) 'if an objection is raised to the jurisdiction of the tribunal and a request is made by either party that the objection be considered as a preliminary matter, the tribunal should do so. The tribunal *may decline to do so when doing so is unlikely to bring about increased efficiency* in the proceedings' (emphasis added). The tribunal further raised the following factors that a tribunal should consider in deciding whether bifurcation would 'increase efficiency' in the proceedings: '(1) whether the objection is substantial inasmuch as the preliminary consideration of a frivolous objection to jurisdiction is very unlikely to reduce the costs of, or time required for, the proceeding; (2) whether the objection to jurisdiction if granted results in a material reduction of the proceedings at the next phase (in other words, the tribunal should consider whether the costs and time required of a preliminary proceedings, even if the objecting party is successful, will be justified in terms of the reduction in costs at the subsequent phase of proceedings); and (3) whether bifurcation is impractical in that the jurisdictional issue identified is so intertwined with the merits that it is very unlikely that there will be any savings in time or cost': para 12.

prongs of the test, the tribunal considered whether bifurcation was 'unlikely to bring about increased efficiency in the proceedings'. The tribunal stated that while none of the objections raised by the respondent were frivolous in nature, two of the respondent's objections would require 'an extensive examination of facts and witnesses relating directly to matters concerning the merits of [the] Claimant's claim'. The tribunal also noted that if the proceedings were bifurcated, a new schedule would have to be established for the consideration of merits and damages, once a jurisdictional award would be rendered—a matter which would require some months in itself.

The other three tribunals, in rejecting requests for bifurcation, also referred to the high risk of procedural inefficiency and the strong link between facts in dispute related to jurisdiction and merits. **5.72**

The importance attributed to decisions on bifurcation is also reflected in the procedural choices of parties and tribunals for the hearing of bifurcation requests. In the cases described above, the tribunal generally decided on bifurcation only after the parties had each filed at least one substantive submission.[56] In many cases, separate submissions on the issue of bifurcation were also made. Some tribunals held a hearing[57] or a teleconference to hear the parties on this issue. **5.73**

Notably, in *Philip Morris v Australia*—a PCA-administered investment treaty arbitration conducted under the 2010 UNCITRAL Rules—the parties disputed *how* the tribunal should decide on bifurcation.[58] Pursuant to an order of the arbitral tribunal, the parties made submissions on the issue of bifurcation,[59] particularly to 'assist the Tribunal in determining the *timing and procedure* for reaching a decision on the bifurcation'.[60] The respondent argued that its objections to jurisdiction should be determined in a preliminary phase of the proceedings, and that the tribunal should move to an immediate determination of the merits of bifurcation.[61] The **5.74**

[56] See also *Guaracachi America Inc and Rurelec PLC v Plurinational State of Bolivia*, PCA Case No 2011-17 (China–Mongolia BIT) (2010 UNCITRAL Rules), Procedural Order No 6, 30 August 2012, where the arbitral tribunal deferred the decision whether to hold a separate hearing on jurisdiction until after the parties would have filed the statement of claim and statement of defence on the merits, as well as two written statements each on jurisdiction.

[57] See eg *Philip Morris Asia Limited v The Commonwealth of Australia*, PCA Case No 2012-12 (Hong Kong–Australia BIT) (2010 UNCITRAL Rules), Procedural Order No 7, 31 December 2012, para 3.5.

[58] *Philip Morris Asia Limited v The Commonwealth of Australia*, PCA Case No 2012-12 (Hong Kong–Australia BIT) (2010 UNCITRAL Rules), Procedural Order No 4, 26 October 2012.

[59] *Philip Morris Asia Limited v The Commonwealth of Australia*, PCA Case No 2012-12 (Hong Kong–Australia BIT) (2010 UNCITRAL Rules), Procedural Order No 2, 3 August 2012, Item 2.

[60] *Philip Morris Asia Limited v The Commonwealth of Australia*, PCA Case No 2012-12 (Hong Kong–Australia BIT) (2010 UNCITRAL Rules) Procedural Order No 4, 26 October 2012, para 20 (emphasis in original).

[61] *Philip Morris Asia Limited v The Commonwealth of Australia*, PCA Case No 2012-12 (Hong Kong–Australia BIT) (2010 UNCITRAL Rules), Procedural Order No 7, 31 December 2012, para 25.

claimant replied that the respondent's jurisdictional objections were 'inchoate', and that 'the procedural efficiency of bifurcation can only be assessed after the submission of full memorials by both Parties'.[62] The tribunal decided to defer its decision until the filing of the respondent's statement of defence, stating that it would not be in a position to decide until 'both sides [had] had an opportunity to make first presentations of their factual and resulting legal arguments on the entire case'. The tribunal also noted that the respondent had specified that it did not waive its right to raise objections to jurisdiction at the latest in its statement of defence and that the tribunal therefore would not be aware of all jurisdictional objections until that time.[63]

5.75 While the above examples under the 1976 and 2010 UNCITRAL Rules arose in arbitrations that involved both states and private parties, requests for bifurcation are not unknown in inter-state arbitration.[64]

5.76 If the proceedings are bifurcated, the jurisdictional phase of the proceedings will often involve two rounds of written submissions by the parties, and, less often, witness statements, document production requests, and post-hearing briefs. It will also generally include a hearing before the tribunal rules on its jurisdiction.[65] A finding that the tribunal lacks jurisdiction will be set forth in a final award,[66] while a finding that the tribunal does have jurisdiction may be contained in what is sometimes called an interim or partial award on jurisdiction. At some arbitral seats, it will not be possible to set aside a decision on jurisdiction until an award on the merits is rendered.[67]

5.77 Article 23(3) also provides that the arbitral proceeding may continue notwithstanding any pending challenge to the tribunal's jurisdiction before a body other than the arbitral tribunal itself. The arbitral tribunal's power to decide on its own competence expressed in Article 23(1) is not necessarily exclusive. While the immunities of states in inter-state cases would normally deprive national courts of

[62] *Philip Morris Asia Limited v The Commonwealth of Australia*, PCA Case No 2012-12 (Hong Kong–Australia BIT) (2010 UNCITRAL Rules), Procedural Order No 7, 31 December 2012, paras 49, 53.

[63] *Philip Morris Asia Limited v The Commonwealth of Australia*, PCA Case No 2012-12 (Hong Kong–Australia BIT) (2010 UNCITRAL Rules), Procedural Order No 7, 31 December 2012, paras 66–8.

[64] See eg *Mauritius v United Kingdom*, PCA Case No 2011-3 (UNCLOS), Procedural Order No 2, 15 January 2013.

[65] See eg *Achmea BV (formerly known as 'Eureko BV') v The Slovak Republic*, PCA Case No 2008-14 (Netherlands–Czech and Slovak Republic BIT) (1976 UNICTRAL Rules), Award on Jurisdiction, Arbitrability and Suspension, 26 October 2010, paras 20–30; *Vito G Gallo v The Government of Canada*, 2008-3 (NAFTA) (1976 UNCITRAL Rules), Award, 15 September 2011, paras 83–110. While there is some ambiguity in Art 17(3) of the Rules as to whether an arbitral tribunal could refuse to hold a hearing on jurisdiction if only one party requests it, in practice arbitral tribunals usually grant such requests without contemplating whether or not they are obliged to do so by the applicable procedural rules.

[66] See eg *Vito G Gallo v The Government of Canada*, 2008-3 (NAFTA) (1976 UNCITRAL Rules), Award, 15 September 2011.

[67] See eg Netherlands Arbitration Act 1986, Arts 1052(4), 1064.

any jurisdiction to decide the tribunal's jurisdiction, the situation is different in the context of contract claims involving private parties and investment treaty claims made outside of the ICSID Convention. In these cases, the tribunal's jurisdiction may, under some laws of arbitral procedure, be challenged at the same time before national courts.[68] An arbitral tribunal's decision on jurisdiction may also be reviewed by national courts. Under Article 23(3), neither of these situations forces the tribunal to suspend the arbitral proceedings. Where the 2010 UNCITRAL Rules refer to any pending challenge before 'a court', the 2012 PCA Rules refer to any pending challenge before 'a competent authority'. In inter-state cases in particular, an arbitral tribunal's jurisdiction would not be subject to challenge before any court without the consent of the parties.[69]

As to the nature of possible objections to jurisdiction, it must be recalled that, as stipulated in Article 1(4) of the 2012 PCA Rules, the nature of the parties to the dispute and whether or not they fall within the scope of Article 1(1) is not relevant to the arbitral tribunal's jurisdiction. **5.78**

H. Further Written Statements—Article 24

> The arbitral tribunal shall decide which further written statements, in addition to the statement of claim and the statement of defence, shall be required from the parties or may be presented by them and shall fix the periods of time for communicating such statements.

Article 24 provides for the arbitral tribunal's discretion to require or allow the parties to file written statements in addition to the statement of claim and statement of defence provided for in Articles 20 and 21. **5.79**

This provision replicates Article 24 of the 2010 UNCITRAL Rules, which, in turn, reproduces the terms of Article 22 of the 1976 UNCITRAL Rules. **5.80**

[68] See eg UNCITRAL Model Law, Art 8: '(1) A court before which an action is brought in a matter which is the subject of an arbitration agreement shall, if a party so requests not later than when submitting his first statement on the substance of the dispute, refer the parties to arbitration unless it finds that the agreement is null and void, inoperative or incapable of being performed. (2) Where an action referred to in paragraph (1) of this article has been brought, arbitral proceedings may nevertheless be commenced or continued, and an award may be made, while the issue is pending before the court'.

[69] For cases where the parties agreed to the ICJ's jurisdiction to review an arbitral tribunal's competence see *Arbitral Award made by the King of Spain on 23 December 1906*, Honduras v Nicaragua, Judgment, 18 November 1960, ICJ Reports, 192, where Honduras challenged an arbitral award made by the King of Spain concerning the determination of the border between Honduras and Nicaragua before the ICJ, on the ground that the king had not been validly appointed as arbitrator under the Gámez-Bonilla Treaty; *Arbitral Award of 31 July 1989*, Guinea-Bissau v Senegal, Judgment, 12 November 1991, ICJ Reports 1991, 53, where Guinea-Bissau challenged the validity of an arbitral award before the ICJ on the basis, among others, that the arbitral tribunal had exceeded its powers by failing to comply with the provisions of the arbitration agreement.

5.81 Written pleadings are an important element of procedure in proceedings conducted under both PCA and UNCITRAL rules. Since it is generally expected that the issues in dispute will be well defined in writing before any hearing is held, written pleadings on substantive issues beyond the statements of claim and defence are filed in almost every case.

5.82 In most PCA-administered proceedings, the arbitral tribunal allows the parties to address substantive issues in two rounds of written pleadings. In other words, after the claimant files a statement of claim, and the respondent files a statement of defence, the claimant files a reply, followed by a rejoinder from the respondent.[70] The parties are often prohibited from submitting new evidence in the reply and rejoinder and are limited to responding to the case made in the preceding submissions.[71] Most tribunals will specify in an early procedural order that written pleadings must be accompanied by all supporting documentation in the form of consecutively numbered exhibits, witness statements, and expert reports (although the latter two could also be assigned their own deadlines).[72]

5.83 If the respondent has filed a counterclaim with its statement of defence, the tribunal may allow the claimant to file an additional written pleading—a rejoinder to the counterclaim.[73] In some cases, the exchange of two rounds of written statements is deemed insufficient, in particular if the parties have filed statements of claim and defence that are not fully detailed or are not accompanied by all the supporting materials. The filing of a further round of written pleadings may then be permitted.[74]

[70] See eg *Guaracachi America Inc and Rurelec PLC v Plurinational State of Bolivia*, PCA Case No 2011-17 (China–Mongolia BIT) (2010 UNCITRAL Rules), Terms of Appointment and Procedural Order No 1, paras 12.1–12.4.

[71] See eg *Guaracachi America Inc and Rurelec PLC v Plurinational State of Bolivia*, PCA Case No 2011-17 (China–Mongolia BIT) (2010 UNCITRAL Rules), Terms of Appointment and Procedural Order No 1, para 12.5 ('The Reply and Rejoinder may only contain evidence that is responsive to the other party's last submission or evidence of new facts'); *Bilcon of Delaware v Canada*, PCA Case No 2009-4 (NAFTA) (1976 UNCITRAL Rules), Procedural Order No 1, 9 April 2009, para 38 ('The Reply and Rejoinder may only contain evidence that is responsive to the other Disputing Party's last preceding submission').

[72] See eg *Guaracachi America Inc and Rurelec PLC v Plurinational State of Bolivia*, PCA Case No 2011-17 (China–Mongolia BIT) (2010 UNCITRAL Rules), Terms of Appointment and Procedural Order No 1, para 12.5 ('Each Party shall include in the... written submissions all allegations of fact and law in support of its claims and annex to such submissions all signed witness statements, signed expert reports, factual exhibits and legal authorities upon which it relied'); *Bilcon of Delaware v Canada*, PCA Case No 2009-4 (NAFTA) (1976 UNCITRAL Rules), Procedural Order No 2, 3 June 2009, paras 2.2–2.3 ('2.2. Evidence in written submissions. Written submissions shall be accompanied by the documentary evidence and the testimonial evidence relied upon by the submitting Disputing Party. 2.3 Legal authorities. A Disputing Party shall submit with its written submissions copies of the legal authorities that it relies upon').

[73] The sequence of submissions is then as follows: (i) statement of claim (claimant); (ii) statement of defence and counterclaim (respondent); (iii) reply and defence to counterclaim (claimant); (iv) rejoinder and reply to defence to counterclaim (respondent); and (v) rejoinder to counterclaim (claimant).

[74] See eg *Bilcon of Delaware v Canada*, PCA Case No 2009-4 (NAFTA) (1976 UNCITRAL Rules), Procedural Order No 1, 9 April 2009, paras 36–7.

A tribunal may also order parties to file post-hearing briefs to address costs or other limited issues that it considers not to have been sufficiently addressed in the written and oral submissions already made.[75]

The tribunal may also order written statements to be filed simultaneously, rather than consecutively. In the PCA's experience, for the first round of written pleadings, this approach is most common in inter-state cases, where the dispute has been submitted to arbitration and the proceeding commenced jointly by the two states.[76] In such circumstances, the terms 'claimant' and 'respondent' may not be appropriate and there may be no basis for requiring one state to submit its written pleading before the other.[77] **5.84**

The simultaneous filing of written pleadings can result in a situation where the parties do not directly address each other's arguments. For this reason, one round of simultaneous submissions is rarely sufficient in the initial written phase of an arbitration. However, where both parties have access to all the relevant information, for instance on costs or witness examination after a hearing, a single round of simultaneous submissions often suffices (although in the most complex cases, two rounds of post-hearing briefs may be allowed). **5.85**

If the arbitration is bifurcated, either between jurisdiction and merits as contemplated in Article 23(3) of the Rules, or between liability and quantum of damages (or otherwise), each stage of the proceeding may involve the entire procedure described above. **5.86**

While the choice of procedure for the filing of written pleadings will depend on the circumstances of each case, the tribunal will always be guided by the principles of fairness and efficiency set out in Article 17(1) of the Rules, taking particular care to ensure that each party is given a reasonable opportunity to present its case. **5.87**

The tribunal's initial decision as to the number and timing of substantive written pleadings may be fully set out in a procedural order issued shortly after the commencement of the arbitration (under the 2012 PCA and 2010 UNCITRAL Rules, in the provisional timetable referred to in Article 17(2)).[78] This timetable may be modified at a later stage as changing circumstances require.[79] In practice, when **5.88**

[75] See eg *Guaracachi America Inc and Rurelec PLC v Plurinational State of Bolivia*, PCA Case No 2011-17 (China–Mongolia BIT) (2010 UNCITRAL Rules), Procedural Order No 19, 12 April 2013, para 1.

[76] See eg *Croatia/Slovenia*, PCA Case No 2012-4, PCA press release, 13 April 2012, <http://www.pca-cpa.org/showpage.asp?pag_id=1443>; *Abyei Arbitration*, the Government of Sudan/the Sudan People's Liberation Movement/Army, PCA Case No 2008-7 (PCA State/Non-State Rules), Arbitration Agreement, Art 8(3).

[77] In one recent PCA case, the parties initially disagreed even as to the order in which their names would appear in the name of the case, finally settling on alphabetical order.

[78] See eg *Guaracachi America Inc and Rurelec PLC v Plurinational State of Bolivia*, PCA Case No 2011-17 (China–Mongolia BIT) (2010 UNCITRAL Rules), Terms of Appointment and Procedural Order No 1, paras 12.1–12.4.

[79] See eg *Guaracachi America Inc and Rurelec PLC v Plurinational State of Bolivia*, PCA Case No 2011-17 (China–Mongolia BIT) (2010 UNCITRAL Rules), Terms of Appointment and

discrete extensions are requested for the filing of written statements, the possibility of maintaining previously fixed hearing dates may play a determinative role in the tribunal's decision to grant an extension.[80] The tribunal may also set deadlines at the outset for only part of the written procedure, leaving the decision on further steps to a later stage.[81] The tribunal may consider that it will be in a better position to decide what more is needed having received the first round of substantive written statements.

5.89 In addition to substantive written statements, written statements on any number of contentious procedural issues (choice of place of arbitration, scheduling, document production, inclusion or exclusion of witnesses, requests for extensions) may also be required. These matters may require only one brief written statement from each side, or even a simple exchange of email.

I. Periods of Time—Article 25

> The periods of time fixed by the arbitral tribunal for the communication of written statements (including the statement of claim and statement of defence) should not exceed 45 days. However, the arbitral tribunal may extend the time limits if it concludes that an extension is justified.

5.90 Article 25 sets a maximum 45-day time limit to be imposed on parties for the filing of the written statements referred to in Articles 20, 21, and 24 of the Rules, and provides for the arbitral tribunal's power to extend any such deadline.

5.91 This provision is identical to Article 25 of the 2010 UNCITRAL Rules and Article 23 of the 1976 UNCITRAL Rules. In contrast, the PCA State/State Rules, State/International Organization Rules, and International Organization/Private Party Rules provide for a 90-day deadline for the filing of written statements.[82]

5.92 The choice between the 45- and 90-day time limits was the subject of discussion within the PCA Drafting Committee, as well as between the PCA Drafting Committee and certain PCA Member States. Ultimately, it was decided not to deviate from the UNCITRAL Rules. With regard to UNCITRAL proceedings generally, commentators report that the 45-day time limit of the UNCITRAL

Procedural Order No 1, 2 July 2012; Procedural Order No 3, 9 August 2012; Procedural Order No 7, 3 September 2012; Procedural Order No 8, 9 October 2012.

[80] See eg *Guaracachi America Inc and Rurelec PLC v Plurinational State of Bolivia*, PCA Case No 2011-17 (China–Mongolia BIT) (2010 UNCITRAL Rules), Terms of Appointment and Procedural Order No 1, 3 September 2012.

[81] See *Bilcon of Delaware v Canada*, PCA Case No 2009-4 (NAFTA) (1976 UNCITRAL Rules), Procedural Order No 1, 9 April 2009, paras 36–7.

[82] PCA State/State Rules, Art 23; PCA State/International Organization Rules, Art 23; PCA International Organization/Private Party Rules, Art 23.

Rules is frequently extended.[83] The PCA Drafting Committee decided, however, to adopt the 45-day time limit of the UNCITRAL Rules as the default time limit as a reminder to parties and arbitrators that they should strive under the PCA Rules, as under the UNCITRAL Rules, to achieve efficiency in the arbitral procedure.

Overall, the time limits for filing substantive written statements in PCA-administered cases vary greatly, depending on the parties' needs. The *Croatia/Slovenia* arbitration provides an example of longer time limits: the parties were given over nine months to simultaneously file their respective memorials, and another nine months to simultaneously file their respective counter-memorials.[84] In contrast, in the *Abyei* arbitration between the Government of Sudan and the Sudan People's Liberation Army/Movement, the parties' arbitration agreement provided for a nine-month time period from the commencement of the arbitration to the issuance of the final award.[85] The stringency of this provision is all the more striking given that the nature of the claims and quantity of evidence were of the sort usually encountered in proceedings lasting several years.[86] The chronology of the filing of written statements was as follows: (i) memorials were filed simultaneously 52 days after the commencement of the arbitration, that is to say 24 days after the first procedural hearing between the parties and the tribunal regarding, inter alia, the timetable for the filing of written statements; (ii) counter-memorials were filed simultaneously 56 days after the filing of the memorials; and (iii) rejoinders were filed simultaneously 15 days thereafter.[87] The parties' choice of an accelerated procedure appears to have been motivated by the role of the arbitration in the larger peace process ongoing between the parties and a desire to avoid any reason for delay of the planned referendum on the independence of South Sudan.[88] Expedited **5.93**

[83] See eg Thomas H Webster, *Handbook of UNCITRAL Arbitration* (Sweet & Maxwell, 2010) para 25-4.

[84] *Croatia/Slovenia*, PCA Case No 2012-4, PCA press releases, 13 April 2013 and 28 February 2013, <http://www.pca-cpa.org/showpage.asp?pag_id=1443>.

[85] *Abyei Arbitration*, the Government of Sudan/the Sudan People's Liberation Movement/Army, PCA Case No 2008-7 (PCA State/Non-State Rules), Arbitration Agreement, Art 4(3): 'The Tribunal shall endeavor to complete the arbitral proceedings including the issuance of the final award within a period of six months from the date of the commencement of the arbitral proceedings subject to three months extension'.

[86] See Brooks W Daly, 'The Abyei Arbitration: Procedural Aspects of an Intra-Border Dispute' (2010) 23 *Leiden Journal of International Law* 801, 818.

[87] See *Abyei Arbitration*, the Government of Sudan/the Sudan People's Liberation Movement/Army, PCA Case No 2008-7 (PCA State/Non-State Rules), Arbitration Agreement, Art 8(3) and the dates of the parties' pleadings, <http://www.pca-cpa.org/showpage.asp?pag_id=1306>.

[88] In *Abyei*, the arbitral tribunal was asked to review the decision of a boundaries commission that had delimited the boundaries of the Abyei area pursuant to the Comprehensive Peace Agreement signed by the parties in 2005 and, if it found the commission to have exceeded the scope of its mandate, to redefine those boundaries (*Abyei Arbitration*, the Government of Sudan/The Sudan People's Liberation Movement/Army, PCA Case No 2008-7 (PCA State/Non-State Rules), Final Award, 22 July 2009, para 6). After the demarcation of the Abyei area, a referendum was to be held entitling the people of South Sudan to vote on whether to secede from Sudan and form an independent country, together with a referendum allowing the population of the Abyei area to choose whether to become part of South or North Sudan (Comprehensive Peace Agreement

proceedings have also been agreed by parties in some investment treaty arbitrations conducted under PCA auspices.

5.94 Arbitral tribunals may require written comments on procedural matters to be submitted within far shorter periods than substantive pleadings, in urgent cases within a period of days or even hours. This may occur, for example, when a tribunal wishes to explore whether a last minute modification to the schedule of an impending meeting or hearing can be agreed with the parties in view of some unforeseen event.

J. Interim Measures—Article 26

1. The arbitral tribunal may, at the request of a party, grant interim measures.
2. An interim measure is any temporary measure by which, at any time prior to the issuance of the award by which the dispute is finally decided, the arbitral tribunal orders a party, for example and without limitation, to:
   (a) Maintain or restore the status quo pending determination of the dispute;
   (b) Take action that would prevent, or refrain from taking action that is likely to cause, (i) current or imminent harm or (ii) prejudice to the arbitral process itself;
   (c) Provide a means of preserving assets out of which a subsequent award may be satisfied; or
   (d) Preserve evidence that may be relevant and material to the resolution of the dispute.
3. The party requesting an interim measure under paragraphs 2(a) to (c) shall satisfy the arbitral tribunal that:
   (a) Harm not adequately reparable by an award of damages is likely to result if the measure is not ordered, and such harm substantially outweighs the harm that is likely to result to the party against whom the measure is directed if the measure is granted; and
   (b) There is a reasonable possibility that the requesting party will succeed on the merits of the claim. The determination on this possibility shall not affect the discretion of the arbitral tribunal in making any subsequent determination.
4. With regard to a request for an interim measure under paragraph 2(d), the requirements in paragraphs 3(a) and (b) shall apply only to the extent the arbitral tribunal considers appropriate.
5. The arbitral tribunal may modify, suspend or terminate an interim measure it has granted, upon application of any party or, in exceptional circumstances and upon prior notice to the parties, on the arbitral tribunal's own initiative.
6. The arbitral tribunal may require the party requesting an interim measure to provide appropriate security in connection with the measure.

---

between the Government of Sudan and The Sudan People's Liberation Movement/Army, 9 January 2005, c II, Art 2.5, c IV, Art 8.1). The first of the two referendums was held in January 2011, leading to the independence of South Sudan in July 2011.

7. The arbitral tribunal may require any party promptly to disclose any material change in the circumstances on the basis of which the interim measure was requested or granted.
8. The party requesting an interim measure may be liable for any costs and damages caused by the measure to any party if the arbitral tribunal later determines that, in the circumstances then prevailing, the measure should not have been granted. The arbitral tribunal may award such costs and damages at any point during the proceedings.
9. A request for interim measures addressed by any party to a judicial authority shall not be deemed incompatible with the agreement to arbitrate, or as a waiver of that agreement.

Article 26 sets out the modalities of the arbitral tribunal's power to grant interim measures. **5.95**

This provision replicates Article 26 of the 2010 UNCITRAL Rules, which was in large part drawn from Article 17 of the UNCITRAL Model Law, as revised in 2006. The 2012 PCA Rules, 2010 UNCITRAL Rules, and UNCITRAL Model Law now provide significantly more detailed regulation of interim measures than did the 1976 UNCITRAL Rules. It has been suggested that national courts might be more likely to enforce interim measures if these are granted by the arbitral tribunal within a defined and explicit framework.[89] The Drafting Committee adopted this provision considering that it reflects common practice in PCA-administered cases. **5.96**

Article 26(1) states the arbitral tribunal's power to grant interim measures—a rule already found in the equivalent provision of the 1976 UNCITRAL Rules. **5.97**

Article 26(2) provides the definition of an interim measure: 'any temporary measure' issued 'at any time prior to the issuance of the award by which the dispute is finally decided' by which a party is ordered to take or not to take one of several listed actions. In an improvement on the text both of the 1976 UNCITRAL Rules and the UNCITRAL Model Law, the list of possible interim measures is introduced by the words 'for example, without limitation to', making it clear that the list is not exhaustive. Under the formulation of Article 26(1) of the 1976 UNCITRAL Rules, it was possible to doubt whether or not the shorter list provided therein was closed. An arbitral tribunal considered this question in a 2008 PCA-administered investment treaty arbitration, in the context of which the respondent requested the tribunal to grant it security for the costs of the arbitration on the basis of its power to grant interim measures. The tribunal found that Article 26(1) of the 1976 UNCITRAL Rules was sufficiently broad to encompass security for costs, but **5.98**

[89] J Castello, 'Generalizing About The Virtues Of Specificity: The Surprising Evolution Of The Longest Article In The UNCITRAL Model Law' (2012) 6:1 *World Arbitration and Mediation Review* 7, 14–17.

ultimately rejected the application, noting that the respondent had failed to demonstrate a significant risk that the claimant would become insolvent.

5.99 The possibility of granting security for costs is now covered by Article 26(2)(c), which contemplates interim measures granted to 'provide a means of preserving assets out of which a subsequent award may be satisfied', as the award in question may also include an order for costs. Under the 2010 UNCITRAL Rules, the *Guaracachi v Bolivia* arbitral tribunal dismissed an application for security for costs in the following terms:

1. Although investment treaty tribunals clearly hold the power to grant provisional measures, an order for the posting of security for costs remains a very rare and exceptional measure. Nevertheless, the lack of precedent—and the cautious approach to such requests suggested by the case law—does not limit the power of this Tribunal to grant such a measure. Article 26 of the UNCITRAL Rules expressly envisages this possibility, as even the Claimants appear to accept. It is thus clear that this arbitral tribunal has the authority to grant the requested *cautio judicatum solvi* (security for costs), provided that the Respondent, as the requesting party, is able to meet its burden of proof and satisfy the conditions of the aforementioned Article 26(3) of the Rules.
2. The Respondent has not, however, been able to supply evidence to justify the extraordinary measure that it requests. As a factual matter, the Respondent has not shown a sufficient causal link such that the Tribunal can infer from the mere existence of third party funding that the Claimants will not be able to pay an eventual award of costs rendered against them, regardless of whether the funder is liable for costs or not. The Respondent's analysis of Rurelec's balance sheet and other related financial documents also does not sufficiently demonstrate that Rurelec will lack the means to pay a costs award or to obtain (additional) funding for that purpose. To the contrary, Rurelec appears to be an ongoing concern with assets beyond those involved in this arbitration and the Claimants have promptly paid all the requested deposits of costs with no suggestion that they have had trouble finding the necessary funds to do so.
3. Given the above, it is unnecessary to look at the issue of the Respondent's good faith—as measured by its payment of its share of the deposits of costs—as a pre-condition for the right to request security for costs (as suggested by one of the Respondent's authorities). Nor is it necessary for the Tribunal to analyze—in accordance with Article 26(3)(b) of the UNCITRAL Rules—whether there is a 'reasonable possibility that the requesting party will succeed on the merits of the claim'. This can be a difficult hypothetical exercise, even with the benefit of the Parties' full written submissions. It is also unwise to risk even the most minor prejudgment of the case so close to the date of the final hearings. Such determinations are therefore best avoided unless absolutely necessary to come to a decision on the request for interim measures, which is not the case here.
4. The same goes for the analysis required by Article 26(3)(a) of the UNCITRAL Rules of the balance of inconvenience, to find whether the harm, if the measure is not granted, 'substantially outweighs the harm that is likely to result to the party against whom the measure is directed if the measure is granted'. The issue—analyzed by scholars and some tribunals—of the appropriate balance between the right of access to justice of entities that have been allegedly

> expropriated and the protection of States against alleged frivolous claims by parties who may not have sufficient assets to guarantee the payment of an adverse costs award is a serious issue. A decision on this issue is not, however, required on the facts of this case.[90]

The PCA has also administered cases under the 1976 UNCITRAL Rules where the tribunal ordered a party to 'maintain . . . the status quo pending determination of the dispute' and to 'take action that would prevent . . . (ii) prejudice to the arbitral process itself' (as it is expressly entitled to do under Article 26(2)(a) and (b) of the 2012 PCA Rules).[91] One facet of preventing 'prejudice to the arbitral process itself' was displayed in a PCA-administered investment treaty arbitration conducted under the 1976 UNCITRAL Rules, in which the arbitral tribunal, at an early stage of the proceedings, ordered the respondent state to locate and return the claimant's 'personal, financial and office and business related Documents' which had been seized by the respondent's 'servants and agents including the Public Prosecutor's Office and its Police' before the commencement of the arbitration. The claimant had argued that it would be prejudiced by waiting until the scheduled time for document production, as this would only take place at the merits stage of the proceedings, while the documents were needed for the claimant to prepare its case on jurisdiction. **5.100**

Unlike the equivalent provision of the UNCITRAL Model Law, which provides that an interim measure may be 'in the form of an award or in another form', the 2010 UNCITRAL Rules and 2012 PCA Rules make no reference to the form in which interim measures may be issued. The UNCITRAL Working Group considered such mention to be unnecessary given that the UNCITRAL Model Law now contains 'provisions permitting the enforcement of interim awards regardless of the form in which they are issued'.[92] Nevertheless, as the arbitration laws of many national jurisdictions do not follow the amended UNCITRAL Model Law approach, arbitral tribunals in arbitrations where such laws are applicable[93] must **5.101**

[90] *Guaracachi America Inc and Rurelec PLC v Plurinational State of Bolivia*, PCA Case No 2011-17 (China–Mongolia BIT) (2010 UNCITRAL Rules), Procedural Order No 14, 11 March 2013 (footnotes removed).

[91] See eg *1 Chevron Corporation and 2 Texaco Petroleum Company v The Republic of Ecuador*, PCA Case No 2009-23 (US–Ecuador BIT), Order for Interim Measures, 9 February 2011, at 3(E); First Interim Award on Interim Measures, 25 January 2012, at 16(2); Second Interim Award on Interim Measures, 16 February 2012, at 2(3). The operative parts of the decisions are reproduced in David D Caron and Lee M Caplan, *The UNCITRAL Arbitration Rules: A Commentary* (2nd edn, Oxford University Press, 2013) 539–43. See also *1 Chevron Corporation and 2 Texaco Petroleum Company v The Republic of Ecuador*, PCA Case No 2009-23 (US–Ecuador BIT), Fourth Interim Award on Interim Measures, 7 February 2013, Part IV(3).

[92] Report of the UNCITRAL Working Group II (Arbitration and Conciliation) on the work of its 47th session, 10–14 September 2009, A/CN.9/641, para 31; see UNCITRAL Model Law, Art 17H.

[93] On the applicability of national legislation in the context of arbitrations involving only states or intergovernmental organizations, see discussion under Art 1(2).

bear in mind the extent to which the form of their decisions (ie award or order) may affect their enforceability.[94] The question of enforcement of interim measures decisions under national law or through national courts does not typically arise in inter-state arbitration, due to the immunity of states in this context to the jurisdiction of national courts.[95]

5.102 Article 26(3) sets out the conditions for the granting of interim measures. It describes the required level of harm, the principle of proportionality, and the requirement that 'there [be] a reasonable possibility that the requesting party will succeed on the merits'. In one interim measures application decided in a PCA-administered investment treaty arbitration under the 2010 UNCITRAL Rules, the arbitral tribunal was particularly cautious in stating its views regarding the strength of the claimant's case on jurisdiction, admissibility, and merits. The case concerned the envisaged expropriation by the respondent state of the claimant's production facilities. The claimant requested the tribunal to order the respondent state to preserve the status quo pending the tribunal's decision on the merits and, in particular, to prevent the competent authorities within the respondent state from issuing or enforcing any measures that would lead to the expropriation of the premises that formed the subject-matter of the arbitration. The tribunal noted that the threshold to satisfy the 'reasonable possibility of success' criterion of the 2010 UNCITRAL Rules was not high and while it found that there was a reasonable possibility of success on the merits, the less said the better so as to 'avoid prejudicing or appearing to prejudice the parties' respective cases on jurisdiction, admissibility and merits'. Ultimately, the tribunal rejected the application on the ground that the claimant had not satisfied the other conditions of Article 26(3)(a).

5.103 Article 26(4) provides that the conditions for interim measures set out in Article 26(3) 'shall apply only to the extent the arbitral tribunal considers appropriate'. This provision confirms that the high level of detail in Article 26 is intended to provide guidance to the parties in arguing interim measures applications and to the arbitral tribunal in deciding them, but not to fetter the arbitral tribunal's ultimate discretion.

[94] The New York Convention, for example, provides for the recognition and enforcement of foreign 'arbitral *awards*' (10 June 1958, 330 UNTS 38, Art 1, emphasis added). See also *1 Chevron Corporation and 2 Texaco Petroleum Company v The Republic of Ecuador*, PCA Case No 2009-23 (United States–Ecuador BIT) (1976 UNCITRAL Rules), Second Interim Award on Interim Measures, 16 February 2012, 1, 9; reproduced in Caron and Caplan (n 92) 539–43, where the arbitral tribunal emphasized that, being an award, its decision would be the type of final and binding decision which the parties had undertaken to carry out without delay both by agreeing to arbitrate under the 1976 UNCITRAL Rules (pursuant to Art 32(2)) and pursuant to the United States–Ecuador BIT. On the enforcement of interim awards generally, see Gary B Born, *International Commercial Arbitration*, vol 2 (Wolters Kluwer, 2009) 2019–28.

[95] See discussion under Art 1.

Paragraphs 5 to 9 of Article 26 provide for the arbitral tribunal's power to: modify the interim measures that it has granted, order the requesting party to provide security, require the parties to disclose any material change in the circumstances on the basis of which interim measures were granted, and award costs and damages suffered by a party due to an interim measure that should not have been granted. All of these provisions are based on the UNCITRAL Model Law and reflect powers already exercised by tribunals under the UNCITRAL Rules before their revision in 2010.[96] Under the 2012 PCA Rules, any deposit of security for costs made pursuant to Article 26(6) will be held by the International Bureau of the PCA, as provided in Article 43(3). **5.104**

Article 26(9), which reproduces Article 26(3) of the 1976 UNCITRAL Rules, provides that a party can make a request for interim measures in a state court without thereby contradicting or waiving the arbitration agreement. It follows that where national law is applicable, state courts may have concurrent jurisdiction with the arbitral tribunal to grant interim measures.[97] Asking interim measures from a state court can facilitate their enforcement in the absence of voluntary compliance. In arbitrations involving only states and intergovernmental organizations, unless otherwise agreed, parties may only be able to seek interim measures from the arbitral tribunal itself. **5.105**

The 2010 UNCITRAL Rules and 2012 PCA Rules do not explicitly provide for the arbitral tribunal's power to issue what the UNCITRAL Model Law refers to as 'preliminary orders'—that is, orders to a party not to take any action during the pendency of an interim measures application which would frustrate the interim measure before the application is decided. The UNCITRAL Working Group considered that given the arbitral tribunal's broad discretion to conduct the proceedings as it sees fit under Article 17, the UNCITRAL Rules 'in and of themselves, [do not] prevent the arbitral tribunal from issuing preliminary orders'.[98] Such limitations may however be found in the applicable procedural law.[99] **5.106**

[96] See eg *1 Chevron Corporation and 2 Texaco Petroleum Company v The Republic of Ecuador*, PCA Case No 2009-23 (US–Ecuador BIT) (1976 UNCITRAL Rules), Order on Interim Measures, 14 May 2010, 2; First Interim Award on Interim Measures, 25 January 2012, IV(3); Second Interim Award on Interim Measures, 16 February 2012, 4, 7; reproduced in Caron and Caplan (n 92) 539–43.

[97] Although under certain national laws, recourse to state courts will be the only possible course of action. See eg Italian Civil Code, Art 818, which prohibits arbitral tribunals from granting 'attachment or other interim measures of protection'.

[98] Report of the UNCITRAL Working Group II (Arbitration and Conciliation) on the work of its 50th session, 9–13 February 2009, A/CN.9/669, para 106.

[99] On the applicability of national legislation in the context of arbitrations involving only states or intergovernmental organizations, see discussion under Art 1(2).

K. Evidence—Article 27

1. Each party shall have the burden of proving the facts relied on to support its claim or defence.
2. Witnesses, including expert witnesses, who are presented by the parties to testify to the arbitral tribunal on any issue of fact or expertise may be any individual, notwithstanding that the individual is a party to the arbitration or in any way related to a party. Unless otherwise directed by the arbitral tribunal, statements by witnesses, including expert witnesses, may be presented in writing and signed by them.
3. At any time during the arbitral proceedings the arbitral tribunal may require the parties to produce documents, exhibits or other evidence within such a period of time as the arbitral tribunal shall determine. The arbitral tribunal may also, after consultation with the parties, perform a site visit.
4. The arbitral tribunal shall determine the admissibility, relevance, materiality and weight of the evidence offered.

5.107 Article 27 is one of the three provisions of the Rules (the other two being Articles 28 and 29) that deal with evidence in the arbitral proceeding.

5.108 This article adopts the text of Article 27 of the 2010 UNCITRAL Rules and adds to it a provision for site visits. Articles 27 and 28 of the 2012 PCA Rules and 2010 UNCITRAL Rules reorganize, with some modifications, Articles 24 and 25 of the 1976 UNCITRAL Rules. Evidential matters that do not concern hearings are now grouped in Article 27, while matters of evidence regarding hearings are found in Article 28.

5.109 Articles 27 and 28 outline a framework for dealing with evidentiary matters, without subjecting either the parties or the arbitral tribunal to any stringent rules. Within this framework, and so long as each party is afforded a reasonable opportunity to present its case (as required by Article 17(1) of the Rules), the arbitral tribunal has discretion to conduct the proceedings in such manner as it considers appropriate. This flexibility is important, as it allows the arbitral process to be adapted to the diverse expectations of arbitrators, counsel, and parties from different legal traditions. This is not to say, however, that arbitrations should proceed on the sole basis of the sparse guidance provided by the Rules. Most arbitral tribunals will consult the parties at an early stage of the proceedings to understand their expectations as to the manner in which evidence is to be presented, and set forth in a procedural order some additional rules that take these expectations into account, to the extent possible. In PCA-administered arbitrations other than inter-state arbitrations, parties sometimes agree to the application of the Rules on the Taking of Evidence in International Arbitration of the International Bar Association 2010 ('IBA Rules').[100]

[100] In rare cases, parties agree to the application of the rules of evidence of a particular jurisdiction.

More often, to preserve the tribunal's discretion, while providing the parties with some direction, the IBA Rules are adopted as 'guidelines'.[101]

Article 27(1) states the generally accepted allocation of the burden of proof in international arbitration. 5.110

Article 27(2) allows the parties to support their legal arguments and factual allegations through witnesses of fact and expert witnesses, and, in particular, through their written statements. In most PCA-administered arbitrations conducted under PCA or UNCITRAL rules, written witness statements are the primary means by which a party introduces witness evidence into the record, oral testimony being used only to confirm the content of a written witness statement and provide an opportunity for the opposing party (and the arbitral tribunal) to put questions to the witness.[102] 5.111

Under Article 27(3), the arbitral tribunal can direct the parties to produce documents. Given the broad wording of this provision, the arbitral tribunal may do so on its own motion or at a party's request. Generally, a procedural order issued at an early stage of the proceeding will provide for one or more rounds of document production requests by the parties. The procedure will usually consist of each party submitting its requests, followed by objections by the other party, if any. The requesting party then generally has a right of reply to any objections and, if the parties fail to agree within a certain period of time, they may submit the requests to the arbitral tribunal for a decision. In terms of criteria for ordering document production, in arbitrations involving private parties, the arbitral tribunal will often refer (explicitly or implicitly) to those set out in Articles 3 and 9 of the IBA Rules. Most requests will be weighed in terms of relevance and materiality, but more 5.112

[101] See eg *Bilcon of Delaware v Canada*, PCA Case No 2009-4 (NAFTA) (1976 UNCITRAL Rules), Procedural Order No 2, 3 June 2009, para 2.1 ('Matters of evidence are governed by the relevant articles of the UNCITRAL Arbitration Rules (1976) . . . In addition, the IBA Rules on the Taking of Evidence in International Commercial Arbitration (1999) . . . will be used as guidelines in these proceedings'); *Guaracachi America Inc and Rurelec PLC v Plurinational State of Bolivia*, PCA Case No 2011-17 (China–Mongolia BIT) (2010 UNCITRAL Rules), Terms of Appointment and Procedural Order No 1, para 14.3 ('the IBA Rules on the Taking of Evidence in International Commercial Arbitration shall be used as non-mandatory guidelines by the Tribunal and the Parties . . .').

[102] See eg *Bilcon of Delaware v Canada*, PCA Case No 2009-4 (NAFTA) (1976 UNCITRAL Rules), Procedural Order No 18, 1 April 2013:

> 4.1 Witness statements shall stand in lieu of direct examination during the oral hearing. . . .
> 4.3 At the hearing, the examination of each witness shall proceed as follows: The Disputing Party summoning the witness may briefly introduce the witness and provide him or her with an opportunity to make corrections or clarifications to his or her statement; the opposing Disputing Party may then cross-examine the witness; the Disputing Party summoning the witness may then re-examine the witness with respect to any matters or issues arising out of the cross-examination. The Tribunal may examine the witness at any time, before, during or after examination by one of the Disputing Parties.

complex issues may arise where one party claims privilege or political sensitivity.[103] The allowed scope of document production will often depend on the complexity of the case and the amount in dispute (if any), as extensive document production may require the expenditure of significant resources.

5.113 The traditional incentive for parties to comply with document production orders is the danger that the arbitral tribunal will draw adverse inferences if it does not consider that its order has been fully complied with. In general, however, parties respect the authority of the tribunal without such threat. National laws, where applicable,[104] may allow the requesting party or the arbitral tribunal to seek the assistance of national courts.[105] Assistance will typically be limited to cases seated in that jurisdiction, although, for example, section 1782 of the United States Code grants US courts the power to order document production 'for use in a proceeding in a foreign or international tribunal', which has sometimes been interpreted to include international arbitral tribunals seated outside the United States.[106]

5.114 An arbitral tribunal is also not typically in a position to direct third parties to produce documents, as they have not agreed to the tribunal's jurisdiction. Here too, the assistance of some national courts may be available.[107] In one recent PCA-administered case under ad hoc procedural rules, a party sought to apply for assistance to the English courts under section 43 of the English Arbitration Act 1996 to obtain documents held by a third party. As with many such provisions, section 43 requires the consent of the other party or the arbitral tribunal as a precondition to the application to the courts. The other party refused to support the application. The arbitral tribunal also declined to provide its agreement, on the ground that the other party was already in the process of obtaining the documents in question from the third party, having been ordered by the tribunal to do so in the context of a regular decision on document production.

5.115 Article 27(3) also provides that the arbitral tribunal may, after consultation with the parties, perform a site visit. There is no equivalent to this provision in the 2010 UNCITRAL Rules, while the 1976 UNCITRAL Rules refer more narrowly to

---

[103] For example, the issues of solicitor-client privilege, work product privilege, and political or institutional sensitivity in the context of document production were grappled with by the arbitral tribunal in *Bilcon of Delaware v Canada*, PCA Case No 2009-4 (NAFTA) (1976 UNCITRAL Rules), Procedural Order No 12, 2 May 2012; Procedural Order No 13, 11 July 2012.

[104] On the applicability of national legislation in the context of arbitrations involving only states or intergovernmental organizations, see discussion under Art 1(2).

[105] See eg UNCITRAL Model Law, Art 27 ('[t]he arbitral tribunal or a party with approval of the arbitral tribunal may request from a competent court of this State assistance in taking evidence. The court may execute the request within its competence and according to its rules on taking evidence'); English Arbitration Act, s 43; US Federal Arbitration Act, 9 USC Art 7.

[106] See *Intel Corporation v Advanced Micro Devices Inc* 542 US 241 (US Supreme Court 2004); *In re Oxus Gold plc*, 2007 WL 1037387 (DNJ 2007); *In re Roz Trading Ltd*, 469 F.Supp.2d 1221 (ND Ga 2006); *In re Babcock Borsig AG*, 583 F.Supp.2d 233, 240 (D.Mass. 2008).

[107] On the applicability of national legislation in the context of arbitrations involving only states or intergovernmental organizations, see discussion under Art 1(2).

the arbitral tribunal's ability to 'meet at any place it deems appropriate for the inspection of goods, other property or documents'.[108] In the 2012 PCA Rules, the expression 'site visit' refers to any visit by the members of the arbitral tribunal to a location relevant to the subject-matter of the dispute. Site visits may be appropriate in many inter-state disputes, in view of the significance of the subject-matter of the dispute (for example, a land or maritime boundary) and the types of issues that may arise.[109] The PCA Drafting Committee chose not to expand upon the possible functions of site visits in Article 27(3). The purpose of a site visit could be for the arbitral tribunal to gather information that might eventually become part of the evidentiary record, or only to obtain a visual impression and a better understanding of the subject-matter of the dispute. The PCA Drafting Committee also did not include in Article 27(3) any direction as to whether explanations given by the parties during a site visit constitute formal oral submissions to which the arbitral tribunal could refer in reaching its decision. These matters are left to be addressed by the tribunal in each case. The practice of international courts and tribunals in inter-state cases to date suggests that there is reluctance to qualify site visits as an exercise in evidence-gathering by the court or tribunal.[110] Nonetheless, parties have made reference to matters presented and questions asked during site visits in the course of their (oral) pleadings.[111]

---

[108] 1976 UNCITRAL Rules, Art 16(3), reproduced in Appendix XI.

[109] Annex VII of UNCLOS, for instance, provides that 'the parties to the dispute shall facilitate the work of the arbitral tribunal' by enabling it when necessary 'to visit the localities to which the case related' (Art 6).

[110] One exception is found in the *Boundary Dispute between Argentina and Chile concerning the Frontier between Boundary Post 62 and Mount Fitzroy*, where, during the site visit, the parties' agents agreed, in the presence of the arbitral tribunal, on the identification of Mount Fitzroy and Boundary Post 62 as the two extreme points of the disputed sector of the boundary between the two countries, and the arbitral tribunal was able to verify an area that had not been explored during an earlier boundary dispute of 1902 (Decision, 21 October 1994, 22 UNRIAA 3, 10, 20, 35).

[111] For example, in the *Gabčíkovo–Nagymaros* case, heard by the ICJ, the original request for a site visit from the Slovak agent indicated that the purpose of the site visit would be to provide contextual information, and not to formally gather evidence in situ (see Peter Tomka and Samuel Wordsworth, 'The First Site Visit of the International Court of Justice in Fulfillment of its Judicial Function' [1998] *AJIL* 92, 134). No official minutes or transcript of the visit were provided to the parties. Instead, both parties made video records, and the registry provided the ICJ with an informal summary of the visit on a daily basis. Both parties referred in the oral hearing to questions and statements by members of the ICJ during the visit: *Gabčíkovo–Nagymaros Project*, Hungary/Slovakia, Judgment, 25 September 1997, ICJ Reports 1997, 7, 13–14. In the 1908 PCA *Grisbådarna* arbitration between Sweden and Norway, the arbitral tribunal conducted a site visit along the demarcation lines proposed by each party as the maritime boundary, while the agents of the parties commented on the specificities of the area (such as the presence of rocks and reefs). The tribunal also visited several islands. The recorded exchanges between the tribunal and the parties indicate that the parties freely communicated with the tribunal during the site visit. During the hearing following the site visit, the president of the tribunal emphasized the usefulness of the site visit and the agents of both parties made periodic references to the site visit in the course of their oral pleadings: *Recueil des Comptes Rendus de la visite des lieux et des protocoles des séances du tribunal arbitral, constitué en vertu de la Convention du 15 Mars 1908, pour juger la question de la délimitation d'une certaine partie de la frontière maritime entre la Norvège et la Suède* (Van Langhuysen Frères, 1909), 1, 38.

5.116 Recently, the seven-member arbitral tribunal in the PCA-administered *Indus Waters Kishenganga Arbitration* between India and Pakistan conducted two site visits. This arbitration concerned the legality of the Kishenganga hydro-electric project, which India intended to build and operate in India-administered Jammu & Kashmir, as well the possible impact of such an installation on a Pakistani hydro-electric project located in the Neelum valley in Pakistan-administered Jammu & Kashmir.[112] The parties agreed during the first procedural meeting that the seven-member arbitral tribunal 'should conduct a site visit to the pertinent facilities and locations of the Kishenganga hydro-electric facility and to those of the Neelum Valley'.[113] A first, week-long site visit to the Indian and Pakistani hydro-electric projects and surrounding areas took place in June 2011.[114] A second, four-day site visit took place the following January, as the arbitral tribunal wished to see the region as it appeared during both the wet and dry season. A delegation composed of only two members of the arbitral tribunal participated in the second site visit.[115] The itinerary of each site visit was agreed by the parties. In the course of each site visit, the arbitral tribunal heard technical presentations, which were video-recorded by the PCA.[116]

5.117 The *Indus Waters Kishenganga Arbitration* is the only case known to the authors where specific procedural and logistical directions made by an international court or tribunal in an inter-state arbitration prior to a site visit are publicly available. Before the first site visit, the arbitral tribunal set out its parameters in a procedural order as follows:

> **1. The Site Visit Program**
>
> 1.1. The Court takes note of the Parties' agreement on the 'broad outline of the itinerary', as follows:
>
> . . .
>
> 1.2. Having found the foregoing acceptable, the Court hereby adopts the outline of the itinerary proposed by the Parties on April 29, 2011.
>
> **2. Size of Delegations**
>
> 2.1 The Court takes note of the Parties' agreement that their respective delegations (including the Agent, Co-Agents, counsel, and experts) each be limited to not more than 10 persons for logistical reasons.

---

[112] *Indus Waters Kishenganga Arbitration*, Pakistan v India, PCA Case No 2011-1 (Indus Waters Treaty 1960), Partial Award, 18 February 2013, paras 126–7, 160.

[113] *Indus Waters Kishenganga Arbitration*, Pakistan v India, PCA Case No 2011-1 (Indus Waters Treaty 1960), Procedural Order No 1, 21 January 2011, Art 8.1; reproduced in *Indus Waters Kishenganga Arbitration*, Pakistan v India, PCA Case No 2011-1 (Indus Waters Treaty 1960), Partial Award, 18 February 2013, para 23.

[114] *Indus Waters Kishenganga Arbitration*, Pakistan v India, PCA Case No 2011-1 (Indus Waters Treaty 1960), PCA Press Release, 22 June 2011, <http://www.pca-cpa.org/showpage.asp?pag_id=1392>.

[115] *Indus Waters Kishenganga Arbitration*, Pakistan v India, PCA Case No 2011-1 (Indus Waters Treaty 1960), Partial Award, 18 February 2013, para 81, n 16; para 86, n 17.

[116] *Indus Waters Kishenganga Arbitration*, Pakistan v India, PCA Case No 2011-1 (Indus Waters Treaty 1960), Procedural Order No 3, 10 May 2011.

2.2 The Court's delegation shall similarly be comprised of not more than 10 persons, including all the Members of the Court, the Registrar, and the members of the Secretariat involved in documentation and logistical support to the Court.

3. Confidentiality; Press Release

3.1 While both Parties have affirmed the importance of the rules on confidentiality in relation to the site visit, the Court takes note of the Parties' lack of agreement on whether a press release should be issued by the Court upon the conclusion of the visit. India has proposed that a press release whose text has been agreed between the Parties be issued by the Court at the end of the visit, while Pakistan maintains that confidentiality is necessary under the circumstances and does not wish the Court to issue such a press release.

3.2 Recalling the principles on confidentiality that govern this arbitration (including Paragraph 7 of Procedural Order No. 1) and taking into account the lack of agreement between the Parties, the Court considers that no public disclosure of the site visit, including any statement to the press emanating from the Court, can be made.

3.3. The Court hereby orders that:

(a) There shall be no advance public announcements of the fact that a site visit shall be conducted, nor of the dates and itineraries thereof. The Parties are enjoined to ensure the absolute confidentiality of all information relating to the site visit until the visit has been concluded.

(b) If both Parties agree at any point before or during the site visit, the Court may issue a press release in consultation with the Parties, to be issued only after the conclusion of the visit on June 21, 2011. However, if both Parties do not so agree, then no press release nor other public statement shall be issued by the Court.

4. Hospitality/Social Events

4.1 The Court takes note of the Parties' agreement that the site visit 'be as discreet as possible without any social events', of India's suggestion that 'this should not exclude any reasonable hospitality by Government authorities', and of Pakistan's request that India clarify the meaning of 'reasonable hospitality'.

4.2 Without limiting the Parties' freedom to reach agreement on this matter, the Court expresses its availability to attend any simple dinner event that a Party may wish to prepare, if that dinner includes and is restricted to the members of both delegations participating in the site visit.

5. Presentations During the Site Visit

5.1 The Court takes note of the Parties' agreement that any presentations made during the site visit be limited to objective, technical presentations made by experts (whether members of the official delegations or other experts), and that legal issues or arguments should not be discussed at any point during such presentations. The Court agrees with this approach and wishes to emphasize that presentations should be succinct and remain neutral in tone.

5.2 The Members of the Court shall be free to put questions at any time during a presentation. No member of any delegation shall be permitted to ask questions during or after a presentation. With the Chairman of the Court's leave, the non-presenting delegation may respond to a point made in a presentation, such response shall be limited strictly to technical or factual matters.

5.3 Any materials meant to be distributed during such presentations (including maps, plans, technical illustrations, and similar documents), shall be provided to the Court and the other Party no later than May 31, 2011.

5.4 For the avoidance of doubt, the site visit (including the presentations made therein) shall not be considered 'oral hearings' or 'oral submissions' within the meaning of Article 14 of the Supplemental Rules of Procedure.

6. Record of the Site Visit

6.1 The Court takes note of Pakistan's statement that 'on the matter of record of the site visit, no doubt that members of the delegation would be taking notes; however, we are of the view that it would be useful to have a permanent record' of the presentations made during the site visit, and of its proposal that the PCA 'make necessary arrangements for a video recording of the entire visit'. For its part, India has suggested that '[e]ither side will arrange videography/photography on its side' while expressing that it is 'open to any directions from the Court' on this point.

6.2 Within their respective delegations, the Parties are free to take their own notes. These need not be shared with the Court or the other Party.

6.3 The Members of the Court and its Secretariat shall be free to take notes and photographs for exclusive use in internal deliberations. The Secretariat shall also take charge of producing a video recording of all presentations made, and shall make a copy thereof for each Party.

7. Costs of the Site Visit

7.1 The Court takes note of the Parties' agreement that each Party shall bear all costs of the site visit within their respective territories, including hotel accommodations and internal transportation.

7.2 Pursuant to Article 21 of the Supplemental Rules of Procedure, all other expenses relating to the site visit shall be borne equally by the Parties.

8. Further Arrangements

8.1 The Court takes note of India's statement that '[i]f the proposed outline programme of the visit to India and Pakistan is generally acceptable to the Court, then we can mutually discuss the further details, including the logistics', and Pakistan's observation that the Parties have yet to 'reach agreement on some of the modalities' of the site visit.

8.2 Within the framework of this Order, the Court invites the Parties to continue conferring on the remaining logistical issues, and to report back to the Court with further points of agreement no later than May 23, 2011. The logistical issues to be agreed upon should include but not necessarily be limited to the following: (a) arrangements to ensure the security of each member of the Court at all times; (b) a detailed (by-the-hour) itinerary, to the extent possible; (c) provisions for medical support; (d) lists of the Parties' delegations and experts that will address the Court during the site visit; (e) hotel arrangements; and (f) modes of internal transportation.[117]

[117] *Indus Waters Kishenganga Arbitration*, Pakistan v India, PCA Case No 2011-1 (Indus Waters Treaty 1960), Procedural Order No 3, 10 May 2011, reproduced in Partial Award, 18 February 2013, para 36.

A procedural order issued prior to the second site visit also provided that: **5.118**

> 'those Members of the Court not present would view the photos and video of the visit taken by the Secretariat;...experts who were not members of the official delegations would be allowed to brief and assist the delegations when *in situ*; and...there would be no advance public announcements of the visit, but a press release containing a text and photograph to be approved by the Parties and the Court would be prepared by the Secretariat for publication on the PCA website following the conclusion of the visit'.[118]

In a separate communication to the parties, the arbitral tribunal also indicated that:

> The purpose of the second site visit is to give the Members of the Court a background impression of the relevant projects and areas surrounding the Kishenganga/Neelum River. As the Secretariat will be providing both Parties with copies of the photographs and video recordings taken, the Parties are free to submit any evidence they deem relevant in their future submissions in accordance with the Supplemental Rules.
>
> ...
>
> The Court is of the view that the second site visit does not constitute a 'transaction of business' within the meaning of Paragraph 11 of Annexure G. The site visit is not an 'oral hearing' in which 'oral submissions' are made by the Parties, and those Members of the Court not present during the second visit will have an opportunity to review the video and photographic materials from the site visit (including videos of any presentations made) individually, just as they each review any submission or communication of the Parties. The Court also assures the Parties that its two physically participating Members shall not by themselves 'transact business' at any point during the visit.[119]

In another letter to the parties, the chairman of the tribunal stated as follows: **5.119**

> I trust that all representatives of the Parties understand the basic rule prohibiting ex parte discussions with Members of the Court during the course of these proceedings. In the case of the second site visit, I trust that any potentially contentious matter, whether of substance or procedure, will not be raised ex parte by any Party representative to any member of the Court or Secretariat.[120]

Article 27(4) of the Rules provides that the arbitral tribunal can determine the **5.120** admissibility, relevance, materiality, and weight of the evidence. The wide discretion given the arbitral tribunal is a key aspect of the flexibility of arbitral proceedings. Generally, arbitral tribunals decide matters of admissibility as they arise during the proceedings (such as when a party objects to the admissibility of a particular piece of evidence), while the relevance, materiality, and weight of the evidence are assessed once the parties have finished presenting their cases.

---

118 *Indus Waters Kishenganga Arbitration*, Pakistan v India, PCA Case No 2011-1 (Indus Waters Treaty 1960), Partial Award, 18 February 2013, para 81.

119 *Indus Waters Kishenganga Arbitration*, Pakistan v India, PCA Case No 2011-1 (Indus Waters Treaty 1960), Partial Award, 18 February 2013, para 82.

120 *Indus Waters Kishenganga Arbitration*, Pakistan v India, PCA Case No 2011-1 (Indus Waters Treaty 1960), Partial Award, 18 February 2013, para 85.

L. Hearings—Article 28

1. In the event of an oral hearing, the arbitral tribunal shall give the parties adequate advance notice of the date, time and place thereof.
2. Witnesses, including expert witnesses, may be heard under the conditions and examined in the manner set by the arbitral tribunal.
3. Hearings shall be held in camera unless the parties agree otherwise. The arbitral tribunal may require the retirement of any witness or witnesses, including expert witnesses, during the testimony of such other witnesses, except that a witness, including an expert witness, who is a party to the arbitration shall not, in principle, be asked to retire.
4. The arbitral tribunal may direct that witnesses, including expert witnesses, be examined through means of telecommunication that do not require their physical presence at the hearing (such as videoconference).

5.121 This provision follows the text of Article 28 of the 2010 UNCITRAL Rules, establishing the flexible framework within which the arbitral tribunal may exercise its discretion regarding the conduct of hearings.

5.122 Article 28(1) is identical to Article 25(1) of the 1976 UNCITRAL Rules. It provides that the arbitral tribunal must give the parties 'adequate advance notice of the date, time and place' of any hearing. While urgent matters, such as a request for interim measures, may require that a hearing be convened on short notice, hearings are generally scheduled months in advance, taking into account the availability and need for preparation of all participants.[121] In the weeks prior to the hearing, the arbitral tribunal may consult the parties, either in writing, by telephone conference, or, in particularly complex cases, at an in-person meeting, concerning any outstanding hearing-related matters, including:

- the time and place of the hearing;
- the daily schedule;
- the order of proceedings (whether there will be opening and/or closing statements, and the order of presentation of witnesses and experts);
- the allocation of hearing time between the parties;
- the procedure for the examination of witnesses;
- the confidentiality or transparency of the hearing;
- the use of hearing bundles (or computer tablets);
- the need for interpretation and/or transcription; and
- any technological requirements that the parties or tribunal may have.

[121] See eg *Guaracachi America Inc and Rurelec PLC v Plurinational State of Bolivia*, PCA Case No 2011-17 (China–Mongolia BIT) (2010 UNCITRAL Rules), Terms of Appointment and Procedural Order No 1, signed in December 2011 and scheduling a hearing for April 2013.

The arbitral tribunal will then confirm any matters agreed by the parties and decide any outstanding matters by letter or procedural order.[122] **5.123**

In PCA-administered cases, the PCA is generally in charge of logistics, such as identifying a hearing facility wherever the parties and tribunal wish to hold the hearing and making arrangements for interpretation, transcription, technological equipment and support (including for video-conferencing or webcasting), and catering. The PCA can arrange for hearing and meeting space at no cost at the Peace Palace in The Hague and at venues in Costa Rica, Mauritius, Singapore, and South Arica. As described in the discussion of Article 16, when hearings are held in the Netherlands, the PCA can also issue safe passage certificates for witnesses. **5.124**

Article 28(2) gives the tribunal, in consultation with the parties, discretion to decide on the manner in which fact and expert witnesses will be heard and examined. This decision may depend on the legal traditions and expectations of the counsel and arbitrators involved. Whatever the content of the chosen rules or guidelines, it is advisable for the parties to agree to them or for the arbitral tribunal to decide what they will be in advance of the hearing. Tribunals generally consider that the written statements of witnesses will contain the whole of their positive evidence. Accordingly, direct examination at the hearing is limited both in time and scope. The tribunal is free to ask questions of the witnesses at any time, although time constraints may cause the presiding arbitrator to limit questions from the tribunal. Just before the commencement of witness examination, the witness is generally asked to read out an oath or affirmation, or is admonished by the tribunal.[123] The approach may vary depending on the personal style of the presiding arbitrator, the views of the parties, and, in some cases, the requirements of applicable law.[124] The tribunal's preferred approach is ideally agreed with the parties and witnesses before any hearing. **5.125**

Article 28(3), which reproduces Article 25(4) of the 1976 UNCITRAL Rules, provides that hearings will be held in camera—in other words, solely in the presence of the arbitral tribunal, the parties, and their representatives (and any supporting personnel, such as the tribunal secretary, interpreters, or court reporters). This default rule can be reversed only by agreement of the parties. **5.126**

[122] See eg *Bilcon of Delaware v Canada*, PCA Case No 2009-4 (NAFTA) (1976 UNCITRAL Rules), Procedural Order No 18, 16 April 2013; *Guaracachi America Inc and Rurelec PLC v Plurinational State of Bolivia*, PCA Case No 2011-17 (China–Mongolia BIT) (2010 UNCITRAL Rules), Procedural Order No 17, 17 March 2013.

[123] An affirmation may be, for fact witnesses: 'I solemnly declare upon my honour and conscience that I shall speak the truth, the whole truth and nothing but the truth'; and, for experts: 'I solemnly declare upon my honour and conscience that my statement will be in accordance with my sincere belief' (ICSID Arbitration Rules, Rule 35).

[124] In some jurisdictions, it is illegal for an arbitral tribunal to administer an oath or affirmation (see eg Swedish Arbitration Act 1999, Art 25).

5.127 In the PCA's experience, hearings are held in camera in the vast majority of cases conducted under the PCA or UNCITRAL rules, even when other aspects of the arbitral proceedings are public (for example, where the parties' written statements and the tribunal's orders and awards are published online). There are, however, some notable exceptions.

5.128 First, the contract, treaty, or other agreement under which the dispute arises, or the arbitration agreement entered into by the parties after the dispute arises (*compromis*), may provide for public hearings. For example, hearings held in arbitrations under the Dominican Republic–Central America–United States Free Trade Agreement ('CAFTA-DR') are open to the public.[125] In the *Abyei* arbitration, the arbitration agreement provided that the '[t]he oral pleading(s) of the Parties shall be open to the media', and, in preparation for the hearing, the parties made known their preference for it to be entirely open to the public.[126]

5.129 Second, the parties may agree to open the hearings to the public once the arbitral proceeding has commenced. In *Guaracachi v Bolivia*, the 'Terms of Appointment and Procedural Order No. 1', signed by both the tribunal and the parties, stated that 'the Tribunal shall conduct hearings open to the public'.[127] In *Bilcon of Delaware v Canada*, the parties chose to expand on the transparency provisions of the North-American Free Trade Agreement (NAFTA) and agreed that hearings would be 'open to the public except when necessary to protect confidential information'.[128]

5.130 The practical application of the standard 'open to the public' varies from case to case. In *Abyei*, the public and the press were welcome in the hearing room. Faced with the practical problem of insufficient seating space in the Great Hall of Justice

---

125 See CAFTA-DR, Art 10.21: 'The tribunal shall conduct hearings open to the public and shall determine, in consultation with the disputing parties, the appropriate logistical arrangements. However, any disputing party that intends to use information designated as protected information in a hearing shall so advise the tribunal. The tribunal shall make appropriate arrangements to protect the information from disclosure'. In one PCA-administered arbitration conducted under the CAFTA-DR, the tribunal provided in a procedural order that the PCA, in consultation with the parties, would make arrangements for public attendance of the hearings (*1 TCW Group, Inc 2 Dominican Energy Holdings LP v the Dominican Republic*, PCA Case No 2008-6 (CAFTA-DR) (1976 UNCITRAL Rules), Procedural Order No 2, 15 August 2008, Art 10.2.3). Ultimately, the case was settled before reaching the hearing stage.

126 *Abyei Arbitration*, the Government of Sudan/the Sudan People's Liberation Movement/Army, PCA Case No 2008-7 (PCA State/Non-State Rules), Arbitration Agreement, Art 8(6); see Brooks W Daly, 'The Abyei Arbitration: Procedural Aspects of an Intra-State Border Arbitration' (2010) 22 *Leiden Journal of International Law* 801, 819.

127 *Guaracachi America Inc and Rurelec PLC v Plurinational State of Bolivia*, PCA Case No 2011-17 (China–Mongolia BIT) (2010 UNCITRAL Rules), Terms of Appointment and Procedural Order No 1, Art 16.2. The full provision reproduced almost exactly the CAFTA-DR provision on the transparency of hearings.

128 *Bilcon of Delaware v Canada*, PCA Case No 2009-4 (NAFTA) (1976 UNCITRAL Rules), Procedural Order No 2 (Confidentiality Order), 4 May 2009, para 2.6.

of the Peace Palace, the PCA arranged a live webcast through its website.[129] The PCA also posted transcripts of the hearing on its website immediately after each day of hearing.[130] In *Guaracachi v Bolivia*, the transcript and audio recording of the hearing were made available on the PCA's website, but the tribunal decided that video recording was 'unnecessary to provide for transparency in the proceeding'.[131] In *Bilcon of Delaware v Canada*, the tribunal decided that the 'open to the public' requirement would be fulfilled by the hearing being 'made accessible to the public in real time, through technical means to be determined in due course'.[132] No provision was made for the physical presence of the public or the press in the hearing room.

Like Article 25(4) of the 1976 UNCITRAL Rules, Article 27(3) of the 2012 PCA Rules and 2010 UNCITRAL Rules provides for the possible sequestration of fact and expert witnesses. In practice, fact witnesses are often excluded from the hearing room (and requested not to read any transcripts) before they testify, on the basis that their testimony may be influenced by hearing other witnesses testify regarding the same or related events. In contrast, the sequestration of expert witnesses is less common because they are testifying to their expertise rather than to a recollection of facts. Many tribunals consider that they are better served when experts can hear one another's testimony, sometimes even seeking to question experts who have the same area of expertise as a group (in a procedure referred to as 'expert conferencing' or 'hot-tubbing').[133] **5.131**

Article 27(3) further specifies that, in principle, a witness who is also a party to the arbitration will not be asked to retire from the hearing room. In light of this provision, tribunals may seek to allay concerns about a party representative who is also a witness being present in the hearing room by ordering that any such person be examined before other witnesses.[134] **5.132**

[129] See Daly (n 127), 819. There were over 2,000 viewers through the webcast from 49 countries (Daly (n 127), 820, n 60). The webcast remains available at <http://www.pca-cpa.org/showpage.asp?pag_id=1306>.

[130] *Abyei Arbitration*, the Government of Sudan/the Sudan People's Liberation Movement/Army, PCA Case No 2008-7 (PCA State/Non-State Rules), Final Award, 22 July 2009, para 85.

[131] *Guaracachi America Inc and Rurelec PLC v Plurinational State of Bolivia*, PCA Case No 2011-17 (China–Mongolia BIT) (2010 UNCITRAL Rules), Procedural Order No 17, 27 March 2013, para 3(1).

[132] *Bilcon of Delaware v Canada*, PCA Case No 2009-4 (NAFTA) (1976 UNCITRAL Rules), Procedural Order No 18, 16 April 2013, para 7.1.

[133] The modalities of a hot-tubbing session should be determined by the tribunal in consultation with the parties in advance of the hearing. For example, it should be decided whether hot-tubbing will follow or replace cross-examination and direct examination by the parties; whether only the tribunal, or both the parties and the tribunal will be allowed to pose questions; whether circulating a list of questions or topics in advance might increase the efficiency of the procedure; and whether the experts should be asked to consult and produce a joint report setting out areas of agreement and disagreement before the hot-tubbing session.

[134] See eg *Guaracachi America Inc and Rurelec PLC v Plurinational State of Bolivia*, PCA Case No 2011-17 (China–Mongolia BIT) (2010 UNCITRAL Rules), Terms of Appointment and Procedural Order No 1, para 13.1 ('the Parties' Representatives who are also witnesses shall be cross-examined before all other witnesses').

5.133 Despite some common practice that may be discerned, disagreement may still emerge between the parties as to whether witnesses in general, and those who are also a party to the arbitration in particular, can be present during the parties' opening statements. Such matters will then fall to the tribunal to decide, taking into account the circumstances of the case.[135]

5.134 Article 27(4) provides for the possibility of examining witnesses through means of telecommunication such as video-conferences. It has no equivalent in the 1976 UNCITRAL Rules.

5.135 The party that has submitted a witness statement is typically responsible for assuring the presence of the witness at the hearing if called for examination by the tribunal or cross-examination by the opposing party. If a witness is requested to attend a hearing, but fails to do so, the admissibility or weight of that witness's statement or report may be negatively impacted. The tribunal's exclusion of a witness statement from the record is a common result. Article 27(4) reflects the possibility that the examination of a witness through means of telecommunication may in certain circumstances be allowed to replace his or her physical presence at the hearing. Nonetheless, the practice of international arbitral tribunals shows that examination of witnesses through means of telecommunication in lieu of personal attendance is not accepted as a matter of course, but requires the showing of good cause and must be weighed against any potential prejudice to the opposing party.

5.136 For example, in *Guaracachi v Bolivia*, a PCA-administered investment treaty arbitration conducted under the 2010 UNCITRAL Rules, the tribunal provided in its first procedural order as follows:

> Failure to make a witness available for cross-examination without good cause shall result in the witness statement or expert report being struck from the record. If a witness is unable to appear personally at the final hearing for reasons of health or force majeure, the Tribunal may permit alternative arrangements (such as video conference facilities).[136]

5.137 In one PCA-administered arbitration conducted under the 1976 UNCITRAL Rules, the arbitral tribunal granted the claimant's request to present seven of its witnesses through a video-conference. In its request, the claimant had stated that 'not all witnesses are easily available to be physically present' and that requiring their attendance would lead to 'substantial additional costs for the Claimant which it can

[135] See eg *Guaracachi America Inc and Rurelec PLC v Plurinational State of Bolivia*, PCA Case No 2011-17 (China–Mongolia BIT) (2010 UNCITRAL Rules), Terms of Appointment and Procedural Order No 17, 27 March 2013, paras 2(f), 3(4).

[136] See eg *Guaracachi America Inc and Rurelec PLC v Plurinational State of Bolivia*, PCA Case No 2011-17 (China–Mongolia BIT) (2010 UNCITRAL Rules), Terms of Appointment and Procedural Order No 1, para 13(3).

hardly bear'. This decision was delivered in a case where it was not clear whether the respondent would participate in the hearing, and where the tribunal, rather than the respondent, had required the presence of the claimant's witnesses at the hearing.

In another PCA-administered arbitration under the 1976 UNCITRAL Rules, the arbitral tribunal rejected a request to provide witness testimony through a video-conference without providing reasons. The party requesting the use of a video-conference had sought to justify its request by referring to the witness's busy agenda, potential costs savings for the parties, and the narrow topic of the witness's statement. **5.138**

In the *Indus Waters Kishenganga Arbitration*, where the applicable procedural rules (as the 1976 UNCITRAL Rules) provided no guidance regarding the possibility of examining witnesses through means of telecommunication, the arbitral tribunal issued the following reasoned decision on a request to present a witness for cross-examination by telephone, inter alia reflecting upon current practice in international arbitration: **5.139**

1. Articles 10 and 14 of the Supplemental Rules establish the procedure for the submission of expert evidence in support of the Parties' factual and legal arguments. A Party wishing to submit such evidence must append to its written pleadings the expert's witness report, which will stand as evidence in chief, while the other Party may request to cross-examine the expert. In accordance with Section 3.3 of Procedural Order No. 9, each Party is responsible for summoning to the hearing those of its experts that the other Party wishes to cross-examine. Consistent with these provisions and with general practice in international arbitration, the expert is expected to appear for cross-examination in person during the scheduled hearing. These provisions provide no guidance for a situation such as this one, where the expert is not presented in person due to a professed prior commitment.
2. At the outset, the Court notes that in international arbitration there are serious consequences to a party's failure to present an expert witness for cross-examination without cogent reasons: in general, that expert's report would be stricken from the record, and would form no part of the evidence on which an award can be based.
3. The Court considers that it is the norm for cross-examination of a witness or expert to be conducted in the physical presence of counsel for the other party and the tribunal. Where, as here, alternative means of cross-examination are proposed, to protect against a violation of the procedural due process rights of the other party, the Court would ordinarily need to be satisfied that: (1) at the time the expert report was presented, the Party did not know that the expert would not be available for cross-examination in person due to a prior commitment; (2) there is good reason, by virtue of the nature of the expert's duties at the time of examination, for excusing the expert's physical presence during the hearing; and (3) the alternative means of cross-examination satisfactorily approximates in-person cross-examination.
4. For reasons of liberality and because of the imminence of the hearing, the Court is willing to forego further analysis of requirements (1) and (2) on a *pro hac vice* basis.

5. As to (3), Pakistan offers to present Dr Acreman for cross-examination by telephone link. In the Court's view, cross-examination by telephone link does not satisfactorily approximate in-person cross-examination, as visual contact with the expert, possible in person but not by telephone, is essential for an effective cross-examination.
6. By contrast, the Court is of the view that video-conferencing is, under certain circumstances, an acceptable substitute for in-person cross-examination. By providing a synchronous audio and visual connection between the witness or expert, the cross-examining counsel, and the arbitral tribunal, video-conferencing can potentially approximate the conditions of in-person cross-examination. The Court notes in this regard that cross-examination of expert and fact witnesses by video-conferencing has been allowed in a number of international arbitral hearings. That said, based on the actual conduct of cross-examination by video-conferencing, the weight to be given to testimony made through that medium rests with the Court.
7. Pakistan contends that Dr Acreman is unable to make himself available for video-conferencing because his assignment involves fieldwork (which presumably requires frequent changes of location), the detailed schedule of which will not be known until some time during the week of August 13, 2012. In this context, it appears that video-conferencing could be arranged once Dr Acreman's schedule and itinerary become known. The hearing is scheduled to take place from August 20 to August 31, 2012, and the Court would be prepared to allow Dr Acreman's cross-examination to take place on any weekday from August 20 to 28, provided that advanced notice of at least three working days is given.
8. The Court therefore *denies* Pakistan's Request and urges Pakistan to present Dr Acreman for cross-examination in person or, if not possible, by video-conferencing.
9. Should cross-examination of Dr Acreman occur not in person but through video-conference, the Court reserves the possibility, in the light of the quality of the video link achieved, of deciding to reconvene at a later stage in order to hear Dr Acreman in person. If so reconvened, the attendant cost consequences will follow.[137]

5.140 When testimony is taken by means of telecommunication, the arbitral tribunal and counsel in charge of the witness's examination will typically be at one location, while the witness is at another location, sometimes accompanied by one counsel from each side or the tribunal's secretary so as to ensure that the witness is neither coerced nor prompted. Exceptionally, the tribunal and the parties may choose not to gather in one location at all. Thus, in one PCA-administered case in 2013, witness testimony was successfully taken by video-conference with each party's legal representatives, the three members of the tribunal, the tribunal's secretary, and the witness being in different locations, for a total of seven video connections. One counsel from the side presenting the witness and an interpreter were present in the room with the witness. A court reporter had an audio connection to all participants.

---

[137] *Indus Waters Kishenganga Arbitration*, Pakistan v India, PCA Case No 2011-1 (Indus Waters Treaty 1960), Procedural Order No 10, 15 August 2012, reproduced in Partial Award, 18 February 2013 (footnotes omitted).

M. Experts Appointed by the Arbitral Tribunal—Article 29

1. After consultation with the parties, the arbitral tribunal may appoint one or more independent experts to report to it, in writing, on specific issues to be determined by the arbitral tribunal. A copy of the expert's terms of reference, established by the arbitral tribunal, shall be communicated to the parties.
2. The expert shall, in principle before accepting appointment, submit to the arbitral tribunal and to the parties a description of his or her qualifications and a statement of his or her impartiality and independence. Within the time ordered by the arbitral tribunal, the parties shall inform the arbitral tribunal whether they have any objections as to the expert's qualifications, impartiality or independence. The arbitral tribunal shall decide promptly whether to accept any such objections. After an expert's appointment, a party may object to the expert's qualifications, impartiality or independence only if the objection is for reasons of which the party becomes aware after the appointment has been made. The arbitral tribunal shall decide promptly what, if any, action to take.
3. The parties shall give the expert any relevant information or produce for his or her inspection any relevant documents or goods that he or she may require of them. Any dispute between a party and such expert as to the relevance of the required information or production shall be referred to the arbitral tribunal for decision.
4. Upon receipt of the expert's report, the arbitral tribunal shall communicate a copy of the report to the parties, which shall be given the opportunity to express, in writing, their opinion on the report. A party shall be entitled to examine any document on which the expert relied in his or her report.
5. If a party so requests or if the arbitral tribunal considers it necessary, the expert shall, after delivery of the report, participate in a hearing where the parties have the opportunity to put questions to him or her and to present expert witnesses in order to testify on the points at issue. The provisions of article 28 shall be applicable to such proceedings.

Article 29 provides for the appointment of independent experts by the arbitral tribunal. It is based on Article 29 of the 2010 UNCITRAL Rules and Article 26 of the UNCITRAL Model Law. **5.141**

While parties often appoint arbitrators for their specialized knowledge, complex scientific, technical, or even legal issues may nevertheless arise in an arbitration that are not within the particular expertise of the arbitral tribunal. In such circumstances, the tribunal may benefit from receiving external assistance. Generally, the tribunal will be assisted by expert evidence presented by the parties in accordance with the procedures set out in Articles 27 and 28 of the Rules. Typically, where counsel consider that expert knowledge would be of assistance to the arbitral tribunal, an expert is engaged by a party and instructed to produce a written report that will be submitted to the tribunal. If requested by the opposing party or the tribunal, the author or authors of the expert report will be presented for examination at an oral hearing. Tribunals may also choose to appoint their own expert in the absence of expert evidence from the parties, or in addition to the **5.142** expert evidence presented by the parties, particularly where this expert evidence is incomplete, appears contradictory, or covers a vast amount of data. Article 29 provides a procedure for seeking such assistance.

5.143 Article 29(1) of the Rules provides that the arbitral tribunal may appoint an independent expert to 'report to it, in writing, on specific issues determined by the arbitral tribunal'. By imparting his or her knowledge on a specific issue to the arbitral tribunal with a written report, the tribunal-appointed expert may play a key role in improving the tribunal's understanding of the issues at hand and, if party-appointed experts have also reported on these issues, in facilitating the tribunal's evaluation of any diverging views.

5.144 An expert may also be appointed by the tribunal, not to advise on any issue, but to independently establish certain facts (although, absent agreement by the parties, the expert's factual findings will not be binding on the parties and the tribunal). For example, while it is more common for a tribunal-appointed expert to be asked to opine directly on the valuation of assets, in one PCA-administered investment treaty arbitration conducted under the 2010 UNCITRAL Rules, the tribunal-appointed expert was appointed to document, for the purposes of a later valuation, the state and characteristics of premises that were in danger of being demolished in the immediate future. In accordance with the mandate drafted jointly by the parties, the expert could take photographs and a video, as well as make drawings and take measurements. The expert could also, 'if necessary', prepare a written report which would set out 'objective information with respect to the state of... [the premises], but [would] not attempt to comment on or color the valuation of the property in any way'.

5.145 In a number of inter-state arbitrations held under PCA auspices concerning maritime and territorial delimitation, experts in cartography and hydrography have been appointed by the arbitral tribunal not only to assist it with understanding the technical aspects of the dispute, but also with articulating its ultimate decision in technical terms. In the *Abyei* arbitration, conducted under the PCA State/Non-State Rules (which contain a provision similar to Article 29 of the 2012 PCA Rules),[138] the

[138] Article 27 of the PCA State/Non-State Rules provides:

1. The arbitral tribunal may appoint one or more experts to report to it, in writing, on specific issues to be determined by the tribunal. A copy of the expert's terms of reference, established by the arbitral tribunal, shall be communicated to the parties.
2. The parties shall give the expert any relevant information or produce for his/her inspection any relevant documents or goods that he/she may request of them. Any dispute between a party and such expert as to the relevance and appropriateness of the required information or production shall be referred to the arbitral tribunal for decision.
3. Upon receipt of the expert's report, the arbitral tribunal shall communicate a copy of the report to the parties who shall be given the opportunity to express, in writing, their opinion on the report. A party shall be entitled to examine any document on which the expert has relied in his/her report.

experts' terms of reference specified that they would assist the tribunal 'in defining (i.e. delimiting) on a map the boundaries of the [Abyei area]' and would 'make themselves available to assist the Tribunal as required by it in the preparation of the Award'.[139] Similarly, in *Guyana v Suriname*, a hydrographer was appointed to assist the arbitral tribunal in 'the drawing and explanation of the maritime boundary line or lines in a technically precise manner' as well as in the 'preparation of the Award'.[140] In another PCA-administered inter-state arbitration conducted under the PCA State/State Rules (which also contain a provision similar to Article 29 of the 2012 PCA Rules), the arbitral tribunal anticipated in its first procedural order the possible appointment of an expert whose role would be to provide 'in addition to the functions contemplated in Article 27 of the [PCA State/State Rules], ongoing assistance to the Arbitral Tribunal in respect of any question within the experts' field of expertise that may arise in the course of the proceedings'.[141]

The need for a tribunal-appointed expert may arise at different stages of the arbitral proceeding. In some cases, the tribunal will realize the complexity of the issues only once the parties submit their own expert reports. In other cases, the need may be apparent from the outset. Exceptionally, in the *Abyei* arbitration, the arbitral tribunal appointed experts before the need for their assistance could be confirmed, so as to ensure that, should the need for expert assistance arise, the tribunal would nevertheless be able to meet the short time limits imposed by the parties' arbitration agreement.[142] **5.146**

4. At the request of either party the expert, after delivery of the report, may be heard at a hearing where the parties shall have the opportunity to be present and to interrogate the expert. At this hearing either party may present expert witnesses in order to testify on the points at issue. The provisions of article 25 shall be applicable to such proceedings.

[139] *Abyei Arbitration*, the Government of Sudan/the Sudan People's Liberation Movement/Army, PCA Case No 2008-7 (PCA State/Non-State Rules), Procedural Order No 2, ss 3.1–3.2, reproduced in Award, 22 June 2009, para 77. The arbitral tribunal circulated a draft of the expert's terms of reference to the parties for their comments before the terms of reference were issued by the tribunal as part of a procedural order.

[140] *Guyana v Suriname*, PCA Case No 2004-4, Procedural Order No 6, 27 November 2006, para 2 and Hydrographer's Terms of Reference, s 3.1, reproduced in Award, 17 September 2007, para 108. The arbitral tribunal issued the procedural order containing the expert's terms of reference after consulting the parties (Award, para 108). With respect to tribunal-appointed experts, the rules of procedure in this arbitration provided as follows (Art 11(3)):

> After having obtained the views of the Parties, the Arbitral Tribunal may upon notice to the Parties appoint one or more experts to report to it, in writing, on specific issues to be determined by the Tribunal. A copy of the expert's terms of reference, established by the Arbitral Tribunal, shall be communicated to the Parties.

[141] The arbitral tribunal further provided in its first procedural order that any tribunal-appointed expert 'would be free to attend the hearing and deliberations of the Arbitral Tribunal, as the Arbitral Tribunal deems necessary'.

[142] *Abyei Arbitration*, the Government of Sudan/the Sudan People's Liberation Movement/Army, PCA Case No 2008-7 (PCA State/Non-State Rules), Award, 22 June 2009, paras 75–6. See discussion of the time limits in the *Abyei* arbitration under Art 25.

5.147 Pursuant to Article 29(1) of the Rules, before appointing an expert, the arbitral tribunal must consult the parties and thereafter communicate to them a copy of the expert's terms of reference. Article 29(2) further provides that before being appointed, an expert must communicate to the tribunal and the parties a description of his or her qualifications and a statement of impartiality and independence, whereupon the parties may object to the expert's appointment within a time period set by the arbitral tribunal. If objections are made, the tribunal will take them into consideration in deciding whether to appoint the proposed expert. The consultation requirement of Article 29(1) and the mechanism for party objections under Article 29(2) are innovations of the 2010 UNCITRAL Rules, which were adopted in the 2012 PCA Rules as reflecting the PCA's experience under previous sets of PCA rules, as well as under the 1976 UNCITRAL Rules. Whether or not they are required to do so, arbitral tribunals often consult the parties not only about the question of appointing an expert in principle, but also regarding the expert's identity and mandate. In some cases, the arbitral tribunal will allow the parties an opportunity to choose the expert themselves. In one PCA-administered investment treaty arbitration conducted under the 2010 UNCITRAL Rules, the arbitral tribunal sought to put the choice of the expert in the parties' hands. When the parties were unable to agree on the expert's identity, the arbitral tribunal presented the parties with a list of four candidates and their curricula vitae and selected the expert after considering the parties' comments. The tribunal may also afford the parties an opportunity to comment on a draft of the expert's terms of reference before adopting them.[143] It can be expected that under the 2012 PCA Rules, a tribunal selecting its own expert (rather than allowing the parties to make this choice themselves) will first enquire as to the expert's qualifications, independence, impartiality, availability, and willingness to be appointed, and thereafter provide the expert's curriculum vitae and statement of independence and impartiality to the parties, setting a time period for any objections. Despite the potential for an increased participation by the parties in the procedure for the appointment of an expert under the 2012 PCA Rules, the ultimate decision on whether or not to appoint remains with the tribunal. Moreover, as the Rules provide that the expert's curriculum vitae and declaration of independence and impartiality must be circulated to the tribunal and parties only 'in principle', the arbitral tribunal may in some cases dispense with this requirement, such as when an expert needs to be appointed urgently, for example to examine perishable goods.[144]

5.148 Article 29(3) allows a tribunal expert to request information from the parties in the form of answers to specific questions, documents, or goods for inspection. The expert may also seek to visit the relevant locale. At the close of the hearing in the *Guyana v Suriname* arbitration, the hydrographer appointed by the arbitral tribunal

[143] See eg *Abyei Arbitration*, the Government of Sudan/the Sudan People's Liberation Movement/Army, PCA Case No 2008-7 (PCA State/Non-State Rules), Award, 22 June 2009, paras 75–6.

[144] Report of the UNCITRAL Working Group II (Arbitration and Conciliation) on the work of its 52nd session, 1–5 February 2010, A/CN.9/688, para 54.

requested a clarification from the parties regarding the precise coordinates of a point previously established by a 1936 Mixed Boundary Commission and referred to as 'Marker "B"' in the parties' pleadings.[145] When the parties were unable to provide a satisfactory answer, the arbitral tribunal authorized the hydrographer to visit the relevant site together with the parties' hydrographic experts.[146] After the visit, the hydrographer set forth his findings as to the precise coordinates of Marker 'B' in a written report, which was accepted by the parties with only some typographic corrections.[147] In its award, the tribunal was able to identify the starting point of the disputed maritime boundary in part through reference to the now clearly identified Marker 'B'.[148]

Requests under Article 29(3) should be made to the relevant party with copies to the opposing party, the arbitral tribunal, and the PCA. **5.149**

Pursuant to Article 29(4), the parties are entitled to comment on any written report of the tribunal-appointed expert and to examine any documents on which the expert's report is based. The parties' comments may be submitted separately or with the parties' written submissions (eg replies, rejoinders, post-hearing briefs). **5.150**

Pursuant to Article 29(5), the parties may also question the tribunal-appointed expert at a hearing, and present their own experts on the relevant issues. Terms of reference should remind the expert of the obligation to attend a hearing. Article 29(5) of the 2012 PCA Rules, based on Article 26(2) of the UNCITRAL Model Law,[149] differs from Article 29(5) of the 2010 UNCITRAL Rules in that it provides that the arbitral tribunal may on its own motion request the presence of the tribunal-appointed expert at a hearing. **5.151**

In contrast to a party-appointed expert, who will be remunerated directly by the party hiring it, the tribunal-appointed expert's agreement regarding remuneration will be with the arbitral tribunal itself (subject to review by the Secretary-General **5.152**

[145] *Guyana v Suriname*, PCA Case No 2004-4 (UNCLOS), Award, 17 September 2007, paras 109–10. Marker 'B' had been described by the Mixed Boundary Commission established by the United Kingdom and the Netherlands, colonial predecessors of Guyana and Suriname, respectively, as a point 220 metres distant on an azimuth of 190° from a fixed point on the west bank of the Corentyne River (known as the '1936 Point' or 'Point 61'), where the Mixed Boundary Commission had recommended that the northern end of the land boundary be fixed.

[146] *Guyana v Suriname*, PCA Case No 2004-4 (UNCLOS), Award, 17 September 2007, paras 111–20.

[147] *Guyana v Suriname*, PCA Case No 2004-4 (UNCLOS), Award, 17 September 2007, paras 123–26; Corrected Report on Site Visit, 30 July 2007.

[148] *Guyana v Suriname*, PCA Case No 2004-4 (UNCLOS), Award, 17 September 2007, para 327.

[149] Article 26(2) of the UNCITRAL Model Law provides:

> Unless otherwise agreed by the parties, if a party so requests or if the arbitral tribunal considers it necessary, the expert shall, after delivery of his written or oral report, participate in a hearing where the parties have the opportunity to put questions to him and to present expert witnesses in order to testify on the points at issue.

of the PCA under Article 41 of the Rules).[150] The agreement on remuneration will typically be part of the expert's terms of reference. The expert's fees and expenses are paid from the deposit established by the parties pursuant to Article 43 of the Rules.

N. Default—Article 30

1. If, within the period of time fixed by these Rules or the arbitral tribunal, without showing sufficient cause:
   (a) The claimant has failed to communicate its statement of claim, the arbitral tribunal shall issue an order for the termination of the arbitral proceedings, unless there are remaining matters that may need to be decided and the arbitral tribunal considers it appropriate to do so;
   (b) The respondent has failed to communicate its response to the notice of arbitration or its statement of defence, the arbitral tribunal shall order that the proceedings continue, without treating such failure in itself as an admission of the claimant's allegations; the provisions of this subparagraph also apply to a claimant's failure to submit a defence to a counterclaim or to a claim for the purpose of a set-off.
2. If a party, duly notified under these Rules, fails to appear at a hearing, without showing sufficient cause for such failure, the arbitral tribunal may proceed with the arbitration.
3. If a party, duly invited by the arbitral tribunal to produce documents, exhibits or other evidence, fails to do so within the established period of time, without showing sufficient cause for such failure, the arbitral tribunal may make the award on the evidence before it.

5.153 Article 30 deals with situations where a party in some way fails to participate in the proceedings.

5.154 This provision replicates the text of Article 30 of the 2010 UNCITRAL Rules.

5.155 Article 30(1)(a) states that the consequence of a claimant's failure to communicate its statement of claim in a timely manner, without showing sufficient cause, is the termination of the arbitral proceedings. The claimant is the arbitration's driving force; the proceedings would not be taking place had the claimant not initiated them. A claimant's failure to file a statement of claim can therefore be seen as tantamount to a withdrawal of its claims. The arbitral tribunal may terminate the proceedings upon the respondent's request or on its own motion.

5.156 However, the arbitral tribunal may also delay the termination of the proceedings if it considers that it needs to decide 'remaining matters', such as a counterclaim or a claim for the costs of the arbitration that the respondent wishes to pursue. Moreover, a termination order, in principle, ends the arbitral proceedings without

[150] See discussion under Art 41.

deciding any claims and therefore does not have *res judicata* effect, leaving the claimant free to initiate a new arbitration dealing with the same dispute at a later time. To prevent abuse, the arbitral tribunal may also decide as 'remaining matters' substantive issues related to the claimant's claim on which the parties have already had a reasonable opportunity to express their views.[151] In practice, awards on such substantive matters should be rare in the absence of a statement of claim, as this document is usually the first submission to set out the claimant's claim in detail.

Other failures to participate by the claimant (such as failing to file other requested written submissions within the prescribed period without showing sufficient cause, or being generally unresponsive) may also lead to the termination of the proceedings under Article 36(2) of the Rules, which provides for termination in cases where 'the continuation of the arbitral proceedings becomes unnecessary or impossible for any reason [other than the parties agreeing on a settlement of the dispute]'. **5.157**

Article 30(1)(b) provides that when a respondent fails to file a response to the notice of arbitration or a statement of defence the arbitral tribunal may decide to continue with the arbitral proceedings. This continuation may mean progressing directly to the next scheduled step of the arbitration, or that some scheduled steps will be skipped. For example, in a PCA-administered investment treaty arbitration conducted under the 1976 UNCITRAL Rules,[152] in which the respondent failed to file a statement of defence in a timely manner despite several extensions granted by the arbitral tribunal, and where the initial procedural calendar provided for the successive filing of two additional written statements by each party after the filing of the statement of defence, the arbitral tribunal ordered the continuation of the proceedings, confirmed that the next step would be for the claimant to file its next pleading, and further indicated that, should the respondent fail to indicate its intention to reply to the claimant's factual and legal allegations within 30 days of the filing of the claimant's pleading, the tribunal would proceed to the oral hearing, skipping the previously scheduled three additional written submissions. Ultimately, the respondent did respond to the claimant's allegations and both parties made subsequent written submissions. While an unjustified failure to file a statement of defence does not, as this example illustrates, necessarily prevent the respondent from denying the claimant's allegations at a later stage, it may prejudice the respondent's ability to file a counterclaim. Pursuant to Article 21(3) of the Rules, a counterclaim may be filed **5.158**

[151] Report of the UNCITRAL Working Group II (Arbitration and Conciliation) on the work of its 51st session, 14–18 September 2009, A/CN.9/684, paras 22–3.

[152] Article 28(1) of the 1976 UNCITRAL Rules also provides that '[i]f, within the period of time fixed by the arbitral tribunal, the respondent has failed to communicate his statement of defence without showing sufficient cause for such failure, the arbitral tribunal shall order that the proceedings continue'.

after the due date of the statement of defence only if the arbitral tribunal decides that the delay is 'justified under the circumstances'. In one PCA-administered investment treaty arbitration, a change of government in the respondent state resulted in an extension granted by the arbitral tribunal. Whatever the obstacle faced by the respondent in filing its submissions, the arbitral tribunal will expect the respondent to take appropriate steps to remove this obstacle in a timely manner. Some purported justifications for delay are likely to be met with scepticism, such as the invocation by a state party of an anti-arbitration injunction rendered by its own courts to justify its failure to participate.[153]

5.159 Pursuant to Article 30(2), the arbitral tribunal may 'proceed with the arbitration' should a party fail to appear at a hearing. In other words, the arbitral tribunal may hold the hearing in the absence of the party that has failed to appear, and then continue the proceedings, either requesting further written comments from the parties or rendering a decision on the subject-matter of the hearing. When a party fails to appear, transcripts or audio recordings of the hearing may be circulated to the parties, allowing the absent party an opportunity to comment. Arbitral tribunals invoke Article 30(2) not only in any cases where a party fails to participate in a hearing on substantive issues, but also when a party is absent from a scheduled meeting with the tribunal, such as a procedural conference. For example, in one PCA-administered investment treaty arbitration, the arbitral tribunal relied on Article 28(2) of the 1976 UNCITRAL Rules, which is identical to Article 30(2) of the 2012 PCA Rules, to hold a first procedural conference in the absence of the respondent. At the procedural conference, a draft procedural order fixing the place of arbitration, the timetable for the arbitration, and other procedural matters was prepared by the tribunal in consultation with the claimant alone. In that case, the arbitral tribunal afforded the respondent another opportunity to comment on the procedural matters in question by inviting its views on the draft procedural order following the first procedural conference.

5.160 Under the 2012 PCA Rules, a respondent's failure to file written submissions, appear at a hearing, or otherwise participate in the arbitral proceedings is not interpreted as an acceptance of the claimant's claims. In cases of default, the burden and standard of proof remain as they would be if both parties were participating fully. In an innovation from the equivalent provision of the 1976 UNCITRAL Rules, Article 30(1)(b) specifically states that a respondent's failure to file a response to the notice of arbitration or a statement of defence should not in itself be treated as 'an admission of the claimant's allegations'. Accordingly, in the absence of participation by the respondent in the proceeding, the arbitral tribunal must weigh the evidence presented to it by the claimant and may adopt a more inquisitorial style

[153] See eg *Himpurna California Energy Ltd Republic of Indonesia*, Interim Award, 26 September 1999, (2000) XXV YB Comm Arb 112, paras 107–15.

in testing the evidence than it otherwise would. Thus, in one PCA-administered investment treaty arbitration conducted under the 1976 UNCITRAL Rules, the arbitral tribunal stated in a letter to the parties that 'should the Respondent choose not to reply to the Claimant's factual allegations or legal arguments, the Tribunal may direct specific questions to the Claimant or request that additional evidence regarding certain factual allegations be adduced prior to the hearing'. In another PCA-administered investment treaty arbitration conducted under the 1976 UNCITRAL Rules, in which the respondent failed to appear at the hearing, the tribunal tested the claimant's allegations by questioning the claimant and three of its six witnesses.

Pursuant to Article 30(3), the consequence of a party's failure to produce evidence as ordered by the arbitral tribunal is that the tribunal may decide on the evidence before it. The case where a party fails to produce evidence because it is not participating in the arbitral proceedings is thus dealt with consistently with the remainder of Article 30: the arbitral tribunal can continue the proceedings and render an award despite the default. In addition, as explained under Article 27, where a party has otherwise participated in the proceedings, but is thought to be withholding relevant documents that it has under its control, the arbitral tribunal may draw adverse inferences as to the content of these documents. **5.161**

The consequences of a failure by the parties to advance the requested amounts for the payment of the fees and expenses of arbitrators, tribunal-appointed experts, and the PCA are addressed in Article 43 of the Rules. **5.162**

O. Closure of Proceedings—Article 31

1. When it is satisfied that the parties have had a reasonable opportunity to present their cases, the arbitral tribunal shall declare the proceedings closed.
2. The arbitral tribunal may, if it considers it necessary owing to exceptional circumstances, decide, on its own initiative or upon application of a party, to reopen the proceedings at any time before the award is made.

Article 31 provides for the mandatory closure and possible reopening of the proceedings by the arbitral tribunal. **5.163**

This provision improves upon Article 31 of the 2010 UNCITRAL Rules in three respects. **5.164**

First, a global terminological change has been introduced: where Article 31 of the 2010 UNCITRAL Rules refers to the closure and reopening of 'hearings', Article 31 of the 2012 PCA Rules refers more precisely to the closure and reopening of the 'proceedings'. The thrust of the two provisions is the same—by declaring under either set of rules that the 'hearings' or 'proceedings' are closed, the arbitral tribunal communicates to the parties that the time for argument and the **5.165** submission of evidence, whether in writing or orally, is over, and that the tribunal will now focus on its deliberations. However, because the reference in the 2010 UNCITRAL Rules to the closure of 'hearings' could be misconstrued as referring to the closure of any oral hearing, rather than to the conclusion of all submissions from the parties,[154] the expression 'closure of proceedings' was adopted in the 2012 PCA Rules.

5.166 Second, Article 31(1) of the 2010 UNCITRAL Rules—'The arbitral tribunal may inquire with the parties if they have any further proof to offer or witnesses to be heard or submissions to make and, if there are none, it may declare the hearings closed'—is modified to read: 'When it is satisfied that the parties have had a reasonable opportunity to present their cases, the arbitral tribunal shall declare the proceedings closed'. The latter formulation, which is similar to Article 22(1) of the 1998 ICC Rules of Arbitration,[155] clarifies that it is for the arbitral tribunal rather than the parties to decide whether or not the time to close the proceedings has come. The primary purpose of this provision is 'to prevent proceedings from dragging on indefinitely once each of the parties has had a reasonable opportunity to present its case'.[156] While Article 31(1) of the 2010 UNCITRAL Rules (as well as the corresponding provision of the 1976 UNCITRAL Rules) has generally been understood to mean that the arbitral tribunal is free to declare the proceedings closed when it chooses, including against the objections of a party, provided the parties have been consulted,[157] a literal reading of this provision could suggest that the proceedings may be closed only once the parties have confirmed that they do not 'have any further proof to offer or witnesses to be heard or submissions to make'. Under such an interpretation, a party could significantly delay the issuance of an award by claiming that it has further evidence to present or arguments to make, thus contradicting the fundamental principle, stated in Article 17(1) of the 2012 PCA Rules, that the parties are entitled to a 'reasonable', but not infinite, opportunity to present their case, and that it is for the arbitral tribunal to decide whether such reasonable opportunity has been afforded in the circumstances. An arbitral tribunal will usually declare the proceedings closed once the parties have had the opportunity to make all the written and oral submissions foreseen

---

[154] Caron and Caplan (n 92), 625, thus call the title of Art 31 of the 2010 UNCITRAL Rules—'Closure of hearings'—'something of a misnomer'.

[155] Article 22(1) of the 1998 ICC Rules of Arbitration provides:

> When it is satisfied that the parties have had a reasonable opportunity to present their cases, the Arbitral Tribunal shall declare the proceedings closed. Thereafter, no further submission or argument may be made, or evidence produced, unless requested or authorized by the Arbitral Tribunal.

[156] Yves Derains and Eric A Schwartz, *Guide to the ICC Rules of Arbitration* (2nd edn, Kluwer Law International, 2005) 291.

[157] See eg Report of the UNCITRAL Working Group II (Arbitration and Conciliation) on the work of its 51st session, 14–18 September 2009, A/CN.9/684, para 34.

in the procedural calendar adopted by the arbitral tribunal in accordance with Article 17(3) of the Rules, as well as any post-hearing submissions authorized by the tribunal.

Third, the 2012 PCA Rules give the closure of proceedings a mandatory character, which contrasts with its optional character under the 2010 UNCITRAL Rules.[158] The PCA Drafting Committee considered that a formal declaration of closure can be useful in every case to ensure that the parties are aware of the status of the proceedings, as well as to prevent proceedings from dragging on due to the submission of additional unsolicited evidence or arguments. While the Rules mandate the arbitral tribunal to declare the proceedings closed only once the parties have had a reasonable opportunity to present their cases, where proceedings are divided into several phases, such as when they are bifurcated between a jurisdiction and a merits phase, the arbitral tribunal may find it helpful to separately declare the closure of each phase of the proceedings at the appropriate time. The arbitral tribunal may also chose to first inform the parties that the evidentiary record is closed, while giving them a further opportunity to make legal arguments. **5.167**

Article 31(2) of the 2012 PCA Rules replicates the text of Article 31(2) of the 2010 UNCITRAL Rules (save that, as explained above, the term 'proceedings' is substituted for 'hearings' throughout Article 31), which, in turn, mostly follows the text of the equivalent provision of the 1976 UNCITRAL Rules. These provisions recognize that exceptional circumstances may justify the reopening of the proceedings, and the acceptance of additional evidence. They have rarely been invoked in PCA-administered arbitrations. **5.168**

P. Waiver of Right to Object—Article 32

> A failure by any party to object promptly to any non-compliance with these Rules or with any requirement of the arbitration agreement shall be deemed to be a waiver of the right of such party to make such an objection, unless such party can show that, under the circumstances, its failure to object was justified.

Article 32 concerns the timing of any objections by the parties on the basis that the arbitral proceedings are not in compliance with the Rules or the parties' arbitration agreement. This provision reproduces Article 32 of the 2010 UNCITRAL Rules. **5.169**

[158] Other sets of procedural rules adopt the same approach as the 2012 PCA Rules. See eg *Eritrea-Ethiopia Boundary Commission*, PCA Case No 2001-1 (Rules of Procedure based on PCA State/State Rules): 'At the end of the hearings, the Commission will declare the hearings closed'; ICSID Arbitration Rules, rule 38: 'When the presentation of the case by the parties is completed, the proceeding shall be declared closed'; 2012 ICC Rules: 'As soon as possible after the last hearing concerning matters to be decided in an award or the filing of the last authorized submissions concerning such matters, whichever is later, the arbitral tribunal *shall*: a) declare the proceedings closed with respect to the matters to be decided in the award…' (emphasis added).

5.170 The procedure for the appointment of the arbitral tribunal and the tribunal's power to conduct proceedings are circumscribed by the terms of the parties' arbitration agreement and any agreed rules of procedure. A party is therefore entitled to object during the arbitral proceedings if it considers that there has been any non-compliance with the arbitration agreement or the procedural rules.

5.171 Article 32 requires that such objections be made promptly, preventing disruption of the proceedings through belated objections. Because a failure to object in a timely manner will, in the absence of a justification, be considered a waiver of the right to object on the basis that 'the composition of the arbitral tribunal or the arbitral procedure was not in accordance with the agreement of the parties', this ground for setting aside awards or for resisting recognition or enforcement will not be available to a party who has not made its complaint known to the arbitral tribunal (or the appointing authority) in a timely manner.[159] To avoid surprises, an arbitral tribunal will often ask the parties at the end of a hearing (shortly before the time when the arbitral proceedings will be declared closed under Article 31) whether they have objections to the manner in which the proceedings have been conducted.[160]

[159] This objection may be available where the New York Convention is applicable, or in UNCITRAL Model Law jurisdictions (New York Convention, 10 June 1958, 330 UNTS 38, Art V; UNCITRAL Model Law, Arts 34, 36). In arbitrations involving only states or intergovernmental organizations, however, the parties in any event have likely not submitted to the jurisdiction of any national courts by virtue of their agreement to arbitrate (see discussion under Art 1(2)).

[160] See eg *Romak SA v The Republic of Uzbekistan*, PCA Case No 2007-7 (Switzerland–Uzbekistan BIT) (1976 UNCITRAL Rules), Award, 26 November 2009, para 88.

6

SECTION IV. THE AWARD

A. Decisions—Article 33

(a) When there is more than one arbitrator, any award or other decision of the arbitral tribunal shall be made by a majority of the arbitrators.
(b) In the case of questions of procedure, when there is no majority or when the arbitral tribunal so authorizes, the presiding arbitrator may decide alone, subject to revision, if any, by the arbitral tribunal.

Article 33 provides for decision-making by an arbitral tribunal of more than one person. **6.01**

This provision replicates Article 33 of the 2010 UNCITRAL Rules, which itself follows the text of Article 31 of the 1976 UNCITRAL Rules with only minor revisions.[1] **6.02**

[1] First, in Art 33(1) of the 2012 PCA Rules and 2010 UNCITRAL Rules, the introductory phrase of Art 31(1) of the 1976 UNCITRAL Rules—'[w]hen there are three arbitrators'—has been replaced by the phrase '[w]hen there is more than one arbitrator' to encompass cases where the number of arbitrators is other than one or three (a possibility foreseen in Art 10(2) of the 2010 UNCITRAL Rules). Second, contrary to Art 31(2) of the 1976 UNCITRAL Rules, which provides that in certain circumstances the presiding arbitrator may decide 'on his own', Art 33(2) of the 2012 PCA Rules and Art 33(2) of the 2010 UNCITRAL Rules provide that the presiding arbitrator can decide 'alone'. This cosmetic change does not affect the meaning of the provision.

6.03 Article 33(1) sets out the general rule pursuant to which the arbitral tribunal's decisions must be made by majority, while Article 33(2) provides the exception allowing the presiding arbitrator to decide alone in certain circumstances on 'questions of procedure'.

6.04 The majority rule of Article 33(1) is typical in international arbitration, appearing in national arbitration legislation[2] and rules of procedure alike,[3] although with various exceptions. In the Rules, the majority rule admits no exception, save as regards 'questions of procedure'. No alternative decision-making rule is provided to deal with an arbitral tribunal's potential inability to reach a majority decision, for example where each of the three members of the tribunal holds a different view as to what the decision of the tribunal should be. Article 31(1) thus imports an obligation for the arbitral tribunal to deliberate and reach a majority decision on all substantive matters. During the revision of the UNCITRAL Rules, text that would have allowed the presiding arbitrator to decide alone in all cases where the arbitral tribunal was not able to reach a majority decision was considered, but ultimately rejected.[4] Such an alternative rule for substantive matters was also left out of the 2012 PCA Rules. Provisions allowing presiding arbitrators to take substantive decisions alone in case of deadlock are not uncommon in rules of procedure designed primarily for arbitration between private parties.[5] For UN Member States represented on the UNCITRAL Working Group, however, such a provision raised the concern that presiding arbitrators might ignore the views of the party-appointed arbitrators, thereby decreasing or eliminating the role of the deliberative process in the tribunal's decision-making. This concern was shared by the PCA Drafting Committee, in particular with respect to cases involving states,

[2] For example, legislation in UNCITRAL Model Law jurisdictions provides that '[i]n arbitral proceedings with more than one arbitrator, any decision of the arbitral tribunal shall be made, unless otherwise agreed by the parties, by a majority of all its members'.

[3] See eg *ARA Libertad Arbitration*, Argentina v Ghana, PCA Case No 2013-11 (UNCLOS), Rules of Procedure, Art 20: 'Decisions of the Arbitral Tribunal, both on procedure and substance, shall be taken by a majority vote of its members, except that questions of administration or routine procedure may be decided by the President of the Arbitral Tribunal, unless the President wishes to have the opinion of the other members of the Arbitral Tribunal or the Parties request a decision of the full Arbitral Tribunal'; UNCLOS, Annex VII, Art 8: 'Decisions of an arbitral tribunal shall be taken by a majority vote of its members'; Iran-United States Claims Tribunal, Rules of Procedure, Art 30(1): 'When there are three arbitrators, any award or other decision of the arbitral tribunal shall be made by a majority of arbitrators'; 2012 ICC Rules, Art 31(1): 'When the arbitral tribunal is composed of more than one arbitrator, an award is made by a majority decision'.

[4] UNCITRAL Working Group II (Arbitration and Conciliation), *Note by the Secretariat: Settlement of commercial disputes: Revision of the UNCITRAL Arbitration Rules*, 49th session, 15–19 September 2008, A/CN.9/WG.II/WP/151/Add.1, para 22.

[5] ICC Rules, Art 31(1): 'If there is no majority, the award shall be made by the president of the arbitral tribunal alone'; LCIA Rules 1998, Art 26.3: 'Failing a majority decision on any issue, the chairman of the Arbitral Tribunal shall decide that issue'.

where the public perception of the legitimacy of arbitral awards is more relevant than in disputes involving exclusively private parties.[6]

Practice under the UNCITRAL Rules shows that the concern with unresolvable deadlocks is largely theoretical, as arbitral tribunals usually succeed in reaching majority decisions.[7] **6.05**

An exception to the majority rule is found in Article 33(2) for decisions concerning 'questions of procedure'. Pursuant to this provision, the presiding arbitrator is empowered to decide alone when there is no majority. The arbitral tribunal may also delegate its decision-making power to the presiding arbitrator. For example, an arbitral tribunal may insert a provision in an early procedural order, authorizing the presiding arbitrator to take procedural decisions alone in all cases, or only in urgent cases, or where the co-arbitrators cannot be reached in a timely manner. A decision taken by the presiding arbitrator alone is subject to subsequent revision by the full tribunal, although this is a rare occurrence. The possibility of revision may be useful where the presiding arbitrator was originally unable to reach his colleagues, but is later faced with their united disagreement. Provided the issue has not yet been overtaken by events, the full tribunal, or a majority composed of the co-arbitrators, can then modify the earlier decision. **6.06**

[6] Notably, the ICJ Statute does not provide any alternative decision-making rule to deal with deadlocks (see Art 55). The role of the majority rule in the deliberative process is clear in the precedent of the Iran–United States Claims Tribunal. See eg *Economy Forms Corporation and Government of the Islamic Republic of Iran*, Award No 55-165-1, 20 June 1983, Concurring Opinion of Howard Holtzmann, reprinted in (1983) 3 Iran-US CTR 55, 55: 'I concur in the Award in this Case. The Award correctly holds that... Unfortunately, however, the damages awarded are only about half of what the governing law requires. Why then do I concur in this inadequate Award, rather than dissenting from it? The answer is based on the realistic old saying that there are circumstances in which "something is better than nothing"... My colleague Dr. Kahani having dissented, I am faced with the choice of either joining in the present Award or accepting the prospect of an indefinite postponement of the Award in this Case... The deliberations in this case have continued long enough... Neither the parties nor the Tribunal will, in my view, benefit from further delay'; *Starrett Housing Corp v Government of the Islamic Republic of Iran*, Interlocutory Award No ITL 32-24-1, 20 December 1983, Concurring Opinion of Howard Holtzmann reprinted in (1983-III) 4 Iran-US CTR 122: 'I concur with reluctance in the Interlocutory Award in this case. I do so in order to form a majority for the key finding that... My concurrence is reluctant because the Interlocutory Award sets the date of taking far later than when it actually occurred. The Interlocutory Award also contains a number of errors'; *Shahin Shaine Ebrahimi v Government of the Islamic Republic of Iran*, Award No 560-44/46/47-3, Separate Opinion of Richard C Allison, 12 October 1994, reprinted in (1994) 30 Iran-US CTR 170, para 1: 'I concur in the result reached in the Award in these Cases in order to form the requisite majority. As set forth herein, however, there are elements of the Award's reasoning with which I cannot agree'.

[7] A deadlock has yet to occur in a PCA-administered case. Under the ICC Rules, which allow the presiding arbitrator to decide alone in case of deadlock, such decisions are 'extremely rare' (Yves Derains and Eric A Schwartz, *Guide to the ICC Rules of Arbitration* (2nd edn, Kluwer Law International, 2005) 306). The effect of such a provision is in fact more likely to be felt within the tribunal, where the presiding arbitrator will possess enhanced power, rather than seen in awards made by the presiding arbitrator alone.

B. Form and Effect of the Award—Article 34

1. The arbitral tribunal may make separate awards on different issues at different times.
2. All awards shall be made in writing and shall be final and binding on the parties. The parties shall carry out all awards without delay.
3. The arbitral tribunal shall state the reasons upon which the award is based, unless the parties have agreed that no reasons are to be given.
4. An award shall be signed by the arbitrators and it shall contain the date on which the award was made and indicate the place of arbitration. Where there is more than one arbitrator and any of them fails to sign, the award shall state the reason for the absence of the signature.
5. An award may be made public with the consent of all parties or where and to the extent disclosure is required of a party by legal duty, to protect or pursue a legal right or in relation to legal proceedings before a court or other competent authority.
6. Copies of the award signed by the arbitrators shall be communicated to the parties by the International Bureau.
7. In cases involving only States, the parties shall communicate to the International Bureau the laws, regulations, or other documents evidencing the execution of the award.

6.07 Article 34 addresses the form and effect of arbitral awards.

6.08 This provision follows the text of Article 34 of the 2010 UNCITRAL Rules, with a minor change to Article 34(6) and the addition of Article 34(7).

6.09 Article 34(1) recognizes the arbitral tribunal's power to make multiple 'separate' awards in the course of a single arbitration. The awards must decide different issues, each award having the force of *res judicata* with respect to the issues it decides, in accordance with Article 34(2). Separate awards are often rendered in cases where the arbitral tribunal has divided the proceedings into separate phases. For example, an arbitral tribunal will render separate awards on jurisdiction (and sometimes admissibility) and the merits of the case if it has decided to rule on jurisdictional objections as a preliminary question (as envisaged in Article 23(3) of the Rules).[8] Alternatively, the arbitral tribunal may choose to first hear the parties and rule on liability, before proceeding to hear the parties and rule on quantum. In these cases, the division of issues may significantly shorten the proceedings if the decision in the first award obviates the need for a second award (a decision on merits being needed only if the tribunal finds that it has jurisdiction, and a decision on quantum, only if there is liability).[9] While these are the most common scenarios,

---

[8] See eg *Achmea BV (formerly known as 'Eureko BV') v The Slovak Republic*, PCA Case No 2008-14 (Netherlands–Czech and Slovak Republic BIT) (1976 UNICTRAL Rules), Award on Jurisdiction, Arbitrability and Suspension, 26 October 2010, para 20 and Final Award, 7 December 2012.

[9] In some cases, bifurcation of proceedings may enhance efficiency, while in others, where issues are common to the decisions to be taken, it may be more efficient to decide all matters in a single award. See discussion of bifurcation between merits and jurisdiction under Art 23.

an arbitral tribunal may choose to rule separately on any substantive issue. In some cases, it only becomes clear that separate awards are appropriate after the tribunal has had the benefit of written and oral pleadings by the parties. For example, in the PCA-administered *Indus Waters Kishenganga Arbitration*, the arbitral tribunal issued a 'partial' award, in which it decided most of the issues in dispute, but, finding that it was missing crucial information, requested the parties to make further submissions on one specific issue, which it left to be decided in a 'final' award.[10] Arbitral tribunals have also rendered separate awards on interim measures,[11] although, where relevant,[12] national arbitration legislation takes varying approaches to recognition and enforcement of such awards.[13]

Article 34(2) requires that arbitral awards be made in writing. It also provides that arbitral awards are 'final and binding on the parties'. In agreeing to arbitration, parties submit their disputes to the arbitral tribunal for final resolution. Arbitral awards under the Rules are final in the sense that, once rendered, they acquire the force of *res judicata* with respect to the issues they decide. Except for the purposes of interpretation and correction as provided for in Articles 37 and 38 of the Rules, which assist tribunals in giving effect to their decisions rather than changing them, the Rules do not foresee any revisiting by the arbitral tribunal of an award that has already been rendered.[14] Where national legislation is applicable,[15] limited recourse against arbitral awards may be available before national courts in setting aside proceedings.[16] **6.10**

In agreeing to arbitration, parties also recognize the binding nature of arbitral awards and undertake to 'carry out awards without delay'. The parties thus manifest their willingness to execute in good faith any award rendered by the arbitral tribunal. Notably, the 1899 Hague Convention already provided that '[t]he **6.11**

[10] See eg *Indus Waters Kishenganga Arbitration*, Pakistan v India, PCA Case No 2011-1 (Indus Waters Treaty 1960), Partial Award, 18 February 2013.

[11] See eg *1 Chevron Corporation and 2 Texaco Petroleum Company v The Republic of Ecuador*, PCA Case No 2009-23 (US–Ecuador BIT), First Interim Award on Interim Measures, 25 January 2012; Second Interim Award on Interim Measures, 16 February 2012, reproduced in David D Caron and Lee M Caplan, *The UNCITRAL Arbitration Rules: A Commentary* (2nd edn, Oxford University Press, 2013) 541–3.

[12] In cases involving only states and intergovernmental organizations, the parties in any event will likely not have submitted to the jurisdiction of any national courts by virtue of their agreement to arbitrate (see discussion under Art 1(2)).

[13] For a detailed discussion of the recognition and enforcement of decisions on interim measures, see Gary B Born, *International Commercial Arbitration*, vol 2 (Wolters Kluwer, 2009) 2019–28.

[14] However, certain national arbitration laws allow tribunals to revise substantive findings of previously-rendered awards when evidence is later produced of fraud, forgery, or concealment of evidence. Fraud, for example, is a basis for revision under French and Swiss law (see *Sovereign Participants International SA v Chadmore Developments Limited* (2001) XXVI YB Comm Arb 299 at 301*ff*; Cass Civ 1re, 25 May 1992, *Fougerolle v Procofrance* [1992] JDI 974).

[15] On the applicability of national legislation to arbitrations involving only states or intergovernmental organizations, see discussion under Art 1(2).

[16] See eg UNCITRAL Model Law, Art 34.

Arbitration Convention implies the engagement to submit loyally to the Award'.[17] In arbitrations between states and intergovernmental organizations on the one hand, and private parties on the other hand, as well as in arbitrations involving exclusively private parties, parties may generally seek the recognition and enforcement of arbitral awards before national courts. The terms on which such recognition and enforcement can be sought in most jurisdictions are found in Article V of the New York Convention, which to date has been adopted by 148 states.[18] In inter-state arbitration, each state's commitment to the peaceful resolution of international disputes and the rule of law is relied upon to assure voluntary compliance with arbitral awards. As arbitral jurisdiction is based on consent, states agreeing to arbitration (particularly after a dispute has arisen) should already have determined that even an adverse award in a fair arbitral proceeding is preferable to having the dispute left unresolved.

6.12 Like the 2010 UNCITRAL Rules, the 2012 PCA Rules contain in an annex a possible waiver of the parties' 'right to any form of recourse against an award to any court or other competent authority', which the parties may include in their arbitration agreement.[19] Where national legislation applies,[20] it will determine the effect of the waiver, as in some jurisdictions certain recourse against arbitral awards will be mandatory and therefore not waivable.[21]

6.13 Reasoned decisions, as required by Article 34(3), reassure parties that the arbitrators have given due attention to their pleadings and have not acted in an arbitrary manner. A decision about which party prevailed on a particular issue derives its legitimacy through a comprehensible explanation of why that party prevailed. In inter-state arbitration, these reasons sustain the political will to fulfill legal obligations. Reasons are also required in cases where enforcement is sought under the

---

[17] Article 18.

[18] See up-to-date list of parties to the New York Convention at <http://www.uncitral.org/uncitral/en/uncitral_texts/arbitration/NYConvention_status.html>.

[19] The annex to the Rules provides as follows:

> *Note—If the parties wish to exclude recourse against the arbitral award that may be available under the applicable law, they may consider adding a provision to that effect as suggested below, considering, however, that the effectiveness and conditions of such an exclusion depend on the applicable law.*
>
> Waiver: The parties hereby waive their right to any form of recourse against an award to any court or competent authority, insofar as such waiver can validly be made under the applicable law.

[20] On the applicability of national legislation in the context of arbitrations involving only states or intergovernmental organizations, see discussion under Art 1(2).

[21] For example, under the English Arbitration Act 1996, parties including the proposed waiver in their arbitration agreement would be waiving their right to appeal points of law before an English court, but not their right to a recourse against an award on the basis of 'serious [procedural] irregularity' (see Arts 68 and 69).

New York Convention or where an effort to set aside an award is made pursuant to national arbitration legislation.[22]

Parties may, however, agree to dispense with reasons in the award. This is most commonly done when the parties have reached a settlement of their dispute through negotiations conducted separate from, but in parallel with, the arbitration. The arbitral tribunal may then be requested to record the settlement as an arbitral award (an 'award on agreed terms' or 'award by consent').[23] Dispensing with reasons allows the tribunal to proceed quickly with the issuance of an award, which may set forth the terms of the settlement or incorporate the terms of the settlement agreement by reference. Often, settlement agreements contain terms considered confidential by the parties, but before signing any award most tribunals will wish to review any settlement terms to be incorporated by reference in the award to be sure that they raise no public policy concerns. **6.14**

Pursuant to Article 34(4), an arbitral award must also be signed by the members of the arbitral tribunal, and indicate the place of arbitration and the date on which it was made. As provided in Article 18(1) of the Rules, the award shall be deemed to have been made at the place of arbitration.[24] The award may in fact be signed at any location convenient to the arbitrators. In cases where the tribunal decides by majority, the dissenting arbitrator typically signs, adding 'dissenting' next to his name.[25] If the dissenting arbitrator refuses to sign or an arbitrator is otherwise unable to sign, the 2012 PCA Rules require that an explanation be provided in the award.[26] If an arbitrator prepares a dissenting opinion, it does not form part of the arbitral award. The majority on the tribunal must decide in what manner a dissenting opinion is to be communicated to the parties.[27] Where national **6.15**

[22] A failure to comply with the requirement of the Rules that awards be reasoned may lead to a refusal of recognition or enforcement or the setting aside of the award on the ground that the 'arbitral procedure was not in accordance with the agreement of the parties' (New York Convention, Art V(d); UNCITRAL Model Law, Art 34(2)(a)(iv)).

[23] For a discussion of awards on agreed terms, see under Art 36.

[24] The consequences of the choice of a place of arbitration are discussed under Art 18.

[25] See eg the award in the *Abyei* arbitration, which was signed by Judge Al-Khasawneh with the mention 'I dissent' underneath his signature (*Abyei Arbitration*, the Government of Sudan/the Sudan People's Liberation Movement/Army, PCA Case No 2008-7 (PCA State/Non-State Rules), Award, 22 June 2009).

[26] For example, in an award rendered in a PCA-administered investment arbitration conducted under the 1976 UNCITRAL Rules, the arbitral tribunal indicated, below the empty signature block of one of the arbitrators: '[i]n a letter to the Presiding Arbitrator dated..., [the dissenting arbitrator] indicated that he would not sign the [award] as he did not agree with the majority of the Arbitral Tribunal. [The dissenting arbitrator] participated in all aspects of the deliberation process'. The arbitrator who had refused to sign the award subsequently issued a reasoned dissent.

[27] While relatively rare in PCA experience, dissents in inter-state arbitrations have usually been communicated to the parties at the same time as the award (see eg *OSPAR Arbitration*, Ireland v United Kingdom, PCA Case No 2001-3, where a separate and a dissenting opinion were communicated as attachments to the final award).

legislation applies,[28] tribunals will have to take this into account when dealing with the dissent.[29]

6.16 Although the requirement that the registrar must sign any awards of the arbitral tribunal, set out in Article 79 of the 1907 Hague Convention,[30] was omitted from later sets of PCA procedural rules and does not appear in the 2012 PCA Rules, it remains the practice for the PCA staff member appointed as registrar in an inter-state arbitration to sign any award rendered by the tribunal.[31] The purpose of this signature is to certify the authenticity of the award.[32]

6.17 Article 34(5) provides the basic rule of confidentiality of the award, which can only be reversed by agreement of the parties or 'where and to the extent disclosure is required of a party by legal duty, to protect or pursue a legal right or in relation to legal proceedings before a court or other competent authority'. Publication of awards in inter-state arbitration is standard, while in other PCA-administered arbitrations a small but growing proportion of awards are made public by consent of the parties.[33] The UNCITRAL Rules on Transparency in Treaty-based Investor-State Arbitration, adopted on 11 July 2013 and to become effective on 1 April 2014, may increase a trend toward public access to documents, third party participation, and award publication.[34] Parties to an investment treaty arbitration may agree to apply the Rules on Transparency to cases under the 2012 PCA Rules.

6.18 Article 34(6) provides that the signed award will be circulated to the parties by the International Bureau of the PCA. This rule is based on the 1990s PCA Rules[35] and reflects practice in PCA-administered cases. Typically, an award will be signed by the arbitrators in multiple originals. These originals, once signed by all the members of the arbitral tribunal, are communicated by the arbitrator who signed last to

---

[28] On the applicability of national legislation in the context of arbitrations involving only states or intergovernmental organizations, see discussion under Art 1(2).

[29] While the Rules implicitly allow dissenting opinions, national arbitration legislation may not. The UNCITRAL Working Group thus notes that 'the question of whether an arbitrator may add his dissenting opinion to the award is left for decision to the law applicable at the place of arbitration' (UNCITRAL, 9th Session, Addendum 1, A/CN.9/112/Add.1, n 97).

[30] Reproduced in Appendix III.

[31] See eg *Indus Waters Kishenganga Arbitration*, Pakistan v India, PCA Case No 2011-1 (Indus Waters Treaty 1960), Partial Award, 18 February 2013; *Abyei Arbitration*, the Government of Sudan/the Sudan People's Liberation Movement/Army, PCA Case No 2008-7 (PCA State/Non-State Rules), Award, 22 June 2009; *Guyana v Suriname*, PCA Case No 2004-4 (UNCLOS), Award, 17 September 2007.

[32] JB Scott (ed.), *Reports to the Hague Conferences of 1899 & 1907* (Clarendon Press, 1917) 232, 276.

[33] All public awards in PCA-administered cases are available on the PCA's website at <http://www.pca-cpa.org/>.

[34] Pre-release publication, 2 October 2013, available at <http://www.uncitral.org/pdf/english/texts/arbitration/rules-on-transparency/pre-release-UNCITRAL-Rules-on-Transparency.pdf>.

[35] PCA State/State Rules, Art 32(6); PCA State/Non-State Rules, Art 32(6); PCA State/International Organization Rules, Art 32(6); PCA International Organization/Private Party Rules, Art 32(6).

the International Bureau, which, in its role as secretary, forwards one copy to each party and each arbitrator for their records, and keeps one for the PCA's archive. In time-sensitive cases, the International Bureau may first issue the award in electronic form, with originally signed versions to follow by mail. In circumstances where political sensitivities require that parties receive the award at precisely the same moment, an award-rendering ceremony may be organized, or a protected website created where the parties can be given access to the award simultaneously at an agreed time. Some national arbitration laws require further steps to be taken after the communication of the award to the parties, such as the deposit of the award with a local court of the place of arbitration.[36]

Article 34(7) is a new provision, which has no equivalent in either set of UNCITRAL Rules. It provides that after the issuance of an award, parties to an inter-state proceeding will communicate to the PCA documents evidencing the execution of the award. This new provision is based on Article 22 of the 1899 Hague Convention and Article 43 of the 1907 Hague Convention, which require that the Member States of the PCA 'communicate to the [International] Bureau the laws, regulations and documents eventually showing the execution of the Awards given by the Court'.[37] This provision aims to encourage compliance, and facilitate the creation of a record of the actions taken by states in execution of arbitral awards. **6.19**

C. Applicable Law, *Amiable Compositeur*—Article 35

1. The arbitral tribunal shall apply the rules of law designated by the parties as applicable to the substance of the dispute. Failing such designation by the parties, the arbitral tribunal shall:
   (a) In cases involving only States, decide such disputes in accordance with international law by applying:
      i. International conventions, whether general or particular, establishing rules expressly recognized by the contesting States;
      ii. International custom, as evidence of a general practice accepted as law;
      iii. The general principles of law recognized by civilized nations;
      iv. Judicial and arbitral decisions and the teachings of the most highly qualified publicists of the various nations, as subsidiary means for the determination of rules of law.
   (b) In cases involving only States and intergovernmental organizations, apply the rules of the organization concerned and the law applicable to any

[36] See eg Dutch Code of Civil Procedure Book IV (Arbitration Act 1986), art 1058(1)(b) ('The arbitral tribunal shall ensure that without delay: . . . (b) the original of the final or partial final award is deposited with the Registry of the District Court within whose district the place of arbitration is located').

[37] This provision was included at the instance of TMC Asser and F de Maartens, representing, the Dutch and Russian delegations, respectively ('Rapport de la troisième commission, relatif au règlement pacifique des conflits internationaux', in Shabtai Rosenne (ed), *Les conférences de la paix de la Haye de 1899 et 1907 et l'arbitrage international—Actes et documents* (Bruylant, 2007) 51).

agreement or relationship between the parties, and, where appropriate, the general principles governing the law of intergovernmental organizations and the rules of general international law.

(c) In cases involving intergovernmental organizations and private parties, have regard both to the rules of the organization concerned and to the law applicable to the agreement or relationship out of or in relation to which the dispute arises, and, where appropriate, to the general principles governing the law of intergovernmental organizations and to the rules of general international law. In such cases, the arbitral tribunal shall decide in accordance with the terms of the agreement and shall take into account relevant trade usages.

(d) In all other cases, apply the law which it determines to be appropriate. In such cases, the arbitral tribunal shall decide in accordance with the terms of the agreement and shall take into account relevant trade usages.

2. The arbitral tribunal shall decide as *amiable compositeur* or *ex aequo et bono* only if the parties have expressly authorized the arbitral tribunal to do so.

6.20 Article 35 prescribes the law to be applied by the arbitral tribunal to the substance of the dispute.

6.21 Adapted from the applicable law provisions of the 1990s PCA Rules[38] and Article 35 of the 2010 UNCITRAL Rules,[39] Article 35 of the 2012 PCA Rules is a unique provision, tailored to the specificities of disputes between the different combinations of parties—states, state-controlled entities, intergovernmental organizations, and private parties—that are expected to have recourse to the Rules.

6.22 Article 35(1) first provides for party autonomy, allowing the parties to designate any rules of law that they see fit for application to the substance of the dispute. The expression 'rules of law' is understood to be wider than the term 'law', including (but not limited to) national laws, various sources of international law, transnational principles such as those set out in the UNIDROIT Principles of International Commercial Contracts, and different combinations of these rules.[40] The PCA Drafting Committee noted in its discussions that parties could, for example, designate the International Law Commission's Draft Articles on Responsibility of States for Internationally Wrongful Acts[41] as applicable rules of law. Agreements on applicable law are usually found in the contract or treaty out of which the dispute arises, or in the parties' agreement to submit an existing dispute to arbitration (*compromis*).[42]

[38] PCA State/State Rules, Art 33; PCA State/International Organization Rules, Art 33; PCA International Organization/Private Party Rules, Art 33.

[39] Reproduced in Appendix XII.

[40] See UNCITRAL Working Group II (Arbitration and Conciliation), *Note by the Secretariat: Settlement of commercial disputes: Revision of the UNCITRAL Arbitration Rules*, 45th session, 11–15 February 2006, A/CN.9/WG.II/WP.143/Add.1, para 30.

[41] International Law Commission, Draft Articles on Responsibility of States for Internationally Wrongful Acts, 53 UN GAOR Supp (No 10) at 43, A/56/10 (2001).

[42] See eg Exchange of Notes constituting an agreement between the Kingdom of the Netherlands and the Kingdom of Belgium on Arbitration concerning the Iron Rhine Railway Line Arbitration

In the absence of agreement by the parties on the applicable law, Article 35(1) provides a default rule for each potential combination of parties: 6.23

- only states (Article 35(1)(a));
- only states and intergovernmental organizations (Article 35(1)(b));
- only intergovernmental organizations and private parties (Article 35(1)(c)); and
- all other combinations of parties (Article 35(1)(d)). This category includes arbitrations between a state and a private party, conducted, for example, pursuant to a state contract or an investment treaty, as well as arbitrations involving a more complex cast (for example, a state, an intergovernmental organization, and a private party).

Article 35(1)(a), dedicated to inter-state arbitration, emulates the PCA State/State Rules by adopting the language of the applicable law provision of the ICJ Statute[43] with one minor change. While arbitration under the 2012 PCA Rules and adjudication by the ICJ differ procedurally, the PCA Drafting Committee decided that, as regards states' substantive rights and obligations, unless the parties agree otherwise, the same law (that is, international law, defined by reference to the same sources) should apply irrespective of the elected dispute resolution forum. In Article 35(1)(a)(iv), the 2012 PCA Rules (like the PCA State/State Rules) add the words 'and arbitral decisions' to the text of Article 38 of the ICJ Statute, making explicit the inclusion of arbitral awards among the subsidiary means for the determination of rules of law, which is implicit in the ICJ Statute.[44] The similarity of the applicable law provision of the 2012 PCA Rules with that of Article 38 of the ICJ Statute should encourage arbitral tribunals to consider ICJ decisions in interpreting Article 35 of the 2012 PCA Rules, thus increasing the consistency and predictability of results thereunder.[45] While the PCA Drafting Committee considered replacing the somewhat archaic expression 'the law of civilized nations' by more modern terminology, it ultimately decided against such an amendment, fearing that it might be understood as a change in the meaning of the provision. Under the 2012 PCA Rules, states are free to modify the default applicable law provision as they find necessary. For example, the rules of procedure of the Eritrea–Ethiopia 6.24

Agreement between the Kingdom of Belgium and the Kingdom of The Netherlands, 23 July 2003, LT/sr A.71.92/3110 (Belgium), which provides that the arbitral tribunal will render its decision 'on the basis of international law, including European law if necessary, while taking into account the Parties' obligations under article 292 of the [Treaty establishing the European Community 1958 (as consolidated in 2002).]'.

[43] 16 June 1945, 59 Stat 1055, Art 38.

[44] Gilbert Guillaume, 'Can Arbitral Awards Constitute a Source of International Law under Article 38 of the ICJ Statute?', in Yas Banifatemi (ed.), *Precedent in International Arbitration*, IAI Series on International Arbitration No 5, 105 (Juris Publishing, 2008): 'Arbitral awards may not serve as a source of law but in accordance with Article 38(d) of the Statute may serve as subsidiary means for the determination of rules of law'.

[45] For an overview of the ICJ's interpretation of Art 38 of the ICJ Statute, see Alain Pellet, 'Article 38', in Zimmermann et al. (eds), *The Statute of the International Court of Justice: A Commentary* (Oxford University Press, 2006) 677.

Claims Commission, which are a modified version of the PCA State/State Rules,[46] retain the text of the ICJ Statute, but add that '[t]he Commission may also refer to national laws in appropriate circumstances'.[47]

6.25 Article 35(1)(b) and (c) of the Rules are based, respectively, on Article 33 of the PCA State/International Organization Rules and Article 33 of the PCA International Organization/Private Party Rules. These provisions enumerate relevant sources of law.

6.26 Article 35(1)(d) adopts the text of Article 35(1) and (3) of the 2010 UNCITRAL Rules with some minor changes. The 2012 PCA Rules provide that the arbitral tribunal must decide on the basis of the terms of the 'agreement', rather than on the terms of the 'contract', because it is anticipated that many disputes submitted to arbitration under the Rules will have arisen out of international treaties rather than contracts. The 2012 PCA Rules, adopting the pithier formulation of Article 21(2) of the 2012 ICC Rules of Arbitration, also provide that the arbitral tribunal will take into account any 'relevant trade usages' rather than 'any usage of trade applicable to the transaction' as provided in the 2010 UNCITRAL Rules.

6.27 Article 35(1) not only lists different sources of applicable law for disputes involving different combinations of parties, but also varies the discretion given to the arbitral tribunal in determining the applicable law, thus preserving the sensitivity of the 1990s PCA Rules to the likely expectations of the parties to the dispute. Where the dispute involves only states, or only states and intergovernmental organizations, the provision prescribes that the tribunal 'shall . . . decide . . . by applying'[48] or 'shall . . . apply'[49] the enumerated sources of law, thus curtailing the discretion of the arbitral tribunal in determining the applicable law. In contrast, where a dispute is between an intergovernmental organization and a private party, the tribunal shall only 'have regard'[50] to the enumerated sources of law; and in all other cases, the tribunal has full discretion to 'apply the law which it determines to be appropriate'.[51]

6.28 Whatever the nature of the parties to the dispute, in accordance with Article 35(2) the arbitral tribunal can decide as *amiable compositeur* or *ex aequo et bono* only with the parties' express authorization. While the Rules do not define the power to decide as *amiable compositeur* or *ex aequo et bono*, this power may be understood broadly as the arbitral tribunal's power to decide on the ground of what it considers to be just and fair in the case at hand without an obligation to strictly apply rules of law.

---

[46] *Eritrea-Ethiopia Claims Commission*, PCA Case No 2001-1, Rules of Procedure, Art 1(1).
[47] *Eritrea-Ethiopia Claims Commission*, PCA Case No 2001-1, Rules of Procedure, Art 19(1).
[48] Rules, Art 35(1)(a); see also PCA State/State Rules, Art 33(1).
[49] Rules, Art 35(1)(b); see also PCA State/International Organization Rules, Art 33(1).
[50] Rules, Art 35(1)(c); see also PCA International Organization/Private Party Rules, Art 33(1).
[51] Rules, Art 35(1)(d); see also 2010 UNCITRAL Rules, Art 35(1).

In the PCA's experience, such authorization is rarely given in arbitrations involving states, state-controlled entities, or intergovernmental organizations.[52] The arbitration agreement establishing the Eritrea–Ethiopia Boundary Commission, which otherwise provided that the Commission's rules of procedure would be based on the PCA State/State Rules (which contain the same applicable law rule for inter-state arbitration as do the 2012 PCA Rules),[53] explicitly stated that the Commission '[would] *not* have the power to make decisions ex aequo et bono'.[54] Instead, the Commission was to fulfill its mandate of delimiting and demarcating the colonial treaty border between Eritrea and Ethiopia based on 'pertinent colonial treaties' and 'applicable international law'.[55] **6.29**

Nevertheless, the applicable law provision of the arbitration agreement in the PCA-administered *Croatia/Slovenia* arbitration conducted under the PCA State/State Rules may be seen as providing an authorization similar to that envisaged by Article 35(2) of the 2012 PCA Rules. The Croatia/Slovenia arbitration agreement provides that the arbitral tribunal will apply: **6.30**

i. the rules and principles of international law for the determination [of the course of the maritime and land boundary between the Republic of Slovenia and the Republic of Croatia];
ii. international law, equity and the principle of good neighbourly relations in order to achieve a fair and just result by taking into account all relevant circumstances for the determinations [of Slovenia's junction to the High Sea and the regime for the use of the relevant maritime areas].[56]

D. Settlement or Other Grounds for Termination—Article 36

1. If, before the award is made, the parties agree on a settlement of the dispute, the arbitral tribunal shall either issue an order for the termination of the arbitral proceedings or, if requested by the parties and accepted by the arbitral tribunal, record the settlement in the form of an arbitral award on agreed terms. The arbitral tribunal is not obliged to give reasons for such an award.

[52] Notably, the ICJ has never been called upon by the parties to decide *ex aequo et bono,* although its Statute provides for this possibility (Statute of the International Court of Justice, June 16, 1945, 59 Stat 1055, Art 38(2)).

[53] Agreement between the Government of the State of Eritrea and the Government of the Federal Democratic Republic of Ethiopia for the resettlement of displaced persons, as well as rehabilitation and peacebuilding in both countries, Algiers, 12 December 2000, 2138 UNTS 94, Art 4(11).

[54] Agreement between the Government of the State of Eritrea and the Government of the Federal Democratic Republic of Ethiopia for the resettlement of displaced persons, as well as rehabilitation and peacebuilding in both countries, Algiers, 12 December 2000, 2138 UNTS 94, Art 4(2) (emphasis added).

[55] Agreement between the Government of the State of Eritrea and the Government of the Federal Democratic Republic of Ethiopia for the resettlement of displaced persons, as well as rehabilitation and peacebuilding in both countries, Algiers, 12 December 2000, 2138 UNTS 94, Art 4(11).

[56] *Croatia/Slovenia*, PCA Case No 2012-4, PCA press release, 18 February 2013, <http://www.pca-cpa.org/showpage.asp?pag_id=1443>.

2. If, before the award is made, the continuation of the arbitral proceedings becomes unnecessary or impossible for any reason not mentioned in paragraph 1, the arbitral tribunal shall inform the parties of its intention to issue an order for the termination of the proceedings. The arbitral tribunal shall have the power to issue such an order unless there are remaining matters that may need to be decided and the arbitral tribunal considers it appropriate to do so.
3. Copies of the order for termination of the arbitral proceedings or of the arbitral award on agreed terms, signed by the arbitrators, shall be communicated by the arbitral tribunal to the parties. Where an arbitral award on agreed terms is made, the provisions of article 34, paragraphs 2, 4 and 5 shall apply.

6.31 Article 36 of the Rules (together with Articles 30(1) and 43(4)) provides for the termination of the arbitral proceedings for reasons other than the issuance of a final award.

6.32 This provision replicates Article 36 of the 2010 UNCITRAL Rules.

6.33 Article 36(1) applies when the parties settle their dispute before it is ruled upon by the arbitral tribunal. Disputes are frequently settled in the course of arbitral proceedings. The commencement of the arbitration may convince the respondent of the claimant's seriousness in pursuing its claims and incline it toward entering into settlement negotiations. The filing of the first round of written submissions may also reveal the relative strength of the parties' cases and encourage amicable dispute resolution. When settlement negotiations take place in parallel with an arbitration, they are generally confidential without notice to the arbitral tribunal. Until there is some indication that settlement negotiations may be successful, claimants may not wish to distract the arbitral tribunal in any way from pushing ahead with the arbitral proceedings. In some cases, however, in order to focus exclusively on their attempt to settle the dispute, the parties may request that the tribunal suspend the proceedings, removing any deadlines for written submissions and, possibly, vacating hearing dates. The PCA has witnessed settlement negotiations involving states that have lasted anywhere between a few days and several years. Therefore, in granting a suspension of proceedings, the tribunal may wish to impose certain conditions, for example requiring the parties to periodically report on the status of negotiations. Should negotiations fail, the proceedings will be resumed and a new procedural calendar established. If the parties inform the tribunal that they have successfully reached a settlement, the tribunal must, under Article 36(1), issue either an order for the termination of proceedings or an award on agreed terms (also sometimes called a consent award).[57]

6.34 The function of a termination order is to declare an end to the proceedings. It does not record or endorse the terms of any settlement agreement that may have been reached by the parties. A termination order will suffice where the terms of the

[57] See eg *TCW Group, Inc and Dominican Energy Holdings, LP v The Dominican Republic*, PCA Case No 2008-6 (CAFTA-DR) (1976 UNCITRAL Rules), Consent Award, 16 July 2009.

settlement are easy to implement, or have already been implemented by the time the tribunal is informed of the settlement. In contrast, an award on agreed terms will record the terms of the settlement, which will either be reproduced verbatim in the award or incorporated by reference.[58] Like all awards under Article 34 of the Rules, an award on agreed terms has the force of *res judicata*.

Under Article 36(1), the tribunal must 'accept' to issue an award on agreed terms; as such, the terms of the settlement can be perceived as bearing the stamp of the tribunal's approval—although it is likely that only very serious reasons would motivate a tribunal to refuse to render an award on agreed terms.[59] **6.35**

A request for an award on agreed terms must have the agreement of all parties to the arbitration. The parties' common intention may be evidenced through a joint request in writing, signed by the parties' respective representatives and enclosing the settlement agreement.[60] In cases where the request is made and the settlement terms communicated to the tribunal by one party on behalf of both, a confirmation by the other party will be necessary before an award is issued. **6.36**

Although this possibility is not explicitly provided for in the Rules, in certain circumstances an arbitral tribunal may issue an award on agreed terms recording a partial settlement and continue the proceedings to resolve remaining claims. **6.37**

As part of a settlement agreement, the parties should agree on the allocation of the costs of arbitration as between the parties.[61] It will remain for the arbitral tribunal, however, to make a final calculation of those costs in accordance with Article 40 when it issues a termination order or award on agreed terms. Article 40(3) of the 1976 UNCITRAL Rules makes it obligatory for the tribunal, when issuing an order for the termination of proceedings or an award on agreed terms, to fix the costs of the arbitration 'in the text of that order or award'. As the 2012 PCA Rules and 2010 UNCITRAL Rules do not contain such a specific requirement, providing only that the arbitral tribunal shall fix the costs of arbitration in a final award or 'another decision' (see Article 40(1)), the tribunal may fix the costs in its termination order or in a separate order or award on costs.[62] **6.38**

[58] See eg *Case Concerning Land Reclamations by Singapore in and around the Straits of Johor*, Malaysia v Singapore, PCA Case No 2004-5 (UNCLOS), Award on Agreed Terms, 1 September 2005, operative part, para 2.

[59] Gary B Born, *International Commercial Arbitration*, vol 1 (Wolters Kluwer, 2009) 2437–8.

[60] See eg *Case Concerning Land Reclamations by Singapore in and around the Straits of Johor*, Malaysia v Singapore, PCA Case No 2004-5 (UNCLOS), Award on Agreed Terms, 1 September 2005, paras 21–2.

[61] In such a case, the parties may seek some indication of the amount of their deposit for tribunal fees and expenses that remains unspent to determine the likely amount of any reimbursement.

[62] In one PCA-administered investment treaty arbitration conducted under the 1976 UNCITRAL Rules, the tribunal issued a so-called 'Order for the Termination of the Proceedings and Award on Costs', ostensibly seeking to achieve a *res judicata* effect for the decision on costs but not the substantive matters at issue between the parties.

6.39 The settlement agreement must, of course, be reached before the tribunal issues any award deciding on the claims at hand. In one PCA-administered investment treaty arbitration conducted under the 1976 UNCITRAL Rules, the parties reached a settlement agreement with suspensive conditions just as the tribunal was about to issue its award on the merits of the case. The PCA was asked to keep signed copies of the tribunal's award under seal, until such time as the suspensive conditions were fulfilled, in which case the PCA was to destroy the awards, or until the stipulated period for the fulfillment of the suspensive conditions passed, in which case the tribunal would, at the request of a party, issue the arbitral award. Ultimately, the settlement agreement's conditions were fulfilled, the PCA destroyed the tribunal's award, and the tribunal issued an order for the termination of the proceedings.

6.40 Article 36(2) provides for termination when 'the continuation of the arbitral proceedings becomes unnecessary or impossible for any reason' other than a settlement. Similar provisions of other PCA and UNCITRAL procedural rules have been invoked in PCA-administered arbitrations in several distinct situations. First, arbitral tribunals have terminated proceedings where a claimant announced the withdrawal of its claims outside the context of a settlement. Second, proceedings have been terminated where the claimant in some way failed to participate in the arbitration. Article 30(1)(a) of the Rules provides for termination exclusively when a claimant fails to file a statement of claim. When a claimant fails to participate in some other aspect of the proceedings, the arbitral tribunal derives its power to terminate the proceedings from Article 36(2). For example, in one PCA-administered arbitration, the tribunal granted the respondent's request for termination of the proceedings on the basis of Article 34(2) of the 1976 UNCITRAL Rules (which closely resembles Article 36(2) of the 2012 PCA Rules), stating that the claimant's 'ongoing failure to obtain legal representation and its . . . failure to respond to the communications of the Tribunal rendered the continuation of [the] proceedings impossible'. Third, the situation where the parties fail to establish the requested deposit for the costs of arbitration can also be seen as falling within the scope of Article 36(2), although Article 43(2) of the Rules expressly refers to this situation.

6.41 Under Article 36(2), the arbitral tribunal may act on its own motion or at the request of a party. It must notify the parties of its intention to issue a termination order, allowing them a brief period to rectify the situation. Article 36(2) is aligned with Article 30(1)(a) because it allows the arbitral tribunal to terminate the proceedings 'unless there are remaining matters that may need to be decided and the arbitral tribunal considers it appropriate to do so'.[63] As under Article 30(1)(a), these

[63] In contrast, Art 34(2) of the 1976 UNCITRAL Rules provides that the arbitral tribunal shall have the power to terminate the proceedings 'unless a party raises justifiable grounds for objections'.

remaining matters may be the parties' costs claims or, in a case of non-participation by the claimant, a counterclaim from the respondent.

Article 36(3) provides that signed copies of the termination order or award on agreed terms shall be communicated to the parties 'by the arbitral tribunal'. This formulation differs from that of Article 34(6), which provides for the circulation of signed copies of awards to the parties by the PCA International Bureau. In practice, the International Bureau, in its role as secretariat pursuant to Article 1(3) of the Rules, may also be requested by the tribunal to circulate termination orders and awards on agreed terms to the parties on its behalf. **6.42**

Article 36(3) further provides that an award on agreed terms must fulfill the requirements applicable to other awards set out in Article 34(2), (4), and (5) of the 2012 PCA Rules. As specified in Article 36(1), however, it need not contain reasons, as the decision results not from the tribunal's consideration of the issues but from the parties' agreement. The requirements of Article 34 applicable to awards do not apply to termination orders; such orders are, however, 'decisions' within the meaning of Article 33 of the Rules. **6.43**

E. Interpretation of the Award—Article 37

1. Within 30 days after the receipt of the award, a party, with notice to the other parties and the International Bureau, may request that the arbitral tribunal give an interpretation of the award.
2. The interpretation shall be given in writing within 45 days after the receipt of the request. The interpretation shall form part of the award and the provisions of article 34, paragraphs 2 to 6, shall apply.

Articles 37 to 39 deal with post-award procedure. Pursuant to Article 37(1), a party has 30 days after receipt of an arbitral award to request that the tribunal give an interpretation of that award. Article 37(2) gives the tribunal 45 days from the receipt of a party's request to issue its interpretation. It also specifies that an interpretation will form part of the original award and must therefore comply with the requirements for a valid award set out in Article 34(2) to (6) of the Rules. **6.44**

Article 37 follows the text of Article 37 of the 2010 UNCITRAL Rules with one modification: it specifies that a request for interpretation must be made with notice to the PCA International Bureau, alerting it to the possibility that the arbitral tribunal may require further assistance and allowing it to archive the request. **6.45**

The short time limits established in Article 37—30 days for a party's request for interpretation and 45 days for the issuance of the tribunal's interpretation—aim at achieving finality for the award as soon as possible following its issuance. **6.46**

6.47 Before issuing any interpretation, the arbitral tribunal should afford the non-requesting party an opportunity to comment with, in some cases, an opportunity for the requesting party to reply.[64]

6.48 As discussed under Article 34, an arbitral award has the force of *res judicata*. Once recorded in an award, the arbitral tribunal's decisions cannot be changed. Accordingly, the interpretation of an award can clarify the tribunal's meaning, but cannot serve as an opportunity for the tribunal to reconsider its decisions. If an arbitral tribunal finds that a request for interpretation is an appeal in disguise or is otherwise abusive (for example, it is aimed at creating delay in the execution of the award), the tribunal may deny the requested interpretation. A denial of a request for interpretation would not form part of the award as it would not have any relevance to the interpretation of its terms.

6.49 A decision of the Eritrea-Ethiopia Boundary Commission provides an example of a refusal to interpret an arbitral award. The Commission's proceedings, administered by the PCA, were conducted pursuant to ad hoc rules of procedure based on the PCA State/State Rules, which contain a provision on interpretation of awards similar to Article 37 of the 2012 PCA Rules.[65] In deciding on a request by Ethiopia for the interpretation and correction of the Commission's Decision on Delimitation of the Border Between Eritrea and Ethiopia, the Commission stated as follows:

> 16. The Ethiopian request appears to be founded on a misapprehension regarding the scope and effect of Articles 28 and 29 of the Commission's Rules of Procedure. The facility accorded to the Parties in Article 28(1) to request the Commission to give an interpretation of the Decision may only be invoked where the meaning of some specific statement in the Decision is unclear and requires clarification in order that the Decision should be properly applied. The concept of interpretation does not open up the possibility of appeal against a decision or the reopening of matters clearly settled by a decision. The Commission, through its President, has already stated 'that the provisions of Articles 28 and 29 of the Rules of Procedure neither allow substantive amendment nor affect the binding quality of the Decision as rendered on 13 April 2002. Re-argument of the case is not permitted'. In this respect, the Commission is adhering to the authoritative views on the limits of interpretation expressed by the Permanent Court of International Justice in the Chorzow Factory Case, (1927, PCIJ, Series A No. 13, at p.21) and the Arbitration Tribunal in the Arbitration on the Delimitation of the Continental Shelf (France-UK), Interpretation Decision of 14 March 1978 (Vol.54, International Law Reports, 1979, at p. 161). 'Interpretation is a process that is merely auxiliary, and may serve

[64] See eg *Eritrea-Ethiopia Boundary Commission*, PCA Case No 2001-1 (Rules of Procedure based on PCA State/State Rules), Decision Regarding the 'Request for Interpretation, Correction and Consultation' Submitted by the Federal Democratic Republic of Ethiopia on 13 May 2012, 24 June 2002, para 1; *Iron Rhine Arbitration*, Belgium v the Netherlands, PCA Case No 2003-2 (Rules of Procedure based on PCA State/State Rules), Interpretation of the Award of the Arbitral Tribunal, 20 September 2005, para 3. The 2012 ICC Rules, for example, explicitly require that non-requesting party be given an opportunity to comment (Art 35(2)).

[65] *Eritrea-Ethiopia Boundary Commission*, PCA Case No 2001-1, Rules of Procedure, paras 1, 28.

to explain, but may not change, what the Court already settled with binding force as res judicata'.

17. The Commission does not find, in any of the items that appear in Section II of the Ethiopian request, anything that identifies an uncertainty in the Decision that could be resolved by interpretation at this time. The same is true of Sections III and IV. Nor is any case made out for revision. Further, the Conclusions of the Request are not so expressed as to invite the Commission to interpret or revise the Decision in any specific respect by reference to applicable considerations of international law or the actual terms of Articles 28 and 29 of the Rules of Procedure.[66]

By contrast, in a PCA-administered investment treaty arbitration conducted under the 1976 UNCITRAL Rules, an arbitral tribunal issued an interpretation clarifying what the tribunal considered to be a real ambiguity in its award on jurisdiction: the operative part of the award explicitly rejected only one of the respondent's objections to jurisdiction, but the respondent's other jurisdictional objections were briefly discussed in the tribunal's reasons, leading the respondent to wonder whether only one or all of its jurisdictional objections had been definitively rejected. In its interpretation, the tribunal clarified that it had intended to decide only the jurisdictional objection referred to in the operative part of the award, while leaving all the others to be considered at a later stage of the proceedings. **6.50**

In the *Iron Rhine Arbitration*, conducted under ad hoc rules of procedure based on the PCA State/State Rules, the arbitral tribunal expressed its interpretive role as follows: **6.51**

The Tribunal has examined carefully the contentions of each of the Parties. At the same time, it notes that it is for the Tribunal to interpret how the Award is to be understood, in the light of its own intentions at the time of rendering the Award. The ensuing paragraphs thus do not respond to the various observations and comments of the Parties but rather constitute an authoritative interpretation by the Tribunal of its own Award under Article 23(1) of the Rules of Procedure.[67]

F. Correction of the Award—Article 38

1. Within 30 days after the receipt of the award, a party, with notice to the other parties and the International Bureau, may request the arbitral tribunal to correct in the award any error in computation, any clerical or typographical error, or any error or omission of a similar nature. If the arbitral tribunal considers that the request is justified, it shall make the correction within 45 days of receipt of the request.

[66] See eg *Eritrea-Ethiopia Boundary Commission*, PCA Case No 2001-1, Decision Regarding the 'Request for Interpretation, Correction and Consultation' Submitted by the Federal Democratic Republic of Ethiopia on 13 May 2002, 24 June 2002, paras 16–17.

[67] *Iron Rhine Arbitration*, Belgium v the Netherlands, PCA Case No 2003-2, Interpretation of the Award of the Arbitral Tribunal, 20 September 2005, para 4.

2. The arbitral tribunal may within 30 days after the communication of the award make such corrections on its own initiative.
3. Such corrections shall be in writing and shall form part of the award. The provisions of article 34, paragraphs 2 to 6, shall apply.

6.52 Article 38 provides for the correction of arbitral awards.

6.53 Like Article 37 of the Rules, Article 38 follows the text of the equivalent provision of the 2010 UNCITRAL Rules, adding only that requests for correction must be notified to the PCA International Bureau.

6.54 A correction under Article 38 is not intended to affect the substance of an award any more than interpretation under Article 37.[68] Article 38(1) states that the arbitral tribunal may correct 'any error of computation, any clerical or typographical error, or any error or omission of a similar nature'. In practice, many corrections of awards only list spelling and punctuation mistakes. It is also common for mathematical errors in the calculation of damages or costs to be corrected.

6.55 In two PCA-administered arbitrations, the tribunal corrected its characterization of a party's argument. In the *Iron Rhine Arbitration* between Belgium and the Netherlands, in which ad hoc rules of procedure based on the PCA State/State Rules applied and contained a provision on the correction of awards similar to that of the 2012 PCA Rules, Belgium requested that the arbitral tribunal bring its re-statement of Belgium's position in line with what was stated in Belgium's submissions. The Netherlands concurred with the request.[69] In a PCA-administered investment treaty arbitration conducted under the 1976 UNCITRAL Rules, the respondent requested that the tribunal correct its statement that the costs claimed by the respondent were in respect of the jurisdictional phase of the proceedings only, as the claim was in fact in respect of the costs of the entire arbitral proceeding. The tribunal noted that the respondent's schedule of costs did not explicitly state this, but nevertheless corrected the award as requested.

6.56 Where national arbitration legislation applies,[70] a correction may also be sought to rectify a situation that could present difficulties in the enforcement of the award, for example if the place of arbitration or date of issuance of the award has not been indicated, as is required by Article 34 of the Rules.[71] In one PCA-administered

---

[68] Report of the UNCITRAL Working Group II (Arbitration and Conciliation) on the work of its 51st session, 14–18 September 2009, A/CN.9/684, para 109.

[69] *Iron Rhine Arbitration*, Belgium v the Netherlands, PCA Case No 2003-2, Correction to the Award of the Arbitral Tribunal, 20 September 2005.

[70] On the applicability of national legislation in the context of an arbitration involving only state or intergovernmental organization parties, see discussion under Art 1(2).

[71] The possibility to correct 'omissions', which was not referred to in the 1976 UNCITRAL Rules, was added to the 2010 UNCITRAL Rules precisely to ensure that errors of this nature could be corrected (UNCITRAL Working Group II (Arbitration and Conciliation), *Note by the Secretariat: Settlement of commercial disputes: Revision of the UNCITRAL Arbitration Rules*, 46th session, 5–9 February 2007, A/CN.9/WG.II/WP.145/Add.1, para 41).

investment treaty arbitration conducted under the 1976 UNCITRAL Rules, a tribunal corrected an award at the claimant's request; while the original award found that the respondent was liable to the claimant for a certain amount in damages, the operative part did not include an explicit order for payment. The claimant expressed concern that the award would be unenforceable. The respondent did not oppose the claimant's request, and the tribunal corrected the award, calling this a case of 'inadvertence or clerical error'.

In contrast with the interpretation of awards under Article 37, which are to be given at a party's request, an arbitral tribunal can make a correction to an award on its own initiative pursuant to Article 38(2). It is necessary that the tribunal have this power for cases where the parties have not, or could not have, noticed an error contained in the award (for example if the tribunal misstated its own fees and expenses). The tribunal's correction must be made within 30 days of the communication of the award to the parties. A tribunal issuing a correction pursuant to a party's request must do so within 45 days.[72] **6.57**

Pursuant to Article 38(3), a correction, like an interpretation, will be part of the original award, and has to comply with the requirements for a valid award set out in Article 34(2) to (6) of the Rules. **6.58**

G. Additional Award—Article 39

1. Within 30 days after the receipt of the termination order or the award, a party, with notice to the other parties and the International Bureau, may request the arbitral tribunal to make an award or an additional award as to claims presented in the arbitral proceedings but not decided by the arbitral tribunal.
2. If the arbitral tribunal considers the request for an award or additional award to be justified, it shall render or complete its award within 60 days after the receipt of the request. The arbitral tribunal may extend, if necessary, the period of time within which it shall make the award.
3. When such an award or additional award is made, the provisions of article 34, paragraphs 2 to 6, shall apply.

Article 39 provides for the making of an additional award to deal with issues that the arbitral tribunal omitted to decide in a previously issued termination order or award. **6.59**

As with Articles 37 and 38, Article 39 of the Rules only departs from the text of the equivalent provision of the 2010 UNCITRAL Rules to require that requests for an additional award be notified to the International Bureau of the PCA. **6.60**

[72] This time limit did not exist under the 1976 UNCITRAL Rules.

6.61 Under Article 39, as well as under Articles 37 and 38, the arbitral tribunal must be careful regarding the scope of its powers. Article 39 authorizes the arbitral tribunal to decide in an additional award claims 'presented in the arbitral proceedings'—that is, only claims that required resolution on the basis of the submissions made by the parties before the issuance of the original termination order or award. In other words, absent an agreement of the parties to this effect, the arbitral tribunal may decide in an additional award only claims that it did not, but should have, decided in its original award.

6.62 For example, in one PCA-administered investment treaty arbitration conducted under the 1976 UNCITRAL Rules, a party's claim for costs was overlooked by the tribunal, which had in the meantime issued a termination order. The tribunal found itself wishing to use the additional award provision despite the fact that it had only issued a termination order rather than an award. Notably, unlike the 2012 PCA Rules and the 2010 UNCITRAL Rules, the 1976 UNCITRAL Rules do not explicitly provide for the making of an additional award further to the issuance of a termination order. They limit additional awards to cases where a previous 'award' did not decide all the relevant claims. The tribunal found that the provision on additional awards of the 1976 UNCITRAL Rules did not apply 'in the strict sense' to the respondent's request, but that the tribunal nevertheless had the authority to decide on the allocation of the costs of arbitration in the form of an additional award. The tribunal explained that:

> To do so would be entirely consistent with the Parties' expectations as well as the obligation of the Tribunal pursuant to Article 40(3) of the Rules. It would also be consistent with the Tribunal's general discretion under Article 15(1) to 'conduct the arbitration in such manner as it considers appropriate, provided that the parties are treated with equality and that at any stage of the proceedings each party is given a full opportunity of presenting its case'.... In addition, the underlying intention of Article 37...is to provide the Tribunal with 'a mechanism for completing [its] mandate'; providing tribunals with the ability to complete their decisions if necessary in order to achieve a final resolution of the parties' dispute.[73]

6.63 As with requests for interpretation and correction, the request for an additional award must be made within 30 days of the party's receipt of the award or termination order. For the issuance of an additional award, Article 39(2) establishes a 60-day time limit that may be extended by the arbitral tribunal. On the one hand, a time limit is necessary to achieve finality as quickly as possible following the issuance of the award. On the other hand, this provision recognizes that complex substantive issues may need to be decided in an additional award, requiring time for the tribunal to seek the views of the parties, perhaps even hold a hearing, and deliberate and draft.[74]

---

[73] Footnotes omitted.

[74] While there were differing interpretations as to whether the 1976 UNCITRAL Rules permit the taking of further evidence and the holding of further hearings before the issuance of

Article 39(3) provides that the requirements for the validity of awards set out in Article 34(2) to (6) apply to additional awards. 6.64

H. Definition of Costs—Article 40

1. The arbitral tribunal shall fix the costs of arbitration in the final award and, if it deems appropriate, in another decision.
2. The term 'costs' includes only:
   (a) The fees of the arbitral tribunal to be stated separately as to each arbitrator and to be fixed by the tribunal itself in accordance with article 41;
   (b) The reasonable travel and other expenses incurred by the arbitrators;
   (c) The reasonable costs of expert advice and of other assistance required by the arbitral tribunal;
   (d) The reasonable travel and other expenses of witnesses to the extent such expenses are approved by the arbitral tribunal;
   (e) The legal and other costs incurred by the parties in relation to the arbitration to the extent that the arbitral tribunal determines that the amount of such costs is reasonable;
   (f) The fees and expenses of the International Bureau, including the fees and expenses of the appointing authority.
3. In relation to interpretation, correction or completion of any award under articles 37 to 39, the arbitral tribunal may charge the costs referred to in paragraphs 2(b) to (f), but no additional fees.

Article 40, one of the Rules' four provisions to deal with the financial aspects of the arbitration (the others being Articles 41 to 43), sets out the arbitral tribunal's obligation to fix the costs of arbitration and defines the term 'costs'. 6.65

This provision follows the text of Article 40 of the 2010 UNCITRAL Rules, adding only in Article 40(2)(f) that the costs of arbitration include 'the fees and expenses of the International Bureau'. Under the 2010 UNCITRAL Rules, when the PCA is chosen by the parties and tribunal to act as registry, its fees and expenses are subsumed under Article 40(2)(c), which provides for the costs of 'other assistance required by the arbitral tribunal'. Given that, under the 2012 PCA Rules, the PCA International Bureau acts as registry in every case, the Drafting Committee considered it appropriate to refer to the PCA's fees and expenses explicitly in these Rules. 6.66

Pursuant to Article 40(1), the tribunal has an obligation to fix the costs of arbitration, ie to indicate precisely the total amounts incurred in the course of the arbitration for each of the cost items listed in Article 40(2). Besides the arbitrators' fees, which must be stated separately as to each arbitrator, and the parties' legal costs, 6.67

an additional award, it is clear that the 2012 PCA Rules and the 2010 UNCITRAL Rules were intended to permit these steps. See Report of the UNCITRAL Working Group II (Arbitration and Conciliation) on the work of its 45th session, 11–15 September, 2006, A/CN.9/614, paras 128–9.

which are unique to each party, a lump sum is usually indicated for each of the other costs items of Article 40(2).[75] The itemized disclosure of arbitrators' fees is intended to 'disciplin[e] the arbitrators and [avoid] exaggerated costs'.[76] Pursuant to Article 40(1), the tribunal 'shall fix the costs of arbitration in the final award *and*, if it deems appropriate, in another decision' (emphasis added). While this phrase may be understood to mean that the tribunal must in every case fix the costs in its final award and may, in some cases, also fix the costs in another decision, the better interpretation of this provision is that while the tribunal must fix the costs of arbitration, it may do so either in its final award or in another decision (or both) at its discretion. The 'other decision' may be an order for the termination of proceedings or a separate award on costs. Having fixed the costs of arbitration, the tribunal may, in the same decision, decide on their allocation between the parties in accordance with Article 42 of the Rules. If expedient, the tribunal can also fix the costs of a discrete part of the proceedings in an order or award issued during the proceedings.[77]

6.68 Article 40(2) exhaustively lists the items comprising the costs of arbitration. The level of discretion enjoyed by the arbitral tribunal in fixing the costs of arbitration varies from one item of costs to another.

6.69 The tribunal's fees and expenses, discussed in greater detail under Article 41, must be 'reasonable in amount' and consistent with the proposal made by the tribunal at the outset of the proceedings as to how it intends to calculate its fees and expenses. The tribunal's fees and expenses are also subject to mandatory review by the Secretary-General of the PCA.

6.70 The 'reasonable costs of expert advice and of other assistance required by the arbitral tribunal' are also subject to mandatory review by the PCA Secretary-General. This item of costs refers to the fees and expenses of service providers hired by the arbitral tribunal in connection with the arbitration, such as tribunal-appointed experts, court reporters, or interpreters. When such services are obtained by the International Bureau, these costs may instead be included in the International Bureau's expenses.

6.71 Regarding the expenses of witnesses and the 'legal and other costs incurred by the parties in relation to the arbitration', the tribunal has discretion to fix the

[75] See eg *Chemtura Corporation (formerly Crompton Corporation) v Canada*, PCA Case No 2008-1 (NAFTA) (1976 UNCITRAL Rules), Award, 2 August 2010, paras 268–71.

[76] Report of the UNCITRAL Working Group II (Arbitration and Conciliation) on the work of its 51st session, 14–18 September 2009, A/CN.9/684, para 121.

[77] In one PCA-administered proceeding conducted pursuant to ad hoc procedural rules, where the parties agreed in mid-proceedings that the respondent would bear the claimant's legal costs in respect of a specific procedural application made by the respondent, the claimant requested that the tribunal immediately assess the amount of its legal costs and order their payment. On the basis of submissions from the parties, the tribunal determined the amount of the claimant's 'reasonable' legal costs, which could be recovered from the respondent, but deferred making an award on costs until the conclusion of the proceedings.

'reasonable' amounts that will form part of the costs of arbitration, as defined in Article 40, and will be the subject of any decision on the allocation of costs under Article 42 of the Rules. While it is understood that it is for a party to provide the statement of its costs of representation, only 'reasonable' costs may be borne by the other party.[78] To arrive at such objectively reasonable amounts, the tribunal will solicit submissions from the parties detailing their actual costs, determine whether they are reasonable, and adjust them if necessary.

Costs of arbitration also include the fees and expenses of the PCA International Bureau. These comprise the fees and expenses of the International Bureau acting as registry and secretariat pursuant to Article 1(3), as well as the fees and expenses of the PCA Secretary-General acting as the appointing authority under Article 6 of the Rules.[79] Time spent by PCA staff in support of an arbitration is charged at an hourly rate set out in the schedule of fees displayed on the PCA's website.[80] International Bureau expenses will also include the travel expenses of its staff if travel is required in connection with an arbitration. **6.72**

Article 40(3) specifies that arbitrators are not entitled to fees for work done in relation to the interpretation, correction, or completion of an award under Articles 37, 38, and 39 of the Rules, so as to encourage the tribunal 'to draft its award with optimal clarity (to the effect that no interpretation or correction would be needed) and to deal expeditiously with any frivolous request for interpretation correction or completion of the award that might be made by a party seeking reversal of the initial award'.[81] **6.73**

States that are parties to the 1899 or 1907 Hague Conventions can seek assistance with meeting the costs of arbitration through the PCA's financial assistance fund. Established in 1994, the fund relies on voluntary contributions[82] and is available to PCA Member States that: (i) have concluded an agreement for the purpose of submitting one or more disputes, whether existing or future, for settlement by any of the means administered by the PCA; and (ii) at the time of requesting financial assistance from the fund, are listed on the 'DAC List of Aid Recipients' prepared by the Organisation for Economic Co-operation and Development. A qualifying **6.74**

---

[78] For example, as decided by one tribunal in a PCA-administered case, an amount of US$87,000 for a short charter jet flight bringing the representative of a party to a hearing is not a 'reasonable' cost that could be apportioned between the parties.

[79] The Secretary-General is the head of the International Bureau of the PCA (Rules Concerning the Organization and Internal Workings of the International Bureau of the Permanent Court of Arbitration, 18 December 1900, <http://www.pca-cpa.org/showpage.asp?pag_id=1191>, Art 1).

[80] For the PCA's schedule of fees as of October 2013, see Appendix VIII.

[81] Report of the UNCITRAL Working Group II (Arbitration and Conciliation) on the work of its 48th session, 4–8 February 2008, A/CN.9/646, para 32.

[82] Since the establishment of the fund, Norway, Cyprus, the United Kingdom, South Africa, the Netherlands, Costa Rica, Saudi Arabia, Switzerland, Lebanon, and France have made contributions.

state may seek financial assistance from the fund by submitting a written request to the Secretary-General of the PCA. An independent board of trustees decides on the request.[83]

I. Fees and Expenses of Arbitrators—Article 41

1. The costs referred to in article 40, paragraphs 2(a), (b) and (c) shall be reasonable in amount, taking into account the amount in dispute, the complexity of the subject matter, the time spent by the arbitrators and any experts appointed by the arbitral tribunal, and any other relevant circumstances of the case.
2. Promptly after its constitution, the arbitral tribunal shall inform the parties as to how it proposes to determine its fees and expenses, including any rates it intends to apply. Within 15 days of receiving that proposal, any party may refer the proposal to the appointing authority for review. If the appointing authority finds that the proposal of the arbitral tribunal is inconsistent with paragraph 1, it shall make any necessary adjustments thereto, which shall be binding upon the arbitral tribunal.
3.
    (a) Before fixing the costs of arbitration pursuant to article 40, the arbitral tribunal shall submit its determination of the costs referred to in article 40, paragraphs 2(a), (b) and (c), with an explanation of the manner in which the corresponding amounts have been calculated, to the appointing authority for review;
    (b) If the appointing authority finds that the arbitral tribunal's determination is inconsistent with the criteria in paragraph 1 or with the arbitral tribunal's proposal (and any adjustments thereto) under paragraph 2, it shall make any necessary adjustments to the arbitral tribunal's determination. Any such adjustments shall be binding upon the arbitral tribunal when it fixes the costs of arbitration pursuant to article 40.
4. Throughout the procedure under paragraphs 2 and 3 of this article, the arbitral tribunal shall proceed with the arbitration, in accordance with article 17, paragraph 1.

6.75 Article 41 focuses on the fees and expenses of arbitrators and tribunal-appointed experts.

6.76 Although it follows the structure of Article 41 of the 2010 UNCITRAL Rules, this provision also includes a novel, mandatory review mechanism of the tribunal's fees and expenses.

6.77 The approach of the UNCITRAL Rules to arbitrators' fees and expenses changed significantly when the UNCITRAL Rules were revised in 2010. The 1976 UNCITRAL Rules required that the amount of arbitrators' fees be 'reasonable', but gave the tribunal discretion to fix its fees, subject only to the obligations to: (i) take

[83] See the financial assistance fund's 'Terms of Reference and Guidelines', and 'Rules Governing the Work of the Board of Trustees', reproduced in Appendices IX and X respectively.

into account, 'to the extent that it considers appropriate in the circumstances of the case', the appointing authority's schedule of fees (if any), and, if no such schedule of fees exists, any statement setting forth a basis for establishing fees issued by the appointing authority at a party's request; and (ii) if requested by a party, consult with the appointing authority prior to fixing its fees. Accordingly, under the 1976 UNCITRAL Rules, the responsibility for ensuring that the tribunal's fees were reasonable lay entirely with the tribunal itself, and any decision taken by it regarding its fees had a definitive character.

Concerned with the potential for abuse, the UNCITRAL Working Group, in revising the UNCITRAL Rules, sought to create a 'neutral mechanism for controlling the fees charged by arbitrators'.[84] Accordingly, the 2010 UNCITRAL Rules maintain the requirement that arbitrators' fees be reasonable, expand this requirement to arbitrators' expenses, and create an obligation for the tribunal to communicate to the parties at the inception of the arbitration how it proposes to determine its fees and expenses. The 2010 UNCITRAL Rules also provide a mechanism through which, upon a party's request, the appointing authority can revise both the tribunal's initial proposal as to the method it wishes to apply for the calculation of its fees and expenses, and the tribunal's final determination of its fees and expenses at the end of a case.[85] **6.78**

With the same goal in mind, the PCA Drafting Committee, in the 2012 PCA Rules, sought to further strengthen the controls on the tribunal's determination of its fees and expenses. The Drafting Committee considered that the PCA, as the appointing authority and administering institution under the Rules, entrusted with the parties' deposits,[86] should have an enhanced ability to safeguard the disbursement of the parties' funds. At the same time, the Drafting Committee did not wish to impose specific schedules of fees on arbitrators and eliminate the PCA's flexibility in tailoring fee arrangements to each case.[87] The Drafting Committee considered that arbitrators should retain a role in determining the price for their own services, provided that they are not unreasonable in so doing. Accordingly, the PCA Drafting Committee maintained the tribunal's primary role in determining its own fees and expenses, adopted the reasonableness requirement of the 2010 UNCITRAL Rules, and, as explained below in paragraphs 6.82–6.92, gave the PCA a strong role, at every stage of the proceedings, for ensuring that the reasonableness requirement is met. **6.79**

---

84 Report of the UNCITRAL Working Group II (Arbitration and Conciliation) on the work of its 48th session, 4–8 February 2008, A/CN.9/646, para 20.

85 See 2010 UNCITRAL Rules, Art 41, reproduced in Appendix XII.

86 See discussion under Art 43.

87 See eg 2012 ICC Rules, Appendix III, Art 4; ICSID Schedule of Fees, <https://icsid.worldbank.org>.

6.80 Because the remuneration of tribunal-appointed experts is typically decided by the arbitral tribunal without input from the parties, the Drafting Committee also considered it appropriate to subject the fees and expenses of tribunal-appointed experts to some of the control mechanisms of Article 41.

6.81 Article 41(1) of the Rules requires, as does the equivalent provision of the 2010 UNCITRAL Rules, that the fees and expenses of arbitrators be reasonable, taking into account relevant circumstances. The 2012 PCA Rules also extend this requirement to the 'costs of expert advice and of other assistance required by the arbitral tribunal'. These costs include the fees and expenses of experts appointed by a tribunal in accordance with Article 29 of the Rules. The 2012 PCA Rules therefore add 'time spent by... any experts appointed by the tribunal' to the list of circumstances relevant in evaluating what is reasonable.

6.82 The PCA is tasked with monitoring compliance with the reasonableness standard of Article 41(1) through three distinct procedures, each applicable at a specific stage of the arbitral proceedings.

6.83 First, at the beginning of the arbitral proceedings, the PCA Secretary-General may be asked by a party to review and adjust a tribunal's proposal as to the manner in which it intends to determine its fees and expenses. This procedure is based on the 2010 UNCITRAL Rules. Pursuant to Article 41(2), the arbitral tribunal must, promptly after its constitution, inform the parties as to 'how it proposes to determine its fees and expenses'. Typically, the tribunal will include this information in its first procedural order, a draft of which will be circulated to the parties for their comments.

6.84 There are different methods for calculating arbitrators' fees. In cases administered by the PCA, arbitrators are most frequently remunerated in accordance with an hourly rate.[88] In a few cases, tribunals have been remunerated on an *ad valorem* basis[89] or have charged a fixed fee for all work in connection with an arbitration. In investment treaty arbitrations, arbitrators may agree to be remunerated in accordance with the ICSID Schedule of Fees.[90] The procedural order setting out the method of calculation of the tribunal's fees often also contains an illustrative list of items that may constitute tribunal expenses.[91]

---

[88] See eg *Bilcon of Delaware v Canada*, PCA Case No 2009-4 (NAFTA) (1976 UNCITRAL Rules), Procedural Order No 1, 1 April 2009, para 12.

[89] Sometimes adopting the *ad valorem* scale of another arbitral institution, such as the ICC.

[90] See eg Detroit International Bridge Company v Canada, Procedural Order No 1, 20 December 2012, at <http://www.international.gc.ca>, s 3; *Guaracachi America Inc and Rurelec PLC v Plurinational State of Bolivia*, PCA Case No 2011-17 (China–Mongolia BIT) (2010 UNCITRAL Rules), Terms of Appointment and Procedural Order No 1.

[91] See eg Detroit International Bridge Company v Canada, Procedural Order No 1, 20 December 2012, at <http://www.international.gc.ca>, s 3; *Guaracachi America Inc and Rurelec PLC v Plurinational State of Bolivia*, PCA Case No 2011-17 (China–Mongolia BIT) (2010 UNCITRAL Rules), Terms of Appointment and Procedural Order No 1, para 11.3.

Within 15 days of receiving the tribunal's proposal, a dissatisfied party can request the PCA Secretary-General to review it. The Secretary-General will adjust the tribunal's proposal if it is inconsistent with the reasonableness requirement set out in Article 41(1) of the Rules. Unlike the 2010 UNCITRAL Rules, the 2012 PCA Rules do not set a 45-day time limit for the Secretary-General's review. Guidance that is appropriate to assist the variety of institutions and individuals that may serve in the role of appointing authority under the 2010 UNCITRAL Rules was considered unnecessary in the 2012 PCA Rules, as under these rules the function of appointing authority will be fulfilled exclusively by the PCA Secretary-General. It is expected that the PCA Secretary-General will complete any requested review in significantly less than 45 days. **6.85**

The second procedure for monitoring compliance with the reasonableness requirement of Article 41(1) is set out in Article 43 of the Rules and is discussed in greater detail thereunder. Pursuant to this provision, the PCA International Bureau is under an obligation throughout the arbitral proceedings to ensure that any disbursements of the parties' deposits to cover arbitrators' fees and expenses are consistent with the criteria of Article 41(1) and the tribunal's proposal (and any adjustments thereto) under Article 41(2). This mechanism has no equivalent in the 2010 UNCITRAL Rules. **6.86**

Finally, at the end of the arbitral proceedings, the Secretary-General of the PCA is called upon to review the tribunal's determination of the fees and expenses of arbitrators and party-appointed experts, before the tribunal formally fixes the costs of arbitration in an award or other decision. **6.87**

Under the 2010 UNCITRAL Rules, an appointing authority can review only the determination of arbitrators' fees and expenses (and not those of tribunal-appointed experts) and only upon referral by a party. Any adjustments made by the appointing authority pursuant to this referral are binding on the tribunal, and must be reflected in the tribunal's award, or, if the award has already been issued, in a correction thereto. Parties may, however, hesitate to invoke the referral procedure before an award is issued, for fear of displeasing the tribunal. In contrast, after an award is rendered, arbitrators may be subjected to unjustified referrals by disgruntled losing parties. **6.88**

The 2012 PCA Rules avoid these difficulties by removing the parties from the review process. Instead, the Rules provide for a mandatory, automatic review by the Secretary-General of the tribunal's determination of the fees and expenses of arbitrators and tribunal-appointed experts. **6.89**

This review takes place before the decision fixing the costs of arbitration is issued. Thus, if the tribunal wishes to fix the costs of arbitration in the same award in which it adjudicates the parties' substantive claims, it must plan to submit its determination of fees and expenses to the PCA Secretary-General for review sufficiently **6.90** in advance of the date on which it wishes to render its award. Alternatively, the tribunal may issue a separate award on costs once the review process is concluded. Because the review process will not delay the issuance of the award, the text of Article 41(6) of the 2010 UNCITRAL Rules, which provides that a referral for review to the appointing authority shall not 'delay the recognition and enforcement of all parts of the award other than those relating to the determination of the arbitral tribunal's fees and expenses', was omitted from the 2012 PCA Rules.

6.91 As with the review of the tribunal's initial proposal for the calculation of its fees and expenses under Article 41(2), the 2012 PCA Rules do not impose the 45-day time limit of the 2010 UNCITRAL Rules for the PCA Secretary-General to act. In addition to the reasons cited with respect to the absent time limit in Article 41(2), the PCA Drafting Committee was also concerned that the relatively long 45-day deadline would imply to some parties and tribunals that multiple submissions from parties and arbitrators regarding fee disputes should be solicited in all cases. Because the PCA will be administering the case in question, it may possess sufficient information to decide the matter quickly. In contrast, the appointing authority under the 2010 UNCITRAL Rules may have had no involvement in the case until the request for review of the tribunal's determination of fees and expenses is received.

6.92 The 2012 PCA Rules also modify the standard of review of the 2010 UNCITRAL Rules. Under both sets of rules, the tribunal's determination of fees and expenses can be revised if it is inconsistent with the proposal made by the tribunal at the outset of the arbitration pursuant to Article 41(2) of the Rules, and any adjustments made to this proposal by the appointing authority. However, whereas under the 2010 UNCITRAL Rules, the appointing authority can otherwise revise the tribunal's determination only if it is 'manifestly excessive', under the 2012 PCA Rules, the Secretary-General may adjust the determination in all cases where it is inconsistent with the reasonableness standard of Article 41(1).

J. Allocation of Costs—Article 42

1. The costs of arbitration shall in principle be borne by the unsuccessful party or parties. However, the arbitral tribunal may apportion each of such costs between the parties if it determines that apportionment is reasonable, taking into account the circumstances of the case.
2. The arbitral tribunal shall in the final award or, if it deems appropriate, in any other award, determine any amount that a party may have to pay to another party as a result of the decision on allocation of costs.

6.93 Article 42 concerns the allocation of the costs of arbitration between the parties.

6.94 This provision replicates Article 42 of the 2010 UNCITRAL Rules, adopting its improvements on the 1976 UNCITRAL Rules.

Article 42(1) provides that the costs of arbitration will in principle be borne by the unsuccessful party, unless the arbitral tribunal decides otherwise. The costs of arbitration are fixed by the tribunal pursuant to Article 40(1), subject to the controls exercised by the PCA Secretary-General under Article 41. The costs of arbitration are exhaustively defined in Article 40(2) and comprise: (i) the fees and expenses of the tribunal; (ii) the fees and expenses of the PCA International Bureau; (iii) the fees and expenses of the PCA Secretary-General acting in his capacity as appointing authority under the Rules; (iv) the costs of expert and other assistance required by the tribunal; (v) the expenses of witnesses; and (vi) the 'legal and other costs incurred by the parties in relation to the arbitration'. Article 42(1) of the 2012 PCA Rules adopts the changes that the 2010 UNCITRAL Rules made to the 1976 UNCITRAL Rules, which provide that the other costs of arbitration, in principle, follow the event, but that the tribunal is 'free to determine' how to allocate the parties' legal costs. Despite the different presumptions, under all these sets of rules, the allocation of costs is ultimately a discretionary decision to be taken by the tribunal. The decision to allocate is an award and should be reasoned in accordance with Article 34(3). **6.95**

In inter-state proceedings, the practice is for each party to bear its own costs of legal representation and half of the other costs of arbitration, regardless of the outcome.[92] By contrast, the exercise of the tribunal's discretion with respect to the allocation of costs has had highly variable results in PCA-administered investment treaty arbitrations conducted under the 1976 UNCITRAL Rules. Thus, some tribunals have noted the existence of a practice in accordance with which the costs follow the event save in exceptional circumstances,[93] some tribunals have concluded that 'a general trend has developed that arbitration costs should be equally apportioned between the Parties, irrespective of the outcome of the dispute',[94] and others have found that practice corresponds to the rule provided in the 1976 UNCITRAL Rules, which distinguishes between the parties' costs of legal representation and assistance and the other costs of arbitration. **6.96**

---

[92] See eg *ARA Libertad Arbitration*, Argentina v Ghana, PCA Case No 2013-11 (UNCLOS), Rules of Procedure, Arts 26–7; *The Mox Plant Case*, Ireland v United Kingdom, PCA Case No 2002-01 (UNCLOS), Rules of Procedure, Art 16(1); *Guyana v Suriname*, PCA Case No 2004-4 (UNCLOS), Rules of Procedure, Arts 18–19; *Barbados v Trinidad and Tobago*, PCA Case No 2004-2 (UNCLOS), Rules of Procedure, Arts 19–20; *Eritrea-Ethiopia Boundary Commission*, PCA Case No 2001-1, Rules of Procedure (based on PCA State/State Rules), Art 31(1)(a); *Iron Rhine Arbitration*, Belgium v the Netherlands, PCA Case No 2003-2, Rules of Procedure (based on PCA State/State Rules), Art 26(1), (4); *The OSPAR Arbitration*, Ireland v United Kingdom, PCA Case No 2001-3, Rules of Procedure, Arts 21–2.

[93] *1 Chevron Corporation and 2 Texaco Petroleum Company v The Republic of Ecuador*, PCA Case No 2007-2 (Ecuador-United States BIT), (1976 UNCITRAL Rules), Final Award, 31 August 2011, para 375; reproduced in David D Caron and Lee M Caplan, *The UNCITRAL Arbitration Rules: A Commentary* (2nd edn, Oxford University Press, 2013) 882.

[94] *Romak SA v The Republic of Uzbekistan*, PCA Case No 2007-6 (1976 UNCITRAL Rules) (Switzerland-Uzbekistan BIT), Award, 26 November 2009, para 250.

6.97 In addition to the degree of success of the parties, tribunals have, when allocating costs, considered other relevant factors, such as the complexity and novelty of the issues in the arbitration,[95] access to justice concerns,[96] the parties' cooperation toward the progression of the proceedings,[97] any abusive behaviour by a party aimed at derailing or delaying the arbitration,[98] as well as the plausibility of the arguments and the professionalism of the unsuccessful party's lawyers.[99]

---

[95] See eg *Romak SA v The Republic of Uzbekistan*, PCA Case No 2007-6 (Switzerland-Uzbekistan BIT), (1976 UNCITRAL Rules) Award, 26 November 2009, para 50, in which the tribunal explains why it considers that, in investment treaty arbitrations, the costs of arbitration should in principle be equally apportioned between the parties:

> One of the reasons for this, as stated in several awards, is that investment treaty tribunals are called upon to apply a novel mechanism and substantive law to the resolution of these disputes (see, for example, *Azinian v. Mexico, Tradex v. Albania*, and *Berschader v. Russia*). Thus, the initiation of a claim that is ultimately unsuccessful is more understandable than would be the case in commercial arbitration, where municipal law applies. With respect to the present dispute, to the Tribunal's knowledge, there has never been an investment treaty claim decided outside the ICSID system in relation to the enforcement of an arbitral award. Other cases, such as *Saipem*, share similar factual elements with the present dispute, but offered no direct analogy.

See also *HICEE BV v The Slovak Republic*, PCA Case No 2009-11 (Netherlands–Slovakia BIT) (1976 UNCITRAL Rules), Partial Award, 23 May 2011; reproduced in Caron and Caplan (n 90), 56–7.

[96] See eg *The Bank for International Settlements*, 1Dr Horst Reineccius 2 First Eagle SoGen Funds, Inc Mr Pierre Mathieu and La Société de Concours Hippique de La Châtre v Bank for International Settlements, PCA Case No 2000-4, Final Award, 19 September 2003, where the arbitral tribunal, noting that 'a correlative of the immunity of international organizations is an obligation to provide for fair access to justice', decided that the respondent, the Bank for International Settlement, should bear the cost of legal representation of one of the claimants, a private shareholder, despite a provision in the applicable arbitration rules stating that each party would bear its own costs (paras 125–9).

[97] See eg *HICEE BV v The Slovak Republic*, PCA Case No 2009-11 (Netherlands–Slovakia BIT) (1976 UNCITRAL Rules), Partial Award, 23 May 2011; reproduced in Caron and Caplan (n 90), paras 56–7: 'the Parties were animated by a sense of practicality and economy in agreeing to hive off the Treaty Interpretation Issue for preliminary decision... their sound judgment in that respect has been vindicated by the events... the Parties are particularly to be commended for their cooperation with the Tribunal and for the concision and precision of their written and oral arguments'.

[98] See eg *Romak SA (Switzerland) v The Republic of Uzbekistan*, PCA Case No 2007-6 (Switzerland-Uzbekistan BIT), (1976 UNCITRAL Rules) Award, 26 November 2009, para 51.

[99] See eg *Polis Fondi Immobiliari di Banche Popolare SGRpA v International Fund for Agricultural Development*, PCA Case No 2010-8 (1976 UNCITRAL Rules), Award, 17 December 2010, paras 225–6, an arbitration between a private party and an intergovernmental organization that arose out of a lease agreement, where the tribunal apportioned the costs of the arbitration between the parties on the following grounds:

> 225. In the present case, both Parties have behaved professionally in presenting their claims and defenses. It is obvious that the Claimant cannot be considered the 'unsuccessful party' in these proceedings within the meaning of Article 40(1) of the UNCITRAL Rules; after all the Claimant ultimately succeeded both in its Claim and in its defense against the Respondent's Counterclaim. On the other hand, however, the Tribunal is mindful of the fact that the Claimant prevailed on both counts—the Claim and the Counterclaim—because the Tribunal has decided to interpret the Parties' conduct in relation to the Lease Agreement in a manner that supports the Claimant's reading of the Lease Agreement, rather than the Respondent's. Everything in this arbitration ultimately

In some cases, the arbitral tribunal has also found that there was no clearly successful party, for example because the claimant largely prevailed on jurisdiction and merits, while the respondent was mostly successful on damages.[100] In cases of settlement, parties most often agree to bear their own costs,[101] but an unequal allocation of costs may also form part of a settlement. In a termination order issued in a PCA-administered multi-party arbitration between two private parties and two states, the arbitral tribunal recorded the parties' agreement that each side would bear the costs of the arbitrator appointed by it and an equal share of the costs of the chairman, and further determined that each side would bear the remainder of the costs of arbitration in equal shares. **6.98**

When proceedings are terminated due to the claimant's failure to participate, tribunals have sometimes chosen to penalize the claimant for wasting the tribunal's time. In one investment treaty arbitration administered by the PCA under the 1976 UNCITRAL Rules, where the proceedings were terminated due to the claimant's failure to supply its share of the requested deposit (while the respondent had dutifully paid its own share), the tribunal found that although no award deciding the claims had been rendered, the claimant nevertheless should be considered as the unsuccessful party, as it had failed 'to meet [its] basic obligations and to orderly prosecute [its] claims'. The tribunal reasoned that the costs of arbitration (other than the respondent's legal costs) had been incurred as a result of the claimant's decision to commence the arbitration and its subsequent refusal to pursue its claims in an efficient manner in accordance with the applicable procedural rules. Nevertheless, the tribunal did not consider it reasonable to order the claimant to reimburse the respondent for its costs of legal representation, finding that the respondent's lawyers had spent an excessive number of hours on the case at an early stage of the proceedings. **6.99**

turned on the threshold issue of the interpretation of the Parties' conduct, and it was not conceivable for either Party to prevail in part on the Claim or the Counterclaim.

226. In the Tribunal's view, the Respondent developed a plausible and coherent line of argument in support of its contention that the Parties adjusted the rate of the rental payment by agreement, taking particular account of the Headquarters Agreement. Having reviewed the facts of the case, the Tribunal disagrees with the Respondent's contention that such an adjustment was indeed agreed between the Parties. The fact that the Respondent's theory did not prevail, however, does not necessarily mean that the Respondent should therefore be penalized with the entirety of the costs of the proceedings.

[100] *1 Chevron Corporation and 2 Texaco Petroleum Company v The Republic of Ecuador*, PCA Case No 2007-2 (Ecuador-United States BIT), (1976 UNCITRAL Rules) Final Award, 31 August 2011, para 376; reproduced in Caron and Caplan (n 90), 882.

[101] See eg *TCW Group Inc and Dominican Energy Holdings LP v The Dominican Republic*, PCA Case No 2008-6 (CAFTA-DR) (1976 UNCITRAL Rules), Consent Award, 16 July 2009.

6.100 Article 42(2) of the Rules specifies that the arbitral tribunal must decide on the allocation of costs in an award and indicate the exact amount that one party may have to pay to the other as a result of this decision. The latter requirement, which did not exist under the 1976 UNCITRAL Rules, was added to avoid any difficulties where enforcement may be sought in national courts.[102]

K. Deposit of Costs—Article 43

1. The International Bureau, following the commencement of the arbitration, may request the parties to deposit an equal amount as an advance for the costs referred to in article 40, paragraphs 2(a), (b), (c), and (f). All amounts deposited by the parties pursuant to this paragraph and paragraph 2 of this article shall be directed to the International Bureau, and disbursed by it for such costs, including, inter alia, fees to the arbitrators, to the appointing authority, and to the International Bureau. The International Bureau shall ensure that any disbursements of arbitral tribunal fees and expenses made prior to the fixing of the costs of arbitration pursuant to article 40 are consistent with the criteria in article 41, paragraph 1 and with the arbitral tribunal's proposal (and any adjustments thereto) under article 41, paragraph 2.
2. During the course of the arbitral proceedings the International Bureau may request supplementary deposits from the parties.
3. Any deposit of security for costs ordered by the arbitral tribunal pursuant to article 26 shall be directed to the International Bureau and disbursed by it upon order from the arbitral tribunal.
4. If the requested deposits are not paid in full within 30 days after the receipt of the request or such other period as may be set by the International Bureau, the International Bureau shall so inform the parties in order that one or more of them may make the required payment. If such payment is not made, the arbitral tribunal may order the suspension or termination of the arbitral proceedings.
5. After a termination order or final award has been made, the International Bureau shall render an accounting to the parties of the deposits received and return any unexpended balance to the parties.

6.101 Article 43 concerns the parties' deposits for the costs of arbitration.

6.102 This provision is based on Article 41 of the PCA State/State Rules, Article 41 of the PCA State/International Organization Rules, and Article 43 of the 2010 UNCITRAL Rules.

6.103 Each of these sets of procedural rules establishes a mechanism whereby the parties deposit equal amounts throughout the arbitral proceedings as advances principally for

[102] Report of the UNCITRAL Working Group II (Arbitration and Conciliation) on the work of its 52nd session, 1–5 February 2010, A/CN.9/688, para 123. However, in cases involving only states and intergovernmental organizations, the parties in any event will likely not have submitted to the jurisdiction of any national courts by virtue of their agreement to arbitrate (see discussion under Art 1(2)).

the fees and expenses of arbitrators, which amounts can be disbursed once services are rendered. This mechanism ensures that arbitrators and others involved in the arbitration are remunerated for their services.

The UNCITRAL Rules, which provide for ad hoc arbitration, put the arbitral tribunal in charge of the parties' deposits. The tribunal has discretion to request, hold, and disburse deposits, with the sole caveat that, upon a party's request, the tribunal must consult the appointing authority prior to fixing the amounts of the deposits.[103] In contrast, the 2012 PCA Rules assign the financial administration of the arbitration to the PCA International Bureau. **6.104**

Financial administration of an arbitration is a function commonly performed by arbitral institutions.[104] Thus, the PCA has assured the financial administration of numerous inter-state arbitrations.[105] In addition, in cases conducted under the UNCITRAL Rules, the PCA routinely assists tribunals in discharging their financial and administrative tasks, proposing estimates for the costs of arbitration in order to fix the amounts of deposits, holding deposits, and disbursing them upon the tribunal's instruction.[106] Entrusting the arbitration's finances to an institution relieves the tribunal from the administrative burden of managing deposits and eliminates any potential concerns arising from the tribunal's unfettered discretion to request and disburse deposits under the UNCITRAL Rules. **6.105**

Specifically, pursuant to Article 43(1) and (2) of the Rules, the PCA International Bureau is empowered: **6.106**

- at the commencement of the arbitration, to request an initial deposit from the parties as an advance for the costs referred to in Article 40(2)(a), (b), (c), and (f)—that is, for the fees and expenses of arbitrators, tribunal-appointed experts, or other assistants, the PCA International Bureau, and the PCA Secretary-General acting as appointing authority;

---

[103] Art 43(3). However, the consultation procedure is rarely used, probably due to the concern that requesting such consultation during the arbitration might not be welcomed by the arbitral tribunal. The Iran-United States Claims Tribunal thus omitted this procedure when adapting the 1976 UNCITRAL Rules for its own rules of procedure.

[104] See eg 2012 ICC Rules, Art 36.

[105] See eg *ARA Libertad Arbitration*, Argentina v Ghana, PCA Case No 2013-11 (UNCLOS), Rules of Procedure, Art 28; *The Mox Plant Case*, Ireland v United Kingdom, PCA Case No 2002-01 (UNCLOS), Rules of Procedure, Art 18; *Guyana v Suriname*, PCA Case No 2004-4 (UNCLOS), Rules of Procedure, Art 18; *Barbados v Trinidad and Tobago*, PCA Case No 2004-2 (UNCLOS), Rules of Procedure, Art 21; *Iron Rhine Arbitration*, Belgium v the Netherlands, PCA Case No 2003-2, Rules of Procedure (based on PCA State/State Rules), Art 27; *The OSPAR Arbitration*, Ireland v United Kingdom, PCA Case No 2001-3, Rules of Procedure, Art 23.

[106] See eg *Bilcon of Delaware v Canada*, PCA Case No 2009-4 (NAFTA) (1976 UNCITRAL Rules), Procedural Order No 1, 1 April 2009, para 14; and *Guaracachi America Inc and Rurelec PLC v Plurinational State of Bolivia*, PCA Case No 2011-17 (China–Mongolia BIT) (2010 UNCITRAL Rules), Terms of Appointment and Procedural Order No 1, Art 7.1.3, providing that the PCA shall manage the deposit.

- in the course of the arbitration, to request supplementary deposits from the parties to cover these same costs; and
- to disburse the parties' deposits to cover the costs for which the deposits were intended.

6.107 It is the International Bureau's responsibility to ensure that, at any given time during the arbitral proceedings, sufficient amounts are held as deposits to cover the costs being incurred, and that the procedural schedule is not held up by the unexpected need to replenish deposits. In practice, in fixing the amount of the initial deposit, the International Bureau usually estimates the costs that are likely to be incurred in the initial months of the proceeding, leaving a margin for unexpected events. It then requests supplementary deposits as the proceedings unfold.

6.108 Pursuant to Article 43(4), the parties must make their deposits within '30 days after the receipt of the request or such other period as may be set by the International Bureau'. This provision finds the middle ground between the fixed 30-day time period set in the 2010 UNCITRAL Rules and the 60-day time period provided in the PCA State/State Rules, State/International Organization Rules, and International Organization/Private Party Rules[107] in recognition of the additional time that may be required by some states and intergovernmental organizations to obtain internal authorizations for the disbursement of funds. As stated in the Explanatory Note to the 2012 PCA Rules, when receiving requests from parties to extend this deadline, the International Bureau will consider the longer deadlines set in corresponding provisions of the 1990s PCA Rules.[108]

6.109 In disbursing the parties' deposits to cover the fees and expenses of arbitrators in the course of the arbitral proceedings, the International Bureau must ensure that these fees and expenses are consistent with the reasonableness requirement of Article 41(1) and the tribunal's initial proposal under Article 41(2) as to how it will determine its fees and expenses. This continuous review obligation is intended to allow the International Bureau to identify any inconsistency with the criteria of Article 41(1) in an arbitrator's billing practices and to inform the concerned arbitrator long before the arbitral tribunal fixes the costs of arbitration pursuant to Article 40(1). In principle, any discrepancies should therefore be dealt with at an early stage, ensuring the smooth and efficient operation of the mandatory review procedure foreseen in Article 41(3). The International Bureau is also in a position to ensure that any calculation errors in arbitrators' invoices are corrected without delay.

6.110 The parties are expected to contribute to any deposit for costs equally. However, pursuant to Article 43(4), if one of the parties fails to pay its share of the deposit

[107] PCA State/State Rules, Art 41(3); PCA State/International Organization Rules, Art 41(3); PCA International Organization/Private Party Rules, Art 41(3). See also PCA Natural Resources/Environmental Rules, Art 41(3).

[108] Explanatory Note, reproduced in Appendix I.

within the specified time period, the other party will be expected to pay the outstanding portion of the deposit, without prejudice to any future decision as to the allocation of costs. While the International Bureau sets the initial deadline for the payment of the parties' deposits, once that deadline has passed it is for the arbitral tribunal to determine when it will take action and either suspend or terminate the proceedings. The tribunal will typically suspend the proceedings in cases where it expects the relevant party to make the requested deposit. However, the tribunal may opt to terminate the proceedings if the deposits are not made within a reasonable period of time.

Article 43(3) deals with deposits made by the parties as security for costs. These **6.111** deposits are made only upon the arbitral tribunal exercising its power to order interim measures under Article 26, and can be disbursed by the International Bureau only upon an order of the tribunal, typically once the tribunal has decided on the allocation of the costs of arbitration pursuant to Article 42. The sole role of the International Bureau is to hold these deposits and disburse them upon the tribunal's instruction.

Article 43(5) of the Rules provides that, at the end of the arbitration, the International **6.112** Bureau shall render an accounting to the parties of the deposits received and return any unexpended balance to the parties. Unexpended deposits will normally be reimbursed to the parties in the same proportion in which they were made, unless another proportion has been agreed.

Appendices

APPENDIX I

Explanatory Note of the International Bureau of the Permanent Court of Arbitration ('PCA') Regarding Time Periods Under the PCA Arbitration Rules 2012 ('2012 PCA Rules')

Certain time periods provided in the 2012 PCA Rules are shorter than those set forth in the PCA arbitration rules adopted in the 1990s ('1990s PCA Rules'). Where the 2012 PCA Rules empower the PCA International Bureau to extend default time periods provided in the Rules (see Articles 4(1), 8(2)(b), 9(3) and 43(4) of the 2012 PCA Rules) and the International Bureau receives a request to extend a time period that it considers justified, the time periods set forth in the 1990s PCA Rules will serve as a guideline for the extensions that the International Bureau may decide to grant.

APPENDIX II

Convention for the Pacific Settlement of International Disputes (1899)[1]

His Majesty the German Emperor, King of Prussia; His Majesty the Emperor of Austria, King of Bohemia, etc. and Apostolic King of Hungary; His Majesty the King of the Belgians; His Majesty the Emperor of China; His Majesty the King of Denmark; His Majesty the King of Spain and in His Name Her Majesty the Queen Regent of the Kingdom; the President of the United States of America; the President of the United Mexican States; the President of the French Republic; Her Majesty the Queen of the United Kingdom of Great Britain and Ireland, Empress of India; His Majesty the King of the Hellenes; His Majesty the King of Italy; His Majesty the Emperor of Japan; His Royal Highness the Grand Duke of Luxembourg, Duke of Nassau; His Highness the Prince of Montenegro; Her Majesty the Queen of the Netherlands; His Imperial Majesty the Shah of Persia; His Majesty the King of Portugal and of the Algarves, etc.; His Majesty the King of Roumania; His Majesty the Emperor of all the Russias; His Majesty the King of Serbia; his Majesty the King of Siam; His Majesty the King of Sweden and Norway; the Swiss Federal Council; His Majesty the Emperor of the Ottomans and His Royal Highness the Prince of Bulgaria;

Animated by a strong desire to work for the maintenance of general peace;

Resolved to promote by their best efforts the friendly settlement of international disputes;

Recognizing the solidarity uniting the members of the society of civilized nations;

Desirous of extending the empire of law, and of strengthening the appreciation of international justice;

Convinced that the permanent institution of a tribunal of arbitration, accessible to all, in the midst of the independent Powers, will contribute effectively to this result;

Having regard to the advantages attending the general and regular organization of the procedure of arbitration;

Sharing the opinion of the august initiator of the International Peace Conference that it is expedient to record in an international agreement the principles of equity and right on which are based the security of States and the welfare of peoples;

Being desirous of concluding a Convention to this effect, have appointed as their plenipotentiaries, to wit:

(Here follow the names of plenipotentiaries.)

Who, after having communicated their full powers, found in good and due form, have agreed on the following provisions:

Title I. On the Maintenance of the General Peace

Article 1

With a view to obviating, as far as possible, recourse to force in the relations between States, the Signatory Powers agree to use their best efforts to insure the pacific settlement of international differences.

---

[1] The text of the Convention reproduced here is a translation of the French text adopted at the 1899 Peace Conference. The French-language version is authoritative.

Title II. On Good Offices and Mediation

Article 2

In case of serious disagreement or conflict, before an appeal to arms the Signatory Powers agree to have recourse, as far as circumstances allow, to the good offices or mediation of one or more friendly Powers.

Article 3

Independently of this recourse, the Signatory Powers recommend that one or more Powers, strangers to the dispute, should, on their own initiative, and as far as circumstances may allow, offer their good offices or mediation to the States at variance.

Powers, strangers to the dispute, have the right to offer good offices or mediation, even during the course of hostilities.

The exercise of this right can never be regarded by one or the other of the parties in conflict as an unfriendly act.

Article 4

The part of the mediator consists in reconciling the opposing claims and appeasing the feelings of resentment which may have arisen between the States at variance.

Article 5

The functions of the mediator are at an end when once it is declared, either by one of the parties to the dispute, or by the mediator himself, that the means of reconciliation proposed by him are not accepted.

Article 6

Good offices and mediation, either at the request of the parties at variance, or on the initiative of Powers strangers to the dispute, have exclusively the character of advice, and never have binding force.

Article 7

The acceptance of mediation cannot, unless there be an agreement to the contrary, have the effect of interrupting, delaying, or hindering mobilization or other measures of preparation for war.

If mediation occurs after the commencement of hostilities, it causes no interruption to the military operations in progress, unless there be an agreement to the contrary.

Article 8

The Signatory Powers are agreed in recommending the application, when circumstances allow, of special mediation in the following form:

In case of a serious difference endangering the peace, the States at variance choose respectively a Power, to whom they intrust the mission of entering into direct communication with the Power chosen on the other side, with the object of preventing the rupture of pacific relations.

For the period of this mandate, the term of which, unless otherwise stipulated, cannot exceed thirty days, the States in conflict cease from all direct communication on the subject of the dispute, which is regarded as referred exclusively to the mediating Powers, who must use their best efforts to settle it.

In case of a definite rupture of pacific relations, these Powers are charged with the joint task of taking advantage of any opportunity to restore peace.

Title III. On International Commissions of Inquiry

Article 9

In differences of an international nature involving neither honour nor vital interests, and arising from a difference of opinion on points of fact, the Signatory Powers recommend that the parties, who have not been able to come to an agreement by means of diplomacy, should, as far as circumstances allow, institute an International Commission of Inquiry, to facilitate a solution of these differences by elucidating the facts by means of an impartial and conscientious investigation.

Article 10

The International Commissions of Inquiry are constituted by special agreement between the parties in conflict.

The Convention for an inquiry defines the facts to be examined and the extent of the Commissioners' powers.

It settles the procedure.

On the inquiry both sides must be heard.

The form and the periods to be observed, if not stated in the Inquiry Convention, are decided by the Commission itself.

Article 11

The International Commissions of Inquiry are formed, unless otherwise stipulated, in the manner fixed by Article 32 of the present Convention.

Article 12

The Powers in dispute engage to supply the International Commission of Inquiry, as fully as they may think possible, with all means and facilities necessary to enable it to be completely acquainted with and to accurately understand the facts in question.

Article 13

The International Commission of Inquiry communicates its Report to the conflicting Powers, signed by all the members of the Commission.

Article 14

The Report of the International Commission of Inquiry is limited to a statement of facts, and has in no way the character of an Arbitral Award. It leaves the conflicting Powers entire freedom as to the effect to be given to this statement.

Title IV. On International Arbitration

Chapter I. On the system of arbitration

Article 15

International arbitration has for its object the settlement of differences between States by judges of their own choice, and on the basis of respect for law.

Article 16

In questions of a legal nature, and especially in the interpretation or application of International Conventions, arbitration is recognized by the Signatory Powers as the most effective, and at the same time the most equitable, means of settling disputes which diplomacy has failed to settle.

Article 17

The Arbitration Convention is concluded for questions already existing or for questions which may arise eventually.

It may embrace any dispute or only disputes of a certain category.

Article 18

The Arbitration Convention implies the engagement to submit loyally to the Award.

Article 19

Independently of general or private Treaties expressly stipulating recourse to arbitration as obligatory on the Signatory Powers, these Powers reserve to themselves the right of concluding, either before the ratification of the present Act or later, new Agreements, general or private, with a view to extending obligatory arbitration to all cases which they may consider it possible to submit to it.

Chapter II. On the Permanent Court of Arbitration

Article 20

With the object of facilitating an immediate recourse to arbitration for international differences, which it has not been possible to settle by diplomacy, the Signatory Powers undertake to organize a Permanent Court of Arbitration, accessible at all times and operating, unless otherwise stipulated by the parties, in accordance with the Rules of Procedure inserted in the present Convention.

Article 21

The Permanent Court shall be competent for all arbitration cases, unless the parties agree to institute a special Tribunal.

Article 22

An International Bureau, established at The Hague, serves as record office for the Court.

This Bureau is the channel for communications relative to the meetings of the Court.

It has the custody of the archives and conducts all the administrative business.

The Signatory Powers undertake to communicate to the International Bureau at The Hague a duly certified copy of any conditions of arbitration arrived at between them, and of any award concerning them delivered by special Tribunals.

They undertake also to communicate to the Bureau the Laws, Regulations, and documents eventually showing the execution of the Awards given by the Court.

Article 23

Within the three months following its ratification of the present Act, each Signatory Power shall select four persons at the most, of known competency in questions of international law, of the highest moral reputation, and disposed to accept the duties of Arbitrators.

The persons thus selected shall be inscribed, as Members of the Court, in a list which shall be notified by the Bureau to all the Signatory Powers.

Any alteration in the list of Arbitrators is brought by the Bureau to the knowledge of the Signatory Powers.

Two or more Powers may agree on the selection in common of one or more Members.

The same person can be selected by different Powers.

The Members of the Court are appointed for a term of six years. Their appointments can be renewed.

In case of the death or retirement of a Member of the Court, his place shall be filled in accordance with the method of this appointment.

Article 24

When the Signatory Powers desire to have recourse to the Permanent Court for the settlement of a difference that has arisen between them, the Arbitrators called upon to form the competent Tribunal to decide this difference, must be chosen from the general list of Members of the Court.

Failing the direct agreement of the parties on the composition of the Arbitration Tribunal, the following course shall be pursued:

Each party appoints two Arbitrators, and these together choose an Umpire.

If the votes are equal, the choice of the Umpire is intrusted to a third Power, selected by the parties by common accord.

If an agreement is not arrived at on this subject, each party selects a different Power, and the choice of the Umpire is made in concert by the Powers thus selected.

The Tribunal being thus composed, the parties notify to the Bureau their determination to have recourse to the Court and the names of the Arbitrators.

The Tribunal of Arbitration assembles on the date fixed by the parties.

The Members of the Court, in the discharge of their duties and out of their own country, enjoy diplomatic privileges and immunities.

Article 25

The Tribunal of Arbitration has its ordinary seat at The Hague.

Except in cases of necessity, the place of session can only be altered by the Tribunal with the assent of the parties.

Article 26

The International Bureau at The Hague is authorized to place its premises and its staff at the disposal of the Signatory Powers for the operations of any special Board of Arbitration.

The jurisdiction of the Permanent Court may, within the conditions laid down in the Regulations, be extended to disputes between non-Signatory Powers, or between Signatory Powers and non-Signatory Powers, if the parties are agreed on recourse to this Tribunal.

Article 27

The Signatory Powers consider it their duty, if a serious dispute threatens to break out between two or more of them, to remind these latter that the Permanent Court is open to them.

Consequently, they declare that the fact of reminding the conflicting parties of the provisions of the present Convention, and the advice given to them, in the highest interests of peace, to have recourse to the Permanent Court, can only be regarded as friendly actions.

Article 28

A Permanent Administrative Council composed of the Diplomatic Representatives of the Signatory Powers accredited to The Hague and of the Netherlands Minister for Foreign Affairs, who will act as President, shall be instituted in this town as soon as possible after the ratification of the present Act by at least nine Powers.

This Council will be charged with the establishment and organization of the International Bureau, which will be under its direction and control.

It will notify to the Powers the constitution of the Court and will provide for its installation.

It will settle its Rules of Procedure and all other necessary Regulations.

It will decide all questions of administration which may arise with regard to the operations of the Court.

It will have entire control over the appointment, suspension or dismissal of the officials and employees of the Bureau.

It will fix the payments and salaries, and control the general expenditure.

At meetings duly summoned the presence of five members is sufficient to render valid the discussions of the Council. The decisions are taken by a majority of votes.

The Council communicates to the Signatory Powers without delay the Regulations adopted by it. It furnished them with an annual Report on the labours of the Court, the working of the administration, and the expenses.

Article 29

The expenses of the Bureau shall be borne by the Signatory Powers in the proportion fixed for the International Bureau of the Universal Postal Union.

Chapter III. On arbitral procedure

Article 30

With a view to encourage the development of arbitration, the Signatory Powers have agreed on the following Rules which shall be applicable to arbitral procedure, unless other Rules have been agreed on by the parties.

Article 31

The Powers who have recourse to arbitration sign a special Act ('Compromis'), in which the subject of the difference is clearly defined, as well as the extent of the Arbitrators' powers. This Act implies the undertaking of the parties to submit loyally to the Award.

Article 32

The duties of Arbitrator may be conferred on one Arbitrator alone or on several Arbitrators selected by the parties as they please, or chosen by them from the Members of the Permanent Court of Arbitration established by the present Act.

Failing the constitution of the Tribunal by direct agreement between the parties, the following course shall be pursued:

Each party appoints two Arbitrators, and these latter together choose an Umpire.

In case of equal voting, the choice of the Umpire is intrusted to a third Power, selected by the parties by common accord.

If no agreement is arrived at on this subject, each party selects a different Power, and the choice of the Umpire is made in concert by the Powers thus selected.

Article 33

When a Sovereign or the Chief of a State is chosen as Arbitrator, the arbitral procedure is settled by him.

Article 34

The Umpire is by right President of the Tribunal.
When the Tribunal does not include an Umpire, it appoints its own President.

Article 35

In case of the death, retirement, or disability from any cause of one of the Arbitrators, his place shall be filled in accordance with the method of his appointment.

Article 36

The Tribunal's place of session is selected by the parties. Failing this selection the Tribunal sits at The Hague.

The place thus fixed cannot, except in case of necessity, be changed by the Tribunal without the assent of the parties.

Article 37

The parties have the right to appoint delegates or special agents to attend the Tribunal, for the purpose of serving as intermediaries between them and the Tribunal.

They are further authorized to retain, for the defence of their rights and interests before the Tribunal, counsel or advocates appointed by them for this purpose.

Article 38

The Tribunal decides on the choice of languages to be used by itself, and to be authorized for use before it.

Article 39

As a general rule the arbitral procedure comprises two distinct phases; preliminary examination and discussion.

Preliminary examination consists in the communication by the respective agents to the members of the Tribunal and to the opposite party of all printed or written Acts and of all documents containing the arguments invoked in the case. This communication shall be made in the form and within the periods fixed by the Tribunal in accordance with Article 49.

Discussion consists in the oral development before the Tribunal of the arguments of the parties.

Article 40

Every document produced by one party must be communicated to the other party.

Article 41

The discussions are under the direction of the President.
They are only public if it be so decided by the Tribunal, with the assent of the parties.
They are recorded in the procès-verbaux drawn up by the Secretaries appointed by the President. These procès-verbaux alone have an authentic character.

Article 42

When the preliminary examination is concluded, the Tribunal has the right to refuse discussion of all fresh Acts or documents which one party may desire to submit to it without the consent of the other party.

Article 43

The Tribunal is free to take into consideration fresh Acts or documents to which its attention may be drawn by the agents or counsel of the parties.

In this case, the Tribunal has the right to require the production of these Acts or documents, but is obliged to make them known to the opposite party.

Article 44

The Tribunal can, besides, require from the agents of the parties the production of all Acts, and can demand all necessary explanations. In case of refusal, the Tribunal takes note of it.

Article 45

The agents and counsel of the parties are authorized to present orally to the Tribunal all the arguments they may think expedient in defence of their case.

Article 46

They have the right to raise objections and points.

The decisions of the Tribunal on those points are final, and cannot form the subject of any subsequent discussion.

Article 47

The members of the Tribunal have the right to put questions to the agents and counsel of the parties, and to demand explanations from them on doubtful points.

Neither the questions put nor the remarks made by members of the Tribunal during the discussions can be regarded as an expression of opinion by the Tribunal in general, or by its members in particular.

Article 48

The Tribunal is authorized to declare its competence in interpreting the 'Compromis' as well as the other Treaties which may be invoked in the case, and in applying the principles of international law.

Article 49

The Tribunal has the right to issue Rules of Procedure for the conduct of the case, to decide the forms and periods within which each party must conclude its arguments, and to arrange all the formalities required for dealing with the evidence.

Article 50

When the agents and counsel of the parties have submitted all explanations and evidence in support of their case, the President pronounces the discussion closed.

Article 51

The deliberations of the Tribunal take place in private.
Every decision is taken by a majority of members of the Tribunal.
The refusal of a member to vote must be recorded in the procès-verbal.

Article 52

The Award, given by a majority of votes, is accompanied by a statement of reasons.
It is drawn up in writing and signed by each member of the Tribunal.
Those members who are in the minority may record their dissent when signing.

Article 53

The Award is read out at a public meeting of the Tribunal, the agents and counsel of the parties being present, or duly summoned to attend.

Article 54

The Award, duly pronounced and notified to the agents of the parties at variance, puts an end to the dispute definitively and without appeal.

Article 55

The parties can reserve in the 'Compromis' the right to demand the revision of the Award.

In this case, and unless there be an agreement to the contrary, the demand must be addressed to the Tribunal which pronounced the Award. It can only be made on the ground of the discovery of some new fact calculated to exercise a decisive influence on the Award, and which, at the time the discussion was closed, was unknown to the Tribunal and to the party demanding the revision.

Proceedings for revision can only be instituted by a decision of the Tribunal expressly recording the existence of the new fact, recognizing in it the character described in the foregoing paragraph, and declaring the demand admissible on this ground.

The 'Compromis' fixes the period within which the demand for revision must be made.

Article 56

The Award is only binding on the parties who concluded the 'Compromis'.

When there is a question of interpreting a Convention to which Powers other than those concerned in the dispute are parties, the latter notify to the former the 'Compromis' they have concluded. Each of these Powers has the right to intervene in the case. If one or more of them avail themselves of this right, the interpretation contained in the Award is equally binding on them.

Article 57

Each party pays its own expenses and an equal share of those of the Tribunal.

General provisions

Article 58

The present Convention shall be ratified as speedily as possible.

The ratifications shall be deposited at The Hague.

A procès-verbal shall be drawn up recording the receipt of each ratification, and a copy duly certified shall be sent, through the diplomatic channel, to all the Powers who were represented at the International Peace Conference at The Hague.

Article 59

The non-Signatory Powers who were represented at the International Peace Conference can adhere to the present Convention. For this purpose they must make known their adhesion to the Contracting Powers by a written notification addressed to the Netherlands Government, and communicated by it to all the other Contracting Powers.

Article 60

The conditions on which the Powers who were not represented at the International Peace Conference can adhere to the present Convention shall form the subject of a subsequent Agreement among the Contracting Powers.

Article 61

In the event of one of the High Contracting Parties denouncing the present Convention, this denunciation would not take effect until a year after its notification made in writing to the Netherlands Government, and by it communicated at once to all the other Contracting Powers.

This denunciation shall only affect the notifying Power.

In faith of which the Plenipotentiaries have signed the present Convention and affixed their seals to it.

Done at The Hague, the 29th July, 1899, in a single copy, which shall remain in the archives of the Netherlands Government, and copies of it, duly certified, be sent through the diplomatic channel to the Contracting Powers.

APPENDIX III

Convention for the Pacific Settlement of International Disputes (1907)[1]

His Majesty the German Emperor, King of Prussia; the President of the United States of America; the President of the Argentine Republic; His Majesty the Emperor of Austria, King of Bohemia, etc., and Apostolic King of Hungary; His Majesty the King of the Belgians; the President of the Republic of Bolivia; the President of the Republic of the United States of Brazil; His Royal Highness the Prince of Bulgaria; the President of the Republic of Chile; His Majesty the Emperor of China; the President of the Republic of Colombia; the Provisional Governor of the Republic of Cuba; His Majesty the King of Denmark; the President of the Dominican Republic; the President of the Republic of Ecuador; His Majesty the King of Spain; the President of the French Republic; His Majesty the King of the United Kingdom of Great Britain and Ireland and of the British Dominions beyond the Seas, Emperor of India; His Majesty the King of the Hellenes; the President of the Republic of Guatemala; the President of the Republic of Haiti; His Majesty the King of Italy; His Majesty the Emperor of Japan; His Royal Highness the Grand Duke of Luxembourg, Duke of Nassau; the President of the United States of Mexico; His Royal Highness the Prince of Montenegro; the President of the Republic of Nicaragua; His Majesty the King of Norway; the President of the Republic of Panama; the President of the Republic of Paraguay; Her Majesty the Queen of the Netherlands; the President of the Republic of Peru; His Imperial Majesty the Shah of Persia; His Majesty the King of Roumania; His Majesty the Emperor of All the Russias; the President of the Republic of Salvador; His Majesty the King of Servia; His Majesty the King of Siam; His Majesty the King of Sweden; the Swiss Federal Council; His Majesty the Emperor of the Ottomans; the President of the Oriental Republic of Uruguay; the President of the United States of Venezuela;

Animated by the sincere desire to work for the maintenance of general peace;

Resolved to promote by all the efforts in their power the friendly settlement of international disputes;

Recognizing the solidarity uniting the members of the society of civilized nations;

Desirous of extending the empire of law and of strengthening the appreciation of international justice;

Convinced that the permanent institution of a Tribunal of Arbitration accessible to all, in the midst of independent Powers, will contribute effectively to this result;

Having regard to the advantages attending the general and regular organization of the procedure of arbitration;

Sharing the opinion of the august initiator of the International Peace Conference that it is expedient to record in an International Agreement the principles of equity and right on which are based the security of States and the welfare of peoples;

Being desirous, with this object, of insuring the better working in practice of Commissions of Inquiry and Tribunals of Arbitration, and of facilitating recourse to arbitration in cases which allow of a summary procedure;

Have deemed it necessary to revise in certain particulars and to complete the work of the First Peace Conference for the pacific settlement of international disputes;

[1] The text of the Convention reproduced here is a translation of the French text adopted at the 1907 Peace Conference. The French-language version is authoritative.

The High Contracting Parties have resolved to conclude a new Convention for this purpose, and have appointed the following as their Plenipotentiaries:

(Here follow the names of Plenipotentiaries.)

Who, after having deposited their full powers, found in good and due form, have agreed upon the following:

Part I. The Maintenance of General Peace

Article 1

With a view to obviating as far as possible recourse to force in the relations between States, the Contracting Powers agree to use their best efforts to ensure the pacific settlement of international differences.

Part II. Good Offices and Mediation

Article 2

In case of serious disagreement or dispute, before an appeal to arms, the Contracting Powers agree to have recourse, as far as circumstances allow, to the good offices or mediation of one or more friendly Powers.

Article 3

Independently of this recourse, the Contracting Powers deem it expedient and desirable that one or more Powers, strangers to the dispute, should, on their own initiative and as far as circumstances may allow, offer their good offices or mediation to the States at variance.

Powers strangers to the dispute have the right to offer good offices or mediation even during the course of hostilities.

The exercise of this right can never be regarded by either of the parties in dispute as an unfriendly act.

Article 4

The part of the mediator consists in reconciling the opposing claims and appeasing the feelings of resentment which may have arisen between the States at variance.

Article 5

The functions of the mediator are at an end when once it is declared, either by one of the parties to the dispute or by the mediator himself, that the means of reconciliation proposed by him are not accepted.

Article 6

Good offices and mediation undertaken either at the request of the parties in dispute or on the initiative of Powers strangers to the dispute have exclusively the character of advice, and never have binding force.

Article 7

The acceptance of mediation cannot, unless there be an agreement to the contrary, have the effect of interrupting, delaying, or hindering mobilization or other measures of preparation for war.

If it takes place after the commencement of hostilities, the military operations in progress are not interrupted in the absence of an agreement to the contrary.

Article 8

The Contracting Powers are agreed in recommending the application, when circumstances allow, of special mediation in the following form:

In case of a serious difference endangering peace, the States at variance choose respectively a Power, to which they intrust the mission of entering into direct communication with the Power chosen on the other side, with the object of preventing the rupture of pacific relations.

For the period of this mandate, the term of which, unless otherwise stipulated, cannot exceed thirty days, the States in dispute cease from all direct communication on the subject of the dispute, which is regarded as referred exclusively to the mediating Powers, which must use their best efforts to settle it.

In case of a definite rupture of pacific relations, these Powers are charged with the joint task of taking advantage of any opportunity to restore peace.

Part III. International Commissions of Inquiry

Article 9

In disputes of an international nature involving neither honour nor vital interests, and arising from a difference of opinion on points of facts, the Contracting Powers deem it expedient and desirable that the parties who have not been able to come to an agreement by means of diplomacy, should, as far as circumstances allow, institute an International Commission of Inquiry, to facilitate a solution of these disputes by elucidating the facts by means of an impartial and conscientious investigation.

Article 10

International Commissions of Inquiry are constituted by special agreement between the parties in dispute.

The Inquiry Convention defines the facts to be examined; it determines the mode and time in which the Commission is to be formed and the extent of the powers of the Commissioners.

It also determines, if there is need, where the Commission is to sit, and whether it may remove to another place, the language the Commission shall use and the languages the use of which shall be authorized before it, as well as the date on which each party must deposit its statement of facts, and, generally speaking, all the conditions upon which the parties have agreed.

If the parties consider it necessary to appoint Assessors, the Convention of Inquiry shall determine the mode of their selection and the extent of their powers.

Article 11

If the Inquiry Convention has not determined where the Commission is to sit, it will sit at The Hague.

The place of meeting, once fixed, cannot be altered by the Commission except with the assent of the parties.

If the Inquiry Convention has not determined what languages are to be employed, the question shall be decided by the Commission.

Article 12

Unless an undertaking is made to the contrary, Commissions of Inquiry shall be formed in the manner determined by Articles 45 and 57 of the present Convention.

Article 13

Should one of the Commissioners or one of the Assessors, should there be any, either die, or resign, or be unable for any reason whatever to discharge his functions, the same procedure is followed for filling the vacancy as was followed for appointing him.

Article 14

The parties are entitled to appoint special agents to attend the Commission of Inquiry, whose duty it is to represent them and to act as intermediaries between them and the Commission.

They are further authorized to engage counsel or advocates, appointed by themselves, to state their case and uphold their interests before the Commission.

Article 15

The International Bureau of the Permanent Court of Arbitration acts as registry for the Commissions which sit at The Hague, and shall place its offices and staff at the disposal of the Contracting Powers for the use of the Commission of Inquiry.

Article 16

If the Commission meets elsewhere than at The Hague, it appoints a Secretary-General, whose office serves as registry.

It is the function of the registry, under the control of the President, to make the necessary arrangements for the sittings of the Commission, the preparation of the Minutes, and, while the inquiry lasts, for the charge of the archives, which shall subsequently be transferred to the International Bureau at The Hague.

Article 17

In order to facilitate the constitution and working of Commissions of Inquiry, the Contracting Powers recommend the following rules, which shall be applicable to the inquiry procedure in so far as the parties do not adopt other rules.

Article 18

The Commission shall settle the details of the procedure not covered by the special Inquiry Convention or the present Convention, and shall arrange all the formalities required for dealing with the evidence.

Article 19

On the inquiry both sides must be heard.

At the dates fixed, each party communicates to the Commission and to the other party the statements of facts, if any, and, in all cases, the instruments, papers, and documents which it considers useful for ascertaining the truth, as well as the list of witnesses and experts whose evidence it wishes to be heard.

Article 20

The Commission is entitled, with the assent of the Powers, to move temporarily to any place where it considers it may be useful to have recourse to this means of inquiry or to send one or more of its members. Permission must be obtained from the State on whose territory it is proposed to hold the inquiry.

Article 21

Every investigation, and every examination of a locality, must be made in the presence of the agents and counsel of the parties or after they have been duly summoned.

Article 22

The Commission is entitled to ask from either party for such explanations and information as it considers necessary.

Article 23

The parties undertake to supply the Commission of Inquiry, as fully as they may think possible, with all means and facilities necessary to enable it to become completely acquainted with, and to accurately understand, the facts in question.

They undertake to make use of the means at their disposal, under their municipal law, to insure the appearance of the witnesses or experts who are in their territory and have been summoned before the Commission.

If the witnesses or experts are unable to appear before the Commission, the parties will arrange for their evidence to be taken before the qualified officials of their own country.

Article 24

For all notices to be served by the Commission in the territory of a third Contracting Power, the Commission shall apply direct to the Government of the said Power. The same rule applies in the case of steps being taken on the spot to procure evidence.

The requests for this purpose are to be executed so far as the means at the disposal of the Power applied to under its municipal law allow. They cannot be rejected unless the Power in question considers they are calculated to impair its sovereign rights or its safety.

The Commission will equally be always entitled to act through the Power on whose territory it sits.

Article 25

The witnesses and experts are summoned on the request of the parties or by the Commission of its own motion, and, in every case, through the Government of the State in whose territory they are.

The witnesses are heard in succession and separately in the presence of the agents and counsel, and in the order fixed by the Commission.

Article 26

The examination of witnesses is conducted by the President.

The members of the Commission may however put to each witness questions which they consider likely to throw light on and complete his evidence, or get information on any point concerning the witness within the limits of what is necessary in order to get at the truth.

The agents and counsel of the parties may not interrupt the witness when he is making his statement, nor put any direct question to him, but they may ask the President to put such additional questions to the witness as they think expedient.

Article 27

The witness must give his evidence without being allowed to read any written draft. He may, however, be permitted by the President to consult notes or documents if the nature of the facts referred to necessitates their employment.

Article 28

A Minute of the evidence of the witness is drawn up forthwith and read to the witness. The latter may make such alterations and additions as he thinks necessary, which will be recorded at the end of his statement.

When the whole of his statement has been read to the witness, he is asked to sign it.

Article 29

The agents are authorized, in the course of or at the close of the inquiry, to present in writing to the Commission and to the other party such statements, requisitions, or summaries of the facts as they consider useful for ascertaining the truth.

Article 30

The Commission considers its decisions in private and the proceedings are secret. All questions are decided by a majority of the members of the Commission. If a member declines to vote, the fact must be recorded in the Minutes.

Article 31

The sittings of the Commission are not public, nor the Minutes and documents connected with the inquiry published except in virtue of a decision of the Commission taken with the consent of the parties.

Article 32

After the parties have presented all the explanations and evidence, and the witnesses have all been heard, the President declares the inquiry terminated, and the Commission adjourns to deliberate and to draw up its Report.

Article 33

The Report is signed by all the members of the Commission.

If one of the members refuses to sign, the fact is mentioned; but the validity of the Report is not affected.

Article 34

The Report of the Commission is read at a public sitting, the agents and counsel of the parties being present or duly summoned.

A copy of the Report is given to each party.

Article 35

The Report of the Commission is limited to a statement of facts, and has in no way the character of an Award. It leaves to the parties entire freedom as to the effect to be given to the statement.

Article 36

Each party pays its own expenses and an equal share of the expenses incurred by the Commission.

Part IV. International Arbitration

Chapter I. The system of arbitration

Article 37

International arbitration has for its object the settlement of disputes between States by Judges of their own choice and on the basis of respect for law.

Recourse to arbitration implies an engagement to submit in good faith to the Award.

Article 38

In questions of a legal nature, and especially in the interpretation or application of International Conventions, arbitration is recognized by the Contracting Powers as the most effective, and, at the same time, the most equitable means of settling disputes which diplomacy has failed to settle.

Consequently, it would be desirable that, in disputes about the above-mentioned questions, the Contracting Powers should, if the case arose, have recourse to arbitration, in so far as circumstances permit.

Article 39

The Arbitration Convention is concluded for questions already existing or for questions which may arise eventually.

It may embrace any dispute or only disputes of a certain category.

Article 40

Independently of general or private Treaties expressly stipulating recourse to arbitration as obligatory on the Contracting Powers, the said Powers reserve to themselves the right of concluding new Agreements, general or particular, with a view to extending compulsory arbitration to all cases which they may consider it possible to submit to it.

Chapter II. The Permanent Court of Arbitration

Article 41

With the object of facilitating an immediate recourse to arbitration for international differences, which it has not been possible to settle by diplomacy, the Contracting Powers undertake to maintain the Permanent Court of Arbitration, as established by the First Peace Conference, accessible at all times, and operating, unless otherwise stipulated by the parties, in accordance with the rules of procedure inserted in the present Convention.

Article 42

The Permanent Court is competent for all arbitration cases, unless the parties agree to institute a special Tribunal.

Article 43

The Permanent Court sits at The Hague.

An International Bureau serves as registry for the Court. It is the channel for communications relative to the meetings of the Court; it has charge of the archives and conducts all the administrative business.

The Contracting Powers undertake to communicate to the Bureau, as soon as possible a certified copy of any conditions of arbitration arrived at between them and of any Award concerning them delivered by a special Tribunal.

They likewise undertake to communicate to the Bureau the laws, regulations, and documents eventually showing the execution of the Awards given by the Court.

Article 44

Each Contracting Power selects four persons at the most, of known competency in questions of international law, of the highest moral reputation, and disposed to accept the duties of Arbitrator.

The persons thus elected are inscribed, as Members of the Court, in a list which shall be notified to all the Contracting Powers by the Bureau.

Any alteration in the list of Arbitrators is brought by the Bureau to the knowledge of the Contracting Powers.

Two or more Powers may agree on the selection in common of one or more Members.

The same person can be selected by different Powers. The Members of the Court are appointed for a term of six years. These appointments are renewable.

Should a Member of the Court die or resign, the same procedure is followed for filling the vacancy as was followed for appointing him. In this case the appointment is made for a fresh period of six years.

Article 45

When the Contracting Powers wish to have recourse to the Permanent Court for the settlement of a difference which has arisen between them, the Arbitrators called upon to form the Tribunal with jurisdiction to decide this difference must be chosen from the general list of Members of the Court.

Failing the direct agreement of the parties on the composition of the Arbitration Tribunal, the following course shall be pursued:

Each party appoints two Arbitrators, of whom one only can be its national or chosen from among the persons selected by it as Members of the Permanent Court. These Arbitrators together choose an Umpire.

If the votes are equally divided, the choice of the Umpire is intrusted to a third Power, selected by the parties by common accord.

If an agreement is not arrived at on this subject each party selects a different Power, and the choice of the Umpire is made in concert by the Powers thus selected.

If, within two months' time, these two Powers cannot come to an agreement, each of them presents two candidates taken from the list of Members of the Permanent Court, exclusive of the members selected by the parties and not being nationals of either of them. Drawing lots determines which of the candidates thus presented shall be Umpire.

Article 46

The Tribunal being thus composed, the parties notify to the Bureau their determination to have recourse to the Court, the text of their 'Compromis', and the names of the Arbitrators.

The Bureau communicates without delay to each Arbitrator the 'Compromis', and the names of the other members of the Tribunal.

The Tribunal assembles at the date fixed by the parties. The Bureau makes the necessary arrangements for the meeting.

The members of the Tribunal, in the exercise of their duties and out of their own country, enjoy diplomatic privileges and immunities.

Article 47

The Bureau is authorized to place its offices and staff at the disposal of the Contracting Powers for the use of any special Board of Arbitration.

The jurisdiction of the Permanent Court may, within the conditions laid down in the regulations, be extended to disputes between non-Contracting Powers or between Contracting Powers and non-Contracting Powers, if the parties are agreed on recourse to this Tribunal.

Article 48

The Contracting Powers consider it their duty, if a serious dispute threatens to break out between two or more of them, to remind these latter that the Permanent Court is open to them.

Consequently, they declare that the fact of reminding the parties at variance of the provisions of the present Convention, and the advice given to them, in the highest interests of peace, to have recourse to the Permanent Court, can only be regarded as friendly actions.

In case of dispute between two Powers, one of them can always address to the International Bureau a note containing a declaration that it would be ready to submit the dispute to arbitration.

The Bureau must at once inform the other Power of the declaration.

Article 49

The Permanent Administrative Council, composed of the Diplomatic Representatives of the Contracting Powers accredited to The Hague and of the Netherlands Minister for Foreign Affairs, who will act as President, is charged with the direction and control of the International Bureau.

The Council settles its rules of procedure and all other necessary regulations.

It decides all questions of administration which may arise with regard to the operations of the Court.

It has entire control over the appointment, suspension, or dismissal of the officials and employees of the Bureau.

It fixes the payments and salaries, and controls the general expenditure.

At meetings duly summoned the presence of nine members is sufficient to render valid the discussions of the Council. The decisions are taken by a majority of votes.

The Council communicates to the Contracting Powers without delay the regulations adopted by it. It furnishes them with an annual Report on the labours of the Court, the working of the administration, and the expenditure. The Report likewise contains a résumé of what is important in the documents communicated to the Bureau by the Powers in virtue of Article 43, paragraphs 3 and 4.

Article 50

The expenses of the Bureau shall be borne by the Contracting Powers in the proportion fixed for the International Bureau of the Universal Postal Union.

The expenses to be charged to the adhering Powers shall be reckoned from the date on which their adhesion comes into force.

Chapter III. Arbitration procedure

Article 51

With a view to encouraging the development of arbitration, the Contracting Powers have agreed on the following rules, which are applicable to arbitration procedure, unless other rules have been agreed on by the parties.

Article 52

The Powers which have recourse to arbitration sign a 'Compromis', in which the subject of the dispute is clearly defined, the time allowed for appointing Arbitrators, the form, order, and time in which the communication referred to in Article 63 must be made, and the amount of the sum which each party must deposit in advance to defray the expenses.

The 'Compromis' likewise defines, if there is occasion, the manner of appointing Arbitrators, any special powers which may eventually belong to the Tribunal, where it shall meet, the language it shall use, and the languages the employment of which shall be authorized before it, and, generally speaking, all the conditions on which the parties are agreed.

Article 53

The Permanent Court is competent to settle the 'Compromis', if the parties are agreed to have recourse to it for the purpose.

It is similarly competent, even if the request is only made by one of the parties, when all attempts to reach an understanding through the diplomatic channel have failed, in the case of:

1. A dispute covered by a general Treaty of Arbitration concluded or renewed after the present Convention has come into force, and providing for a 'Compromis' in all disputes and not either explicitly or implicitly excluding the settlement of the 'Compromis' from the competence of the Court. Recourse cannot, however, be had to the Court if the other party declares that in its opinion the dispute does not belong to the category of disputes which can be submitted to compulsory arbitration, unless the Treaty of Arbitration confers upon the Arbitration Tribunal the power of deciding this preliminary question.
2. A dispute arising from contract debts claimed from one Power by another Power as due to its nationals, and for the settlement of which the offer of arbitration has been accepted. This arrangement is not applicable if acceptance is subject to the condition that the 'Compromis' should be settled in some other way.

Article 54

In the cases contemplated in the preceding Article, the 'Compromis' shall be settled by a Commission consisting of five members selected in the manner arranged for in Article 45, paragraphs 3 to 6.

The fifth member is President of the Commission *ex officio*.

Article 55

The duties of Arbitrator may be conferred on one Arbitrator alone or on several Arbitrators selected by the parties as they please, or chosen by them from the Members of the Permanent Court of Arbitration established by the present Convention.

Failing the constitution of the Tribunal by direct agreement between the parties, the course referred to in Article 45, paragraphs 3 to 6, is followed.

Article 56

When a Sovereign or the Chief of a State is chosen as Arbitrator, the arbitration procedure is settled by him.

Article 57

The Umpire is President of the Tribunal *ex officio*.

When the Tribunal does not include an Umpire, it appoints its own President.

Article 58

When the 'Compromis' is settled by a Commission, as contemplated in Article 54, and in the absence of an agreement to the contrary, the Commission itself shall form the Arbitration Tribunal.

Article 59

Should one of the Arbitrators either die, retire, or be unable for any reason whatever to discharge his functions, the same procedure is followed for filling the vacancy as was followed for appointing him.

Article 60

The Tribunal sits at The Hague, unless some other place is selected by the parties.

The Tribunal can only sit in the territory of a third Power with the latter's consent.

The place of meeting once fixed cannot be altered by the Tribunal, except with the consent of the parties.

Article 61

If the question as to what languages are to be used has not been settled by the 'Compromis', it shall be decided by the Tribunal.

Article 62

The parties are entitled to appoint special agents to attend the Tribunal to act as intermediaries between themselves and the Tribunal.

They are further authorized to retain for the defence of their rights and interests before the Tribunal counsel or advocates appointed by themselves for this purpose.

The Members of the Permanent Court may not act as agents, counsel, or advocates except on behalf of the Power which appointed them Members of the Court.

Article 63

As a general rule, arbitration procedure comprises two distinct phases: pleadings and oral discussions.

The pleadings consist in the communication by the respective agents to the members of the Tribunal and the opposite party of cases, counter-cases, and, if necessary, of replies; the parties annex thereto all papers and documents called for in the case. This communication shall be made either directly or through the intermediary of the International Bureau, in the order and within the time fixed by the 'Compromis'.

The time fixed by the 'Compromis' may be extended by mutual agreement by the parties, or by the Tribunal when the latter considers it necessary for the purpose of reaching a just decision.

The discussions consist in the oral development before the Tribunal of the arguments of the parties.

Article 64

A certified copy of every document produced by one party must be communicated to the other party.

Article 65

Unless special circumstances arise, the Tribunal does not meet until the pleadings are closed.

Article 66

The discussions are under the control of the President. They are only public if it be so decided by the Tribunal, with the assent of the parties.

They are recorded in minutes drawn up by the Secretaries appointed by the President. These minutes are signed by the President and by one of the Secretaries and alone have an authentic character.

Article 67

After the close of the pleadings, the Tribunal is entitled to refuse discussion of all new papers or documents which one of the parties may wish to submit to it without the consent of the other party.

Article 68

The Tribunal is free to take into consideration new papers or documents to which its attention may be drawn by the agents or counsel of the parties.

In this case, the Tribunal has the right to require the production of these papers or documents, but is obliged to make them known to the opposite party.

Article 69

The Tribunal can, besides, require from the agents of the parties the production of all papers, and can demand all necessary explanations. In case of refusal the Tribunal takes note of it.

Article 70

The agents and the counsel of the parties are authorized to present orally to the Tribunal all the arguments they may consider expedient in defence of their case.

Article 71

They are entitled to raise objections and points. The decisions of the Tribunal on these points are final and cannot form the subject of any subsequent discussion.

Article 72

The members of the Tribunal are entitled to put questions to the agents and counsel of the parties, and to ask them for explanations on doubtful points.

Neither the questions put, nor the remarks made by members of the Tribunal in the course of the discussions, can be regarded as an expression of opinion by the Tribunal in general or by its members in particular.

Article 73

The Tribunal is authorized to declare its competence in interpreting the 'Compromis', as well as the other Treaties which may be invoked, and in applying the principles of law.

Article 74

The Tribunal is entitled to issue rules of procedure for the conduct of the case, to decide the forms, order, and time in which each party must conclude its arguments, and to arrange all the formalities required for dealing with the evidence.

Article 75

The parties undertake to supply the Tribunal, as fully as they consider possible, with all the information required for deciding the case.

Article 76

For all notices which the Tribunal has to serve in the territory of a third Contracting Power, the Tribunal shall apply direct to the Government of that Power. The same rule applies in the case of steps being taken to procure evidence on the spot.

The requests for this purpose are to be executed as far as the means at the disposal of the Power applied to under its municipal law allow. They cannot be rejected unless the Power in question considers them calculated to impair its own sovereign rights or its safety.

The Court will equally be always entitled to act through the Power on whose territory it sits.

Article 77

When the agents and counsel of the parties have submitted all the explanations and evidence in support of their case the President shall declare the discussion closed.

Article 78

The Tribunal considers its decisions in private and the proceedings remain secret. All questions are decided by a majority of the members of the Tribunal.

Article 79

The Award must give the reasons on which it is based. It contains the names of the Arbitrators; it is signed by the President and Registrar or by the Secretary acting as Registrar.

Article 80

The Award is read out in public sitting, the agents and counsel of the parties being present or duly summoned to attend.

Article 81

The Award, duly pronounced and notified to the agents of the parties, settles the dispute definitively and without appeal.

Article 82

Any dispute arising between the parties as to the interpretation and execution of the Award shall, in the absence of an Agreement to the contrary, be submitted to the Tribunal which pronounced it.

Article 83

The parties can reserve in the 'Compromis' the right to demand the revision of the Award.

In this case and unless there be an Agreement to the contrary, the demand must be addressed to the Tribunal which pronounced the Award. It can only be made on the ground of the discovery of some new fact calculated to exercise a decisive influence upon the Award and which was unknown to the Tribunal and to the party which demanded the revision at the time the discussion was closed.

Proceedings for revision can only be instituted by a decision of the Tribunal expressly recording the existence of the new fact, recognizing in it the character described in the preceding paragraph, and declaring the demand admissible on this ground.

The 'Compromis' fixes the period within which the demand for revision must be made.

Article 84

The Award is not binding except on the parties in dispute.

When it concerns the interpretation of a Convention to which Powers other than those in dispute are parties, they shall inform all the Signatory Powers in good time. Each of these Powers is entitled to intervene in the case. If one or more avail themselves of this right, the interpretation contained in the Award is equally binding on them.

Article 85

Each party pays its own expenses and an equal share of the expenses of the Tribunal.

Chapter IV. Arbitration by summary procedure

Article 86

With a view to facilitating the working of the system of arbitration in disputes admitting of a summary procedure, the Contracting Powers adopt the following rules, which shall be observed in the absence of other arrangements and subject to the reservation that the provisions of Chapter III apply so far as may be.

Article 87

Each of the parties in dispute appoints an Arbitrator. The two Arbitrators thus selected choose an Umpire. If they do not agree on this point, each of them proposes two candidates taken from the general list of the Members of the Permanent Court exclusive of the members appointed by either of the parties and not being nationals of either of them; which of the candidates thus proposed shall be the Umpire is determined by lot. The Umpire presides over the Tribunal, which gives its decisions by a majority of votes.

Article 88

In the absence of any previous agreement the Tribunal, as soon as it is formed, settles the time within which the two parties must submit their respective cases to it.

Article 89

Each party is represented before the Tribunal by an agent, who serves as intermediary between the Tribunal and the Government who appointed him.

Article 90

The proceedings are conducted exclusively in writing. Each party, however, is entitled to ask that witnesses and experts should be called. The Tribunal has, for its part, the right to demand oral explanations from the agents of the two parties, as well as from the experts and witnesses whose appearance in Court it may consider useful.

Part V. Final Provisions

Article 91

The present Convention, duly ratified, shall replace, as between the Contracting Powers, the Convention for the Pacific Settlement of International Disputes of the 29th July, 1899.

Article 92

The present Convention shall be ratified as soon as possible.

The ratifications shall be deposited at The Hague.

The first deposit of ratifications shall be recorded in a *procès-verbal* signed by the Representatives of the Powers which take part therein and by the Netherlands Minister for Foreign Affairs.

The subsequent deposits of ratifications shall be made by means of a written notification, addressed to the Netherlands Government and accompanied by the instrument of ratification.

A duly certified copy of the *procès-verbal* relative to the first deposit of ratifications, of the notifications mentioned in the preceding paragraph, and of the instruments of ratification, shall be immediately sent by the Netherlands Government, through the diplomatic channel, to the Powers invited to the Second Peace Conference, as well as to those Powers which have adhered to the Convention. In the cases contemplated in the preceding paragraph, the said Government shall at the same time inform the Powers of the date on which it received the notification.

Article 93

Non-Signatory Powers which have been invited to the Second Peace Conference may adhere to the present Convention.

The Power which desires to adhere notifies its intention in writing to the Netherlands Government, forwarding to it the act of adhesion, which shall be deposited in the archives of the said Government.

This Government shall immediately forward to all the other Powers invited to the Second Peace Conference a duly certified copy of the notification as well as of the act of adhesion, mentioning the date on which it received the notification.

Article 94

The conditions on which the Powers which have not been invited to the Second Peace Conference may adhere to the present Convention shall form the subject of a subsequent Agreement between the Contracting Powers.

Article 95

The present Convention shall take effect, in the case of the Powers which were not a party to the first deposit of ratifications, sixty days after the date of the *procès-verbal* of this deposit, and, in the case of the Powers which ratify subsequently or which adhere, sixty days after the notification of their ratification or of their adhesion has been received by the Netherlands Government.

Article 96

In the event of one of the Contracting Parties wishing to denounce the present Convention, the denunciation shall be notified in writing to the Netherlands Government, which shall immediately communicate a duly certified copy of the notification to all the other Powers informing them of the date on which it was received.

The denunciation shall only have effect in regard to the notifying Power, and one year after the notification has reached the Netherlands Government.

Article 97

A register kept by the Netherlands Minister for Foreign Affairs shall give the date of the deposit of ratifications effected in virtue of Article 92, paragraphs 3 and 4, as well as the date on which the notifications of adhesion (Article 93, paragraph 2) or of denunciation (Article 96, paragraph 1) have been received.

Each Contracting Power is entitled to have access to this register and to be supplied with duly certified extracts from it.

In faith whereof the Plenipotentiaries have appended their signatures to the present Convention.

Done at The Hague, the 18th October, 1907, in a single copy, which shall remain deposited in the archives of the Netherlands Government, and duly certified copies of which shall be sent, through the diplomatic channel, to the Contracting Powers.

APPENDIX IV

Agreement Concerning the Headquarters of the Permanent Court of Arbitration

between
the Permanent Court of Arbitration,
and
The Kingdom of the Netherlands

Whereas the Conventions for the Pacific Settlement of International Disputes, establishing the Permanent Court of Arbitration were concluded on 29 July, 1899 and 18 October, 1907, and the Kingdom of the Netherlands is a Contracting Power to both Conventions,

Whereas the seat of the International Bureau of the Permanent Court of Arbitration is The Hague, Kingdom of the Netherlands, pursuant to Article 22, paragraph 1, of the Convention of 1899 and Article 43 of the Convention of 1907,

Having regard to the provisions set forth in Article 24 of the 1899 Convention and Article 46, paragraph 4, of the 1907 Convention, establishing, respectively, the diplomatic privileges and immunities of the Members of the Court and members of Tribunals,

Having regard to exchanges of letters in 1930, 1937 and 1972-1974 between the International Bureau of the Permanent Court of Arbitration and the Ministry of Finance of the Netherlands in which provisions were made for exemption from direct tax in respect of salaries for the Secretary-General and the personnel of the Permanent Court of Arbitration, including Netherlands citizens,

Whereas the Parties first named above desire to conclude a more comprehensive agreement,

They have therefore agreed as follows:

Article 1

Definitions

1. '1899 Convention' shall mean the Convention for the Pacific Settlement of International Disputes, concluded at The Hague on 29 July, 1899, and '1907 Convention' shall mean the Convention for the Pacific. Settlement of International Disputes, concluded at The Hague on 18 October, 1907;
2. 'PCA' shall mean the International Bureau of the Permanent Court of Arbitration;
3. 'Government' shall mean the Government of the Kingdom of the Netherlands;
4. 'Appropriate Authorities' shall mean such State, municipal or other authorities of the Kingdom of the Netherlands as may be appropriate in the context of the relevant provisions of this Agreement and in accordance with the laws and customs applicable in the Kingdom of the Netherlands;
5. 'Parties' shall mean the PCA and the Kingdom of the Netherlands;
6. 'Headquarters' shall mean the area and any building, including conference facilities, parts of buildings, land or facilities ancillary thereto, irrespective of ownership, used by the PCA on a permanent basis or from time to time, to carry out official functions;
7. 'PCA Proceedings' shall mean dispute resolution administered by or under the auspices of the PCA, whether or not pursuant to the 1899 Convention, the 1907 Convention, or any of the PCA's optional rules of procedure, in which at least one party is a State, a State-controlled entity, or an intergovernmental organization;

8. 'PCA Adjudicator' shall mean an arbitrator, mediator, conciliator, or member of a commission of inquiry taking part in a hearing, meeting or other activity in relation to PCA Proceedings;
9. 'Participant in Proceedings' shall mean a witness, expert, counsel, party, agent or other party representative, taking part in a hearing, meeting or other activity in relation to PCA Proceedings;
10. 'PCA Meeting' shall mean any meeting of any of the organs or subsidiary organs of the PCA, or any internal conference or other gathering convened by the PCA or under its sponsorship;
11. 'Secretary-General' shall mean the head of the International Bureau of the PCA as set out in Article VIII of the Rules of Procedure of the Administrative Council and Article I of the Rules Concerning the Organization and Internal Working of the International Bureau of the Permanent Court of Arbitration, or in his absence the First Secretary as established in Article IV of the aforementioned rules;
12. 'Officials of the PCA' shall mean the Secretary-General and all members of the staff of the PCA;
13. 'Property' shall mean all property, assets and funds, belonging to the PCA or held or administered by the PCA in furtherance of its functions, including any funds held on deposit for the benefit of PCA Proceedings and any Provident Fund to be established by or conducted under the authority of the PCA, and all income of the PCA;
14. 'Archives of the PCA' shall mean all records, correspondence, documents, manuscripts, computer and media data, photographs, films, video and sound recordings belonging to or held by the PCA or any of its staff members in an official function, or in the possession of any PCA Adjudicator or Participant in Proceedings, and any other material which the Secretary-General and the Government may agree shall form part of the archives of the PCA;
15. 'The Vienna Convention' shall mean the Vienna Convention on Diplomatic Relations of 18 April 1961.

Article 2

Legal personality

The PCA shall possess full legal personality. In particular, it shall have the capacity to contract, to acquire and dispose of immovable and movable property; and to institute legal proceedings.

Article 3

Immunity from legal process; immunity of property from other actions

1. The PCA, and its Property, wherever located and by whomsoever held, shall enjoy immunity from every form of legal process, except in the case of:
   (a) express waiver by the PCA of immunity in a particular case;
   (b) civil action by a third party for damages arising out of an accident caused by a motor vehicle belonging to, or operated on behalf of, the PCA where these damages are not recoverable from insurance.
2. The Headquarters of the PCA shall be inviolable. The Property of the PCA, wherever situated, shall be immune from search, requisition, confiscation, expropriation and any other form of interference, whether by executive, administrative, judicial or legislative action except in so far as the PCA shall have expressly waived its immunity. It is, however, understood that no waiver of immunity shall extend to any measure of execution.
3. The Archives of the PCA, wherever situated, shall be inviolable at all times.

Article 4

The Headquarters

The Appropriate Authorities shall take whatever reasonable action may be necessary, within their powers, to ensure that the PCA shall not be dispossessed of all or any part of the Headquarters. To the extent necessary, the Kingdom of the Netherlands shall either facilitate the acquisition on its territory, in accordance with its laws, by the PCA of premises necessary for its Headquarters or assist the latter in obtaining accommodation in some other way.

Article 5

Law and authority in the Headquarters

1. The Netherlands authorities may not enter the Headquarters except with the consent of, or given on behalf of, the Secretary-General. Any person who enters the Headquarters with the permission of the Secretary-General shall, if so requested by or on behalf of the Secretary-General, leave the Headquarters immediately.
2. This Article shall not prevent the reasonable application of fire protection regulations by the Appropriate Authorities. In addition in any situation posing an immediate threat to life or property, the consent of the Secretary-General to entry into the Headquarters shall be presumed if he or his authorised representative cannot be reached in time.
3. Service of legal process may take place within the Headquarters only with the prior consent of, and under conditions approved by, the Secretary-General.
4. The Secretary-General shall prevent the Headquarters from being used to harbour persons who are:
   (a) avoiding arrest under any law of the Kingdom of the Netherlands;
   (b) endeavouring to evade service of legal process; or
   (c) wanted by the Government for extradition or expulsion to another State.
5. The PCA shall have the right to use a flag and emblem, and to fly its flag at the Headquarters.

Article 6

Protection of the Headquarters

1. The Appropriate Authorities shall exercise due diligence to ensure that the security and tranquillity of the Headquarters are not impaired by any person or group of persons attempting unauthorised entry into, or creating disturbances in, the immediate vicinity of the Headquarters. As may be required for this purpose, the appropriate authorities shall provide adequate police protection on the boundaries and in the vicinity of the Headquarters.
2. If so requested by the Secretary-General, the Appropriate Authorities shall provide a sufficient number of police for the preservation of law and order in the Headquarters.

Article 7

Exemption of the PCA and its property from taxes and duties

1. Within the scope of its official activities, the PCA shall be exempt from all direct taxes, whether levied by national, provincial or local authorities.
2. Within the scope of its official activities, the PCA shall be exempt from:
   (a) motor vehicle tax (*motorrijtuigenbelasting*);
   (b) tax on passenger motor vehicles and motorcycles (*BPM*);
   (c) value-added tax (*omzetbelasting*) paid on all goods and services supplied on a recurring basis or involving considerable expenditure;
   (d) excise duties (*accijnzen*) included in the price of alcoholic beverages and hydrocarbons;
   (e) import taxes and duties (*belastingen bij invoer*);
   (f) insurance tax (*assurantiebelasting*);
   (g) real property transfer tax (*overdrachtsbelasting*);
   (h) any other taxes and duties of a substantially similar character to the taxes and duties provided for in this paragraph, imposed by the Netherlands subsequent to the date of signature of this Agreement.
3. The exemptions provided for in subparagraphs 2(c), 2(d), 2(f), 2(g) and 2(h) of this Article may be granted by way of a refund under conditions to be agreed upon by the PCA and the Government.
4. No exemption shall be accorded in respect of taxes and duties which represent charges for specific services rendered.
5. Goods acquired or imported under the terms set out in paragraph 2 of this Article shall not be sold, let out, given away or otherwise disposed of, except in accordance with conditions agreed upon with the Government.

Article 8

Transit and residence

1. The Government shall take all reasonable measures to facilitate and allow the entry into and sojourn in the territory of the Kingdom of the Netherlands of the persons listed below, whatever their nationality:
   (a) PCA Adjudicators and their partners;
   (b) Officials of the PCA, their partners and dependent members of their household;
   (c) Participants in Proceedings;
   (d) Persons attending PCA Meetings.
2. The Government shall take all reasonable measures to ensure that any visas which may be required for any of the persons referred to in this Article are issued as promptly as possible in order to allow the timely conduct of official business with the PCA. Visas shall be granted without charge to those persons referred to under 1(a) (b) and (c), above.
3. No activity performed by any person referred to in this Article in his capacity with respect to the PCA as indicated in paragraph 1 of this Article shall constitute a reason for preventing his entry into or his departure from the territory of the Kingdom of the Netherlands or for requiring him to leave such territory.

Article 9

Immunities of PCA adjudicators and participants in proceedings

1. PCA Adjudicators shall, in the exercise of their duties, enjoy such immunities as are accorded to diplomatic agents pursuant to the Vienna Convention.
2. Participants in Proceedings shall enjoy immunity from criminal, civil and administrative jurisdiction in respect of acts performed in the fulfilment of their duties in PCA Proceedings.

Article 10

Privileges and immunities of the Secretary-General and other officials of the PCA

1. Except with respect to (i) a motor traffic offence committed by an Official of the PCA, and (ii) a civil action by a third party for damage arising from an accident caused by a motor vehicle belonging to or driven by an Official of the PCA:
   (a) The Secretary-General shall be accorded the privileges and immunities, exemptions and facilities accorded to the head of a diplomatic mission pursuant to the Vienna Convention;
   (b) Officials of the PCA other than the Secretary-General shall be accorded the same privileges and immunities, exemptions and facilities as the Government accords to members of diplomatic missions of comparable rank pursuant to the Vienna Convention.
2. In addition to the immunities specified in paragraph 1 of this Article, Officials of the PCA shall enjoy within and with respect to the Kingdom of the Netherlands the following privileges and immunities:
   (a) exemption from taxation in respect of the salaries and emoluments paid by the PCA with the exception of pensions and annuities paid to former officials of the PCA and their dependants;
   (b) the same protection and repatriation facilities with respect to themselves, their partners, their dependent relatives and other members of their households as are accorded in time of international crisis to comparably-ranked members of the staffs of diplomatic missions accredited to the Kingdom of the Netherlands.

Article 11

Notification

1. The PCA shall promptly notify the Government of:
   (a) the appointment of the Secretary-General, the First Secretary, and other Officials of the PCA, their arrival and their final departure, or the termination of their functions with the PCA;

(b) the arrival and final departure of the partners and dependent members of the households of the persons referred to in subparagraph 1(a) of this Article and, where appropriate, the fact that a person has ceased to form part of the household.

2. The Government shall issue to the Secretary-General, the First Secretary and to other Officials of the PCA and their partners and dependent members of their household an identity card bearing the photograph of the holder. This card shall serve to identify the holder in relation to all authorities of the Kingdom of the Netherlands.

Article 12

Social security

1. In the event that the PCA shall have established its own social security system or shall adhere to a social security system offering comparable coverage to the coverage under Netherlands' legislation, the PCA and its staff members and other employees to whom the aforementioned scheme applies, shall be exempt from social security provisions in the Netherlands, unless the staff members and other employees to whom the aforementioned scheme applies take up a gainful activity in the Netherlands.
2. The provisions of paragraph 1 of this Article shall apply, mutatis mutandis, to the dependent members of the families forming part of the households of the persons referred to in paragraph 1, unless they are employed otherwise than by the PCA or self-employed or unless they receive Netherlands' social security benefits.

Article 13

Employment

1. Persons who have been recognised by the Government as
   (a) partners of Officials of the PCA; or
   (b) dependent children of Officials of the PCA who have not yet reached the age of 18 shall be authorised by the Appropriate Authorities to engage in gainful employment for the duration of the employment of the said Officials.
2. Persons who obtain employment under paragraph 1 of this Article shall have no immunity from criminal civil and administrative jurisdiction with respect to matters arising in the course of or in connection with such employment provided that measures of execution can be taken without infringing the inviolability of their person or their residence.
3. Employment referred to in paragraph 1 of this Article shall be in accordance with the laws of the Kingdom of the Netherlands.

Article 14

Additional provisions on privileges and immunities

1. The privileges and immunities granted under the provisions of this Agreement are conferred in the interest of the PCA and not for the personal benefit of the individuals themselves. It is the duty of the PCA and all persons enjoying such privileges and immunities to observe in all respects the laws and regulations of the Kingdom of The Netherlands.
2. This Agreement shall apply irrespective of whether the Government maintains or does not maintain diplomatic relations with the State of origin of the person concerned and irrespective of whether the State of origin of the person concerned grants similar privileges or immunities to the diplomatic envoys or citizens of the Kingdom of the Netherlands.
3. The privileges and immunities granted to Officials of the PCA under the provisions of this Agreement are granted on the understanding that the PCA shall waive the immunity of the persons concerned in any circumstances in which the PCA considers that such immunity would impede the course of justice, and whenever it can be waived without prejudice to the purpose for which it was granted.
4. The PCA shall cooperate at all times with the appropriate authorities of the Kingdom of the Netherlands to facilitate the proper administration of justice and shall prevent any abuse of the privileges and immunities granted under the provisions of this Agreement by Officials of the PCA.

5. Should the Government consider that an abuse by an Official of the PCA or an expert of a privilege or immunity conferred by this Agreement has occurred, the Secretary-General shall, upon request, consult with the appropriate Netherlands authorities to determine whether any such abuse has occurred. If such consultations fail to achieve a result satisfactory to the Secretary-General and to the Government, the matter shall be determined in accordance with the procedures set out in Article 16, paragraph 2 of this Agreement.
6. The Secretary-General shall have the right and the duty to waive the immunity of any Official of the PCA in cases in which the immunity would impede the course of justice and can be waived without prejudice to the interests of the PCA. In respect of the Secretary-General, the PCA has a similar right and duty, which shall be performed by the Administrative Council.

Article 15

International responsibility of the Kingdom of the Netherlands

The Kingdom of the Netherlands shall not incur by reason of the location of the Headquarters of the PCA within its territory any international responsibility for acts or omissions of the PCA or of Officials of the PCA acting or abstaining from acting within the scope of their functions, other than the international responsibility which the Kingdom of the Netherlands would incur on the same footing as other Contracting Powers to the 1899 Convention and/or the 1907 Convention.

Article 16

Settlement of disputes

1. The PCA shall make provisions for appropriate methods of settlement of:
   (a) disputes arising out of contracts and disputes of a private law character to which the PCA is party; and
   (b) disputes involving an Official of the PCA who, by reason of his official position, enjoys immunity, if such immunity has not been waived by the PCA.
2. Any dispute, controversy or claim arising between the PCA and the Government out of or relating to the interpretation, application or performance of this Agreement, including its existence, validity or termination, or any question affecting the Headquarters or the relationship between the PCA and the Government, which is not settled amicably within six months of the date on which one Party notifies the other of the existence of such dispute, shall be settled by final and binding arbitration in accordance with the Permanent Court of Arbitration Optional Rules for Arbitration Involving International Organisations and States (the 'Rules'), as in force on the date of signature of this Agreement. The number of arbitrators shall be one. The language to be used in the arbitral proceedings shall be English. The appointing authority shall be the Netherlands Arbitration Institute. In any such arbitration proceedings, the registry, archive and secretariat services of the PCA, referred to in Article 1, paragraph 3 and Article 25, paragraph 3 of the Rules, will not be available, and the PCA shall not be empowered to request, hold or disburse deposits of costs as provided in Article 41, paragraph 1 of the Rules.

Article 17

Operation of this Agreement

1. This Agreement shall be construed in the light of its primary purpose of enabling the PCA at its Headquarters in the Kingdom of the Netherlands fully and efficiently to discharge its responsibilities and fulfil its purpose.
2. Whenever this Agreement imposes obligations on the appropriate authorities of the Kingdom of the Netherlands, the ultimate responsibility for the fulfilment of such obligations shall rest with the Government.

Article 18

Termination of the Agreement

This Agreement may be terminated by either Party by giving notice to the other Party at least two years in advance of the effective date of termination.

Article 19

Amendments

1. This Agreement may be amended at any time.
2. Any such amendment shall be agreed by mutual consent and shall be effected by an Exchange of Notes.
3. Consultations with respect to amendment of this Agreement may be entered into by the PCA and the Government at the request of either Party.

Article 20

Entry into force

1. This Agreement shall enter into force on the day after both Parties have notified each other in writing that the legal requirements for entry into force have been complied with.
2. With respect to the Kingdom of the Netherlands, this Agreement shall apply to the part of the Kingdom in Europe only.

Done at The Hague on 30 March 1999 in two originals in the English language.

For the Permanent Court of Arbitration (signed)

For the Kingdom of the Netherlands (signed)

APPENDIX V

Exchange of Notes constituting an Agreement supplementing the Agreement concerning the Headquarters of the Permanent Court of Arbitration

Ministry of Foreign Affairs
Treaties Division

MINBUZA-2012.12246

The Ministry of Foreign Affairs of the Kingdom of the Netherlands presents its compliments to the Permanent Court of Arbitration and, with reference to the Agreement concerning the Headquarters of the Permanent Court of Arbitration of 30 March 1999, has the honour to propose that the following provisions shall apply with regard to witnesses in PCA Proceedings, in addition to Article 9, paragraph 2 of the Agreement concerning the Headquarters of the Permanent Court of Arbitration.

1. Witnesses shall enjoy the following privileges, immunities and facilities to the extent necessary for their appearance in PCA Proceedings for purposes of giving evidence, subject to the production of the document referred to in paragraph 2:
   (a) immunity from personal arrest or detention or any other restriction of their liberty in respect of acts or convictions prior to their entry into the territory of the Kingdom of the Netherlands;
   (b) immunity from seizure of their personal baggage unless there are serious grounds for believing that the baggage contains articles the import or export of which is prohibited by law or controlled by the quarantine regulations of the Kingdom of the Netherlands;
   (c) immunity from legal process of every kind in respect of words spoken or written and all acts performed by them in the course of their testimony, which immunity shall continue to be accorded even after their appearance and testimony in PCA Proceedings;
   (d) inviolability of all papers, documents in whatever form and materials relating to their testimony;
   (e) for purposes of their communications in relation to PCA Proceedings and with their counsel in connection with their testimony, the right to receive and send papers and documents in whatever form;
   (f) exemption from immigration restrictions or alien registration when they travel for purposes of their testimony;
   (g) the same repatriation facilities in time of international crisis as are accorded to diplomatic agents under the Vienna Convention.
2. Witnesses shall be provided by the PCA with a document certifying that their appearance is required by the PCA and specifying a time period during which such appearance is necessary. This document shall be withdrawn prior to its expiry if the witness's appearance in PCA Proceedings, or his or her presence at the seat of the PCA is no longer required.
3. The privileges, immunities and facilities referred to in paragraph 1 shall cease to apply after fifteen consecutive days following the date on which the presence of the witness concerned is no longer required by the PCA, provided such witness had an opportunity to leave the Kingdom of the Netherlands during that period.
4. Witnesses who are nationals or permanent residents of the Kingdom of the Netherlands shall enjoy only the following privileges, immunities and facilities to the extent necessary for their appearance or testimony in PCA Proceedings:
   (a) immunity from personal arrest or detention or any other restriction of their liberty;

(b) immunity from legal process of every kind in respect of words spoken or written and all acts performed by them in the course of their appearance or testimony, which immunity shall continue to be accorded even after their appearance or testimony;
(c) inviolability of all papers, documents in whatever form and materials relating to their appearance or testimony;
(d) for the purpose of their communications in relation to PCA Proceedings and with their counsel in connection with their appearance or testimony, the right to receive and send papers in whatever form.

5. Witnesses shall not be subjected by the Kingdom of the Netherlands to any measure which may affect their appearance or testimony in PCA Proceedings.

If this proposal is acceptable to the Permanent Court of Arbitration, the Ministry proposes that this Note and the Permanent Court of Arbitration's affirmative reply to it shall together constitute an Agreement between the Kingdom of the Netherlands and the Permanent Court of Arbitration. This Agreement shall enter into force on the date of receipt of the Permanent Court of Arbitration's reply by the Ministry.

The Ministry of Foreign Affairs of the Kingdom of the Netherlands avails itself of this opportunity to renew to the Permanent Court of Arbitration the assurances of its highest consideration.

The Hague, 6 June 2012

To the Permanent Court of Arbitration

at

The Hague

COUR PERMANENTE D'ARBITRAGE—PERMANENT COURT OF ARBITRATION

Supplementary agreement to the Agreement concerning the Headquarters of the Permanent Court of Arbitration

NOTE IN REPLY

The Permanent Court of Arbitration presents its complements to the Ministry of Foreign Affairs of the Kingdom of the Netherlands and has the honour to acknowledge the receipt of the latter's Note No. MINBUZA-2012.12246 of 6 June 2012, which reads as follows:

> The Ministry of Foreign Affairs of the Kingdom of the Netherlands presents its compliments to the Permanent Court of Arbitration and, with reference to the Agreement concerning the Headquarters of the Permanent Court of Arbitration of 30 March 1999, has the honour to propose that the following provisions shall apply with regard to witnesses in PCA Proceedings, in addition to Article 9, paragraph 2 of the Agreement concerning the Headquarters of the Permanent Court of Arbitration.

1. Witnesses shall enjoy the following privileges, immunities and facilities to the extent necessary for their appearance in PCA Proceedings for purposes of giving evidence, subject to the production of the document referred to in paragraph 2:
   (a) immunity from personal arrest or detention or any other restriction of their liberty in respect of acts or convictions prior to their entry into the territory of the Kingdom of the Netherlands;
   (b) immunity from seizure of their personal baggage unless there are serious grounds for believing that the baggage contains articles the import or export of which is prohibited by law or controlled by the quarantine regulations of the Kingdom of the Netherlands;
   (c) immunity from legal process of every kind in respect of words spoken or written and all acts performed by them in the course of their testimony, which immunity shall continue to be accorded even after their appearance and testimony in PCA Proceedings;
   (d) inviolability of all papers, documents in whatever form and materials relating to their testimony;
   (e) for purposes of their communications in relation to PCA Proceedings and with their counsel in connection with their testimony, the right to receive and send papers and documents in whatever form;

(f) exemption from immigration restrictions or alien registration when they travel for purposes of their testimony;
(g) the same repatriation facilities in time of international crisis as are accorded to diplomatic agents under the Vienna Convention.

2. Witnesses shall be provided by the PCA with a document certifying that their appearance is required by the PCA and specifying a time period during which such appearance is necessary. This document shall be withdrawn prior to its expiry if the witness's appearance in PCA Proceedings, or his or her presence at the seat of the PCA is no longer required.
3. The privileges, immunities and facilities referred to in paragraph 1 shall cease to apply after fifteen consecutive days following the date on which the presence of the witness concerned is no longer required by the PCA, provided such witness had an opportunity to leave the Kingdom of the Netherlands during that period.
4. Witnesses who are nationals or permanent residents of the Kingdom of the Netherlands shall enjoy only the following privileges, immunities and facilities to the extent necessary for their appearance or testimony in PCA Proceedings:
   (a) immunity from personal arrest or detention or any other restriction of their liberty;
   (b) immunity from legal process of every kind in respect of words spoken or written and all acts performed by them in the course of their appearance or testimony, which immunity shall continue to be accorded even after their appearance or testimony;
   (c) inviolability of all papers, documents in whatever form and materials relating to their appearance or testimony;
   (d) for the purpose of their communications in relation to PCA Proceedings and with their counsel in connection with their appearance or testimony, the right to receive and send papers in whatever form.
5. Witnesses shall not be subjected by the Kingdom of the Netherlands to any measure which may affect their appearance or testimony in PCA Proceedings.

If this proposal is acceptable to the Permanent Court of Arbitration, the Ministry proposes that this Note and the Permanent Court of Arbitration's affirmative reply to it shall together constitute an Agreement between the Kingdom of the Netherlands and the Permanent Court of Arbitration. This Agreement shall enter into force on the date of receipt of the Permanent Court of Arbitration's reply by the Ministry.

The Ministry of Foreign Affairs of the Kingdom of the Netherlands avails itself of this opportunity to renew to the Permanent Court of Arbitration the assurances of its highest consideration.

The Permanent Court of Arbitration has the honour to inform the Ministry that the proposals set out in the Ministry's Note are acceptable to the Permanent Court of Arbitration and to confirm that the Ministry's Note and this Note, shall constitute an Agreement between the Kingdom of the Netherlands and the Permanent Court of Arbitration. This Agreement shall enter into force on the date of receipt of this affirmative Note in reply by the Ministry.

The Permanent Court of Arbitration avails itself of this opportunity to renew to the Ministry of Foreign Affairs of the Kingdom of the Netherlands the assurances of its highest consideration.

The Hague, 6 June 2012

APPENDIX VI

List of PCA Rules of Procedure[1]

PCA Arbitration Rules 2012 (2012)
PCA Optional Rules for Arbitration of Disputes Relating to Outer Space Activities (2011)
PCA Optional Rules for Conciliation of Disputes Relating to Natural Resources and/or the Environment (2002)
PCA Optional Rules for Arbitration of Disputes Relating to Natural Resources and/or the Environment (2001)
PCA Optional Rules for Fact-finding Commissions of Inquiry (1997)
PCA Optional Conciliation Rules (1996)
PCA Optional Rules for Arbitration Involving International Organizations and States (1996)
PCA Optional Rules for Arbitration between International Organizations and Private Parties (1996)
PCA Optional Rules for Arbitrating Disputes between Two Parties of Which Only One Is a State (1993)[2]
PCA Optional Rules for Arbitrating Disputes between Two States (1992)

[1] The PCA's earliest procedural rules are found in Part IV, Chapter 3 of the 1899 Hague Convention and Part IV, Chapter 3 of the 1907 Hague Convention. However, they have been overtaken by developments in international arbitration and their use is not recommended.

[2] As stated in their introduction, these procedural rules superseded the PCA 1962 Rules of Arbitration and Conciliation for Settlement of International Disputes between Two Parties of Which Only One Is a State.

APPENDIX VII

Drafting Groups of PCA Rules of Procedure

1. PCA Arbitration Rules 2012

Drafting Committee

Jan Paulsson (Chairman)	Michael Hwang
Lise Bosman	Gabrielle Kaufmann Kohler
Brooks W. Daly	Salim Moolan
Alvaro Galindo	Michael Pryles
Alejandro Garro	Jamal Seifi
Christopher Greenwood	Jernej Sekolec

2. PCA Optional Rules for Arbitration of Disputes Relating to Outer Space Activities (2011)

Advisory Group

Fausto Pocar (Chairman)	Ram S. Jakhu
Tare Brisibe	Armel Kerrest
Frans G. Von der Dunk	Justine C. Limpitlaw
Jose Monserrat Filho	Francis Lyall
Joanne Irene Gabrynowicz	V.S. Mani
Zhao Haifeng	Maureen Williams
Stephan Hobe	

3. PCA Optional Rules for Arbitration of Disputes Relating to Natural Resources and the Environment (2001) and PCA Optional Rules for Conciliation of Disputes Relating to Natural Resources and/or the Environment (2002)

Working Group[1]

Philippe Sands (Chairman)	Christopher Pinto
G. Aguilar Rojas	Amedeo Postiglione
W. Bernhard Boer	P.S. Rao
James Crawford	Thomas Schoenbaum
Pierre-Marie Dupuy	Patrick Szell

(*Continued*)

[1] The Working Group recommended the development of rules of procedure for disputes relating to natural resources and the environment.

Hiroji Isozaki	Jakob von Uexkull
Kheng Lian Koh	Agni Vlavianos-Arvanitis
Kenneth McCallion	Xianliang Yi
Hiroko Onishi	Christopher Weeramantry
R.S. Pathak	

Drafting Group

Philippe Sands (Chairman)	Hans Lammers
Mohammed Bekhechi	Thomas Mensah
Charles Di Leva	Francisco Orrego Vicuña
Florentino Feliciano	Alfred Rest
Parvez Hassan	

4. PCA Optional Rules for Arbitration Involving International Organizations and States (1996), PCA Optional Rules for Arbitration between International Organizations and Private Parties (1996), PCA Optional Conciliation Rules (1996), PCA Optional Rules for Fact-finding Commissions of Inquiry (1997)

Steering Committee

N. Ang Sánchez	Nasrollah Kazemi Kamyab
Andrés Aguilar Mawsdley	Mohamed Lejmi
M. Ali	Mary Catherine Malin
Prince Bola Ajibola	E Martin
Ion Anghel	HM Natabaya
Vladimir Astapenka	Jean-Dieudonné Ntsama
Arturo Hernandez Basave	Shigeru Oda
Marin Buhoara	Juan Andrés Pacheco Ramirez
Carlos José Argüello Gomez	José Antonio Pastor Ridruejo
Mohammed M Bedjaoui	Stefan Paulliny
Prafullachandra N. Bhagwati	Pierre Pescatore (Rapporteur)
A. Bos	Christopher Pinto
Bengt Broms	Serguei Pounjine
Lucius Caflisch	Raymond Ranjeva
Zhou Congwu	Shabtai Rosenne
Gerardo Girardo Crocini	W. Schlote
Jan Van Ettinger	Mr Shimbura
Luigi Ferrari Bravo	T. Simonsen
G. Figueroa	Leonid A. Skotnikov
K. Fujishita	Krusztof Skubiszewski
Gavan Griffith	Louis B. Sohn
Claudia Guevara	Mr Stavinotte
Gilbert Guillaume	Catherine Lisa Steains
Atilla Gunay	Stefan Stoïca

(*Continued*)

Conrad K Harper	T. Tabapssi
Ferdinand Hess	M.A. Tageldin
Albert J. Hoffmann	Michael Carter Tate
Howard M. Holtzmann	R. Valcarce
Koorosh-Hossein Ameli	Christian Verdonck
Sir Robert Y. Jennings	Manuel Gonzalo Viera Merola
Xiao Jianguo	José Villegas
Shi Jiuyong	R. Zdravkov
P. Kaukoranta	Bernardo Zuluaga

5. PCA Optional Rules for Arbitrating Disputes between Two States (1992) and PCA Optional Rules for Arbitrating Disputes between Two Parties of Which Only One Is a State (1993)

Expert Group

Manfred Lachs (Chairman)	P.J.H. Jonkman
Ion M. Anghel	Simon Marti
Andrés Aguilar Mawsdley	Abel Meguid
Koorosh-Hossein Ameli	Shigeru Oda
Carlos Argüello Gómez	Pierre Pescadore
Mohammed Bedjaoui	Christopher Pinto
J. Bleich	P.M.L. Plompen
A. Bos	P.S. Rao
Bengt Broms	Jacques H. Schraven
Hans Corell	Stephen M. Schwebel
Achol Deng	Leonid A. Skotnikov
Luigi Ferrari-Bravo	Breman Smedes
L. Hardenberg	Jorge Antonio Tapia-Valdés
Reinhard Hilger	C.A. Whomersley
Howard M. Holtzmann	

6. Convention for the Pacific Settlement of Disputes (1907)

Committee of Examination A

Léon Bourgeois (President)	Knut Hjalmar Leonard de Hammarskjöld
T.M.C. Asser	Mr Kriege
Ruy Barbosa	Henri Lammasch
Francisco L. de la Barra	Christian Lous Lange
Baron Marschall de Bierberstein	Frederic de Martens

(*Continued*)

Gaston Carlin	Gaëtan Mérey von Kapos-Mére
Luis M. Drago	Milovan Milovanovitch
Gonzalo A. Esteva	Alberto d'Oliveira
Baron d'Estournelles de Constant	Chevalier Guido Pompilj
Mr Fromageot	Horace Porter
Sir Edward Fry	James Brown Scott
Guido Fusinato	Georges Streit
Baron Guillaume	Count Joseph Tornielli

Committee of Examination C

Mr Fusinato (President)	Mr Kriege
Eyre Crowe	Henri Lammasch
Mr Fromageot	Christian Lous Lange
Sir Edward Fry	Alberto d'Oliveira
Baron Guillaume	James Brown Scott

7. Convention for the Pacific Settlement of Disputes (1899)

Committee of Examination[2]

Chevalier Descamps (President)	**Frederic de Martens**
T.M.C. Asser	Count Nigra
Léon Bourgeois	**Edouard Odier**
Baron d'Estournelles de Constant	Sir Julian Pauncefote
Frederick W. Holls	Jarousse de Sillac
Jonkheer A.P.C. van Karnebeek	Mr Stall
Henri Lammasch	**Mr Zorn**

[2] This Committee prepared the draft of the 1899 Hague Convention that was presented to the Third Commission on Pacific Settlement of International Disputes before being proposed to the First Peace Conference. The persons whose names are indicated in bold were appointed to the Committee, while the others participated in its work without having been formally appointed ('Report to the Conference from the Third Commission on Pacific Settlement of International Disputes', reproduced in Shabtai Rosenne (ed.), *The Hague Peace Conferences of 1899 and 1907 and International Arbitration: Reports and Documents* (TMC Asser Press, 2001, 29).

APPENDIX VIII

PCA Schedule of Fees and Costs

This Schedule of Fees and Costs applies to the following PCA services as of October 2013. All amounts are subject to change.

Acting as an Appointing Authority (for example, pursuant to the 2012 PCA Arbitration Rules or the UNCITRAL Arbitration Rules)

Non-refundable processing fee	€1,500

Designation of an Appointing Authority (for example, pursuant to the UNCITRAL Arbitration Rules)

Non-refundable processing fee	€750

Registry Services provided by the PCA International Bureau

Secretary-General	€250/hour
Deputy Secretary-General	€250/hour
Senior Legal Staff	€175/hour
Junior Legal Staff	€125/hour
Secretarial/Clerical	€50/hour

The International Bureau can arrange for estimates for the following on request: verbatim transcription, interpretation, translation, document reproduction, sound and audiovisual equipment, tele- and videoconferencing, etc.

Hearing/Meeting Facilities

Hearing and meeting rooms at the Peace Palace in The Hague, and in Costa Rica, Mauritius, Singapore, and South Africa are available free of charge to arbitral tribunals and commissions for which the PCA serves as registry. Ancillary equipment is charged separately.

The following rates apply to guest tribunals for which the PCA does not serve as registry:

Arbitration Suite

Hearing space only	€1,000/day
Entire suite	€1,750/day

Reservations can be made by e-mail to bureau@pca-cpa.org.

APPENDIX IX

Permanent Court of Arbitration Financial Assistance Fund for Settlement of International Disputes—Terms of Reference and Guidelines

(as approved by the PCA Administrative Council on 11 December 1995)

Establishment of a Financial Assistance Fund

1. The Hague Conventions for the Pacific Settlement of International Disputes of 1899 and 1907 brought into being what is today the oldest existing global system for the peaceful settlement of international disputes. They established the Permanent Court of Arbitration, and provided for the settlement of such disputes by States Parties through arbitration and other peaceful means of their own choice.
2. States Parties to the Conventions undertake to use their best efforts to ensure the peaceful settlement of their disputes. However, there may be instances when States are deterred from recourse to international arbitration or other means of settlement offered by the Conventions because they find it difficult at the time to allocate funds to meet the costs involved. Such costs may include the fees and expenses of members of an arbitral or other body entrusted with settling the dispute; the expenses of implementing an award or other decision or recommendation of such a body; payments to agents, counsel, experts and witnesses; and operational or administrative expenses connected with oral or written proceedings. Making funds available to meet costs of this nature could facilitate recourse to arbitration or other means of settlement, thus advancing the aims and purposes of the Conventions, and promoting friendly relations and cooperation among States.
3. Accordingly, the Secretary-General of the Permanent Court of Arbitration (the 'Secretary-General') has, with the approval of the Administrative Council, established a Financial Assistance Fund for the Settlement of International Disputes (the 'Fund'). The Fund will provide financial assistance to Qualifying States (as defined herein), in accordance with the terms and conditions specified herein, to enable them to meet, in whole or in part, expenses of the type referred to in paragraph 2.

Contributions to the Fund

4. The Fund shall consist of voluntary financial contributions by States, intergovernmental organizations, national institutions, as well as natural and legal persons.

Request for Financial Assistance from the Fund

5. For purposes of this document, 'Qualifying State' shall mean a State that is a party to the Convention of 1899 or 1907, or any institution or enterprise owned and controlled by such State, which has concluded an agreement for the purpose of submitting one or more disputes, whether existing or future, for settlement under the auspices of the Permanent Court of Arbitration by any of the means administered by the Permanent Court of Arbitration, and which State, at the time of requesting financial assistance from the Fund, is listed on the 'DAC List of Aid Recipients' prepared by the Organization for Economic Cooperation and Development (OECD).

6. Any Qualifying State may seek financial assistance from the Fund, by submitting a written request therefor to the Secretary-General, accompanied by:
   (i) A copy of the abovementioned dispute resolution agreement, as well as, in the case of an agreement to submit future disputes, a brief description of the specific dispute concerned;
   (ii) An itemized statement of the estimated costs for which financial assistance is sought from the Fund;
   (iii) An undertaking that the requesting State shall supply a final statement of account providing details of the expenditures made from the approved amounts, audited by an independent accountant acceptable to the International Bureau of the Permanent Court of Arbitration.

Implementing Office

7. The International Bureau of the Permanent Court of Arbitration shall be the implementing office for the Fund, and shall be responsible for the administration of the Fund. The International Bureau shall make no allocations or disbursements from the Fund, other than pursuant to a decision of the Board of Trustees, as set forth below.

Board of Trustees

8. For purposes of deciding on requests for financial assistance from the fund, there shall be a Board of Trustees (the 'Board'), composed of no fewer than three and no more than seven members who have experience in international dispute resolution and are of the highest moral standing. Members shall be appointed by the Secretary-General with the approval of the Administrative Council, and shall serve for a term of four years, which may be renewed. The Secretary-General shall be entitled to fill any vacancy occurring in the membership of the Board with immediate effect, pending approval by the Administrative Council at its next following meeting.
9. The Secretary-General shall serve as chairman of the Board. He shall conduct and participate fully in meetings of the Board, but shall not vote on any request for financial assistance from the Fund.
10. The Board shall examine requests for financial assistance from the Fund, and shall determine the amount of financial assistance to be given, if any, the categories of expenses to which it may be applied, as well as any terms and conditions it deems appropriate.
11. After having consulted the Board of Trustees, the Secretary-General shall adopt rules governing, *inter alia*, the manner in which the work of the Board is to be conducted. The work of the Board shall be conducted in strict confidentiality.
12. In considering a request for disbursement, the Board shall be guided, *inter alia*, by the financial needs of the requesting State and the availability of funds.
13. Members of the Board shall not be entitled to receive fees for their services, or reimbursement of expenses incurred in that connection. The Secretary-General may, in exceptional cases and in his sole discretion, determine the amount to be paid to a member by way of reimbursement of expenses for travel and subsistence incurred in connection with the rendering of services to the Board.
14. Upon the approval of a request for financial assistance, the amount granted shall be disbursed to the requesting State out of the Fund, pursuant to the terms and conditions set forth by the Board in its decision.
15. The decision of the Board concerning a request for financial assistance from the Fund shall be final, and not subject to recourse or review.

Reporting

16. The Secretary-General shall report to the Administrative Council at least once annually in detail on the activities and transactions relative to the Fund, including contributions pledged and received, and allocations and disbursements made. The Annual Report of the PCA shall contain a summary report on the activities of the Fund.

APPENDIX X

Permanent Court of Arbitration Financial Assistance Fund for Settlement of International Disputes Rules Governing the Work of the Board of Trustees

1. These Rules Governing the Work of the Board of Trustees have been adopted by the Secretary-General of the Permanent Court of Arbitration ('PCA') pursuant to paragraph 11 of the Terms of Reference and Guidelines for the PCA's Financial Assistance Fund, approved by the Administrative Council on 3 October 1994 (the 'Guidelines'). Terms used herein that are not defined shall, unless the context requires otherwise, have the meaning given to them in the Guidelines.
2. The Guidelines established the PCA's Financial Assistance Fund (the 'Fund'), and provided for creation of a Board of Trustees (the 'Board') for the purpose of deciding on requests for financial assistance from the Fund.
3. Upon receipt of a request for financial assistance from the Fund, the Secretary-General shall conduct an initial screening, for the purpose of determining:
   a. Whether the State making the request is a Qualifying State as defined in paragraph 5 of the Guidelines, and
   b. Whether the request is accompanied by the documents required pursuant to paragraph 6 of the Guidelines.
4. If the State making the request is not a Qualifying State, the Secretary-General shall inform that State that the request cannot be submitted to the Board for its consideration.
5. If one or more of the accompanying documents has not been submitted, the Secretary-General shall inform the State making the request accordingly, indicating that the request cannot be submitted to the Board for its consideration until all required documents have been received.
6. As soon as the Secretary-General has determined that (a) the State making the request is a Qualifying State, and (b) all required documentation has been submitted, the Secretary-General shall transmit copies of the request and accompanying documents to each of the members of the Board. The Secretary-General shall inform the members of the Board of the current status of the Fund, the availability of funds capable of being allocated to the request, and of any limitations imposed by contributors to the Fund that might affect the allocation, and shall make a recommendation as to the action to be taken by the Board in response to the request.
7. The members of the Board may communicate with each other, and with the Secretary-General, by any available means, including mail, telephone, facsimile and electronic mail. The Secretary-General shall, if necessary, coordinate and act as a conduit for such communications.
8. Upon the request of either the Secretary-General or of at least one member of the Board, the Board shall meet in person for the purpose of deliberating and deciding on a request for assistance. The Secretary-General shall give written notice of any such meeting, by mail, facsimile or electronic mail, to the members of the Board at least seven (7) days prior to the date of the meeting.
9. For reasons of efficiency, the Board may conduct its business without a meeting. Each member of the Board shall communicate his views on the request to the Secretary-General no later than two (2) weeks following receipt of the documents referred to in section 6. A Board member who does not respond within that time period shall be deemed to agree with the recommendation of the Secretary-General.

10. At any meeting, the presence of three (3) of the members of the Board shall constitute a quorum for the purpose of conducting business and taking decisions.
11. The Board's decision on a request for assistance shall be taken by a simple majority of those participating in the decision-making.
12. A member of the Board shall not participate in the deliberations or decision-making concerning any request for assistance with respect to which there exist any grounds that may cause doubt as to his independence or impartiality, including, but not limited to, any personal or professional relationship with a party or an arbitrator, or any personal or professional interest in the outcome of the arbitration. Notwithstanding the foregoing, the mere fact that a member of the Board is a national of a requesting State shall not constitute such a ground.
13. The Board shall convey its decision in writing, signed by the members of the Board, to the Secretary-General. A member who does not agree with the decision may refuse to sign, but this shall have no effect on the validity or finality of the decision, if duly adopted. The decision shall set forth the amount of financial assistance granted, if any; the categories of expenses to which it may be applied; and any terms and conditions that the Board considers necessary or expedient. Upon receipt of the Board's decision, the Secretary-General shall inform the requesting State of its contents. If arbitration proceedings have already been initiated, and the Board grants financial assistance to the requesting State, the Secretary-General shall inform the opposing party, without disclosing the specific sums involved, that the requesting State has been granted financial assistance. If arbitration proceedings have not yet been initiated, the Secretary-General shall give such notice to the opposing party as soon as practicable after the initiation of proceedings.
14. The members of the Board shall preserve the confidential nature of the Board's deliberations and decisions.
15. The Secretary-General shall make the necessary arrangements with the requesting State for disbursement of the funds, record-keeping, and compliance with any terms and conditions of the decision.
16. The decision of the Board concerning a request for financial assistance from the Fund shall be final, and not subject to recourse or review.

The Hague, 17 July 1995

APPENDIX XI

UNCITRAL Arbitration Rules 1976

Section I. Introductory Rules

Scope of application

Article 1

1. Where the parties to a contract have agreed in writing* that disputes in relation to that contract shall be referred to arbitration under the UNCITRAL Arbitration Rules, then such disputes shall be settled in accordance with these Rules subject to such modification as the parties may agree in writing.
2. These Rules shall govern the arbitration except that where any of these Rules is in conflict with a provision of the law applicable to the arbitration from which the parties cannot derogate, that provision shall prevail.

Notice, calculation of periods of time

Article 2

1. For the purposes of these Rules, any notice, including a notification, communication or proposal, is deemed to have been received if it is physically delivered to the addressee or if it is delivered at his habitual residence, place of business or mailing address, or, if none of these can be found after making reasonable inquiry, then at the addressee's last-known residence or place of business. Notice shall be deemed to have been received on the day it is so delivered.
2. For the purposes of calculating a period of time under these Rules, such period shall begin to run on the day following the day when a notice, notification, communication or proposal is received. If the last day of such period is an official holiday or a non-business day at the residence or place of business of the addressee, the period is extended until the first business day which follows. Official holidays or non-business days occurring during the running of the period of time are included in calculating the period.

Notice of arbitration

Article 3

1. The party initiating recourse to arbitration (hereinafter called the 'claimant') shall give to the other party (hereinafter called the 'respondent') a notice of arbitration.
2. Arbitral proceedings shall be deemed to commence on the date on which the notice of arbitration is received by the respondent.
3. The notice of arbitration shall include the following:
   (a) A demand that the dispute be referred to arbitration;
   (b) The names and addresses of the parties;

---

* MODEL ARBITRATION CLAUSE

Any dispute, controversy or claim arising out of or relating to this contract, or the breach, termination or invalidity thereof, shall be settled by arbitration in accordance with the UNCITRAL Arbitration Rules as at present in force.

Note - Parties may wish to consider adding:

(a) The appointing authority shall be . . . (name of institution or person);
(b) The number of arbitrators shall be . . . (one or three);
(c) The place of arbitration shall be . . . (town or country);
(d) The language(s) to be used in the arbitral proceedings shall be . . .

(c) A reference to the arbitration clause or the separate arbitration agreement that is invoked;
(d) A reference to the contract out of or in relation to which the dispute arises;
(e) The general nature of the claim and an indication of the amount involved, if any;
(f) The relief or remedy sought;
(g) A proposal as to the number of arbitrators (i.e. one or three), if the parties have not previously agreed thereon.

4. The notice of arbitration may also include:
   (a) The proposals for the appointments of a sole arbitrator and an appointing authority referred to in article 6, paragraph 1;
   (b) The notification of the appointment of an arbitrator referred to in article 7;
   (c) The statement of claim referred to in article 18.

Representation and assistance

Article 4

The parties may be represented or assisted by persons of their choice. The names and addresses of such persons must be communicated in writing to the other party; such communication must specify whether the appointment is being made for purposes of representation or assistance.

Section II. Composition of the Arbitral Tribunal

Number of arbitrators

Article 5

If the parties have not previously agreed on the number of arbitrators (i.e. one or three), and if within fifteen days after the receipt by the respondent of the notice of arbitration the parties have not agreed that there shall be only one arbitrator, three arbitrators shall be appointed.

Appointment of arbitrators (Articles 6 to 8)

Article 6

1. If a sole arbitrator is to be appointed, either party may propose to the other:
   (a) The names of one or more persons, one of whom would serve as the sole arbitrator; and
   (b) If no appointing authority has been agreed upon by the parties, the name or names of one or more institutions or persons, one of whom would serve as appointing authority.
2. If within thirty days after receipt by a party of a proposal made in accordance with paragraph 1 the parties have not reached agreement on the choice of a sole arbitrator, the sole arbitrator shall be appointed by the appointing authority agreed upon by the parties. If no appointing authority has been agreed upon by the parties, or if the appointing authority agreed upon refuses to act or fails to appoint the arbitrator within sixty days of the receipt of a party's request therefor, either party may request the Secretary-General of the Permanent Court of Arbitration at The Hague to designate an appointing authority.
3. The appointing authority shall, at the request of one of the parties, appoint the sole arbitrator as promptly as possible. In making the appointment the appointing authority shall use the following list-procedure, unless both parties agree that the list-procedure should not be used or unless the appointing authority determines in its discretion that the use of the list-procedure is not appropriate for the case:
   (a) At the request of one of the parties the appointing authority shall communicate to both parties an identical list containing at least three names;
   (b) Within fifteen days after the receipt of this list, each party may return the list to the appointing authority after having deleted the name or names to which he objects and numbered the remaining names on the list in the order of his preference;
   (c) After the expiration of the above period of time the appointing authority shall appoint the sole arbitrator from among the names approved on the lists returned to it and in accordance with the order of preference indicated by the parties;
   (d) If for any reason the appointment cannot be made according to this procedure, the appointing authority may exercise its discretion in appointing the sole arbitrator.

4. In making the appointment, the appointing authority shall have regard to such considerations as are likely to secure the appointment of an independent and impartial arbitrator and shall take into account as well the advisability of appointing an arbitrator of a national other than the nationalities of the parties.

Article 7

1. If three arbitrators are to be appointed, each party shall appoint one arbitrator. The two arbitrators thus appointed shall choose the third arbitrator who will act as the presiding arbitrator of the tribunal.
2. If within thirty days after the receipt of a party's notification of the appointment of an arbitrator the other party has not notified the first party of the arbitrator he has appointed:
   (a) The first party may request the appointing authority previously designated by the parties to appoint the second arbitrator; or
   (b) If no such authority has been previously designated by the parties, or if the appointing authority previously designated refuses to act or fails to appoint the arbitrator within thirty days after receipt of a party's request therefor, the first party may request the Secretary-General of the Permanent Court of Arbitration at The Hague to designate the appointing authority. The first party may then request the appointing authority so designated to appoint the second arbitrator. In either case, the appointing authority may exercise its discretion in appointing the arbitrator.
3. If within thirty days after the appointment of the second arbitrator the two arbitrators have not agreed on the choice of the presiding arbitrator, the presiding arbitrator shall be appointed by an appointing authority in the same way as a sole arbitrator would be appointed under article 6.

Article 8

1. When an appointing authority is requested to appoint an arbitrator pursuant to article 6 or article 7, the party which makes the request shall send to the appointing authority a copy of the notice of arbitration, a copy of the contract out of or in relation to which the dispute has arisen and a copy of the arbitration agreement if it is not contained in the contract. The appointing authority may require from either party such information as it deems necessary to fulfill its function.
2. Where the names of one or more persons are proposed for appointment as arbitrators, their full names, addresses and nationalities shall be indicated, together with a description of their qualifications.

Challenge of arbitrators (Articles 9 to 12)

Article 9

A prospective arbitrator shall disclose to those who approach him in connexion with his possible appointment any circumstances likely to give rise to justifiable doubts as to his impartiality or independence. An arbitrator, once appointed or chosen, shall disclose such circumstances to the parties unless they have already been informed by him of these circumstances.

Article 10

1. Any arbitrator may be challenged if circumstances exist that give rise to justifiable doubts as to the arbitrator's impartiality or independence.
2. A party may challenge the arbitrator appointed by him only for reasons of which he becomes aware after the appointment has been made.

Article 11

1. A party who intends to challenge an arbitrator shall send notice of his challenge within fifteen days after the appointment of the challenged arbitrator has been notified to the challenging party or within fifteen days after the circumstances mentioned in articles 9 and 10 became known to that party.
2. The challenge shall be notified to the other party, to the arbitrator who is challenged and to the other members of the arbitral tribunal. The notification shall be in writing and shall state the reasons for the challenge.

3. When an arbitrator has been challenged by one party, the other party may agree to the challenge. The arbitrator may also, after the challenge, withdraw from his office. In neither case does this imply acceptance of the validity of the grounds for the challenge. In both cases the procedure provided in articles 6 or 7 shall be used in full for the appointment of the substitute arbitrator, even if during the process of appointing the challenged arbitrator a party had failed to exercise his right to appoint or to participate in the appointment.

Article 12

1. If the other party does not agree to the challenge and the challenged arbitrator does not withdraw, the decision on the challenge will be made:
   (a) When the initial appointment was made by an appointing authority, by that authority;
   (b) When the initial appointment was not made by an appointing authority, but an appointing authority has been previously designated, by that authority;
   (c) In all other cases, by the appointing authority to be designated in accordance with the procedure for designating an appointing authority as provided for in article 6.
2. If the appointing authority sustains the challenge, a substitute arbitrator shall be appointed or chosen pursuant to the procedure applicable to the appointment or choice of an arbitrator as provided in articles 6 to 9 except that, when this procedure would call for the designation of an appointing authority, the appointment of the arbitrator shall be made by the appointing authority which decided on the challenge.

Replacement of an arbitrator

Article 13

1. In the event of the death or resignation of an arbitrator during the course of the arbitral proceedings, a substitute arbitrator shall be appointed or chosen pursuant to the procedure provided for in articles 6 to 9 that was applicable to the appointment or choice of the arbitrator being replaced.
2. In the event that an arbitrator fails to act or in the event of the *de jure* or *de facto* impossibility of his performing his functions, the procedure in respect of the challenge and replacement of an arbitrator as provided in the preceding articles shall apply.

Repetition of hearings in the event of the replacement of an arbitrator

Article 14

If under articles 11 to 13 the sole or presiding arbitrator is replaced, any hearings held previously shall be repeated; if any other arbitrator is replaced, such prior hearings may be repeated at the discretion of the arbitral tribunal.

Section III. Arbitral Proceedings

General provisions

Article 15

1. Subject to these Rules, the arbitral tribunal may conduct the arbitration in such manner as it considers appropriate, provided that the parties are treated with equality and that at any stage of the proceedings each party is given a full opportunity of presenting his case.
2. If either party so requests at any stage of the proceedings, the arbitral tribunal shall hold hearings for the presentation of evidence by witnesses, including expert witnesses, or for oral argument. In the absence of such a request, the arbitral tribunal shall decide whether to hold such hearings or whether the proceedings shall be conducted on the basis of documents and other materials.
3. All documents or information supplied to the arbitral tribunal by one party shall at the same time be communicated by that party to the other party.

Place of arbitration

Article 16

1. Unless the parties have agreed upon the place where the arbitration is to be held, such place shall be determined by the arbitral tribunal, having regard to the circumstances of the arbitration.

2. The arbitral tribunal may determine the locale of the arbitration within the country agreed upon by the parties. It may hear witnesses and hold meetings for consultation among its members at any place it deems appropriate, having regard to the circumstances of the arbitration.
3. The arbitral tribunal may meet at any place it deems appropriate for the inspection of goods, other property or documents. The parties shall be given sufficient notice to enable them to be present at such inspection.
4. The award shall be made at the place of arbitration.

Language

Article 17

1. Subject to an agreement by the parties, the arbitral tribunal shall, promptly after its appointment, determine the language or languages to be used in the proceedings. This determination shall apply to the statement of claim, the statement of defence, and any further written statements and, if oral hearings take place, to the language or languages to be used in such hearings.
2. The arbitral tribunal may order that any documents annexed to the statement of claim or statement of defence, and any supplementary documents or exhibits submitted in the course of the proceedings, delivered in their original language, shall be accompanied by a translation into the language or languages agreed upon by the parties or determined by the arbitral tribunal.

Statement of claim

Article 18

1. Unless the statement of claim was contained in the notice of arbitration, within a period of time to be determined by the arbitral tribunal, the claimant shall communicate his statement of claim in writing to the respondent and to each of the arbitrators. A copy of the contract, and of the arbitration agreement if not contained in the contract, shall be annexed thereto.
2. The statement of claim shall include the following particulars:
   (a) The names and addresses of the parties;
   (b) A statement of the facts supporting the claim;
   (c) The points at issue;
   (d) The relief or remedy sought.

   The claimant may annex to his statement of claim all documents he deems relevant or may add a reference to the documents or other evidence he will submit.

Statement of defence

Article 19

1. Within a period of time to be determined by the arbitral tribunal, the respondent shall communicate his statement of defence in writing to the claimant and to each of the arbitrators.
2. The statement of defence shall reply to the particulars (b), (c) and (d) of the statement of claim (article 18, para. 2). The respondent may annex to his statement the documents on which he relies for his defence or may add a reference to the documents or other evidence he will submit.
3. In his statement of defence, or at a later stage in the arbitral proceedings if the arbitral tribunal decides that the delay was justified under the circumstances, the respondent may make a counter-claim arising out of the same contract or rely on a claim arising out of the same contract for the purpose of a set-off.
4. The provisions of article 18, paragraph 2, shall apply to a counter-claim and a claim relied on for the purpose of a set-off.

Amendments to the claim or defence

Article 20

During the course of the arbitral proceedings either party may amend or supplement his claim or defence unless the arbitral tribunal considers it inappropriate to allow such amendment having regard to the delay in making it or prejudice to the other party or any other circumstances. However, a claim may not be amended in such a manner that the amended claim falls outside the scope of the arbitration clause or separate arbitration agreement.

Pleas as to the jurisdiction of the arbitral tribunal

Article 21

1. The arbitral tribunal shall have the power to rule on objections that it has no jurisdiction, including any objections with respect to the existence or validity of the arbitration clause or of the separate arbitration agreement.
2. The arbitral tribunal shall have the power to determine the existence or the validity of the contract of which an arbitration clause forms a part. For the purposes of article 21, an arbitration clause which forms part of a contract and which provides for arbitration under these Rules shall be treated as an agreement independent of the other terms of the contract. A decision by the arbitral tribunal that the contract is null and void shall not entail *ipso jure* the invalidity of the arbitration clause.
3. A plea that the arbitral tribunal does not have jurisdiction shall be raised not later than in the statement of defence or, with respect to a counter-claim, in the reply to the counter-claim.
4. In general, the arbitral tribunal should rule on a plea concerning its jurisdiction as a preliminary question. However, the arbitral tribunal may proceed with the arbitration and rule on such a plea in their final award.

Further written statements

Article 22

The arbitral tribunal shall decide which further written statements, in addition to the statement of claim and the statement of defence, shall be required from the parties or may be presented by them and shall fix the periods of time for communicating such statements.

Periods of time

Article 23

The periods of time fixed by the arbitral tribunal for the communication of written statements (including the statement of claim and statement of defence) should not exceed forty-five days. However, the arbitral tribunal may extend the time-limits if it concludes that an extension is justified.

Evidence and hearings (Articles 24 and 25)

Article 24

1. Each party shall have the burden of proving the facts relied on to support his claim or defence.
2. The arbitral tribunal may, if it considers it appropriate, require a party to deliver to the tribunal and to the other party, within such a period of time as the arbitral tribunal shall decide, a summary of the documents and other evidence which that party intends to present in support of the facts in issue set out in his statement of claim or statement of defence.
3. At any time during the arbitral proceedings the arbitral tribunal may require the parties to produce documents, exhibits or other evidence within such a period of time as the tribunal shall determine.

Article 25

1. In the event of an oral hearing, the arbitral tribunal shall give the parties adequate advance notice of the date, time and place thereof.
2. If witnesses are to be heard, at least fifteen days before the hearing each party shall communicate to the arbitral tribunal and to the other party the names and addresses of the witnesses he intends to present, the subject upon and the languages in which such witnesses will give their testimony.
3. The arbitral tribunal shall make arrangements for the translation of oral statements made at a hearing and for a record of the hearing if either is deemed necessary by the tribunal under the circumstances of the case, or if the parties have agreed thereto and have communicated such agreement to the tribunal at least fifteen days before the hearing.
4. Hearings shall be held in camera unless the parties agree otherwise. The arbitral tribunal may require the retirement of any witness or witnesses during the testimony of other witnesses. The arbitral tribunal is free to determine the manner in which witnesses are examined.
5. Evidence of witnesses may also be presented in the form of written statements signed by them.

6. The arbitral tribunal shall determine the admissibility, relevance, materiality and weight of the evidence offered.

Interim measures of protection

Article 26

1. At the request of either party, the arbitral tribunal may take any interim measures it deems necessary in respect of the subject-matter of the dispute, including measures for the conservation of the goods forming the subject-matter in dispute, such as ordering their deposit with a third person or the sale of perishable goods.
2. Such interim measures may be established in the form of an interim award. The arbitral tribunal shall be entitled to require security for the costs of such measures.
3. A request for interim measures addressed by any party to a judicial authority shall not be deemed incompatible with the agreement to arbitrate, or as a waiver of that agreement.

Experts

Article 27

1. The arbitral tribunal may appoint one or more experts to report to it, in writing, on specific issues to be determined by the tribunal. A copy of the expert's terms of reference, established by the arbitral tribunal, shall be communicated to the parties.
2. The parties shall give the expert any relevant information or produce for his inspection any relevant documents or goods that he may require of them. Any dispute between a party and such expert as to the relevance of the required information or production shall be referred to the arbitral tribunal for decision.
3. Upon receipt of the expert's report, the arbitral tribunal shall communicate a copy of the report to the parties who shall be given the opportunity to express, in writing, their opinion on the report. A party shall be entitled to examine any document on which the expert has relied in his report.
4. At the request of either party the expert, after delivery of the report, may be heard at a hearing where the parties shall have the opportunity to be present and to interrogate the expert. At this hearing either party may present expert witnesses in order to testify on the points at issue. The provisions of article 25 shall be applicable to such proceedings.

Default

Article 28

1. If, within the period of time fixed by the arbitral tribunal, the claimant has failed to communicate his claim without showing sufficient cause for such failure, the arbitral tribunal shall issue an order for the termination of the arbitral proceedings. If, within the period of time fixed by the arbitral tribunal, the respondent has failed to communicate his statement of defence without showing sufficient cause for such failure, the arbitral tribunal shall order that the proceedings continue.
2. If one of the parties, duly notified under these Rules, fails to appear at a hearing, without showing sufficient cause for such failure, the arbitral tribunal may proceed with the arbitration.
3. If one of the parties, duly invited to produce documentary evidence, fails to do so within the established period of time, without showing sufficient cause for such failure, the arbitral tribunal may make the award on the evidence before it.

Closure of hearings

Article 29

1. The arbitral tribunal may inquire of the parties if they have any further proof to offer or witnesses to be heard or submissions to make and, if there are none, it may declare the hearings closed.
2. The arbitral tribunal may, if it considers it necessary owing to exceptional circumstances, decide, on its own motion or upon application of a party, to reopen the hearings at any time before the award is made.

Waiver of rules

Article 30

A party who knows that any provision of, or requirement under, these Rules has not been complied with and yet proceeds with the arbitration without promptly stating his objection to such non-compliance, shall be deemed to have waived his right to object.

Section IV. The Award

Decisions

Article 31

1. When there are three arbitrators, any award or other decision of the arbitral tribunal shall be made by a majority of the arbitrators.
2. In the case of questions of procedure, when there is no majority or when the arbitral tribunal so authorizes, the presiding arbitrator may decide on his own, subject to revision, if any, by the arbitral tribunal.

Form and effect of the award

Article 32

1. In addition to making a final award, the arbitral tribunal shall be entitled to make interim, interlocutory, or partial awards.
2. The award shall be made in writing and shall be final and binding on the parties. The parties undertake to carry out the award without delay.
3. The arbitral tribunal shall state the reasons upon which the award is based, unless the parties have agreed that no reasons are to be given.
4. An award shall be signed by the arbitrators and it shall contain the date on which and the place where the award was made. Where there are three arbitrators and one of them fails to sign, the award shall state the reason for the absence of the signature.
5. The award may be made public only with the consent of both parties.
6. Copies of the award signed by the arbitrators shall be communicated to the parties by the arbitral tribunal.
7. If the arbitration law of the country where the award is made requires that the award be filed or registered by the arbitral tribunal, the tribunal shall comply with this requirement within the period of time required by law.

Applicable law, *amiable compositeur*

Article 33

1. The arbitral tribunal shall apply the law designated by the parties as applicable to the substance of the dispute. Failing such designation by the parties, the arbitral tribunal shall apply the law determined by the conflict of laws rules which it considers applicable.
2. The arbitral tribunal shall decide as *amiable compositeur* or *ex aequo et bono* only if the parties have expressly authorized the arbitral tribunal to do so and if the law applicable to the arbitral procedure permits such arbitration.
3. In all cases, the arbitral tribunal shall decide in accordance with the terms of the contract and shall take into account the usages of the trade applicable to the transaction.

Settlement or other grounds for termination

Article 34

1. If, before the award is made, the parties agree on a settlement of the dispute, the arbitral tribunal shall either issue an order for the termination of the arbitral proceedings or, if requested by both parties and accepted by the tribunal, record the settlement in the form of an arbitral award on agreed terms. The arbitral tribunal is not obliged to give reasons for such an award.

2. If, before the award is made, the continuation of the arbitral proceedings becomes unnecessary or impossible for any reason not mentioned in paragraph 1, the arbitral tribunal shall inform the parties of its intention to issue an order for the termination of the proceedings. The arbitral tribunal shall have the power to issue such an order unless a party raises justifiable grounds for objection.
3. Copies of the order for termination of the arbitral proceedings or of the arbitral award on agreed terms, signed by the arbitrators, shall be communicated by the arbitral tribunal to the parties. Where an arbitral award on agreed terms is made, the provisions of article 32, paragraphs 2 and 4 to 7, shall apply.

Interpretation of the award

Article 35

1. Within thirty days after the receipt of the award, either party, with notice to the other party, may request that the arbitral tribunal give an interpretation of the award.
2. The interpretation shall be given in writing within forty-five days after the receipt of the request. The interpretation shall form part of the award and the provisions of article 32, paragraphs 2 to 7, shall apply.

Correction of the award

Article 36

1. Within thirty days after the receipt of the award, either party, with notice to the other party, may request the arbitral tribunal to correct in the award any errors in computation, any clerical or typographical errors, or any errors of similar nature. The arbitral tribunal may within thirty days after the communication of the award make such corrections on its own initiative.
2. Such corrections shall be in writing, and the provisions of article 32, paragraphs 2 to 7 shall apply.

Additional award

Article 37

1. Within thirty days after the receipt of the award, either party, with notice to the other party, may request the arbitral tribunal to make an additional award as to claims presented in the arbitral proceedings but omitted from the award.
2. If the arbitral tribunal considers the request for an additional award to be justified and considers that the omission can be rectified without any further hearings or evidence, it shall complete its award within sixty days after the receipt of the request.
3. When an additional award is made, the provisions of article 32, paragraphs 2 to 7, shall apply.

Costs (Articles 38 to 40)

Article 38

The arbitral tribunal shall fix the costs of arbitration in its award. The term 'costs' includes only:

(a) The fees of the arbitral tribunal to be stated separately as to each arbitrator and to be fixed by the tribunal itself in accordance with article 39;
(b) The travel and other expenses incurred by the arbitrators;
(c) The costs of expert advice and of other assistance required by the arbitral tribunal;
(d) The travel and other expenses of witnesses to the extent such expenses are approved by the arbitral tribunal;
(e) The costs for legal representation and assistance of the successful party if such costs were claimed during the arbitral proceedings, and only to the extent that the arbitral tribunal determines that the amount of such costs is reasonable;
(f) Any fees and expenses of the appointing authority as well as the expenses of the Secretary-General of the Permanent Court of Arbitration at The Hague.

Article 39

1. The fees of the arbitral tribunal shall be reasonable in amount, taking into account the amount in dispute, the complexity of the subject-matter, the time spent by the arbitrators and any other relevant circumstances of the case.

2. If an appointing authority has been agreed upon by the parties or designated by the Secretary-General of the Permanent Court of Arbitration at The Hague, and if that authority has issued a schedule of fees for arbitrators in international cases which it administers, the arbitral tribunal in fixing its fees shall take that schedule of fees into account to the extent that it considers appropriate in the circumstances of the case.
3. If such appointing authority has not issued a schedule of fees for arbitrators in international cases, any party may at any time request the appointing authority to furnish a statement setting forth the basis for establishing fees which is customarily followed in international cases in which the authority appoints arbitrators. If the appointing authority consents to provide such a statement, the arbitral tribunal in fixing its fees shall take such information into account to the extent that it considers appropriate in the circumstances of the case.
4. In cases referred to in paragraphs 2 and 3, when a party so requests and the appointing authority consents to perform the function, the arbitral tribunal shall fix its fees only after consultation with the appointing authority which may make any comment it deems appropriate to the arbitral tribunal concerning the fees.

Article 40

1. Except as provided in paragraph 2, the costs of arbitration shall in principle be borne by the unsuccessful party. However, the arbitral tribunal may apportion each of such costs between the parties if it determines that apportionment is reasonable, taking into account the circumstances of the case.
2. With respect to the costs of legal representation and assistance referred to in article 38, paragraph (e), the arbitral tribunal, taking into account the circumstances of the case, shall be free to determine which party shall bear such costs or may apportion such costs between the parties if it determines that apportionment is reasonable.
3. When the arbitral tribunal issues an order for the termination of the arbitral proceedings or makes an award on agreed terms, it shall fix the costs of arbitration referred to in article 38 and article 39, paragraph 1, in the text of that order or award.
4. No additional fees may be charged by an arbitral tribunal for interpretation or correction or completion of its award under articles 35 to 37.

Deposit of costs

Article 41

1. The arbitral tribunal, on its establishment, may request each party to deposit an equal amount as an advance for the costs referred to in article 38, paragraphs (a), (b) and (c).
2. During the course of the arbitral proceedings the arbitral tribunal may request supplementary deposits from the parties.
3. If an appointing authority has been agreed upon by the parties or designated by the Secretary-General of the Permanent Court of Arbitration at The Hague, and when a party so requests and the appointing authority consents to perform the function, the arbitral tribunal shall fix the amounts of any deposits or supplementary deposits only after consultation with the appointing authority which may make any comments to the arbitral tribunal which it deems appropriate concerning the amount of such deposits and supplementary deposits.
4. If the required deposits are not paid in full within thirty days after the receipt of the request, the arbitral tribunal shall so inform the parties in order that one or another of them may make the required payment. If such payment is not made, the arbitral tribunal may order the suspension or termination of the arbitral proceedings.
5. After the award has been made, the arbitral tribunal shall render an accounting to the parties of the deposits received and return any unexpended balance to the parties.

APPENDIX XII

UNCITRAL Arbitration Rules 2010[1]

Section I. Introductory Rules

Scope of application*

Article 1

1. Where parties have agreed that disputes between them in respect of a defined legal relationship, whether contractual or not, shall be referred to arbitration under the UNCITRAL Arbitration Rules, then such disputes shall be settled in accordance with these Rules subject to such modification as the parties may agree.
2. The parties to an arbitration agreement concluded after 15 August 2010 shall be presumed to have referred to the Rules in effect on the date of commencement of the arbitration, unless the parties have agreed to apply a particular version of the Rules. That presumption does not apply where the arbitration agreement has been concluded by accepting after 15 August 2010 an offer made before that date.
3. These Rules shall govern the arbitration except that where any of these Rules is in conflict with a provision of the law applicable to the arbitration from which the parties cannot derogate, that provision shall prevail.

Notice and calculation of periods of time

Article 2

1. A notice, including a notification, communication or proposal, may be transmitted by any means of communication that provides or allows for a record of its transmission.
2. If an address has been designated by a party specifically for this purpose or authorized by the arbitral tribunal, any notice shall be delivered to that party at that address, and if so delivered shall be deemed to have been received. Delivery by electronic means such as facsimile or email may only be made to an address so designated or authorized.
3. In the absence of such designation or authorization, a notice is:
   (a) received if it is physically delivered to the addressee; or
   (b) deemed to have been received if it is delivered at the place of business, habitual residence or mailing address of the addressee.
4. If, after reasonable efforts, delivery cannot be effected in accordance with paragraphs 2 or 3, a notice is deemed to have been received if it is sent to the addressee's last-known place of business, habitual residence or mailing address by registered letter or any other means that provides a record of delivery or of attempted delivery.
5. A notice shall be deemed to have been received on the day it is delivered in accordance with paragraphs 2, 3 or 4, or attempted to be delivered in accordance with paragraph 4. A notice

---

* A model arbitration clause for contracts can be found in the annex to the Rules.

[1] On 11 July 2013, UNCITRAL adopted a new set of arbitration rules, which will come into effect on 1 April 2014. The new rules reproduce the language of the 2010 UNCITRAL Rules, with the addition of a new Art 1(4), which provides:

> For investor-State arbitration initiated pursuant to a treaty providing for the protection of investments or investors, these Rules include the UNCITRAL Rules on Transparency in Treaty-based Investor-State Arbitration ('Rules on Transparency'), subject to article 1 of the Rules on Transparency.

transmitted by electronic means is deemed to have been received on the day it is sent, except that a notice of arbitration so transmitted is only deemed to have been received on the day when it reaches the addressee's electronic address.

6. For the purpose of calculating a period of time under these Rules, such period shall begin to run on the day following the day when a notice is received. If the last day of such period is an official holiday or a non-business day at the residence or place of business of the addressee, the period is extended until the first business day which follows. Official holidays or non-business days occurring during the running of the period of time are included in calculating the period.

Notice of arbitration

Article 3

1. The party or parties initiating recourse to arbitration (hereinafter called the 'claimant') shall communicate to the other party or parties (hereinafter called the 'respondent') a notice of arbitration.
2. Arbitral proceedings shall be deemed to commence on the date on which the notice of arbitration is received by the respondent.
3. The notice of arbitration shall include the following:
   (a) A demand that the dispute be referred to arbitration;
   (b) The names and contact details of the parties;
   (c) Identification of the arbitration agreement that is invoked;
   (d) Identification of any contract or other legal instrument out of or in relation to which the dispute arises or, in the absence of such contract or instrument, a brief description of the relevant relationship;
   (e) A brief description of the claim and an indication of the amount involved, if any;
   (f) The relief or remedy sought;
   (g) A proposal as to the number of arbitrators, language and place of arbitration, if the parties have not previously agreed thereon.
4. The notice of arbitration may also include:
   (a) A proposal for the designation of an appointing authority referred to in article 6, paragraph 1;
   (b) A proposal for the appointment of a sole arbitrator referred to in article 8, paragraph 1;
   (c) Notification of the appointment of an arbitrator referred to in articles 9 or 10.
5. The constitution of the arbitral tribunal shall not be hindered by any controversy with respect to the sufficiency of the notice of arbitration, which shall be finally resolved by the arbitral tribunal.

Response to the notice of arbitration

Article 4

1. Within 30 days of the receipt of the notice of arbitration, the respondent shall communicate to the claimant a response to the notice of arbitration, which shall include:
   (a) The name and contact details of each respondent;
   (b) A response to the information set forth in the notice of arbitration, pursuant to article 3, paragraphs 3 (c) to (g).
2. The response to the notice of arbitration may also include:
   (a) Any plea that an arbitral tribunal to be constituted under these Rules lacks jurisdiction;
   (b) A proposal for the designation of an appointing authority referred to in article 6, paragraph 1;
   (c) A proposal for the appointment of a sole arbitrator referred to in article 8, paragraph 1;
   (d) Notification of the appointment of an arbitrator referred to in articles 9 or 10;
   (e) A brief description of counterclaims or claims for the purpose of a set-off, if any, including where relevant, an indication of the amounts involved, and the relief or remedy sought;
   (f) A notice of arbitration in accordance with article 3 in case the respondent formulates a claim against a party to the arbitration agreement other than the claimant.

3. The constitution of the arbitral tribunal shall not be hindered by any controversy with respect to the respondent's failure to communicate a response to the notice of arbitration, or an incomplete or late response to the notice of arbitration, which shall be finally resolved by the arbitral tribunal.

Representation and assistance

Article 5

Each party may be represented or assisted by persons chosen by it. The names and addresses of such persons must be communicated to all parties and to the arbitral tribunal. Such communication must specify whether the appointment is being made for purposes of representation or assistance. Where a person is to act as a representative of a party, the arbitral tribunal, on its own initiative or at the request of any party, may at any time require proof of authority granted to the representative in such a form as the arbitral tribunal may determine.

Designating and appointing authorities

Article 6

1. Unless the parties have already agreed on the choice of an appointing authority, a party may at any time propose the name or names of one or more institutions or persons, including the Secretary-General of the Permanent Court of Arbitration at The Hague (hereinafter called the 'PCA'), one of whom would serve as appointing authority.
2. If all parties have not agreed on the choice of an appointing authority within 30 days after a proposal made in accordance with paragraph 1 has been received by all other parties, any party may request the Secretary-General of the PCA to designate the appointing authority.
3. Where these Rules provide for a period of time within which a party must refer a matter to an appointing authority and no appointing authority has been agreed on or designated, the period is suspended from the date on which a party initiates the procedure for agreeing on or designating an appointing authority until the date of such agreement or designation.
4. Except as referred to in article 41, paragraph (4), if the appointing authority refuses to act, or if it fails to appoint an arbitrator within 30 days after it receives a party's request to do so, fails to act within any other period provided by these Rules, or fails to decide on a challenge to an arbitrator within a reasonable time after receiving a party's request to do so, any party may request the Secretary-General of the PCA to designate a substitute appointing authority.
5. In exercising their functions under these Rules, the appointing authority and the Secretary-General of the PCA may require from any party and the arbitrators the information they deem necessary and they shall give the parties and, where appropriate, the arbitrators, an opportunity to present their views in any manner they consider appropriate. All such communications to and from the appointing authority and the Secretary-General of the PCA shall also be provided by the sender to all other parties.
6. When the appointing authority is requested to appoint an arbitrator pursuant to articles 8, 9, 10 or 14, the party making the request shall send to the appointing authority copies of the notice of arbitration and, if it exists, any response to the notice of arbitration.
7. The appointing authority shall have regard to such considerations as are likely to secure the appointment of an independent and impartial arbitrator and shall take into account the advisability of appointing an arbitrator of a nationality other than the nationalities of the parties.

Section II. Composition of the Arbitral Tribunal

Number of arbitrators

Article 7

1. If the parties have not previously agreed on the number of arbitrators, and if within 30 days after the receipt by the respondent of the notice of arbitration the parties have not agreed that there shall be only one arbitrator, three arbitrators shall be appointed.

2. Notwithstanding paragraph 1, if no other parties have responded to a party's proposal to appoint a sole arbitrator within the time limit provided for in paragraph 1 and the party or parties concerned have failed to appoint a second arbitrator in accordance with articles 9 or 10, the appointing authority may, at the request of a party, appoint a sole arbitrator pursuant to the procedure provided for in article 8, paragraph 2 if it determines that, in view of the circumstances of the case, this is more appropriate.

Appointment of arbitrators (articles 8 to 10)

Article 8

1. If the parties have agreed that a sole arbitrator is to be appointed and if within 30 days after receipt by all other parties of a proposal for the appointment of a sole arbitrator the parties have not reached agreement thereon, a sole arbitrator shall, at the request of a party, be appointed by the appointing authority.
2. The appointing authority shall appoint the sole arbitrator as promptly as possible. In making the appointment, the appointing authority shall use the following list-procedure, unless the parties agree that the list-procedure should not be used or unless the appointing authority determines in its discretion that the use of the list-procedure is not appropriate for the case:
   (a) The appointing authority shall communicate to each of the parties an identical list containing at least three names;
   (b) Within 15 days after the receipt of this list, each party may return the list to the appointing authority after having deleted the name or names to which it objects and numbered the remaining names on the list in the order of its preference;
   (c) After the expiration of the above period of time the appointing authority shall appoint the sole arbitrator from among the names approved on the lists returned to it and in accordance with the order of preference indicated by the parties;
   (d) If for any reason the appointment cannot be made according to this procedure, the appointing authority may exercise its discretion in appointing the sole arbitrator.

Article 9

1. If three arbitrators are to be appointed, each party shall appoint one arbitrator. The two arbitrators thus appointed shall choose the third arbitrator who will act as the presiding arbitrator of the arbitral tribunal.
2. If within 30 days after the receipt of a party's notification of the appointment of an arbitrator the other party has not notified the first party of the arbitrator it has appointed, the first party may request the appointing authority to appoint the second arbitrator.
3. If within 30 days after the appointment of the second arbitrator the two arbitrators have not agreed on the choice of the presiding arbitrator, the presiding arbitrator shall be appointed by the appointing authority in the same way as a sole arbitrator would be appointed under article 8.

Article 10

1. For the purposes of article 9, paragraph 1, where three arbitrators are to be appointed and there are multiple parties as claimant or as respondent, unless the parties have agreed to another method of appointment of arbitrators, the multiple parties jointly, whether as claimant or as respondent, shall appoint an arbitrator.
2. If the parties have agreed that the arbitral tribunal is to be composed of a number of arbitrators other than one or three, the arbitrators shall be appointed according to the method agreed upon by the parties.
3. In the event of any failure to constitute the arbitral tribunal under these Rules, the appointing authority shall, at the request of any party, constitute the arbitral tribunal and, in doing so, may revoke any appointment already made and appoint or reappoint each of the arbitrators and designate one of them as the presiding arbitrator.

Disclosures by and challenge of arbitrators (articles 11 to 13)**

Article 11

When a person is approached in connection with his or her possible appointment as an arbitrator, he or she shall disclose any circumstances likely to give rise to justifiable doubts as to his or her impartiality or independence. An arbitrator, from the time of his or her appointment and throughout the arbitral proceedings, shall without delay disclose any such circumstances to the parties and the other arbitrators unless they have already been informed by him or her of these circumstances.

Article 12

1. Any arbitrator may be challenged if circumstances exist that give rise to justifiable doubts as to the arbitrator's impartiality or independence.
2. A party may challenge the arbitrator appointed by it only for reasons of which it becomes aware after the appointment has been made.
3. In the event that an arbitrator fails to act or in the event of the *de jure* or *de facto* impossibility of his or her performing his or her functions, the procedure in respect of the challenge of an arbitrator as provided in article 13 shall apply.

Article 13

1. A party that intends to challenge an arbitrator shall send notice of its challenge within 15 days after it has been notified of the appointment of the challenged arbitrator, or within 15 days after the circumstances mentioned in articles 11 and 12 became known to that party.
2. The notice of challenge shall be communicated to all other parties, to the arbitrator who is challenged and to the other arbitrators. The notice of challenge shall state the reasons for the challenge.
3. When an arbitrator has been challenged by a party, all parties may agree to the challenge. The arbitrator may also, after the challenge, withdraw from his or her office. In neither case does this imply acceptance of the validity of the grounds for the challenge.
4. If, within 15 days from the date of the notice of challenge, all parties do not agree to the challenge or the challenged arbitrator does not withdraw, the party making the challenge may elect to pursue it. In that case, within 30 days from the date of the notice of challenge, it shall seek a decision on the challenge by the appointing authority.

Replacement of an arbitrator

Article 14

1. Subject to paragraph (2), in any event where an arbitrator has to be replaced during the course of the arbitral proceedings, a substitute arbitrator shall be appointed or chosen pursuant to the procedure provided for in articles 8 to 11 that was applicable to the appointment or choice of the arbitrator being replaced. This procedure shall apply even if during the process of appointing the arbitrator to be replaced, a party had failed to exercise its right to appoint or to participate in the appointment.
2. If, at the request of a party, the appointing authority determines that, in view of the exceptional circumstances of the case, it would be justified for a party to be deprived of its right to appoint a substitute arbitrator, the appointing authority may, after giving an opportunity to the parties and the remaining arbitrators to express their views: (a) appoint the substitute arbitrator; or (b) after the closure of the hearings, authorize the other arbitrators to proceed with the arbitration and make any decision or award.

Repetition of hearings in the event of the replacement of an arbitrator

Article 15

If an arbitrator is replaced, the proceedings shall resume at the stage where the arbitrator who was replaced ceased to perform his or her functions, unless the arbitral tribunal decides otherwise.

** Model statements of independence pursuant to article 11 can be found in the annex to the Rules.

Exclusion of liability

Article 16

Save for intentional wrongdoing, the parties waive, to the fullest extent permitted under the applicable law, any claim against the arbitrators, the appointing authority and any person appointed by the arbitral tribunal based on any act or omission in connection with the arbitration.

Section III. Arbitral Proceedings

General provisions

Article 17

1. Subject to these Rules, the arbitral tribunal may conduct the arbitration in such manner as it considers appropriate, provided that the parties are treated with equality and that at an appropriate stage of the proceedings each party is given a reasonable opportunity of presenting its case. The arbitral tribunal, in exercising its discretion, shall conduct the proceedings so as to avoid unnecessary delay and expense and to provide a fair and efficient process for resolving the parties' dispute.
2. As soon as practicable after its constitution and after inviting the parties to express their views, the arbitral tribunal shall establish the provisional timetable of the arbitration. The arbitral tribunal may, at any time, after inviting the parties to express their views, extend or abridge any period of time prescribed under these Rules or agreed by the parties.
3. If at an appropriate stage of the proceedings any party so requests, the arbitral tribunal shall hold hearings for the presentation of evidence by witnesses, including expert witnesses, or for oral argument. In the absence of such a request, the arbitral tribunal shall decide whether to hold such hearings or whether the proceedings shall be conducted on the basis of documents and other materials.
4. All communications to the arbitral tribunal by one party shall be communicated by that party to all other parties. Such communications shall be made at the same time, except as otherwise permitted by the arbitral tribunal if it may do so under applicable law.
5. The arbitral tribunal may, at the request of any party, allow one or more third persons to be joined in the arbitration as a party provided such person is a party to the arbitration agreement, unless the arbitral tribunal finds, after giving all parties, including the person or persons to be joined, the opportunity to be heard, that joinder should not be permitted because of prejudice to any of those parties. The arbitral tribunal may make a single award or several awards in respect of all parties so involved in the arbitration.

Place of arbitration

Article 18

1. If the parties have not previously agreed on the place of arbitration, the place of arbitration shall be determined by the arbitral tribunal having regard to the circumstances of the case. The award shall be deemed to have been made at the place of arbitration.
2. The arbitral tribunal may meet at any location it considers appropriate for deliberations. Unless otherwise agreed by the parties, the arbitral tribunal may also meet at any location it considers appropriate for any other purpose, including hearings.

Language

Article 19

1. Subject to an agreement by the parties, the arbitral tribunal shall, promptly after its appointment, determine the language or languages to be used in the proceedings. This determination shall apply to the statement of claim, the statement of defence, and any further written statements and, if oral hearings take place, to the language or languages to be used in such hearings.
2. The arbitral tribunal may order that any documents annexed to the statement of claim or statement of defence, and any supplementary documents or exhibits submitted in the course

of the proceedings, delivered in their original language, shall be accompanied by a translation into the language or languages agreed upon by the parties or determined by the arbitral tribunal.

Statement of claim

Article 20

1. The claimant shall communicate its statement of claim in writing to the respondent and to each of the arbitrators within a period of time to be determined by the arbitral tribunal. The claimant may elect to treat its notice of arbitration referred to in article 3 as a statement of claim, provided that the notice of arbitration also complies with the requirements of paragraphs 2 to 4 of this article.
2. The statement of claim shall include the following particulars:
   (a) The names and contact details of the parties;
   (b) A statement of the facts supporting the claim;
   (c) The points at issue;
   (d) The relief or remedy sought;
   (e) The legal grounds or arguments supporting the claim.
3. A copy of any contract or other legal instrument out of or in relation to which the dispute arises and of the arbitration agreement shall be annexed to the statement of claim.
4. The statement of claim should, as far as possible, be accompanied by all documents and other evidence relied upon by the claimant, or contain references to them.

Statement of defence

Article 21

1. The respondent shall communicate its statement of defence in writing to the claimant and to each of the arbitrators within a period of time to be determined by the arbitral tribunal. The respondent may elect to treat its response to the notice of arbitration referred to in article 4 as a statement of defence, provided that the response to the notice of arbitration also complies with the requirements of paragraph 2 of this article.
2. The statement of defence shall reply to the particulars (b) to (e) of the statement of claim (article 20, paragraph 2). The statement of defence should, as far as possible, be accompanied by all documents and other evidence relied upon by the respondent, or contain references to them.
3. In its statement of defence, or at a later stage in the arbitral proceedings if the arbitral tribunal decides that the delay was justified under the circumstances, the respondent may make a counterclaim or rely on a claim for the purpose of a set-off provided that the arbitral tribunal has jurisdiction over it.
4. The provisions of article 20, paragraphs 2 to 4 shall apply to a counterclaim, a claim under article 4, paragraph (2) (f) and a claim relied on for the purpose of a set-off.

Amendments to the claim or defence

Article 22

During the course of the arbitral proceedings, a party may amend or supplement its claim or defence, including a counterclaim or a claim for the purpose of a set-off, unless the arbitral tribunal considers it inappropriate to allow such amendment or supplement having regard to the delay in making it or prejudice to other parties or any other circumstances. However, a claim or defence, including a counterclaim or a claim for the purpose of a set-off, may not be amended or supplemented in such a manner that the amended or supplemented claim or defence falls outside the jurisdiction of the arbitral tribunal.

Pleas as to the jurisdiction of the arbitral tribunal

Article 23

1. The arbitral tribunal shall have the power to rule on its own jurisdiction, including any objections with respect to the existence or validity of the arbitration agreement. For that purpose, an

arbitration clause that forms part of a contract shall be treated as an agreement independent of the other terms of the contract. A decision by the arbitral tribunal that the contract is null shall not entail automatically the invalidity of the arbitration clause.

2. A plea that the arbitral tribunal does not have jurisdiction shall be raised no later than in the statement of defence or, with respect to a counterclaim or a claim for the purpose of a set-off, in the reply to the counterclaim or to the claim for the purpose of a set-off. A party is not precluded from raising such a plea by the fact that it has appointed, or participated in the appointment of, an arbitrator. A plea that the arbitral tribunal is exceeding the scope of its authority shall be raised as soon as the matter alleged to be beyond the scope of its authority is raised during the arbitral proceedings. The arbitral tribunal may, in either case, admit a later plea if it considers the delay justified.
3. The arbitral tribunal may rule on a plea referred to in paragraph 2 either as a preliminary question or in an award on the merits. The arbitral tribunal may continue the arbitral proceedings and make an award, notwithstanding any pending challenge to its jurisdiction before a court.

Further written statements

Article 24

The arbitral tribunal shall decide which further written statements, in addition to the statement of claim and the statement of defence, shall be required from the parties or may be presented by them and shall fix the periods of time for communicating such statements.

Periods of time

Article 25

The periods of time fixed by the arbitral tribunal for the communication of written statements (including the statement of claim and statement of defence) should not exceed 45 days. However, the arbitral tribunal may extend the time limits if it concludes that an extension is justified.

Interim measures

Article 26

1. The arbitral tribunal may, at the request of a party, grant interim measures.
2. An interim measure is any temporary measure by which, at any time prior to the issuance of the award by which the dispute is finally decided, the arbitral tribunal orders a party, for example and without limitation, to:
   (a) Maintain or restore the status quo pending determination of the dispute;
   (b) Take action that would prevent, or refrain from taking action that is likely to cause, (i) current or imminent harm or (ii) prejudice to the arbitral process itself;
   (c) Provide a means of preserving assets out of which a subsequent award may be satisfied; or
   (d) Preserve evidence that may be relevant and material to the resolution of the dispute.
3. The party requesting an interim measure under paragraphs 2 (a) to (c) shall satisfy the arbitral tribunal that:
   (a) Harm not adequately reparable by an award of damages is likely to result if the measure is not ordered, and such harm substantially outweighs the harm that is likely to result to the party against whom the measure is directed if the measure is granted; and
   (b) There is a reasonable possibility that the requesting party will succeed on the merits of the claim. The determination on this possibility shall not affect the discretion of the arbitral tribunal in making any subsequent determination.
4. With regard to a request for an interim measure under paragraph 2 (d), the requirements in paragraphs 3 (a) and (b) shall apply only to the extent the arbitral tribunal considers appropriate.
5. The arbitral tribunal may modify, suspend or terminate an interim measure it has granted, upon application of any party or, in exceptional circumstances and upon prior notice to the parties, on the arbitral tribunal's own initiative.

6. The arbitral tribunal may require the party requesting an interim measure to provide appropriate security in connection with the measure.
7. The arbitral tribunal may require any party promptly to disclose any material change in the circumstances on the basis of which the interim measure was requested or granted.
8. The party requesting an interim measure may be liable for any costs and damages caused by the measure to any party if the arbitral tribunal later determines that, in the circumstances then prevailing, the measure should not have been granted. The arbitral tribunal may award such costs and damages at any point during the proceedings.
9. A request for interim measures addressed by any party to a judicial authority shall not be deemed incompatible with the agreement to arbitrate, or as a waiver of that agreement.

Evidence

Article 27

1. Each party shall have the burden of proving the facts relied on to support its claim or defence.
2. Witnesses, including expert witnesses, who are presented by the parties to testify to the arbitral tribunal on any issue of fact or expertise may be any individual, notwithstanding that the individual is a party to the arbitration or in any way related to a party. Unless otherwise directed by the arbitral tribunal, statements by witnesses, including expert witnesses, may be presented in writing and signed by them.
3. At any time during the arbitral proceedings the arbitral tribunal may require the parties to produce documents, exhibits or other evidence within such a period of time as the arbitral tribunal shall determine.
4. The arbitral tribunal shall determine the admissibility, relevance, materiality and weight of the evidence offered.

Hearings

Article 28

1. In the event of an oral hearing, the arbitral tribunal shall give the parties adequate advance notice of the date, time and place thereof.
2. Witnesses, including expert witnesses, may be heard under the conditions and examined in the manner set by the arbitral tribunal.
3. Hearings shall be held *in camera* unless the parties agree otherwise. The arbitral tribunal may require the retirement of any witness or witnesses, including expert witnesses, during the testimony of such other witnesses, except that a witness, including an expert witness, who is a party to the arbitration shall not, in principle, be asked to retire.
4. The arbitral tribunal may direct that witnesses, including expert witnesses, be examined through means of telecommunication that do not require their physical presence at the hearing (such as videoconference).

Experts appointed by the arbitral tribunal

Article 29

1. After consultation with the parties, the arbitral tribunal may appoint one or more independent experts to report to it, in writing, on specific issues to be determined by the arbitral tribunal. A copy of the expert's terms of reference, established by the arbitral tribunal, shall be communicated to the parties.
2. The expert shall, in principle before accepting appointment, submit to the arbitral tribunal and to the parties a description of his or her qualifications and a statement of his or her impartiality and independence. Within the time ordered by the arbitral tribunal, the parties shall inform the arbitral tribunal whether they have any objections as to the expert's qualifications, impartiality or independence. The arbitral tribunal shall decide promptly whether to accept any such objections. After an expert's appointment, a party may object to the expert's qualifications, impartiality or independence only if the objection is for reasons of which the party becomes aware after the appointment has been made. The arbitral tribunal shall decide promptly what, if any, action to take.

3. The parties shall give the expert any relevant information or produce for his or her inspection any relevant documents or goods that he or she may require of them. Any dispute between a party and such expert as to the relevance of the required information or production shall be referred to the arbitral tribunal for decision.
4. Upon receipt of the expert's report, the arbitral tribunal shall communicate a copy of the report to the parties, which shall be given the opportunity to express, in writing, their opinion on the report. A party shall be entitled to examine any document on which the expert has relied in his or her report.
5. At the request of any party, the expert, after delivery of the report, may be heard at a hearing where the parties shall have the opportunity to be present and to interrogate the expert. At this hearing, any party may present expert witnesses in order to testify on the points at issue. The provisions of article 28 shall be applicable to such proceedings.

Default

Article 30

1. If, within the period of time fixed by these Rules or the arbitral tribunal, without showing sufficient cause:
   (a) The claimant has failed to communicate its statement of claim, the arbitral tribunal shall issue an order for the termination of the arbitral proceedings, unless there are remaining matters that may need to be decided and the arbitral tribunal considers it appropriate to do so;
   (b) The respondent has failed to communicate its response to the notice of arbitration or its statement of defence, the arbitral tribunal shall order that the proceedings continue, without treating such failure in itself as an admission of the claimant's allegations; the provisions of this subparagraph also apply to a claimant's failure to submit a defence to a counterclaim or to a claim for the purpose of a set-off.
2. If a party, duly notified under these Rules, fails to appear at a hearing, without showing sufficient cause for such failure, the arbitral tribunal may proceed with the arbitration.
3. If a party, duly invited by the arbitral tribunal to produce documents, exhibits or other evidence, fails to do so within the established period of time, without showing sufficient cause for such failure, the arbitral tribunal may make the award on the evidence before it.

Closure of hearings

Article 31

1. The arbitral tribunal may inquire of the parties if they have any further proof to offer or witnesses to be heard or submissions to make and, if there are none, it may declare the hearings closed.
2. The arbitral tribunal may, if it considers it necessary owing to exceptional circumstances, decide, on its own initiative or upon application of a party, to reopen the hearings at any time before the award is made.

Waiver of right to object

Article 32

A failure by any party to object promptly to any noncompliance with these Rules or with any requirement of the arbitration agreement shall be deemed to be a waiver of the right of such party to make such an objection, unless such party can show that, under the circumstances, its failure to object was justified.

Section IV. The Award

Decisions

Article 33

1. When there is more than one arbitrator, any award or other decision of the arbitral tribunal shall be made by a majority of the arbitrators.

2. In the case of questions of procedure, when there is no majority or when the arbitral tribunal so authorizes, the presiding arbitrator may decide alone, subject to revision, if any, by the arbitral tribunal.

Form and effect of the award

Article 34

1. The arbitral tribunal may make separate awards on different issues at different times.
2. All awards shall be made in writing and shall be final and binding on the parties. The parties shall carry out all awards without delay.
3. The arbitral tribunal shall state the reasons upon which the award is based, unless the parties have agreed that no reasons are to be given.
4. An award shall be signed by the arbitrators and it shall contain the date on which the award was made and indicate the place of arbitration. Where there is more than one arbitrator and any of them fails to sign, the award shall state the reason for the absence of the signature.
5. An award may be made public with the consent of all parties or where and to the extent disclosure is required of a party by legal duty, to protect or pursue a legal right or in relation to legal proceedings before a court or other competent authority.
6. Copies of the award signed by the arbitrators shall be communicated to the parties by the arbitral tribunal.

Applicable law, *amiable compositeur*

Article 35

1. The arbitral tribunal shall apply the rules of law designated by the parties as applicable to the substance of the dispute. Failing such designation by the parties, the arbitral tribunal shall apply the law which it determines to be appropriate.
2. The arbitral tribunal shall decide as *amiable compositeur* or *ex aequo et bono* only if the parties have expressly authorized the arbitral tribunal to do so.
3. In all cases, the arbitral tribunal shall decide in accordance with the terms of the contract, if any, and shall take into account any usage of trade applicable to the transaction.

Settlement or other grounds for termination

Article 36

1. If, before the award is made, the parties agree on a settlement of the dispute, the arbitral tribunal shall either issue an order for the termination of the arbitral proceedings or, if requested by the parties and accepted by the arbitral tribunal, record the settlement in the form of an arbitral award on agreed terms. The arbitral tribunal is not obliged to give reasons for such an award.
2. If, before the award is made, the continuation of the arbitral proceedings becomes unnecessary or impossible for any reason not mentioned in paragraph 1, the arbitral tribunal shall inform the parties of its intention to issue an order for the termination of the proceedings. The arbitral tribunal shall have the power to issue such an order unless there are remaining matters that may need to be decided and the arbitral tribunal considers it appropriate to do so.
3. Copies of the order for termination of the arbitral proceedings or of the arbitral award on agreed terms, signed by the arbitrators, shall be communicated by the arbitral tribunal to the parties. Where an arbitral award on agreed terms is made, the provisions of article 34, paragraphs 2, 4 and 5 shall apply.

Interpretation of the award

Article 37

1. Within 30 days after the receipt of the award, a party, with notice to the other parties, may request that the arbitral tribunal give an interpretation of the award.

2. The interpretation shall be given in writing within 45 days after the receipt of the request. The interpretation shall form part of the award and the provisions of article 34, paragraphs 2 to 6, shall apply.

Correction of the award

Article 38

1. Within 30 days after the receipt of the award, a party, with notice to the other parties, may request the arbitral tribunal to correct in the award any error in computation, any clerical or typographical error, or any error or omission of a similar nature. If the arbitral tribunal considers that the request is justified, it shall make the correction within 45 days of receipt of the request.
2. The arbitral tribunal may within 30 days after the communication of the award make such corrections on its own initiative.
3. Such corrections shall be in writing and shall form part of the award. The provisions of article 34, paragraphs 2 to 6, shall apply.

Additional award

Article 39

1. Within 30 days after the receipt of the termination order or the award, a party, with notice to the other parties, may request the arbitral tribunal to make an award or an additional award as to claims presented in the arbitral proceedings but not decided by the arbitral tribunal.
2. If the arbitral tribunal considers the request for an award or additional award to be justified, it shall render or complete its award within 60 days after the receipt of the request. The arbitral tribunal may extend, if necessary, the period of time within which it shall make the award.
3. When such an award or additional award is made, the provisions of article 34, paragraphs 2 to 6, shall apply.

Definition of costs

Article 40

1. The arbitral tribunal shall fix the costs of arbitration in the final award and, if it deems appropriate, in another decision.
2. The term 'costs' includes only:
   (a) The fees of the arbitral tribunal to be stated separately as to each arbitrator and to be fixed by the tribunal itself in accordance with article 41;
   (b) The reasonable travel and other expenses incurred by the arbitrators;
   (c) The reasonable costs of expert advice and of other assistance required by the arbitral tribunal;
   (d) The reasonable travel and other expenses of witnesses to the extent such expenses are approved by the arbitral tribunal;
   (e) The legal and other costs incurred by the parties in relation to the arbitration to the extent that the arbitral tribunal determines that the amount of such costs is reasonable;
   (f) Any fees and expenses of the appointing authority as well as the fees and expenses of the Secretary-General of the PCA.
3. In relation to interpretation, correction or completion of any award under articles 37 to 39, the arbitral tribunal may charge the costs referred to in paragraphs 2 (b) to (f), but no additional fees.

Fees and expenses of arbitrators

Article 41

1. The fees and expenses of the arbitrators shall be reasonable in amount, taking into account the amount in dispute, the complexity of the subject matter, the time spent by the arbitrators and any other relevant circumstances of the case.

2. If there is an appointing authority and it applies or has stated that it will apply a schedule or particular method for determining the fees for arbitrators in international cases, the arbitral tribunal in fixing its fees shall take that schedule or method into account to the extent that it considers appropriate in the circumstances of the case.
3. Promptly after its constitution, the arbitral tribunal shall inform the parties as to how it proposes to determine its fees and expenses, including any rates it intends to apply. Within 15 days of receiving that proposal, any party may refer the proposal to the appointing authority for review. If, within 45 days of receipt of such a referral, the appointing authority finds that the proposal of the arbitral tribunal is inconsistent with paragraph 1, it shall make any necessary adjustments thereto, which shall be binding upon the arbitral tribunal.
4. (a) When informing the parties of the arbitrators' fees and expenses that have been fixed pursuant to article 40, paragraphs 2 (a) and (b), the arbitral tribunal shall also explain the manner in which the corresponding amounts have been calculated.
   (b) Within 15 days of receiving the arbitral tribunal's determination of fees and expenses, any party may refer for review such determination to the appointing authority. If no appointing authority has been agreed upon or designated, or if the appointing authority fails to act within the time specified in these Rules, then the review shall be made by the Secretary-General of the PCA.
   (c) If the appointing authority or the Secretary-General of the PCA finds that the arbitral tribunal's determination is inconsistent with the arbitral tribunal's proposal (and any adjustment thereto) under paragraph 3 or is otherwise manifestly excessive, it shall, within 45 days of receiving such a referral, make any adjustments to the arbitral tribunal's determination that are necessary to satisfy the criteria in paragraph 1. Any such adjustments shall be binding upon the arbitral tribunal.
   (d) Any such adjustments shall either be included by the arbitral tribunal in its award or, if the award has already been issued, be implemented in a correction to the award, to which the procedure of article 38, paragraph 3 shall apply.
5. Throughout the procedure under paragraphs 3 and 4, the arbitral tribunal shall proceed with the arbitration, in accordance with article 17, paragraph 1.
6. A referral under paragraph 4 shall not affect any determination in the award other than the arbitral tribunal's fees and expenses; nor shall it delay the recognition and enforcement of all parts of the award other than those relating to the determination of the arbitral tribunal's fees and expenses.

Allocation of costs

Article 42

1. The costs of the arbitration shall in principle be borne by the unsuccessful party or parties. However, the arbitral tribunal may apportion each of such costs between the parties if it determines that apportionment is reasonable, taking into account the circumstances of the case.
2. The arbitral tribunal shall in the final award or, if it deems appropriate, in any other award, determine any amount that a party may have to pay to another party as a result of the decision on allocation of costs.

Deposit of costs

Article 43

1. The arbitral tribunal, on its establishment, may request the parties to deposit an equal amount as an advance for the costs referred to in article 40, paragraphs 2 (a) to (c).
2. During the course of the arbitral proceedings the arbitral tribunal may request supplementary deposits from the parties.
3. If an appointing authority has been agreed upon or designated, and when a party so requests and the appointing authority consents to perform the function, the arbitral tribunal shall fix the

amounts of any deposits or supplementary deposits only after consultation with the appointing authority, which may make any comments to the arbitral tribunal that it deems appropriate concerning the amount of such deposits and supplementary deposits.

4. If the required deposits are not paid in full within 30 days after the receipt of the request, the arbitral tribunal shall so inform the parties in order that one or more of them may make the required payment. If such payment is not made, the arbitral tribunal may order the suspension or termination of the arbitral proceedings.
5. After a termination order or final award has been made, the arbitral tribunal shall render an accounting to the parties of the deposits received and return any unexpended balance to the parties.

Annex

Model arbitration clause for contracts

Any dispute, controversy or claim arising out of or relating to this contract, or the breach, termination or invalidity thereof, shall be settled by arbitration in accordance with the UNCITRAL Arbitration Rules.

Note—Parties should consider adding:

(a) The appointing authority shall be... (name of institution or person);
(b) The number of arbitrators shall be... (one or three);
(c) The place of arbitration shall be... (town and country);
(d) The language to be used in the arbitral proceedings shall be....

Possible waiver statement

Note—If the parties wish to exclude recourse against the arbitral award that may be available under the applicable law, they may consider adding a provision to that effect as suggested below, considering, however, that the effectiveness and conditions of such an exclusion depend on the applicable law.

Waiver:

The parties hereby waive their right to any form of recourse against an award to any court or other competent authority, insofar as such waiver can validly be made under the applicable law.

Model statements of independence pursuant to Article 11 of the Rules

No circumstances to disclose:

I am impartial and independent of each of the parties and intend to remain so. To the best of my knowledge, there are no circumstances, past or present, likely to give rise to justifiable doubts as to my impartiality or independence. I shall promptly notify the parties and the other arbitrators of any such circumstances that may subsequently come to my attention during this arbitration.

Circumstances to disclose:

I am impartial and independent of each of the parties and intend to remain so. Attached is a statement made pursuant to article 11 of the UNCITRAL Arbitration Rules of (a) my past and present professional, business and other relationships with the parties and (b) any other relevant circumstances. [Include statement] I confirm that those circumstances do not affect my independence and impartiality. I shall promptly notify the parties and the other arbitrators of any such further relationships or circumstances that may subsequently come to my attention during this arbitration.

Note—Any party may consider requesting from the arbitrator the following addition to the statement of independence:

I confirm, on the basis of the information presently available to me, that I can devote the time necessary to conduct this arbitration diligently, efficiently and in accordance with the time limits in the Rules.

APPENDIX XIII

Procedure for Requesting the PCA Secretary-General to Designate an Appointing Authority Pursuant to the UNCITRAL Arbitration Rules

Application

Requests for designation of an appointing authority should be directed to:

The Secretary-General
Permanent Court of Arbitration
Peace Palace
Carnegieplein 2
2517 KJ The Hague
The Netherlands
Tel: +31 70 302 4165
Fax: +31 70 302 4167
E-mail: bureau@pca-cpa.org

The request should be accompanied by:

1. A copy of the arbitration clause or agreement establishing the applicability of the UNCITRAL Arbitration Rules;
2. A copy of the Notice of Arbitration served upon the respondent, as well as the date of such service;
3. A copy of any response to the Notice of Arbitration;
4. An indication of the nationalities of the parties;
5. The names and nationalities of the arbitrators already appointed, if any;
6. The names of any institutions or persons that the parties had considered selecting as appointing authority but which have been rejected;
7. A power of attorney evidencing the authority of the person making the request; and
8. Payment of the non-refundable administrative fee.

Administrative Fee

The non-refundable administrative fee for the analysis of a request for the designation of an appointing authority is €750, which includes the cost of the designation of an appointing authority if that is the next appropriate step. The fee is required to be paid in advance and is non-refundable, and should be made to the PCA by bank transfer or by cheque (details at www.pca-cpa.org).

Please mention the UNCITRAL arbitration case, and whether the payment is made for the claimant or the respondent, as a payment reference on your bank transfer, or in the accompanying letter with your cheque.

APPENDIX XIV

Procedure for Requesting the PCA Secretary-General to Act as Appointing Authority

Application

Where the PCA Arbitration Rules 2012 apply, or where the PCA Secretary-General is otherwise empowered to act as appointing authority by agreement of the parties, requests that the Secretary-General take any action as appointing authority should be directed to:

The Secretary-General
Permanent Court of Arbitration
Peace Palace
Carnegieplein 2
2517 KJ The Hague
The Netherlands
Tel: +31 70 302 4165
Fax: +31 70 302 4167
E-mail: bureau@pca-cpa.org

and be accompanied by:

1. A copy of the arbitration clause, agreement, or other instrument establishing the applicability of the PCA Arbitration Rules 2012 or the designation of the Secretary-General as appointing authority;
2. A copy of the notice of arbitration served upon the respondent, as well as the date of such service;
3. An indication of the nationalities of the parties;
4. The names and nationalities of the arbitrators already appointed, if any;
5. A power of attorney evidencing the authority of the person making the request; and
6. Payment of the non-refundable appointing authority fee.

Administrative Fee

The non-refundable administrative fee for the Secretary-General of the PCA to act as appointing authority is €1,500. The fee is required to be paid in advance and is non-refundable, and should be made to the PCA by bank transfer or by cheque (details at www.pca-cpa.org).

Please mention the case number, and whether the payment is made for the claimant or the respondent, as a payment reference on your bank transfer, or in the accompanying letter with your cheque.

APPENDIX XV

Model Declaration of Acceptance and Statement of Impartiality and Independence for Cases under the 2012 PCA Rules

PCA CASE NO. [ ]:

[Claimant]

v.

[Respondent]

(Please check the relevant box or boxes)

I, the undersigned,

Last Name: ________________________ First Name: ________________________

Non-acceptance

☐ hereby declare that **I decline** to serve as arbitrator in the above-referenced case. (If you wish to state the reasons for checking this box, please do so and submit on a separate sheet.)

Acceptance

☐ hereby declare that **I accept** to serve as arbitrator under the 2012 PCA Rules in the instant case. In so declaring, I confirm that I have familiarized myself with the requirements of the 2012 PCA Rules and am able and available to serve as an arbitrator in accordance with all of the requirements of those Rules.

Impartiality and Independence

(If you accept to serve as arbitrator, please also check one of the two following boxes. The choice of which box to check will be determined after you have taken into account, inter alia, whether there exists any past or present relationship, direct or indirect, with any of the parties or their counsel, whether financial, professional or of another kind and whether the nature of any such relationship is such that disclosure is called for pursuant to the criteria set out below. Any doubt should be resolved in favour of disclosure.)

☐ **I am impartial and independent** of each of the parties and intend to remain so. To the best of my knowledge, there are no circumstances, past or present, that need be disclosed because they are likely to give rise to justifiable doubts as to my impartiality or independence. I shall promptly notify the parties and other arbitrators of any such circumstances that may subsequently come to my attention during this arbitration.

OR

☐ **I am impartial and independent** of each of the parties and intend to remain so. **However**, in consideration of my disclosure obligation under the 2012 PCA Rules,* I attach a statement

* *PCA Arbitration Rules 2012, Article 11: 'When a person is approached in connection with his or her possible appointment as an arbitrator, he or she shall disclose any circumstances likely to give rise to justifiable doubts as to his or her impartiality or independence. An arbitrator, from the time of his or her appointment and throughout the arbitral proceedings, shall without delay disclose any such circumstances to the parties and the other arbitrators unless they have already been informed by him or her of these circumstances.'*

of (a) my past and present professional, business and other relationships with the parties and (b) any other relevant circumstances. I confirm that these circumstances do not affect my independence and impartiality. I shall promptly notify the parties and other arbitrators of any such further relationships or circumstances that may subsequently come to my attention during this arbitration. (Use separate sheet for disclosure.)

Date: ______________________________Signature: ______________________________

APPENDIX XVI

Model Clause for PCA Services under the UNCITRAL Arbitration Rules

Any dispute, controversy, or claim arising out of or relating to this contract, or the breach, termination, or invalidity thereof, shall be settled by arbitration in accordance with the UNCITRAL Arbitration Rules in effect on the date of this contract.

The appointing authority shall be the Secretary-General of the Permanent Court of Arbitration.

Note: parties might wish to consider adding:

(a) The number of arbitrators shall be... [one or three].
(b) The place of arbitration shall be... [town, country].
(c) The language(s) to be used in the arbitral proceedings shall be... [insert choice].
(d) [*For cases involving a State, a State-controlled entity or an intergovernmental organization*] The case shall be administered by the International Bureau of the Permanent Court of Arbitration.

APPENDIX XVII

Sample Procedural Order No 1[1]

IN THE MATTER OF AN ARBITRATION PURSUANT TO [RELEVANT CONTRACT, TREATY, OR OTHER AGREEMENT] AND THE PERMANENT COURT OF ARBITRATION ARBITRATION RULES 2012

(the 'PCA Rules')

-between-

[NAME OF THE CLAIMANT]

(the 'Claimant')

-and-

[NAME OF THE RESPONDENT]

(the 'Respondent', and together with the Claimant, the 'Parties')

PROCEDURAL ORDER NO 1

Tribunal[2]

[Name of the presiding arbitrator] (Presiding Arbitrator)

[Name of the arbitrator appointed by the Claimant]

[Name of the arbitrator appointed by the Respondent]

Registry

Permanent Court of Arbitration

[Date]

---

[1] A hallmark of international arbitration is its procedural flexibility. Arbitral tribunals constituted under the 2012 PCA Rules have wide discretion in their conduct of proceedings (subject to the requirements of Article 17(1) and, in arbitrations involving private parties, the mandatory provisions of the *lex arbitri*). Accordingly, the particular circumstances of every dispute, the legal traditions of arbitrators and counsel, and their personal style and preferences will exert a defining influence on the conduct of proceedings, resulting in a variety of approaches being taken on the same or similar procedural issues (regarding the benefits of tailoring the procedure to the specific case, see Lucy Greenwood, 'Tear up the Procedural Schedule: Reducing Time and Costs in International Commercial Arbitration' (2010) 76 *Arbitration* 563). This sample procedural order, together with the sample procedural order found in Appendix XVIII, reflects the way some tribunals have dealt with the most common procedural issues that may arise in the early stages of an international arbitration. They are intended to give practitioners examples of some provisions that the PCA has seen used successfully in proceedings under its auspices without creating a presumption in favour of their terms or limiting the freedom of tribunals and parties to adopt them as needed or craft very different approaches.

This sample is intended for arbitrations conducted under the 2012 PCA Rules. Where an arbitration conducted under the 2010 UNCITRAL Rules (with PCA administration) would call for different provisions, these are included in footnotes. While this sample foresees that it will be signed exclusively by the arbitral tribunal, some tribunals may include in a first procedural order undertakings by the parties, which would call for signature of the procedural order by the parties, as well as by the arbitral tribunal.

[2] With the exception of Section 4, this model assumes an arbitral tribunal of three members.

1. Parties

The Claimant	Counsel for the Claimant
[Name][3]	**[Name]** [Postal address] Tel.: [telephone number] Fax: [facsimile number] E-mail: [e-mail address]
The Respondent	**Counsel for the Respondent**
[Name]	**[Name]** [Postal address] Tel.: [telephone number] Fax: [facsimile number] E-mail: [e-mail address]

2. Representation

2.1 The Parties have designated their respective representatives listed above as being authorized to act on their behalf in these arbitration proceedings.

2.2 To the extent they have not already done so, the Parties shall confirm these designations by each providing to the other Party copies of the powers of attorney or letter of representation granted to its representative(s).

2.3 In the event of any change by a Party of its representatives or of the contact details of any of its representatives, that change shall be notified promptly in writing to opposing counsel, to each member of the Tribunal, and to the Permanent Court of Arbitration (the '**PCA**'). Failing such notification, communications sent to the addresses set out above shall be valid.

3. Dispute and Commencement of Arbitration

3.1 According to the Claimant, a dispute has arisen between the Claimant and the Respondent under the [relevant contract, treaty, or other agreement].

3.2 The Claimant submitted a Notice of Arbitration dated [date], pursuant to [relevant provision of contract, treaty, or other agreement] and Article 3 of the PCA Rules. The Notice of Arbitration was received by the Respondent on [date].

3.3 In accordance with Article 3(2) of the PCA Rules, these arbitration proceedings are deemed to have commenced on [date], the date on which the Respondent received the Notice of Arbitration.

4. Appointment of the Tribunal

Option 1: Sole Arbitrator

4.1 On [date], the Parties appointed [name], a national of [country], as the Sole Arbitrator. [name]'s contact details are as follows:

[Name]

[Postal address]

Tel: [Telephone number]

Fax: [Facsimile number]

E-mail: [E-mail address]

[3] The contact details (postal address, telephone number, facsimile number, and/or email address) of any party who has not appointed a legal representative should be indicated here.

Or

On [date], The Secretary-General of the PCA appointed [name], a national of [country], as the Sole Arbitrator. [name]'s contact details are as follows:

[Name]

[Postal address]

Tel: [Telephone number]

Fax: [Facsimile number]

E-mail: [E-mail address]

Option 2: Three-member tribunal

4.2 In the Notice of Arbitration, the Claimant notified the Respondent of the appointment of [name], a national of [country], as the first arbitrator. [name]'s contact details are as follows:

[Name]

[Postal address]

Tel: [Telephone number]

Fax: [Facsimile number]

E-mail: [E-mail address]

4.3 In its Response to the Notice of Arbitration dated [date], the Respondent appointed [name], a national of [country], as the second arbitrator. [name]'s contact details are as follows:

Or

The Secretary-General of the PCA appointed [name], a national of [country], as the second arbitrator on [date]. [name]'s contact details are as follows:

[Name]

[Postal address]

Tel: [Telephone number]

Fax: [Facsimile number]

E-mail: [E-mail address]

4.4 The two co-arbitrators appointed [name], a national of [country], as presiding arbitrator on [date]. [name]'s contact details are as follows:

Or

The Secretary-General of the PCA appointed [name], a national of [country], as presiding arbitrator on [date]. [name]'s contact details are as follows:

[Name]

[Postal address]

Tel: [Telephone number]

Fax: [Facsimile number]

E-mail: [E-mail address]

Option 3: Five-member tribunal

4.5 In the Notice of Arbitration, the Claimant notified the Respondent of the appointment of [name], a national of [country], as the first arbitrator. [name]'s contact details are as follows:

[Name]

[Postal address]

Tel: [Telephone number]

Fax: [Facsimile number]

E-mail: [E-mail address]

4.6 In its Response to the Notice of Arbitration dated [date], the Respondent appointed [name], a national of [country], as the second arbitrator. [name]'s contact details are as follows:

<u>Or</u>

The Secretary-General of the PCA appointed [name], a national of [country], as the second arbitrator on [date]. [name]'s contact details are as follows:

[Name]

[Postal address]

Tel: [Telephone number]

Fax: [Facsimile number]

E-mail: [E-mail address]

4.7 The two party-appointed arbitrators appointed [name], a national of [country], as the third arbitrator on [date]. [name]'s contact details are as follows:

<u>Or</u>

The Secretary-General of the PCA appointed [name], a national of [country], as the third arbitrator on [date]. [name]'s contact details are as follows:

[Name]

[Postal address]

Tel: [Telephone number]

Fax: [Facsimile number]

E-mail: [E-mail address]

4.8 On [date], the two party-appointed arbitrators appointed [name], a national of [country], as the fourth arbitrator. [name]'s contact details are as follows:

<u>Or</u>

The Secretary-General of the PCA appointed [name], a national of [country], as the fourth arbitrator on [date]. [name]'s contact details are as follows:

[Name]

[Postal address]

Tel: [Telephone number]

Fax: [Facsimile number]

E-mail: [E-mail address]

4.9 On [date], the two party-appointed arbitrators appointed [name], a national of [country], as the fifth arbitrator. [name]'s contact details are as follows:

<u>Or</u>

The Secretary-General of the PCA appointed [name], a national of [country], as the fifth arbitrator on [date]. [name]'s contact details are as follows:

[Name]

[Postal address]

Tel: [Telephone number]

Fax: [Facsimile number]

E-mail: [E-mail address]

4.10 The two party-appointed arbitrators designated [name of the third, fourth, or fifth arbitrator] as the presiding arbitrator.

Or

The Secretary-General of the PCA designated [name of the third, fourth, or fifth arbitrator] as the presiding arbitrator.

For all options:

4.11 The members of the Tribunal are and shall remain impartial and independent of the Parties.

4.12 The members of the Tribunal confirm that they have disclosed, to the best of their knowledge, all circumstances likely to give rise to justifiable doubts as to their impartiality or independence and that they will promptly disclose any such circumstances that may arise or come to their attention during the arbitration.

4.13 The Tribunal notes that the Parties have confirmed that the Tribunal has been validly appointed in accordance with the [relevant contract, treaty, or other agreement] and the PCA Rules, and that they have no objection to the appointment of any member of the Tribunal on the grounds of conflict of interest or lack of independence or impartiality in respect of matters known to them as at the date of their comments on the draft of this Order.[4]

5. Applicable Procedural Rules

5.1 The arbitration shall be conducted in accordance with the PCA Rules.

5.2 In accordance with Article 6 of the PCA Rules, the Secretary-General of the PCA shall act as the appointing authority in this arbitration for all purposes under the PCA Rules.

5.3 Procedural decisions shall be issued by the presiding arbitrator after consultation with his co-arbitrators or, in cases of urgency or if a co-arbitrator cannot be reached, by him alone, subject to possible reconsideration of such decisions by the full Tribunal. Procedural orders issued on behalf of the full Tribunal may be signed by the presiding arbitrator only.

6. Place of Arbitration

Option 1: If the place of arbitration is agreed by the parties

6.1 The place of arbitration (or 'legal seat') shall be [city, country].

6.2 Meetings and hearings may take place at other locations if so decided by the Tribunal after consultation with the Parties. The Tribunal may meet at any location it considers appropriate for deliberations.

Option 2: If the place of arbitration is to be decided by the tribunal

6.3 Pursuant to the PCA Rules, the Tribunal will determine the place (or 'legal seat') of the arbitration having regard to the circumstances of the case, after consultation with the Parties.

6.4 Meetings and hearings may take place at other locations if so decided by the Tribunal after consultation with the Parties. The Tribunal may meet at any location it considers appropriate for deliberations.

7. Language[5]

Option 1: If the language of arbitration is agreed by the parties

[4] If this document is intended to be signed by the parties as well as the arbitral tribunal, this provision may be replaced with the following text:

> The Parties confirm that the Tribunal has been validly appointed in accordance with the [relevant contract, treaty, or law] and the PCA Rules and have no objection to the appointment of any member of the Tribunal on the grounds of conflict of interest or lack of independence or impartiality in respect of matters known to them as at the date of signature of this document.

[5] In most cases, a single language is preferred in view of the added cost, time, and issues of interpretation that may arise in multilingual proceedings. Multilingual proceedings, however, are possible under the Rules. See discussion under Art 19.

7.1 The language of the proceedings shall be [language].

__Option 2: If the language of arbitration is to be decided by the tribunal__

7.2 Pursuant to the PCA Rules, the Tribunal will determine the language of the proceedings, after consultation with the Parties.

7.3 Until such time as the Tribunal determines the language of the proceedings, communications shall be made in [language].

8. Case Administration

8.1 In accordance with Article 1(3) of the PCA Rules, the PCA serves as registry and provides secretariat services in this matter. The PCA's services are provided on the following terms:

8.1.1 In consultation with the Tribunal, the Secretary-General of the PCA shall appoint a legal officer of the International Bureau to act as Tribunal Secretary.[6]

8.1.2 The PCA shall maintain an archive of filings of correspondence and submissions.

8.1.3 Pursuant to Article 43 of the PCA Rules, the PCA shall manage Party deposits to cover the costs of the arbitration.

8.1.4 If needed, the PCA shall make its hearing and meeting rooms at the Peace Palace in The Hague or at certain other venues in Costa Rica, Mauritius, Singapore, and South Africa available to the Parties and the Tribunal at no charge. Costs of catering, court reporting, or other technical support associated with hearings or meetings at the Peace Palace or elsewhere shall be borne by the Parties.

8.1.5 The PCA shall carry out administrative tasks on behalf of the Tribunal, the primary purpose of which would be to reduce the costs that would otherwise be incurred by the Tribunal carrying out purely administrative tasks. Work carried out by the PCA shall be billed in accordance with the PCA's schedule of fees.

8.1.6 PCA fees and expenses shall be paid in the same manner as the Tribunal's fees and expenses.

8.2 The contact details of the PCA are as follows:

Permanent Court of Arbitration
Attn: [name of the PCA legal officer appointed as Tribunal Secretary]
Peace Palace
Carnegieplein 2
2517 KJ The Hague
The Netherlands
Tel: +31 70 302 4140
Fax: +31 70 302 4167
E-mail: [e-mail address of the PCA legal officer appointed as Tribunal Secretary]
bureau@pca-cpa.org

9. Tribunal Fees and Expenses

9.1 Each member of the Tribunal shall be remunerated at the rate of [amount] per hour plus VAT, if applicable, for all time spent in connection with the arbitration.

9.2 Members of the Tribunal shall be remunerated in the amount of 50 per cent of their fees, for each day reserved for the hearing, based on an eight-hour day, in respect of any hearing or other meeting for which they are asked to reserve more than one day and that is cancelled, or postponed by more than one week, by one or both of the Parties within four weeks from the first day of such hearing or meeting. This remuneration will be in addition to any fees due in respect of hourly charges actually incurred in preparation for any cancelled hearing prior to the cancellation being notified to the Tribunal.

[6] In inter-state arbitrations, this legal officer would typically be referred to as the 'Registrar'.

9.3 Members of the Tribunal shall be reimbursed for all disbursements and charges reasonably incurred in connection with the arbitration, including but not limited to travel expenses, telephone, fax, delivery, printing, and other expenses.

9.4 Members of the Tribunal may bill for reimbursement of disbursements and charges as and when they are incurred, and may submit to the PCA periodic bills in respect of fees.

9.5 All payments to the Tribunal shall be made from the deposit administered by the PCA pursuant to Article 43 of the Rules.[7]

10. Procedural Meeting

10.1 Further procedural details and in particular a schedule for submissions and the determination of the place and language of arbitration shall be discussed and, as far as possible, agreed at a procedural meeting to be held with the Parties in person or by telephone conference call. The results of the procedural meeting shall be included in a further procedural order of the Tribunal.

11. Communications

11.1 Further details regarding communications shall be discussed at the procedural meeting. Subject to any modification arising from the procedural meeting, the following provisions shall apply.

11.2 The Parties and their representatives shall not engage in any oral or written communications with any member of the Tribunal *ex parte* in connection with the subject-matter of the arbitration or any procedural issues which are related to the arbitration.

11.3 The Parties shall send all communications for the attention of the Tribunal by e-mail simultaneously to opposing counsel, each member of the Tribunal, and the PCA.

<u>Or</u>

The Parties shall send all communications for the attention of the Tribunal by e-mail simultaneously to opposing counsel and the PCA. The PCA shall promptly transmit all communications received from the Parties to each member of the Tribunal.

11.4 A hard copy of all communications exceeding 30 pages (including all attached documents) shall also be sent by courier on the day of their transmission by e-mail.

11.5 The Parties shall send copies of correspondence between them to the Tribunal and the PCA only if such correspondence relates to a matter where the Tribunal is required to take action or to abstain from acting or if it gives notice of a relevant event that the Tribunal and the PCA should be apprised of.

12. Immunity from Suit

12.1 The Parties shall not seek to make the Tribunal or any of its members liable in respect of any act or omission in connection with any matter related to the arbitration.

12.2 The Parties shall not require any member of the Tribunal to be a party or witness in any judicial, administrative, or other proceedings arising out of or in connection with the arbitration.

---

[7] If this document is intended to be signed by the parties as well as the arbitral tribunal, the following text may be added:

> Payment of all outstanding fees and disbursements must be made before any award or interim award will be released to the Parties. In the event of a settlement by agreement between the Parties before an award is made, any outstanding fees and expenses not covered by the deposit will be paid by the Parties within three weeks of receipt of the invoice in respect thereof.
>
> Notwithstanding any order as to the payment of costs by one Party to another made by the Tribunal, the Parties shall be jointly and severally liable for the Tribunal's fees and expenses.

13. Signature of this Order

13.1 This Order may be signed in counterparts, collectively forming one composite signed document.[8]

THE TRIBUNAL:

______________________________	______________________________
[Name of arbitrator appointed by the Claimant]	[Name of arbitrator appointed by the Respondent]
Date:	Date:

____

[Name of presiding arbitrator]

(Presiding Arbitrator)

Date:

[8] In a case conducted under the 2010 UNCITRAL Rules (with PCA administration), the arbitral tribunal's first procedural order would also usually include a provision dealing with the deposit for the costs of arbitration, for example as follows:

In accordance with the UNCITRAL Rules and in order to assure sufficient funds for the Tribunal's fees and expenses, the Parties shall establish an initial deposit of [amount] with the PCA by [30 days from the date of this Order] by wire transfer to the following account:

Bank:	ING Bank N.V. Schenkkade 65 2519 AS The Hague The Netherlands
Account number:	[Details from the PCA website, depending on the currency]
IBAN:	[Details from the PCA website, depending on the currency]
BIC:	[Details from the PCA website, depending on the currency]
Name of beneficiary:	Permanent Court of Arbitration
Reference:	[Case reference/Party]

The PCA will review the adequacy of the deposit from time to time and may invite the Parties to make supplementary deposits.

The unused balance held on deposit at the end of the arbitration shall be returned to the Parties.

APPENDIX XVIII

Sample Procedural Order No 2[1]

IN THE MATTER OF AN ARBITRATION PURSUANT TO [RELEVANT CONTRACT, TREATY, OR OTHER AGREEMENT] AND THE PERMANENT COURT OF ARBITRATION ARBITRATION RULES 2012

(the 'PCA Rules')

-between-

[NAME OF THE CLAIMANT]

(the 'Claimant')

-and-

[NAME OF THE RESPONDENT]
(the 'Respondent', and together with the Claimant, the 'Parties')

PROCEDURAL ORDER NO 2

Tribunal

[Name of the presiding arbitrator] (Presiding Arbitrator)
[Name of the arbitrator appointed by the Claimant]
[Name of the arbitrator appointed by the Respondent]

Registry
Permanent Court of Arbitration

[Date]

---

[1] A hallmark of international arbitration is its procedural flexibility. Arbitral tribunals constituted under the 2012 PCA Rules have wide discretion in their conduct of proceedings (subject to the requirements of Article 17(1) and, in arbitrations involving private parties, the mandatory provisions of the *lex arbitri*). Accordingly, the particular circumstances of every dispute, the legal traditions of arbitrators and counsel, and their personal style and preferences will exert a defining influence on the conduct of proceedings, resulting in a variety of approaches being taken on the same or similar procedural issues (regarding the benefits of tailoring the procedure to the specific case see Lucy Greenwood, 'Tear up the Procedural Schedule: Reducing Time and Costs in International Commercial Arbitration' (2010) 76 Arbitration 563). This sample procedural order, together with the sample procedural order found in Appendix XVII, reflects the way some tribunals have dealt with the most common procedural issues that may arise in the early stages of an international arbitration. They are intended to give practitioners examples of some provisions that the PCA has seen used successfully in proceedings under its auspices without creating a presumption in favour of their terms or limiting the freedom of tribunals and parties to adopt them as needed or craft very different approaches.

This sample is intended for arbitrations conducted under the 2012 PCA Rules. Where an arbitration conducted under the 2010 UNCITRAL Rules (with PCA administration) would call for different provisions, these are included in footnotes.

1. Place of Arbitration

1.1 The place of arbitration (or 'legal seat') is fixed at [city, country].

1.2 Meetings and hearings may take place at other locations if so decided by the Tribunal after consultation with the Parties. The Tribunal may meet at any location it considers appropriate for deliberations.

2. Language[2]

2.1 The language of the proceedings shall be [language].

2.2 Documents originally written in a language other than [the language of the proceedings] shall be submitted to the Tribunal with a translation into [the language of the proceedings]. Whenever a Party considers that the content of a document of more than five pages in length is not relevant in its entirety, the translation may be limited to all relevant excerpts together with such other portions of the document as necessary to put such excerpts in proper context. A full translation shall be provided if the Tribunal decides that the document is relevant in its entirety at the request of a party or upon the Tribunal's own initiative. Informal translations will be accepted as accurate unless contested by the other Party, in which case the Parties will attempt to reach agreement on the translation (including if needed through the introduction of certified translations). Documents produced pursuant to Sections 5.2 and 5.3.6 of this Order may be in their original language.

2.3 Witness statements and expert reports in a language other than [the language of the proceedings] shall be submitted with an informal translation in [the language of the proceedings], which will be accepted as accurate unless contested by the other Party, in which case the Parties will attempt to reach agreement on the translation.

2.4 Oral testimony given in a language other than [the language of the proceedings] shall be interpreted into [the language of the proceedings]. The PCA shall make appropriate arrangements for interpretation at the hearing, in consultation with the Parties.

3. Schedule of Proceedings

3.1 The schedule of proceedings shall be as follows:

Example 1: If no bifurcation request is foreseen

Event	Date
Claimant's Statement of Claim	[date]
Respondent's Statement of Defence	[date]
Requests for document production[3]	[date]
Objections to requests for document production	[date]
Responses to objections to document production	[date]
Tribunal's decision on document production	On or around [date]
Production of documents	[date]
Claimant's Reply	[date]
Respondent's Rejoinder	[date]
Pre-hearing Conference	On or around [date](at least 30 days before the hearing)
Hearing on jurisdiction, admissibility, and merits	[date(s)]

[2] This provision assumes that there is one language of the proceedings. In most cases, a single language is preferred in view of the added cost, time, and issues of interpretation that may arise in multilingual proceedings. Multilingual proceedings, however, are possible under the Rules. See discussion under Art 19.

[3] Although relatively common in international arbitration, document production may not be called for in some proceedings, in which case this row and the following four would not be necessary.

Example 2: If a bifurcation request between merits and jurisdiction is foreseen

Event	Date
Claimant's Statement of Claim	[date]
Respondent's request for bifurcation	[date]
Claimant's reply to the request for bifurcation	[date]
Tribunal's decision on bifurcation	On or around [date]
Option 1: If the Tribunal grants the request for bifurcation:	
Respondent's Memorial on jurisdiction and admissibility	[date]
Claimant's Counter-Memorial on jurisdiction and admissibility	[date]
Requests for document production[4]	[date]
Objections to requests for document production	[date]
Responses to objections to document production	[date]
Tribunal's decision on document production	On or around [date]
Production of documents	[date]
Respondent's Reply on jurisdiction and admissibility	[date]
Claimant's Rejoinder on jurisdiction and admissibility	[date]
Pre-hearing Conference	On or around [date](at least 30 days before the hearing)
Hearing on jurisdiction and admissibility	[date(s)]
In the event that the Tribunal upholds its jurisdiction in whole or in part, the time periods that appear below under Option 2 shall be used for the schedule of the merits phase of the proceedings, counting from the date of the Tribunal's decision on jurisdiction	–
Option 2: If the Tribunal denies the request for bifurcation:	
Respondent's Statement of Defence	[date]
Requests for document production[5]	[date]
Objections to requests for document production	[date]
Responses to objections to document production	[date]
Tribunal's decision on document production	If at all possible, [date]
Production of documents	[date]
Claimant's Reply	[date]
Respondent's Rejoinder	[date]
Pre-hearing Conference	On or around [date] (at least 30 days before the hearing)
Hearing on jurisdiction, admissibility, and merits	[date(s)]

[4] See n 3. Document production is somewhat less common in a jurisdictional phase, particularly when jurisdictional objections are based predominantly on questions of law rather than fact.

[5] See n 3.

3.2 Unless otherwise provided, all time limits shall refer to 6 p.m. at the place of arbitration on the day of the deadline.
3.3 Short extensions may be agreed by the Parties as long as they do not affect later dates in the schedule and the Tribunal is informed before the original due date.

4. Communications

4.1 On or before the due date, the submitting Party shall send its submission, together with witness statements and expert reports (if any), but without exhibits or attachments, by e-mail simultaneously to the opposing Party, each member of the Tribunal, and the PCA.

Or

On the due date, the submitting Party shall send its submission, together with witness statements and expert reports (if any), but without exhibits or attachments, by e-mail simultaneously to the opposing Party and the PCA for onward transmission to the Tribunal.

4.2 To facilitate filing, citations, and word processing, all written submissions, including witness statements and expert reports, shall be provided as searchable Adobe Portable Document Format ('PDF') files, preceded by a hyper-linked table of contents.
4.3 On the day of the submission of pleadings and accompanying documents by e-mail, hard copies of the pleadings and exhibits shall be sent to the opposing Party, each member of the Tribunal, and the PCA by courier, unbound in ring binders, organized in chronological order with a separate tab for each document, and preceded by a list describing each document by exhibit number, date, type of document, author, and recipient (as applicable). Documents shall also be submitted in electronic form on a USB flash memory drive, preferably as searchable PDF files.
4.4 For any simultaneous submissions, each side will submit all electronic and hard copies to the PCA. The PCA will then distribute copies to the Tribunal and opposing counsel once both submissions have been received.

5. Document Production

5.1 Each Party may request the production of documents from the other Party in accordance with the above schedule.
5.2 Requests for the production of documents shall be in writing and set forth reasons for the request in respect of each document or class of documents requested. Unless the requested Party objects to production, it shall produce the requested documents within the time limit set above.
5.3 If the requested Party objects to production, the following procedure shall apply:
  5.3.1 The requested Party shall submit a response stating which documents or classes of document it objects to producing. The response shall state the reasons for each objection and shall indicate the documents, if any, that the Party would be prepared to produce instead of those requested.
  5.3.2 The requesting Party shall respond to the other Party's objection, indicating, with reasons, whether it disputes the objection.
  5.3.3 The Parties shall seek agreement on production requests to the greatest extent possible.
  5.3.4 To the extent that agreement cannot be reached between the requesting and the requested Party, the Parties shall jointly submit all outstanding requests to the Tribunal for decision. All other correspondence or documents exchanged in the course of this process shall not be copied to the Tribunal.
  5.3.5 Document production requests submitted to the Tribunal for decision must be in the form of a 'Redfern Schedule', detailing (i) the documents or category of documents requested; (ii) their relevance and materiality according to the requesting Party; (iii) the reasoned objection to the request by the objecting Party; and (iv) a brief response to the objection to the document production request by the requesting Party.
  5.3.6 The Tribunal shall rule on any such application and may for this purpose refer to the *IBA Rules on the Taking of Evidence in International Arbitration 2010*. Documents ordered by the Tribunal to be disclosed shall be produced within the time limit set above.

5.3.7 Should a Party fail to produce documents as ordered by the Tribunal, the Tribunal shall draw the inferences it deems appropriate, taking into consideration all relevant circumstances.

5.4 The Tribunal may also request the production of documents on its own motion.

5.5 Documents produced according to the above procedure shall not be considered on record unless and until a Party subsequently submits them in accordance with the provisions regarding the schedule of proceedings above.

6. Evidence and Legal Authorities

6.1 In addition to the provisions on document production above, the Tribunal may use, as an additional guideline, the *IBA Rules on the Taking of Evidence in International Arbitration 2010* when considering matters of evidence.

6.2 The Parties shall submit with their written submissions all evidence and authorities on which they intend to rely in support of the factual and legal arguments advanced therein, including witness statements, expert reports, documents, and all other evidence in whatever form.

6.3 In their rebuttal submissions on jurisdiction and admissibility and/or the merits (i.e., Reply and Rejoinder), the Parties shall submit only additional written witness testimony, expert opinion testimony and documentary or other evidence to respond to or rebut matters raised in the other Party's immediately prior written submission, except for new evidence they receive through document production.

6.4 Following submission of the Reply and Rejoinder, the Tribunal shall not consider any evidence that has not been introduced as part of the written submissions of the Parties, unless the Tribunal grants leave on the basis of exceptional circumstances. Should such leave be granted to one side, the other side shall have an opportunity to submit counter-evidence.

6.5 The Parties shall identify each exhibit submitted to the Tribunal with a distinct number. Each exhibit submitted by the Claimant shall begin with a letter 'C' followed by the applicable number (i.e., C-1, C-2, etc.); each exhibit submitted by the Respondent shall begin with a letter 'R' followed by the applicable number (i.e., R-1, R-2, etc.). The Parties shall use sequential numbering throughout the proceedings.

6.6 The Parties shall identify each legal authority submitted to the Tribunal with a distinct number. Each legal authority submitted by the Claimant shall begin with the letters 'CLA' followed by the applicable number (i.e., CLA-1, CLA-2, etc.); each legal authority submitted by the Respondent shall begin with the letters 'RLA' followed by the applicable number (i.e., RLA-1, RLA-2, etc.). The Parties shall use sequential numbering throughout the proceedings.

6.7 All evidence submitted to the Tribunal shall be deemed to be authentic and complete, including evidence submitted in the form of copies, unless a Party disputes within a reasonable time its authenticity or completeness, or the Party submitting the evidence indicates the respects in which any document is incomplete.

7. Witnesses

7.1 Any person may present evidence as a witness, including a Party or a Party's officer, employee, or other representative.

7.2 For each witness, a written and signed witness statement shall be submitted to the Tribunal. Where in exceptional circumstances a party is unable to obtain such a statement from a witness, the evidence of that witness shall be admitted only with leave of the Tribunal and in accordance with its directions.

7.3 Each witness statement shall contain at least the following:

7.3.1 the name, date of birth, and present address of the witness;

7.3.2 a description of the witness's position and qualifications, if relevant to the dispute or to the contents of the statement;

7.3.3 a description of any past and present relationship between the witness and the Parties, counsel, or members of the Tribunal;

7.3.4 a description of the facts on which the witness's testimony is offered and, if applicable, the source of the witness's knowledge; and

7.3.5 the signature of the witness.

7.4 Witness statements shall be numbered discretely from other documents and properly identified as such (i.e., 'CWS' (Claimant's witness statements) or 'RWS' (Respondent's witness statements), followed by the applicable number).

7.5 Witness statements shall stand in lieu of direct examination. Accordingly, witnesses shall testify at the oral hearing only if they are called by the opposing party or the Tribunal for examination or cross-examination, at least [number] days before the commencement of such hearing.

<u>Or</u>

Before any oral hearing, and not less than [number] days before the commencement of such hearing, a Party may be called upon by the Tribunal or the other Party to produce at the hearing for examination and cross-examination any witness or expert whose written testimony has been submitted with the written submissions. Should a Party wish to present any of its own witnesses or experts for examination at the hearing who have not been called by the Tribunal or the other Party, it shall request leave from the Tribunal not less than [number] days before the commencement of the hearing.

7.6 Each Party shall be responsible for summoning its own witnesses to the applicable hearing, except when the other Party has waived cross-examination of a witness and the Tribunal does not direct his or her appearance. In accordance with Article 28(4) of the PCA Rules, the Tribunal may direct that witnesses be examined through means of telecommunication that do not require their physical presence at the hearing (such as video-conference).

7.7 The Tribunal may, on its own initiative or at the request of a Party, summon any other witness to appear.

7.8 If a witness who has been called to testify by the Tribunal or the other Party does not appear to testify at the hearing, either in person or by means of telecommunication, as directed by the Tribunal, the witness's testimony shall be stricken from the record, unless the Tribunal determines that a valid reason has been provided for failing to appear. In such case, the Tribunal may summon the witness to appear a second time if satisfied that the testimony of the witness is relevant and material.

7.9 Each Party shall cover the costs of appearance of its own witnesses. The Tribunal will decide upon the appropriate allocation of such costs in its final award.

7.10 At any hearing, the examination of each witness shall proceed as follows:
   (a) the presiding arbitrator shall admonish the witness;
   (b) the party presenting the witness may conduct a brief direct examination lasting no more than 15 minutes;
   (c) the adverse Party may then cross-examine the witness on relevant matters that were addressed or presented in the witness statement;
   (d) the Party summoning the witness may then re-examine the witness with respect to any matters or issues arising out of the cross-examination;
   (e) the Tribunal may examine the witness at any time, either before, during or after examination by one of the Parties.

7.11 The Tribunal shall, at all times, have complete control over the procedure for hearing a witness. The Tribunal may in its discretion:
   (a) refuse to hear a witness if it considers that the facts with respect to which the witness will testify are either proven by other evidence or are irrelevant;
   (b) limit or refuse the right of a Party to examine a witness when it appears that a question has been addressed by other evidence or is irrelevant; or
   (c) direct that a witness be recalled for further examination at any time.

7.12 Unless the Parties agree otherwise, a factual witness shall not be present in the hearing room during the hearing of oral testimony, discuss the testimony of any other witness, or read any transcript of any oral testimony, prior to his or her examination.[6]

[6] See discussion under Art 28.

8. Experts

8.1 Each Party may retain and submit the evidence of one or more experts to the Tribunal.

8.2 Expert reports shall be accompanied by any documents or information upon which they rely, unless such documents or information have already been submitted with the Parties' written submissions.

8.3 With the exception of section 7.13 above, the provisions set out in relation to witnesses shall apply, *mutatis mutandis*, to the evidence of experts. Unless the parties agree otherwise, expert witnesses shall be allowed to be present in the hearing room at any time.

8.4 The Tribunal may, on its own initiative or at the request of a Party, appoint one or more experts. The Tribunal shall consult with the Parties on the selection, terms of reference (including expert fees), and conclusions of any such expert.

9. Hearings

9.1 After consultation with the Parties, the Arbitral Tribunal shall determine the place, time, agenda, and all other technical and ancillary aspects of any hearing.

9.2 Hearings shall be recorded and shall be transcribed in English using LiveNote or a similar software so that the transcript is available on a real-time basis. At the end of each day of hearings, or as soon as practicable, the Parties shall be provided with the transcript of that day.

9.3 No new evidence may be presented at the hearing except with leave of the Tribunal. Demonstrative exhibits may, however, be shown using documents submitted earlier in accordance with this Order. Should the Tribunal grant leave to a party to present new evidence in the course of the hearing, it should grant the other party the opportunity to introduce new evidence to rebut it.

10. Confidentiality[7]

Place of Arbitration: [city, country]

____

[Name of the presiding arbitrator]

(Presiding Arbitrator)

On behalf of the Tribunal

[7] If the parties agree on any confidentiality/publicity provisions that differ from those provided in the 2012 PCA Rules, these may be recorded here or in a separate procedural order.

INDEX

The manufacturer's authorised representative in the EU for product safety is Oxford University Press España S.A. of El Parque Empresarial San Fernando de Henares, Avenida de Castilla, 2 - 28830 Madrid (www.oup.es/en or product.safety@oup.com). OUP España S.A. also acts as importer into Spain of products made by the manufacturer.
Printed and bound by CPI Group (UK) Ltd, Croydon, CR0 4YY
14/09/2026
02216287-0017